# ABUSED BODIES IN ROMAN EPIC

Greco-Roman martial epic poetry, from Homer and Virgil to Neronian and Flavian epic, is obsessed with the treatment of dead bodies. Sometimes corpses take centre stage in grand funerals; sometimes, disturbingly, they are objects of physical violence or malign neglect. In this book – the first full-length examination of corpse mistreatment in epic – Andrew M. McClellan explores the motif of *post mortem* abuse in Greco-Roman epic, especially the Latin poems of early imperial Rome: Lucan's *Bellum ciuile*, Valerius Flaccus' *Argonautica*, Statius' *Thebaid*, and Silius' *Punica*. He counters the pervasive tendency to view epic violence from the perspective of the abuser by shifting the focus to the object of abuse. In signalling the corpse as a critical 'character' and not simply a by-product of war, he offers a fundamental re-evaluation of violence and warfare in Latin epic, and through close study of intertextualities indicates the distinctive features of each author's treatment of the dead.

ANDREW M. MCCLELLAN is the Stepsay Family Postdoctoral Fellow in Classics at San Diego State University. His research interests range widely across Greek and Latin literature, especially epic poetry, drama, historiography, and classical reception. He is particularly interested in the intersections of war, violence, and death in Roman epic poetry and society.

# ABUSED BODIES IN ROMAN EPIC

### ANDREW M. MCCLELLAN

*San Diego State University*

# CAMBRIDGE
## UNIVERSITY PRESS

University Printing House, Cambridge CB2 8BS, United Kingdom

One Liberty Plaza, 20th Floor, New York, NY 10006, USA

477 Williamstown Road, Port Melbourne, VIC 3207, Australia

314–321, 3rd Floor, Plot 3, Splendor Forum, Jasola District Centre,
New Delhi – 110025, India

79 Anson Road, #06–04/06, Singapore 079906

Cambridge University Press is part of the University of Cambridge.

It furthers the University's mission by disseminating knowledge in the pursuit of
education, learning, and research at the highest international levels of excellence.

www.cambridge.org
Information on this title: www.cambridge.org/9781108482622
DOI: 10.1017/9781108697118

First published 2019

Printed and bound in Great Britain by Clays Ltd, Elcograf S.p.A.

*A catalogue record for this publication is available from the British Library.*

*Library of Congress Cataloging-in-Publication Data*
NAMES: McClellan, Andrew M., 1984– author.
TITLE: Abused bodies in Roman epic / Andrew M. McClellan.
DESCRIPTION: Cambridge : Cambridge University Press, 2019. | Includes bibliographical
references and index.
IDENTIFIERS: LCCN 2019002790 | ISBN 9781108482622 (alk. paper)
SUBJECTS: LCSH: Dead in literature. | Mutilation in literature. | Epic poetry, Latin – History
and criticism.
CLASSIFICATION: LCC PA6029.D43 M33 2019 | DDC 870.09/3561–dc23
LC record available at https://lccn.loc.gov/2019002790

ISBN 978-1-108-48262-2 Hardback

*For Zana and Zafir*

# Contents

vii

# *Preface*

My justifications for writing this book and an outline of its structure and arguments are laid out in the Introduction. Here it's a great pleasure to express my gratitude to a number of people who have provided their time and support as I brought this project to life. The present work began as a doctoral dissertation submitted to the University of British Columbia in 2015. First thanks go to Susanna Braund, my supervisor. She has for many years now been my first and best reader. I cannot begin to express or do justice to my many debts to her, academic and otherwise. In alphabetical order, Keyne Cheshire, Francesca D'Alessandro Behr, Laurel Fulkerson, Kyle Gervais, Stephen Guy-Bray, Philip Hardie, Toph Marshall, Siobhán McElduff, Tim Stover, and Gernot Wieland all read drafts of the book, or select chapters, at various stages of composition. Each has offered valuable feedback that has immeasurably improved this final product. I'd like to thank CUP's two anonymous readers for brilliant suggestions, for making me think harder, and for their enthusiasm, which has proved enormously heartening. Audiences in Bryn Mawr, Boston, Boulder, New Brunswick (NJ), Provo, Seattle, Tallahassee, Vancouver, Waco, and Winnipeg have endured bits and pieces of this project. I am grateful for helpful comments on what was often very much work-in-progress. Students in my courses the last few years deserve credit for being my sounding-board for theories and irrationalities; I note in particular seminars on Lucan, Ovid, and the survey 'Epic and History' on Virgil, Lucan, and Silius, at Florida State University. Everyone I've mentioned has saved me from countless blunders. In cases where my stubbornness has won out, they will wish they had saved me from more. All errors that remain are my own responsibility.

I owe many thanks to faculty and friends in the Department of Classical, Near Eastern, and Religious Studies at UBC, and the Classics Department at FSU, two exceptional places to work and learn filled with exceptional people. I single out especially (and for brevity) Susanna Braund, Francis Cairns, Jessica Clark, Laurel Fulkerson, Charmaine Gorrie, Trevor Luke,

Toph Marshall, Daniel Pullen, Tim Stover, and Erika Weiberg for advice and kindness along the way. The final typescript was completed in October 2018 during my first few months in the wonderful Humanities and Classics Department at San Diego State University. Many thanks to Michael Caldwell, Raechel Dumas, Risa Levitt Kohn, Joseph Smith, Jennifer Starkey and the rest of the department for immediately embracing me. Michael Sharp was excited about the project from our first conversation and has been encouraging and helpful ever since. Thanks to Les and Leslie Varley for treating me like family (more than I could have hoped for), and for being my home away from home. Thanks to Erica Cobb for showing me the way and also for some last-minute editing. Karen and Michael McClellan have provided constant encouragement and support. They are the best of parents. And extra-special thanks to my wife, Zana, for putting up with me and for indulging my tastes for gore, even if our conversations sometimes give her nightmares. She also read the entire manuscript and offered enormously helpful advice. Though it's ultimately an inadequate (and morbid?) expression of my gratitude, I offer her and our son Zafir this book nonetheless.

Part of Chapter 1 is a revised and trimmed-down version of a piece that originally appeared as 'The death and mutilation of Imbrius in *Iliad* 13', in the *Yearbook of Ancient Greek Epic*, vol. 1, eds. Ready and Tsagalis (Leiden, 2017): 159–74.

# Notes on Texts and Abbreviations

For the main epic authors discussed in this monograph, I have used the following editions (exceptions/emendations cited in notes): Monro and Allen (1920) for Homer's *Iliad*, Vian (1974–1981) for Apollonius' *Argonautica*, Mynors (1969) for Virgil's *Aeneid*, Housman (1927 2nd ed.) for Lucan's *Bellum ciuile*, Ehlers (1980) for Valerius Flaccus' *Argonautica*, Hill (1983) for Statius' *Thebaid*, and Delz (1987) for Silius Italicus' *Punica*. Other Greek and Latin quotations are from the *Thesaurus Linguae Graecae* and the Packard Humanities Institute. All translations are my own though I have often leaned on earlier versions; my aim has been for utility, not artistry.

In general, abbreviations for Classical authors and their works follow Hornblower, Spawforth, and Eidinow, eds. (2012), *The Oxford Classical Dictionary*, 4th ed. (Oxford), with occasional expansions for the sake of clarity. The main exceptions are Apollonius' *Argonautica* (AR), Lucan's *Bellum ciuile* (*BC*), and Valerius Flaccus' *Argonautica* (VF). Journal abbreviations follow the system of *L'Année philologique*. Note also:

| | |
|---|---|
| *ANRW* | Temporini, H., and W. Haase (1972–), *Aufstieg und Niedergang der römischen Welt*. Berlin. |
| *CIL* | (1862–), *Corpus Inscriptionum Latinarum*. Berlin. |
| *C&S* | *Cultura e scuola* |
| *FGrH* | Jacoby F., et al., (1923–), *Die Fragmente der griechischen Historiker*. Berlin. |
| *ILS* | Dessau, H. (1892–1916), *Inscriptiones Latinae Selectae*. Berlin. |
| *LIMC* | (1982–2009), *Lexicon Iconographicum Mythologiae Classicae*. Zurich. |
| *LSJ* | Liddell, H.G. and R. Scott (1940), *A Greek–English Lexicon*, 9th ed., rev. H. Stuart-Jones, with a revised supplement, ed. P.G.W. Glare (1996). Oxford. |
| *OLD* | Glare, P.G.W. ed. (1968–82), *The Oxford Latin Dictionary*. Oxford. |
| *ORA* | *Oxford Research Archive* |
| *TLL* | (1900–), *Thesaurus Linguae Latinae*. Leipzig. |

# Introduction

In the Introduction to his *Violence: Six Sideways Reflections* Slavoj Žižek offers what amounts to an *apologia* for taking a dispassionate approach to critical analysis of societal violence; by looking 'sideways' at the content we in certain ways highlight our own implicature in it: 'there is a sense in which a cold analysis of violence somehow reproduces and participates in its horror'.[1] While my own approach to the violence in Greek and Roman literature and culture is inherently dispassionate and academic, I do share similar concerns.[2] This is a book about the mistreatment of dead bodies. It's about both the physical abuse directed at enemy corpses and the denial, withholding, perversion, and distortion of funeral rites. These categories involve actions taken consciously against what I shall call the 'rights' owed to dead bodies by more or less universal Greco-Roman customs and standards: corporeal preservation or integrity, funeral ritual, familial and/or communal rites of mourning, the last kiss, the closing of the eyes; also (depending on wealth and status) commemoration, procession, ritual *laudationes* or panegyrics, and so on.[3] It's also a book about literature, about poetry, specifically the Latin epic poems of the early imperial period. But it was not composed in an insular literary vacuum. My writing has coincided with the brutally violent uprising of the so-called Islamic State (ISIS, ISIL, IS, The Caliphate, Daesh, etc.), whose establishment and ascendancy in 2014 are inextricably linked to body and corpse abuses splashed worldwide across the Internet.[4] ISIS does not have anything close to a monopoly on modern violence, but their means and manner of

---

[1] Žižek (2008): 4.

[2] Cf. Evans and Giroux (2015): 40: 'Violence as a subject is seldom broached with ethical care or duty of thought in terms of its political or cultural merit.'

[3] See e.g. Toynbee (1971): 33–72, Hopkins (1983): 201–55, Garland (1985), Flower (1996): 91–127, Lindsay (2000): 161–9.

[4] The group's leader Abu Bakr al-Baghdadi declared the birth of the 'Islamic State' on 28 June 2014 from the pulpit of the Great Mosque of al-Nuri in Mosul, Iraq. In reality the jihadist militant organization has existed in various instantiations since it was founded as 'The Organisation of

disseminating *evidence* of body abuse deserves singular attention here upfront. Let me unpack this a bit more.

The terrorist group is most notorious for a series of snuff films – a fusion of ultra-violent global psychological warfare and mass-media propaganda tool[5] – of brutal decapitations beginning with American journalist James Foley in August 2014. Similar videos of escalating cruelty followed suit,[6] each made more disturbing by the amount of detail and attention paid to production and cinematography: ISIS employs hundreds of videographers and editors responsible for scripting, filming, cutting, and disseminating these films as well as publishing the monthly issue of *Dabiq*, the group's own propaganda magazine.[7] These are performative, spectacularized productions of corporeal mistreatment.

The awful 'artistic' stylization of *actual* body abuse puts my Latin epic material, always at least in part mitigated by time and space and refracted through a generic prism, into much higher relief. The abuses perpetrated by ISIS and its enemies in Iraq and Syria (ISIS' ultra-violence has had an infectious ricocheting effect on all sides of the recent civil wars) viscerally actualize and often mirror the *post mortem* violence contained in Greco-Roman epic's most brutal scenery. ISIS' forum-style Hudud Squares become public venues for decapitations, mutilations, corpse exposure, and heads on pikes;[8] the pick-up truck has replaced the chariot as gruesome vehicle for the dragging of corpses;[9] bodies are summarily dumped in the Tigris or Euphrates, or crucified, or hung from electricity poles, or left to suppurate in fields or by the side of the road as fodder for scavenging animals.[10]

Individual acts of grotesquery proliferate: Hezbollah Brigades fighters have uploaded videos to YouTube of playing 'bongos' with severed human heads; a militiaman whose *nom de guerre* is Abu Azrael ('Angel of Death') 'is shown cutting slices of charred human flesh from an upside-down corpse as though it were shawarma'.[11] The food analogy in Michael

---

Monotheism and Jihad' by Jordanian Abu Musab al-Zarqawi in 2000; see Weiss and Hassan (2016): 1–22.

[5]  Carr (2014); Weiss and Hassan (2016): 173–85; Georgy (2017). Evans and Giroux (2015): 226 call the filmic violence the 'psychological weaponization of imagery'.

[6]  See Cottee (2015) on the 'demonic nature' of ISIS' exponentially horrific videographic terrorism campaign.

[7]  Weiss and Hassan (2016): 173. Cf. Chulov (2016).

[8]  Report by the United Nations commission: www.theguardian.com/world/2014/aug/27/syria-isis-war-crimes-united-nations-un; Weiss and Hassan (2016): xi, 180, 200, 209, 337.

[9]  MacSwan (2016); Weiss and Hassan (2016): 247, 308.

[10]  Weiss and Hassan (2016): 64, 81, 121, 252, 342; Dearden (2017); Georgy (2017).

[11]  Weiss and Hassan (2016): 244.

Weiss and Hassan Hassan's frightening description might recall for epic audiences the brutal cannibalistic threats of Achilles and Hecuba in Homer's *Iliad* (22.345–7; 24.212–13) and the literal and wilful anthropophagous acts of Polyphemus and the Laestrygonians in the *Odyssey* (9.287–93; 10.116, 124; cf. Enn. *Ann.* 319–20 Skutsch; Ov. *Met.* 14.192–212, 233–8), Erichtho in Lucan's *Bellum ciuile* (6.549, 564–9), Tydeus in Statius' *Thebaid* (8.760–2), and Laevinus in Silius Italicus' *Punica* (6.47–53).

As Richard Spencer has noted, all implicit suggestion is shattered in the case of Independent Omar al-Farouq Brigade leader Khaled al-Hamad (aka Abu Sakkar) who in March 2013 was filmed biting the heart and liver he had cut from a Syrian regime soldier's corpse.[12] The video was circulated with enormous fanfare. Spencer cites Achilles' threat to Hector at *Iliad* 22.345–7 as one of the earliest and (probably) most famous literary comparanda: μή με κύον γούνων γουνάζεο μη δὲ τοκήων· | αἲ γάρ πως αὐτόν με μένος καὶ θυμὸς ἀνείη | ὤμ' ἀποταμνόμενον κρέα ἔδμεναι, οἶα ἔοργας, 'do not beg me by my knees or parents, you dog. I wish that my might and heart would impel me to carve up your flesh and devour it, for what you've done.' Hecuba, I might add, will later deride Achilles as a 'raw flesh eater', a sub-human (24.207: ὠμηστής) for his savage behaviour on (and, by implication, off) the battlefield. Her anger degenerates into an amplified threat that she might be able to eat Achilles raw (212–13: τοῦ ἐγὼ μέσον ἧπαρ ἔχοιμι | ἐσθέμεναι προσφῦσα). What Spencer doesn't mention is that al-Hamad's own boast in the video moments before his grisly act is nearly identical to Achilles', with the added component of the raw flesh eating from Hecuba's threat: 'I swear to God, you soldiers of Bashar [al-Assad], you dogs, we will eat from your hearts and livers.'[13]

The use of corpse mistreatment as a form of staged psychological warfare is not a modern phenomenon. In the same geographic territory as the heart of ISIS' self-proclaimed Caliphate in northern Syria and Iraq, the Neo-Assyrian Empire (911–612 BCE) deployed corpse abuse as a form of power-politics. Both the annalistic royal inscriptions and monuments punctuating the capital cities – especially during the bloody reign of Aššurbanipal (668–627 BCE) – betray a 'confection of gore' (both real and artistic) with mutilated, impaled, decapitated, and flayed bodies and limbs creating a public spectacle meant to terrorize subjects and enemies of the Assyrian imperial war machine.[14] Moving westwards, the panoply of heads adorning the Roman fora during various civil wars were not (simply) decorative: this was performative violence showcasing

---

[12] Spencer (2013). On ISIS and Iliadic violence generally see, briefly, Nicolson (2014).

[13] Bouckaert (2013) provides the translation.

[14] See Richardson (2007): 196–200; cf. Bleibtreu (1991), Bahrani (2008): 23–55.

the steep price paid by those declared (or deemed) *hostes* to the state or to a particular political cause. Only the heads of senators or elites were singled out for display: these were the most recognizable and carried the most visual and symbolic – and indeed monetary – value (App. *B Civ.* 1.71; Dio Cass. 30–35 fr. 102.9).[15] Centuries later, Genghis Khan used catapults to hurl rotting corpses over siege walls as a form of psychological warfare, and after sacking Samarkand in 1220 he created a massive pyramid outside the city of severed citizens' heads 'as a signal to everyone that the Mongols meant business'.[16] The Byzantine Greek historian Chalcondyles (*Hist.* 9.104) records that upon seeing over 20,000 impaled Turks outside the Wallachian capital of Târgoviște in June 1462, the Ottoman king Mehmed II, overwhelmed by such an atrocious sight, decided not to attack Vlad the Impaler and his army. I could go on.

Spectacularized violence of this sort is intended to invoke audience gaze. But more disturbing is its ability to *attract* it. In her gripping book *Severed: A History of Heads Lost and Heads Found*, Frances Larson documents the simultaneous repulsion and allure of terrorist decapitation videos (from *Wall Street Journal* reporter Daniel Pearl in 2002 to more recent execution videos) and other graphic snuff films released by jihadist groups, through search-engine statistics, downloads, and mass-media attention.[17] Despite overwhelming revulsion in the face of acts perpetrated by the murderers, audiences appear to be captivated by the sick 'drama' of the videos. These films are for many, quite frankly, entertainment. Audience attraction to public executions has for centuries been definitively intoxicating, as Larson details.[18] What has changed in much more recent history is not interest in the spectacle, but a general sense of impropriety associated with it:

> [It] was not that the sights on the scaffold became unseemly, it was that the persistently enthralled spectators became something of an embarrassment, and also, perhaps, a threat to social order. Public executions came to an end, not because of the executions themselves but because of a widening gap between the sensibilities of spectators who came to see them and the definition of acceptable behaviour among the elite.[19]

Access to these videos via the Internet permits indiscretion and provides space: we have front row seats to a horror show we don't need to be 'on-set' to witness: the Internet mediates our gaze. Despite – or more accurately,

---

[15] See Jervis (2001): 133–5 on Marius and Cinna's display of the heads of elite rivals.
[16] Grayling (2017): 60.     [17] Larson (2014): 77–84; also Larson (2015).
[18] Larson (2014): 84–108.     [19] Larson (2014): 84–5.

*because of* – the graphic violence, many millions of viewers consciously tune in. The point here is that body-horror and violence are inherently alluring. We strangely 'enjoy' (in a frightening and self-defeating Kantian or Lacanian sense) the horrific images. But we should at least take the time to acknowledge our own captivation and our role in the grisly spectacle, both as wilful readers and viewers. It's a role with which the perpetrators of this perverse art-horror seem acutely *au fait*.

Lost amidst the tragic artistic and cultural casualties of ISIS' takeover and destruction of much of Palmyra's (Homs Governorate, Syria) ancient relics in the summer of 2015 was another video in which child-soldiers were made to line up twenty-five Assad regime soldiers and shoot them in the back of the head. What was the venue for this staged atrocity? The centre of the city's Roman theatre.[20] Over forty years ago terrorism expert Bryan Jenkins argued forcefully that at its core terrorism is theatre;[21] can we call this literally staged violence at Palmyra 'metatheatrical terrorism'? ISIS propaganda videos routinely splice pirated material from Hollywood blockbusters like *The Lord of the Rings: The Return of the King* (2003), *Kingdom of Heaven* (2005), *Flags of Our Fathers* (2006), *G.I. Joe: The Rise of Cobra* (2009) (etc.) with real-life footage of murder and terror.[22] More striking perhaps are scenes that explicitly re-create famous shots and motifs from action films (e.g. *The Hunger Games* (2012), *Sniper* (2014), *Mad Max: Fury Road* (2015)) and video games (*Halo*, the *Call of Duty* franchise, *Gears of War*),[23] granting them 'life' in a world that frighteningly blurs or collapses the distinction between reality and fiction. The aim is to appeal and appal, to traffic in horror by actualizing the stylized violence of Hollywood 'myth' that has otherwise always maintained a fictionalized distance.

Is this all that far from Rome's theatricalized 'fatal charades', wherein myth and mytho-history served as a baseline for painfully real 're-enactments' on the arena's bloody stage?[24] Similarly for Roman audiences, the appeal seems to rest on the 'violation of the theatrical by the actual', as Shadi Bartsch notes; the 'conflation' of fiction and reality adds 'a certain frisson to the experience of the spectators'.[25] The rupturing of the distinction between reality and fiction forms a more broadly pervasive facet of the 'political theatre' of the early imperial period, as Bartsch and others have argued.[26] Role-playing, something for which aristocratic Romans trained

---

[20] Weiss and Hassan (2016): 273.
[21] Jenkins (1974), cited in Cottee (2014); cf. Larson (2014): 83–4; Evans and Giroux (2015): 228–9.
[22] Bond (2017); Ma (2018).    [23] Kang (2014); Parkin (2016); Bond (2017).    [24] Coleman (1990).
[25] Bartsch (1994): 51. Cf. Fagan (2011): 235–7.
[26] E.g. Bartsch (1994); Boyle (2006): esp. 162–4, 176–88.

in declamation were acutely prepared, became a vital way of negotiating the complexities of living under *principes*. Sometimes the *princeps* 'acted out' atrocities on stage, as Nero seems to have done, playing mythic roles (Canace, Orestes, Oedipus, Hercules) that echoed the real-life violence he committed against his own family (Suet. *Ner.* 21.3).[27] The world of imperial Rome was suffused with actors and spectators, reality itself a 'spectacle' designed to be *viewed* (Sen. *Ot.* 5.3: *spectatores nos tantis rerum spectaculis*). The impact of this rupturing of the real into the imaginary, and the imaginary into the real, on the epic literature composed at this time is, as we shall see, pervasive.

Audience has a major role to play in the action, and authors (film and literary) know this and toy with our voyeuristic interest with varying levels of sadism. Our engagement with Rome's epic poetry is never as real as ISIS' video executions, of course. The poetic violence is fictionalized. But it isn't pure fiction, and I will stress repeatedly that corpse abuse in the Latin epics everywhere reflects and reacts upon the very real violence perpetrated in Rome from the end of the Republic through the early empire. Repeated allusions in the texts to actual violence and corpse mistreatment committed by Romans destabilizes the mythic or mytho-historic framework of the fictionalized epic world, blending fiction and reality in ways that nod to the inherent theatricality of the imperial socio-political system.

Although he invokes, generically, 'Medieval' (not Roman) violence in a *New York Times* article detailing the staggering production quality of ISIS' abhorrent videos, David Carr provocatively suggests that: 'Video beheadings are a triple death – murder and defilement in a public way – and YouTube becomes the pike on which the severed heads are displayed.'[28] There has been, as in Rome, no shortage of eager *spectatores*. Though the medium through which audiences experience this material provides an important detachment or distancing effect, the literary (or theatrical/filmic) façade must not blind us to the realities of body abuse across human history (and into the present); it must not blind us to our own capacity to strangely *enjoy* the abuses. As Larson aptly notes regarding the terrifying allure of severed heads: 'The dead human face is a siren: dangerous but irresistible.'[29]

[27] Boyle (2006): 184.    [28] Carr (2014).
[29] Larson (2014): 8; cf. Kristeva (2012): 89: 'no one looks at a severed head except art lovers, voyeurs like you and me'.

## 'Viewing' Epic Corpses

As book 8 of Lucan's *Bellum ciuile* builds to a crescendo, with Pompey the Great's relentlessly foreshadowed death and mutilation fast approaching, the poet describes the paradoxical reaction of Pompey's wife Cornelia to what awaits her doomed husband. Cornelia and Pompey have only just arrived in Egypt after Pompey's devastating loss to Julius Caesar and his renegade army at the decisive battle of Pharsalus in Thessaly (48 BCE). They are greeted by the feigned hospitality of assassins sent by the boy-Pharaoh, Ptolemy XIII. This pretence fools no one. Cornelia levels protests at Pompey as he knowingly leaves the relative safety of his fleet for the tiny death-boat that will serve as the stage for his grisly murder and decapitation. Paralyzed, Cornelia fixes her gaze reluctantly upon him (*BC* 8.589–92):

> haec ubi frustra
> effudit, prima pendet tamen anxia puppe,
> attonitoque metu nec quoquam auertere uisus
> nec Magnum spectare potest.

> When she vainly poured out
> these words, still anxiously she hangs over the stern's edge,
> and, with thunderstruck with fear, she can neither turn away her gaze,
> nor look at Magnus.

This scene has received virtually no critical reaction from scholars[30] despite its almost kindred connection to an earlier moment of paradoxical paralysis that has been posited as a launching pad for recent debate about the 'competing voices' in Lucan's narrative. Before he describes the extreme horrors of the battle of Pharsalus between Pompey's Republican forces and Caesar's army, Lucan attempts to relegate his subject to darkness and to silence (7.552–6):

> hanc fuge, mens, partem belli tenebrisque relinque,
> nullaque tantorum discat me uate malorum,
> quam multum bellis liceat ciuilibus, aetas.
> a potius pereant lacrimae pereantque querellae:
> quidquid in hac acie gessisti, Roma, tacebo.

> Mind, flee this part of the war and abandon it in shadows,
> and let no age learn of such evils from me as a poet
> how much is permitted in civil wars.
> It's better that these tears and protests vanish:
> whatever you did in this battle, Rome, I'll keep quiet.

---

[30] Though see Rimell (2015): 244.

The events of the civil war's climax are too horrible to narrate, yet Lucan, by continuing his narrative, betrays his own obsession with its horrifying content as this *praeteritio* makes way immediately for a bizarre but detailed description of the battle that should not be described (the civil war is *nefas* and thus 'unspeakable'[31]). This is an *internal* struggle; Lucan's *mens* has replaced the traditional epic *Musa*.[32]

But the paradox here is a larger feature of Lucan's poetic programme, as Jamie Masters has articulated: 'In the struggle between Caesar and Pompey, then, lies the paradigm of Lucan's narrative technique: the conflict between the will to tell the story and the horror which shies from telling it.'[33] If Lucan's narratorial dilemma describes something like a distorted metapoetics of writing about epic *nefas*, then in Cornelia's frozen stare is to be found a programmatic metapoetic marker for a system of viewing or reading it. Her vision of the scene we are about to witness, presaged from the outset (and imbued with forewarning both intratextual and historical) as a *post mortem* mutilation, is the perspective through which we are invited to view the abuses we know will follow; the scene is 'focalized' through Cornelia.[34] Yet the outcome of this perspective alignment is unsettling. For Cornelia, the paradox proves too much: she faints (8.661–2) before Pompey's head is ultimately severed and thrust onto a pike. She cannot 'read' any further, but we must, with Lucan, go on.

This scene powerfully articulates both the difficulties involved in viewing/reading scenes of corpse mistreatment and the simultaneous allure and attraction to abuses that provoke horror and enjoyment. Cornelia's paralyzed reaction to viewing Pompey's decapitation (in effect, an execution) chillingly evokes the psychologizing explicit in the title of Larson's *CNN* article on the topic of viewer reactions to terrorist decapitation videos: 'ISIS beheadings: why we're too horrified to watch, too fascinated to turn away.' Cornelia cannot help but watch the tragedy unfolding before her eyes, she's paralyzed, until the inherent paradox conquers her and she simply passes out. We read on (or we don't), but like Lucan's Cornelia, as an audience for this cruelty we may find ourselves caught in what Noël Carroll calls the 'horror paradox':[35] we want to watch (or read) yet we feel the moral

---

[31] O'Higgins (1988): 217 n.28; Feeney (1991): 276–7; Martindale (1993): 72.
[32] Narducci (2002): 175.
[33] Masters (1992): 9, and further 147–8, 210–15. See also Henderson (1998): 185–6, O'Higgins (1988): 215–16, Feeney (1991): 277.
[34] The pioneering studies on focalization and classical literature are de Jong (1987) and Fowler (1990).
[35] Carroll (1990). Ganiban (2007): 49 invokes Carroll's work in his important study of horror and *nefas* in Statius' *Thebaid*.

implications of viewing something horrific, something almost always signalled to us by the narrator or other intratextual characters as unwatchable or unspeakable and, in the act of viewing, we become paralyzed by these incongruous emotional reactions.[36]

Philosophizing and theorizing (ancient and modern) have focused directly on the corpse as an instigator of paralyzing horror. Plato and Aristotle recognized a similar paradoxical phenomenon of the simultaneous attraction and aversion to rotting corpses. Plato describes the disturbing situation at *Republic* 439e–40a, where one Leontius is unable to pull his eyes away from corpses festering in the street despite his revulsion both at their sight and at his own inability to look away:

ἀλλ᾽, ἦν δ᾽ ἐγώ, ποτὲ ἀκούσας τι† πιστεύω τούτῳ· ὡς ἄρα Λεόντιος ὁ Ἀγλαΐωνος ἀνιὼν ἐκ Πειραιῶς ὑπὸ τὸ βόρειον τεῖχος ἐκτός, αἰσθόμενος νεκροὺς παρὰ τῷ δημίῳ κειμένους, ἅμα μὲν ἰδεῖν ἐπιθυμοῖ, ἅμα δὲ αὖ δυσχεραίνοι καὶ ἀποτρέποι ἑαυτόν, καὶ τέως μὲν μάχοιτό τε καὶ παρακαλύπτοιτο, κρατούμενος δ᾽ οὖν ὑπὸ τῆς ἐπιθυμίας, διελκύσας τοὺς ὀφθαλμούς, προσδραμὼν πρὸς τοὺς νεκρούς, 'Ἰδοὺ ὑμῖν', ἔφη, 'ὦ κακοδαίμονες, ἐμπλήσθητε τοῦ καλοῦ θεάματος'.

'But', I said, 'I heard a story once, one which I believe, that Leontius the son of Aglaion, coming up from the Peiraeus under the outside of the north wall, noticing the dead bodies sprawled out by the public executioner, both desired to look at them, and simultaneously was unable to look, turning himself away, and that for a long time he struggled and covered his head; but conquered nonetheless by his desire, having opened his eyes wide, he ran up to the corpses and said, "there, you evil things, sate yourselves on the beautiful spectacle".'

His powerlessness to avert his gaze, caught between incompatible responses of desire (ἐπιθυμοῖ . . . ἐπιθυμίας) and disgust (δυσχεραίνοι), is so disturbing to him that Leontius curses his own eyes (ὦ κακοδαίμονες). Aristotle describes a similar reaction but as it applies to the *mimesis* of horrific images at *Poetics* 1448b10-12: ἃ γὰρ αὐτὰ λυπηρῶς ὁρῶμεν, τούτων τὰς εἰκόνας τὰς μάλιστα ἠκριβωμένας χαίρομεν θεωροῦντες, οἷον θηρίων τε μορφὰς τῶν ἀτιμοτάτων καὶ νεκρῶν, 'we enjoy looking at the most precise images of things which are naturally painful for us to see, e.g. the forms of the most wretched animals and of corpses' (cf. Arist. *Rh.* 1371b4-10). Aristotle does not elaborate beyond stating that mimetic objects, no matter how horrific, are inherently (σύμφυτος) enjoyable to everyone (τὸ χαίρειν . . . πάντας)

---

[36] On gaze and vision in Greco-Roman epic see Lovatt's (2013) monumental study.

because imitation sparks learning and the pursuit of knowledge, both of which elicit pleasure.

For Julia Kristeva the corpse is the ultimate form of abjection which pulls and repels the viewer simultaneously: 'It is death infecting life',[37] and this at the same time 'beckons to us and ends up engulfing us'.[38] Though Kristeva doesn't cite him, in his *Critique of the Power of Judgment*, Immanuel Kant had similarly articulated the troubling physico-pathemic reaction of viewers to images/scenes of extreme 'ugliness' (*Hässlichkeit*) that produce 'disgust' (*Ekel*), but a disgust that he argues is actively tied to an experience of 'enjoyment' (*Genuss*: tantamount to Lacanian/Kristevan *jouissance*).[39] The result is a corporeal petrifaction brought about by the opposite pull of these seemingly antithetical reactions. Slavoj Žižek sums up nicely: 'Do we not get here [in Kant] an echo of what Kristeva calls abject? The object of enjoyment is by definition *disgusting*, and what makes it disgusting is a weird superego injunction that appears to emanate from it, a call to enjoy it even if (and precisely because) we find it ugly and desperately try to resist being dragged into it.'[40] William Ian Miller's work on disgust identifies this same paradox (the corpse for Miller is a feature of the categorical 'uncanny'): 'we cannot avoid one of the most troubling aspects of the disgusting: it attracts as well as repels. The disgusting has an allure; it exerts a fascination which manifests itself in the difficulty of averting our eyes at a gory accident . . . or in the attraction of horror films.'[41] Disgust, according to Carolyn Korsmeyer, provokes a strange autonomic 'magnetism'.[42] The situation is not dissimilar to Augustine's famous story of his friend Alypius who is dragged against his will to the Colosseum only to be sucked into the intoxicating visual spectacle of bodily violence.[43] Despite his best efforts he eventually 'drinks in' the games with rabid brio and cannot pull his eyes away (*Conf.* 6.8.13): *ut enim uidit illum sanguinem, immanitatem simul ebibit et non se auertit, sed fixit aspectum et hauriebat furias et nesciebat, et delectabatur scelere certaminis et cruenta uoluptate inebriabatur*, 'for when he saw that blood, he gulped down the savagery and did not pull himself away, but he fixed his gaze and drank in the madness mindlessly, and was delighting in the wickedness of the contest and became drunk on cruel pleasure'.

Adriana Cavarero expands upon the notion of viewer paralysis when confronted with scenes of horror (the *Horrorism* of her book's title), by

[37] Kristeva (1982): 4.   [38] Kristeva (1982): 4.
[39] Guyer (2000): 190–1, 203. See Parret (2009), Žižek (2016): 154–8.   [40] Žižek (2016): 157.
[41] Miller (1997): 22 *et passim*.   [42] Korsmeyer (2011): 113–35.
[43] Cf. Sen. *Ep.* 7. On the 'lure of the arena' see Coleman (1990): 57–9, Fagan (2011).

focusing on the dead body which has itself been broken, dismembered, mutilated, mangled, exploded, dehumanized (she zeroes in on suicide bombings): 'movement is blocked in total paralysis, and each victim is affected on its own. Gripped by revulsion in the face of a form of violence that appears more inadmissible than death, the body reacts as if nailed to the spot, hairs standing on end.'[44] She identifies a true psychosomatic reaction to the viewing of horrific images that, in many ways, perfectly applies to Lucan's aphoristic psychologizing of Cornelia's ekplectic gaze at Pompey in *BC* 8.

Yet all of these analyses identify the corpse as an endpoint, as a limit. Even Cavarero's discussion of violence that rips the body to pieces focuses on the moment of death; the experience of horror doesn't extend beyond violence that is life-ending.[45] But for the Roman epicists of the early imperial period death was a limit that needed to be ruptured and explored, it needed to be *viewed*. Violence in these imperial epics is presented as an aesthetic 'spectacle' that has the power to both repel and attract our gaze. That our extratextual implicatedness in the violence aimed at dead bodies has an effect on our *own* bodies, made manifest through a kind of readerly paralysis, is a masterstroke of the more perverse elements of post-Augustan epic poetics. The audience takes on a virtual choral role, watching, participating even (through our voyeuristic gaze) in the abuses, but unable to intervene.

The mistreated body in these poems is foremost a (mimetic) visual/corporeal specimen of violence or malign neglect. But it's worth stressing here upfront the semantic capaciousness of the body both in the Roman context and in Western thought generally. Bodies – and indeed corpses – in these poems are almost never simply *just* bodies. To take the most enduring symbolic construct, politics posits the human body as an ordering metaphor (the 'body politic'), comprised of 'social members', e.g. head(s), limbs, and appendages of state (*caput, membra, partes*, etc.) which must work together to function properly. If they do not work together or if a part has defected or has been severed from the whole, chaos ensues. The likening of a political body to a human body had a long tradition in Rome, as Menenius Agrippa's parable suggests. Livy tells us that in order to quell a plebeian revolt in 494 BCE, Menenius Agrippa delivered a speech comparing the revolt to the rebellion of various body parts from what they perceived to be a gluttonous and lazy belly (2.32.8–12). The details and date are less important than the lasting symbolic impact. And it's clear that by

[44] Cavarero (2009): 8.     [45] See the important critique in Miller (2014): 109–15.

the last few decades of the Republic, the rupturing of the state could naturally inspire comparisons with a bloodless, lifeless body (Cic. *Att.* 4.18.2), or a body infected with plague or poison (Sall. *Cat.* 10.6, 11.3) or a gangrenous body (Varro fr. 123 Riposati), or a body torn to pieces (Sall. *Jug.* 41).[46] The metaphorical imagery of bodily dissolution mirrors the *physical* violence visited upon the Roman citizenry during the internecine violence of the end of the Republic; the State doubles as victim for the atrocities aimed at its collective *corpus*.

   This 'organological' metaphor has a considerable *Nachleben* in the West. The body politic rounds into form in the Middle Ages and the Renaissance, most explicitly spawned from John of Salisbury's political treatise *Policraticus* (c. 1159). Drawing on imagery from Cicero, Livy, and Seneca, John's state (*res publica*) is a living – yet static, unageing, undying – male body composed of various functional parts, susceptible only to internal disease and infection. Tudor and Stuart England gave rise to the theory of the king's 'two bodies': one physical and perishable, the other political and, in effect, immortal. For Thomas Hobbes – building upon William Harvey's politicized language of the body's cardiovascular system – the commonwealth is a political 'automaton', a human construction mimicking God's creative venture;[47] the famous frontispiece of his *Leviathan* is a symbolic justification for the sovereign authority of the monarch, whose body is shown (massively) comprised of the pixilated people he represents and governs. For writers on either side of the 'Revolution Controversy' in England in the late eighteenth and early nineteenth centuries, events across the Channel in France conjured parricidal images of revolutionary children mutilating and murdering the parental body of the *ancien régime*.[48] Imagery in the post-Augustan epics of bodies and/as *state* bodies ripped to pieces as a result of violence and war plays a seismic role both in the Roman imperial literary system and in the development of successive political metaphorizing.

   Literary works themselves were also endowed with corporeality in ancient literary criticism. Latin could comfortably pun *corpus* as a 'body of work' (*OLD* s.v. *corpus* 16a; *TLL* iv 1020–1021), language we similarly use today. The vocabulary deployed to describe an ancient 'book' borrowed bodily terminology: the scroll came wrapped in a *membrana* of parchment; the papyrus roll's edge was the *frons*; the papyrus itself was wound around the *umbilicus*.[49] Roman rhetorical handbooks referred to the structure and sections of a speech through corporeal signification (*corpus, membra, caput,*

---

[46] See Walters (2011); also succinctly Mebane (2016): 194–9.   [47] Cavarero (2002).
[48] McClellan (2018).   [49] Farrell (2007): 184–5, and the more expansive study in Farrell (1999).

etc.),[50] imagery going back at least to Plato (*Phdr.* 264c, 265e; cf. Arist. *Poet.* 1459a20). And the language of poetic metrics was explicitly bodily: Horace (*Sat.* 2.6.17; *Ars P.* 7–8) and Ovid (*Am.* 1.1.1–4, 3.1.7–10; *Tr.* 3.1.56) for instance have fun with metrical 'feet' (*pes/pedes*). More specific to literary content and style, a poem could be 'thin' or 'fat/bloated', ruggedly 'masculine' or 'effeminate/soft', sententious and thus 'amputated' or 'mutilated'.[51] Horace famously compares a well-crafted poem to an aesthetically/proportionally pleasing physical body (in visual art) in contrast to malformed hybrid monsters (*Ars P.* 1–12; cf. Tac. *Dial.* 21.8 on oratory), while Seneca's paratactic *sententiae* create, for Quintilian, a 'dismembered' and incoherent literary *corpus* (Quint. *Inst.* 10.1.130).

The treatment of both living and dead bodies in these texts has, then, pointed metapoetic potential.[52] Shattered and scattered *corpora* can be seen to reflect syntactical, stylistic, and narrative dismemberment:[53] but so too the *corpus* of an earlier author can serve as a site for 'revivified' allusion and surgical probing. In *Satires* 1.4, to take a well-worn but important example for our purposes, Horace claims that if one were to tear (1.4.57: *eripias*) Lucilius' satirical poetry from its context and rhythmic structures it would be impossible to identify even the 'limbs of a dismembered poet' in his Latin (62: *disiecti membra poetae*). The issue here is poetic register and what differentiates Lucilian satire from epic poetry, and Horace enjoins the reader to play along by slicing up and comparing Lucilian and Ennian verses.[54] But this metaphorical image of *imagined* butchered poetic 'limbs' follows in the satire itself a 'dismembered' chunk of Ennius which Horace hews from the earlier poet's *corpus* and affixes to his own poem (60–1). The *membrum* of Ennius – which, Horace claims not without wit, we could never fully decontextualize through excision or *metathesis* – is both a 'limb' of the long-dead poet and a fragment of the poet's poetic *corpus* (*Annales* 225–6 Skutsch). The presence of an Ennian citation in this satire and an explicit invitation to chop up the verses and redistribute their parts might remind us of the invasive and probing procedure of allusive *compositio* and of Horace's own engagement with earlier literary *materia*; we are,

---

[50]  Keith (1999): 41 with n.4.

[51]  Most (1992): 406–8; Keith (1999); Rimell (2002); Lovatt (2005): 209–11; Bartsch (2015): Chapter 1.

[52]  See Kennedy (2018) for some observations similar to those that follow here; his source text is the scene of Hippolytus' 'reassembly' at the end of Seneca's *Phaedra*; note also Lohmar (2013): 116–18.

[53]  E.g. Most (1992): 408 on Senecan and Lucanian style; Quint (1993): 140–7 on Lucanian narrative fragmentation.

[54]  Horace includes his own satire with Lucilius' in this comparative example, but only ironically.

in a sense, invited into the poet's intertextual workshop before he has supplied the *extrema manus*.

Horace plays upon the well-established semantic range of *corpus*. Ennius' physical body is long gone, but his poetic *corpus* is gifted a somewhat bizarre afterlife in the resurrected *membra* that later poets, like Horace himself, conjure in their fragmented allusions to that other body he's left behind. The poet's physical body is (ideally) inviolable, sacred yet perishable; his symbolically inextricable literary *corpus*, however, is a site for critical necroscopic analysis, dissection, mutilation, and repurposing. The juxtaposition in 'treatments' here is sharp, and the violence of Horace's imagery should not elude us.[55] The content/context of the Ennian passage he excises is, not accidentally, *Discordia* and the opening of the gates of war in *Annales* 7. War instigates violence, death, and the physical rupturing of bodies on the field of battle just the way Horace describes treating his forebears' (literary) bodies and initiates his own fragmenting of Ennius' epic.

We might usefully compare Macrobius' playful investigation of intertextual correspondences between Lucretius and Virgil in the sixth book of the *Saturnalia*.[56] Macrobius stockpiles a series of fragmented sketches linking the two poets' works. He then puns, like Horace, on the double meaning of *membra* by asking his audience to notice allusive resonances in the chunks of text he has just reproduced and compared (*Sat.* 6.2.14): *nonne uobis uidentur membra huius descriptionis ex uno fonte manasse?* 'does it not seem to you that the *membra* of this description derive from a single source?' Again the context from which these poetic 'limbs' have been severed is telling and amplifies Macrobius' morbid joke: the material is drawn from horror scenes of plague-ridden and festering *corpora* at Lucr. 6.1138–1286 and *Georgics* 3.478–566.

Given the obsession in epic poetry with corpses, the metapoetic system outlined here has ramifications. One way of reading the mistreatment of the dead in the early imperial epics that occupy the present study is through the lens of a Bloomian/Oedipal corporeal metapoetics of reception. In these hyper-intertextual poems the fates of endless parades of violated bodies suggest a viciously self-conscious competitive poetics aimed at and spawned from the *corpora* of literary precedence.[57] In this light creative imitation doubles as generative '*corpus* abuse' as each successive author

---

[55] Freudenburg (1993): 148; Oliensis (1998): 23–4; Bartsch (2015): 21.  [56] Butler (2011): 59.
[57] Lohmar (2013) argues along similar lines, reading Roman epic violence (corpse mistreatment is not a focus) through the lens of Derridean *différance*.

picks his way through a vast poetical graveyard for material to repurpose, shape, and re-embody.

This intertextual system is complex and cumulative. What Homer does with corpse treatment in the *Iliad* is re-examined and repurposed by Virgil, whose engagement with the motif is then repurposed by Lucan, who is also (simultaneously) reading Homer through Virgil's reading of Homer, and also, at times, reading Homer irrespective of Virgil's reading of Homer, and so on. Scholars have termed this system of intertextual gymnastics 'double allusion', or 'window reference' in the system of epic poetics.[58] The allusive games at play here can feel labyrinthine, and though I do not necessarily subscribe to Jacques Derrida's conception of analyzing complex literature (in his case reading Joyce's *Finnegans Wake*) as a 'war' between author and reader to reconstruct 'meaning',[59] sometimes it does feel this way when reading Latin epic.

A quick note, then, on intertextuality. When I refer to allusions or intertexts linking the work of a later author to an earlier author's 'model' text, I am making assumptions about the creative and allusive process of composition and poetic engagement. Authorial intentionality in the analysis of intertextuality has been a major point of debate in classical philology. Recovering the intention of the alluding author does not necessarily affect our ability to interpret intertexts in a void; nor does it mean that we should ignore intentionality altogether even if we can't prove it, as this process of (attempted) 'recovery' is useful for a deeper engagement with the texts.[60] In this way I align myself generally with Stephen Hinds and Joseph Farrell (and others) who have sought to revive the role of the author in reader-response criticism, in many ways as a reaction to the semiological reader-oriented intertextual framework that aims to eliminate the author from the picture entirely.[61] I will make claims at times about an author's unknowable intentions, yet the importance of these claims will ultimately rest on my ability to convince readers that there is something meaningful that emerges from the relationship between the specific texts I highlight, whether that relationship was 'intended' or not. Roman epic is so vastly self-reflexive, intra-/extra-critical, and self-conscious of generic literary

---

[58] Thomas (1986): 188–9: 'window reference'; McKeown (1987): 37–45: 'double allusion'. Noted by Hardie (1989): 4, with 17 n.8, as 'double imitation'.

[59] Derrida (1985): 145–58; see Miller (2014): 160–73. Cf. Eagleton (2008): 71: 'It is always worth testing out any literary theory by asking: How would it work with Joyce's *Finnegans Wake?*'

[60] E.g. Hinds (1998): 50: this process is 'good to think with'.

[61] Hinds (1998): 47–51, 144; Farrell (2005). For reader-oriented approaches see Fowler (1997a), Gale (2000): 4–6, Edmunds (2001). See the succinct summation in Ganiban (2007): 6–8.

history, that intertextual cues are as much an orchestrated open-armed invitation to the reader as a Derridean challenge to interpretative warfare.

Something like an elaborate poetic dialogue is discernible through the texts, but text-focused philological readings are importantly inseparable from cultural-historical, ideological, readings of these poems. This should be obvious, so much so that over twenty years ago Alessandro Barchiesi could compare dissenters on either side to Japanese snipers in the jungle fighting a war lost long ago.[62] That the poetic intertexts are everywhere supplemented by presupposed cultural-historical referents adds a deeper context to the poetic dialogue, and with it creates a cohesive system for unpacking meaning. For my purposes, the reference point for the Roman epics is most crucially Roman civil wars and the abuses that inevitably came along with them. Amphitheatrical display is also important, though there we are dealing more with violence inflicted upon *living* bodies.[63] Corpse abuse and funeral denial were hallmarks of the civil wars, both Republican and imperial,[64] and the impact of witnessing these abuses cannot have been insignificant to the authors and their audiences. The *Aeneid* is loaded with civil war imagery teasing at the internecine violence Virgil lived through which precipitated the establishment of the principate (Chapter 1). Lucan wrote an entire epic detailing the civil war between Caesar and Pompey that Virgil alludes to elliptically (Chapters 2, 3). The Flavian epicists fill their verses with civil war, and while this plays off earlier epic civil war themes, the events of 68–69 CE, which brought about the establishment of the Flavian dynasty, provide constant cultural-historical reference points for the horrors contained in those poems (Chapters 4, 5, and 6).

## Origins and Aims

To steal a line from Mary Roach's wonderfully morbid book *Stiff: The Curious Lives of Human Cadavers*: 'A book about dead bodies is a conversational curveball.'[65] This has mostly been my experience talking to colleagues, friends, and family. But more to the point, it has also been my experience perusing scholarship on issues related to corpse mistreatment in epic poetry. I leave more extended discussion of secondary sources to later

---

[62] Barchiesi (2001): 147, originally published in Barchiesi (1997). See more generally the programmatic discussion in Barchiesi (2015): Chapters 3 and 4.

[63] Leigh (1997); see also Most (1992).

[64] Hinard (1984) on corpse abuse during the proscriptions; Voisin (1985) on 'head-hunting'; see also Kyle (1998), Richlin (1999), Hope (2000), Barry (2008).

[65] Roach (2003): 14.

analyses and my footnotes, but in general little has been written in any length or depth about corpse abuse in Roman epic, and when scholars do broach the topic, the discussions are most often selective, with individual scenes or individual poems singled out as cases for analysis. My present work is an attempt at a more expansive and synoptic examination of a collective body of epic material related to corpse mistreatment.

There are of course exceptions,[66] but even when scholars do enter into the discussion of corpse mistreatment more broadly it's usually deployed as a means of describing the behaviour of the abuser, while the corpse itself is something of an afterthought, 'collateral damage' to larger interests in human *furor* and rage, or exegeses on madness, bloodlust, and so on. My aim has been to start from the perspective of the corpse and work backwards like, as Giovanni De Luna describes it in his book on corpse treatment in modern warfare, 'looking at the grass from the perspective of the roots'.[67] That is, I am attempting to signal the corpse as a crucial entryway into analyses of the violence and abuses of war in these epic poems and not simply as a physical by-product of war. I privilege the corpse as a critical 'character' in these poems, a character with a bizarre *post mortem* existence that defies the typical limitation imposed by death. These poets, by guiding reader attention to the now-lifeless body, demand that the corpse is worthy of the same attention that the living person had been. This shift in focus is revelatory for the functioning of each poet's epic universe. My study offers a fundamental re-evaluation of violence and warfare in Latin epic poetry through this readjustment of interpretative perspective.

I say 'Latin epic' since there are a number of excellent works on the motif of corpse mistreatment in the *Iliad* that deserve special mention. Charles Segal's *The Theme of the Mutilation of the Corpse in the Iliad* is the seminal study, and many of Segal's conclusions form the basis of later examinations by (especially) James Redfield, Emily Vermeule, Jasper Griffin, and Jean-Pierre Vernant.[68] These studies have in many ways served as my launch-pad, and this book represents a concerted attempt to provide for the later Roman epic material on corpses something like what these Homeric scholars have done for the *Iliad*.

---

[66] See e.g. Burck (1981); Pagán (2000); Berno (2004); Erasmo (2008): esp. Chapter 4.

[67] De Luna (2006): 42: 'È come guardare l'erba dalla parte delle radici'. De Luna's book details mass globalized violence in war, with a focus on the twentieth century, from the perspective of the treatment of corpses in those wars. Each chapter works outwardly from a single photograph displaying corpse mistreatment in a particular warzone – the effect mimics (unintentionally?) Bertold Brecht's photo-epigrammatic *Kriegsfibel*.

[68] Segal (1971); Redfield (1975); Vermeule (1979), Griffin (1980); Vernant (1991). See also most recently Kucewicz (2016), McClellan (2017).

A central driving force of these analyses of corpse treatment in the *Iliad* concerns the 'limits' placed on violence in war. This has obvious implications for individual actors (victors and victims, killers and killed), but also for the larger picture in the poem of the institution of warfare and its intrinsic parameters. This last point has been less clearly articulated but it has ramifications for my interests in the Roman epics and thus deserves a brief comment. While the aims of war and warring are circumstantial and variable – war can be about economics and supply-lines, territory, politics, restitution, religion, or ideology – warfare itself, especially ancient warfare, provides killing and death as a brutal but reasonable way of negotiating the 'transaction' of the conflict, whatever it is about exactly.[69] As Carl von Clausewitz, Georges Betaille, Roger Caillois, and others have articulated, warfare is rationalized, organized, institutionalized killing and violence. Killing and death are necessary, requisite characteristics of this transaction of war; they are definable and measurable. The violence becomes a real problem only if the actors fail to appreciate it as the appropriate limit of the use of force in war (a disruption of the categorical *ius in bello*).[70]

When Achilles abuses Hector's corpse, when he refuses him death rights, and refuses his family and city the rights of ritual mourning over his body, he not only demonstrates his own savagery but also instigates an attack upon these parameters of war. This act, or rather the repeated attempts to mutilate Hector's corpse, provides a redefinition of the basic nature of the Trojan War, and the final books of the poem set about analyzing (and ultimately righting) the wrongs of Achilles' transgressions of the normative and regulative features of the institution of war. We know that he has crossed some discernible threshold related to the use of violence because the gods tell us he has gone too far (not to mention the outrage of the human actors in the poem). His actions especially provoke Apollo's complaints and disgust (*Il.* 24.33–54), and lead to Zeus's own intervention and a return to the codes of humanity, which amount to the proper upholding of the rights owed to the dead in war. The real issue is not that Hector has been killed but rather what happens *after* he's killed. It is the mistreatment of his corpse that precipitates chaos and instigates divine action. Given that the *Iliad* is the Ur-text of war, the parameters of war defined therein are crucial for the shaping of subsequent articulations of war in literature, particularly epic literature, and so the system of

---

[69] See Grayling (2017): 117–61 for a wide-ranging discussion of the 'causes of war', broadly defined.

[70] Grayling (2017): 195–8, 204–15 on wartime codes of behaviour in various instantiations of 'just war theory' from Aquinas and Hugo Grotius to the present.

'appropriate' (and inappropriate) expressions of violence in the transaction of war in later literature and culture ultimately are reflected by and reflect back upon this Iliadic model.

Among Étienne Balibar's reflections on 'extreme violence' is his insistence on the uncontrollability of war in its relation to warfare's tendency to revert to extremes of violence, which everywhere serve to destabilize the very definitions of the limits of violence in war. There is some acknowledgement of and adaptation from Clausewitz's basic logic that war, principally defined as a duel between opposing forces, naturally passes to extremes of violence: 'war is an act of force, and there is no logical limit to the application of that force. Each side, therefore, compels its opponent to follow suit; a reciprocal action is started which must lead, in theory, to extremes.'[71] Balibar is interested in these extremes and how far the use of violence can push them. The limits of extreme violence are elusive, mobile, and contested – they are 'heterogeneous' since each war has different ways of measuring what constitutes a transgression of the limits of violence – but they always constitute a transition from the 'appropriate' wartime exercise of might, or 'violence-of-power' (*Gewalt*) to the implementation of *cruelty*.[72]

In considering the treatment of Hector's corpse, what is intrinsically cruel about Achilles' actions is their utter gratuitousness and redundancy. Apollo identifies this, though somewhat obliquely, when he complains to Zeus and the other gods in a striking turn of phrase that Achilles is attempting to mutilate 'mute earth' (*Il.* 24.53–4: μὴ ἀγαθῷ περ ἐόντι νεμεσσηθέωμέν οἱ ἡμεῖς· | κωφὴν γὰρ δὴ γαῖαν ἀεικίζει μενεαίνων, 'though he's a brave man, let him be careful not to anger us; for look, in his rage he mutilates mute earth').[73] Achilles' actions are monstrous, sub-human. He has lost control of his 'might', his 'violence' (βίη, 24.42; βία (Att.) = *uis* = 'violence'), and is attacking lifeless flesh that cannot fight back or protect itself.[74] Moreover Achilles' actions are situated beyond the immediate context of battle inasmuch as they do not occur during the course of regular combat and so signify precisely the sort of action that ruptures the limit of death as the final act of violence in war. With Hector dead,

---

[71] Clausewitz (1976): 77.

[72] Balibar (2002): esp. 136–7 and (2015). See also Žižek (2008): 63–5 expanding on Simone Weil's observations on the limitlessness of the 'desires' inherent in human conflicts (there is a basic undercurrent here of Lacanian *plus-de-jouir*); Miller (1993): 70–1.

[73] Cf. Antony's address to Caesar's corpse in Shakespeare's Julius Caesar as 'thou bleeding piece of earth' (3.1.254).

[74] Segal (1971): 57–9.

nothing more can or need be gained save a demonstration of outright cruelty. Achilles has gone too far and the gods intervene.

De Luna discusses Achilles' treatment of Hector as an entry-point for his analysis of corpse abuse in modern warfare. Some of his conclusions share commonalities with Balibar's interest in extreme violence and its limits. He identifies the extremity of Achilles' violence by psychologizing his actions, focusing on the 'existential void' (*vuoto esistenziale*) the dead enemy leaves his victor. With no one alive to fight, the dead enemy removes all reason for hostilities, and this should correspond to an end of violence. Hector's death, however, will not provide a limit or an end for Achilles' cruelty, it is only the beginning: 'Instead Achilles doesn't stop, his fury is not appeased by the corpse of Hector, the war persists no longer against the enemy but against his dead body.'[75] The physical state of Hector's corpse (as in the state of all corpses in all wars) becomes an 'extraordinary document' for uncovering the nature of his killer, which in turn offers a valuable glimpse and insight into the nature of the war itself.[76]

Yet despite his efforts, what is so crucial here, and what is so crucial for our understanding of the limits of violence in the *Iliad* is that Achilles finds himself repeatedly and definitively *unable* to successfully carry out the mutilation of Hector's corpse. The gods prevent Achilles' cruelty reaching fruition (e.g. *Il.* 23.184–91, 24.18–20, 411–23). His actions signify an act of war directed against the parameters of war, but the poet does not allow the actual act to materialize fully. Achilles may not be able to be trusted to care for the body of Hector, but larger forces ensure its protection. There is still in the *Iliad* some limit to extreme violence in war (dictated by poetic, aesthetic, and moral factors) often despite the best efforts of individual characters who would seek to transgress that limit.

I have lingered here on Achilles' treatment of Hector in the *Iliad* to stress the point that my study explicitly and contrastingly targets moments in epic poetry where the extremes of violence utterly disrupt this system of limitation. Achilles' mistreatment of Hector is the *locus classicus* of epic corpse abuse, but in reality it doesn't fully qualify as abuse since Hector's body is protected from all of Achilles' attacks against it. Roman epic's greatest innovation on the theme of violence in a genre defined by violence is to shatter the limits Homeric epic placed on the extremity of violence in war. And this is expressed most emphatically in the abuses dealt to the

---

[75] De Luna (2006): 53: 'E invece Achille non si ferma, la sua furia non si placa davanti al cadavere di Ettore, la guerra continua non più contro il nemico, ma contro il suo corpo morto.'
[76] De Luna (2006): 53–4.

dead. What differentiates the extremes of violence in Homer and the post-Augustan epicists is that the Latin poets are all aestheticians of overwhelming cruelty.

The imperial epics disrupt the system of limitation related to violence contained in Homer's and (to a certain degree) Virgil's poems for a reason. There are obvious aesthetic considerations, and these are of primary concern to this study. I have already stressed epic poetry's intimate interest in generic self-referentiality and competitive poetics, and scenes of violence are no exception to this competitive poetic engagement: in many ways literary violence helps define the implicitly 'violent' act of *compositio*.[77] Epicists strive to stand out among the crowd of generations of prior tradition, and the creative manipulation of earlier model scenes, especially violent ones,[78] provided a powerful path to poetic notoriety. Visceral violence – the politically sponsored, endorsed, and monopolized extreme violence in Rome (civil war abuses, 'head-hunting', gladiatorial competition, exposure on the *Scalae Gemoniae* and in the forum, corpse-dumping in the Tiber, and so on) – was everywhere pushing against (and through) the limit of killing as an endpoint to violence. Corpse mistreatment becomes a mainstay of the fabric of imperial epic in many ways because it reflected precisely the politically motivated extreme violence that defined the establishment and continuation of the Roman principate; epic abuses resonate because they reflect the real-world violence endemic in a society intimately bound to the horrors of war.

Not only extreme violence, but an obsession with extremity in general defined the early imperial period, as Carlin Barton has articulated.[79] By examining the collective psychology of Romans from the end of the Republic through the first two centuries CE, particularly concerning boundaries, transgressions, and the limits of human endurance, Barton provocatively argues that all strata of Roman society participated in an overindulgent, self-defeating 'theatre of excess'. While she does not discuss corpse mistreatment directly, she homes in on the excess of cruelty and violence that became so rampant as to create (through the tendencies of our sources) a 'trivialization' of violence and an indifference to suffering where deaths as entertainment had ceased to scandalize. Barton surely goes too far

[77] See Hardie (1993): esp. 105–19 for a Bloomian reading of intertextual engagement.
[78] On the popularity of scenes of violence see succinctly Harrison (1988) and (1991): xxi–xxii (on the *Aeneid*).
[79] Barton (1993): esp. 46–81; cf. Hopkins (1983): 27–30, Fagan (2011): 25–7.

when she claims that Rome was a 'frolicking theatre of violence',[80] but it is true that many of our sources aim to betray a playful indifference to the abuses and displays of cruelty. In many ways this indifference and mockery were perhaps the most reasonable way to deal with the often horrific levels of violence that were a daily occurrence in Rome.

The discussion so far has more or less pointed the way toward my approach to reading this poetic material, but I should be explicit. This book is a sort of methodological *mélange* drawing upon a range of interpretive networks and axes including intertextuality, horror theory, visual theory (focalization and the gaze), body studies, death studies, theories of war, metapoetics, social history, political theory, philosophy, and aesthetics. The range indicates both my scope and also the importance of the body – and indeed the dead body – as a narrative and thematic *Mittelpunkt* in the epic poems I analyze. Most of the theoretical lenses I have indicated here overlap in important ways and prioritizing one over the others seems, for my purposes, unnecessarily reductive. My aim has been to approach the text from multiple angles and perspectives and always with a view to larger theoretical and socio-historical issues. Although the discussion here will be most accessible to students and scholars of Latin poetry, my goal is that the material will have something to say across disciplines, to scholars of the epic tradition, comparative literature, war, violence, critical theory, and reception.

This project could have been much larger. I have tried to cast a wide net, but often this has led to the underdevelopment of particular poems or particular scenes related to corpse mistreatment that deserve more consideration than I provide. This is not so much a book about war as a book about bodies in and at war. Consequently, I have privileged the martial epics as the dead are among the most visceral and tangible 'objects' that fill the pages of this genre. Homer's *Iliad* and Virgil's *Aeneid* share a chapter upfront, and the bulk of discussion falls upon subsequent treatments of Lucan, Valerius Flaccus, Statius, and Silius. My chapter on Valerius Flaccus (Chapter 4) is supplemented with a detailed analysis of corpse abuse in Apollonius' *Argonautica*, and some significant discussion of Ovid's *Metamorphoses* throughout the book offers a juxtaposition to tendencies to read Virgil as the singular 'father-figure' of post-Augustan epic.

---

[80] Barton (1993): 62. Cf. Rohmann (2006) who argues that the influence of lived violence in Rome had much less influence on our texts than most scholars assume, and that literary violence is largely the combined product of a competitive intertextual aesthetic and a unifying language of aristocratic despair under imperial rule (see esp. p.54–92, 144–203). See now the nuanced survey by Gale and Scourfield (2018): 1–13.

My study is not exhaustive but should make it possible to follow the motif of corpse mistreatment through variations on the theme in a significant range of epic material.

## The Body of the Book

Chapter 1 examines the motif of corpse treatment in Homer's *Iliad* and Virgil's *Aeneid*. The chapter sets a 'baseline' for the motif by looking at two foundational and familiar works, with the intention of establishing a normative framework which will prove valuable for highlighting deviations from the norm in the treatment of corpses in imperial epic. The first section, on the *Iliad*, demonstrates the basic pattern of corpse treatment in the poem with examples that fully flesh out the general observations I have stressed above. In particular, I highlight Sarpedon, Patroclus, and Hector, all of whose corpses receive some form of attempted abuse but are eventually rescued from that abuse by the gods. Much of this follows the general consensus among scholarship that corpse mistreatment is threatened, feared, and even attempted in the poem, but ultimately unfulfilled. Yet despite the overwhelming emphasis on corpse preservation in the *Iliad*, scholars have almost universally ignored the case of Imbrius in book 13. My discussion of Locrian Ajax's *post mortem* decapitation of Imbrius (*Il.* 13.201–5) aims to problematize this general picture of corpse 'preservation' in the poem, and I offer some larger structural, aesthetic, and thematic insights into the functioning of this scene in the epic.

The next section considers Virgil's narrative strategies concerning the abuse of corpses in the *Aeneid*. While it is clear that Virgil departs from Homer in allowing a wider range of corpse abuse into his poem, in every case Virgil pulls back from describing it and blankets the abuse in narrative silence. I argue that Virgil's allegiance to Homeric poetics allowed him to go only so far: while the *Iliad* expresses a moral horror of carrying out the mutilation of corpses, there is in the *Aeneid* a moral horror of describing the abuses that we know have happened, even though Virgil is willing to concede that corpse abuse actually does occur. The section also offers a consideration of the civil war violence and corpse mistreatment from Marius and Sulla to Actium and the establishment of the principate, as a means of contextualizing some of the (silent) abuses contained within the *Aeneid*.

Chapter 2 is a detailed examination of three scenes (one each from Lucan, Statius, and Silius) that directly target and exploit the most brutal form of epic mistreatment: decapitation and further abuses aimed at the 'capital organ'.[81] The first section analyzes the death and abuse of Pompey in Lucan *BC* 8 in a small skiff off the coast of Egypt. The following section looks, first, at the decapitation of Melanippus in Statius' *Thebaid* 8, and Tydeus' cannibalizing of Melanippus' head, and second at the Thebans' abuse of Tydeus' own corpse in book 9. The final section treats the decapitation of the Carthaginian general's ally Asbyte by Theron in Silius' *Punica* 2, and Hannibal's subsequent abuse of Theron's corpse in retaliation for Theron's slaying of Asbyte. These scenes are all built explicitly upon model scenes in the *Iliad* and *Aeneid* which the later epicists have infused with elements of *post mortem* abuse and grotesquery either ignored or only insinuated in the earlier poems. Through consideration of the ways in which Lucan, Statius, and Silius expand upon their models, this chapter offers a vivid glimpse into the dark evolution of the motif of corpse mistreatment from the 'classic' texts of Homer and Virgil, who had sought (in their own unique ways) to set a limit on the level of violence congruent with the world of epic poetry. Although this chapter consists of close readings of a specific moment in each poem, these particular scenes also function crucially as emblematic of major themes that permeate each work, and I develop these points as I work through the material as a means of foregrounding further discussion in subsequent chapters.

   The next four chapters take a more macroscopic view of corpse mistreatment, focusing on one poem at a time, in contrast to Chapter 2 which seeks to unpack a particular substratum of abuse across multiple poems. Chapter 3 focuses on funeral denial and perversion broadly in Lucan's *Bellum ciuile*. The first section details the elderly survivor's recollection of the civil war between Marius and Sulla in *BC* 2. This flashback is crucial for Lucan's handling of the issues of funeral rites as it anticipates the horrors to come, particularly the warped funeral for Pompey in book 8, which I discuss next. Lucan expands Pompey's death, abuse, and funeral rites over the final three books of the epic (with material anticipating his funeral(s) and also looking beyond the space provided by the epic framework). The disparate scenes create a patchwork of repeated but slightly altered funeral rites, none of which function as a legitimate 'whole'. Next I consider Caesar's position vis-à-vis funeral rites by exploring four scenes that demonstrate his rejection of or lack of interest in what happens to the human body after death (including his own body). The chapter ends with the witch Erichtho's 'zombie' prophetic corpse-soldier, his quasi-prophecy predictive of further death, and Erichtho's paradoxical, almost loving funeral for the corpse-soldier in book 6. I argue briefly in closing that Lucan lingers on issues of death-in-life, and life-in-death, as a means of highlighting his perception of Neronian Rome as a slavish 'death-world'.

Chapter 4 offers a reading of corpse abuse in both the Hellenistic and Flavian *Argonautica* poems, though the emphasis falls on Valerius' epic. The treatment of the dead comes to the fore particularly in the intestine violence in Valerius' depiction of the Lemnian massacre in VF 2 and in the Colchian war between the brothers Perses and Aeetes in book 6. In each case the conflict is tinged with the stain of Lucanesque civil war, culminating in a degeneration of violence with abuses aimed not just at the living, but the dead. Valerius' most extensive engagement with the theme of corpse mistreatment comes during the Argonauts' confrontation with the Bebrycian king Amycus, whose rustic cave is a horror-show of corporal savagery and sadism. The major scene of corpse abuse in Apollonius' *Argonautica* occurs when Jason murders Medea's brother Absyrtus and ritually truncates his still-warm corpse in AR 4. Though this particular mythic scene does not appear in Valerius' epic (Absyrtus is still alive at the end of the Flavian epic), the influence of what I would term 'sparagmatic' violence (from *sparagmos*, dismemberment) in Apollonius' poem sends clear shockwaves through the Flavian epic. While Valerius' poem shows evidence of Apollonian and Lucanian influence in the handling of *post mortem* violence, it importantly pushes back upon these more visceral expositions by reviving Virgilian distancing effects in rendering corpse mistreatment.

Chapter 5 looks at funeral denial and perversion in Statius' *Thebaid*. My discussion of these motifs in Statius' poem focuses on Creon's funeral abnegation decree at *Thebaid* 11.661–4. This point marks the official moment when death rites are denied, but the theme has been building steadily over the course of the epic. The chapter also considers a series of bizarre funeral perversions, particularly the funerals for the fallen Argive leaders, all of whom receive a warping of traditional rites. I examine also the role of women and their attempts to provide funerals for their loved ones, specifically Hypsipyle, Argia and Antigone, and the Argive women. The final section details Iris' 'preservation' of the dead Argive leaders, and the strange case of Maeon's corpse in book 3.

Chapter 6 explores funeral rites in Silius' *Punica* with special focus on the figure of Hannibal. My interest concerns the Carthaginian leader's perversions of Roman funeral practice when he conducts rites over the corpses of three slain Roman generals (L. Aemilius Paulus, T. Sempronius Gracchus, and M. Claudius Marcellus). This analysis sets the stage for an

examination of Hannibal's quasi-funeral rites that close the poem in book
17, mimicking and masking the triumphal parade for Scipio Africanus that,
I argue, simultaneously doubles as a funeral parade. In all three of the
chapters on Flavian epic, I contextualize and supplement my arguments by
considering the role of the civil wars following the death of Nero in 68 CE,
which brought an end to Julio-Claudian reign and ushered in the Flavian
dynasty. Most crucial are the *post mortem* abuses and exposures in the wars
of 68–69 CE, the cyclical death and 'rebirth' of Roman autocracy, and the
burning of the Capitol and the Temple of Jupiter Capitolinus.

    In what follows below I demonstrate the variety of ways in which the
imperial Latin epicists address issues of corpse mistreatment and their
ingenuity in reworking a major epic motif. This poetic engagement functions largely as a disruption of Homeric and Virgilian interests in corpse
treatment in the *Iliad* and *Aeneid*, but my analyses of particular scenes in
the post-Augustan epics illustrate that the referential dialogue is far more
complex than this. The Neronian Lucan becomes a crucial 'canonical' text
for the Flavian epicists, who everywhere draw on his morbid and self-
defeating poetics to highlight the horrors of their own epic universes. In
addition, these epics are, importantly, products of their times. Just as
Virgil's *Aeneid* is inseparable from the context of the civil wars that plagued
Rome for decades before and during his writing, so too the imperial epics
are bound to the principate that emerged from the horrors Virgil grapples
with in his poetry. For Lucan, the civil wars that spawned Caesarism had
not ended. Neronian Rome is simply an extension and repetition of the
abuses that destroyed the Republic. The civil wars that rocked Rome
following the collapse of the Julio-Claudian dynasty in 68 CE must have
made Lucan seem a grim *uates* for his successors, and the Flavian poets
evoke Lucanian darkness as they feed imagery of Rome's civil war abuses
into their epics of mytho-historical retreat.

# CHAPTER I

# Setting the Stage: Corpse Abuse in Homer and Virgil

Homer's *Iliad* and Virgil's *Aeneid* are the 'classic' martial epic texts in Greek and Latin, and the ways in which they address issues of corpse mutilation and funeral abnegation provide critical poetic context for the post-Augustan epicists' engagement with these themes. In the *Iliad* we find numerous examples of threatened, feared, and attempted corpse mistreatment, and the theme of abuse builds steadily until Achilles slays Hector and refuses to return his body to his family for proper obsequies. Ultimately the gods intervene, and all threats and acts of abuse are unfulfilled, except in the anomalous case of Imbrius in book 13 which problematizes this picture. Virgil follows Homer in placing significant emphasis on corpse treatment, and even goes beyond Homer by allowing a greater range of abuse to seep into his poem. But he too places a certain limit on the abuse by refusing to narrate the scenes of mutilation that we know occur. In Homer there exists a moral horror of carrying out the abuse of a corpse; in Virgil there exists a moral horror of describing the abuses that the poet does allow into his poem.

## The *Iliad*

The *Iliad* is a poem obsessively concerned with the composition, or, probably better, the decomposition of the human body.[1] Warriors are hacked to pieces with alarming and breathtaking variety and ingenuity in the heat of battle. Yet there exists a special focus in the poem on what *might* be inflicted on the body once the warrior has been killed. Attempts at corpse mutilation abound, as do threats and fears of abuse voiced by characters. Concomitant with this is the poem's emphasis on proper funeral practice. Efforts to deny this most basic rite are poignantly highlighted as deviating from the norm,

---

[1] Vermeule (1979): 95–9 is particularly instructive.

which finds its model in the extravagant funeral of Patroclus occupying the
bulk of book 23.

In the *Iliad* the main focus on corpses concerns the treatment and
preservation of dead heroes. Minor or unnamed characters occupy little
narrative space with regard to their treatment, though Homer does provide a
description of the collective funeral rites of mostly insignificant fighters on
either side after a momentary truce (7.421–32; cf. 327–38, 375–8, 394–7);[2] rites
are also granted to the nameless many lost to Apollo's plague at 1.52. But the
funeral rites here are collective and cursory.[3] Far more narrative space is
granted to the treatment of Hector's corpse by Achilles and of Sarpedon's
during the bloody *Leichenkampf* (battle over the corpse), both of which
represent the fullest examples of the physical affront to dead bodies in the
*Iliad*.

After the death of Sarpedon there follows a lengthy skirmish between the
Achaeans and Trojans to recover his corpse (16.562–665) – the first instance
in the poem of the fate of a dead warrior's body becoming a point of
consideration.[4] That the two sides would risk further bloodshed to claim
the body of a fallen warrior indicates the importance of proper treatment
from his comrades' perspective (the Trojans) and of the withholding of
that rite by his enemies (the Achaeans). Patroclus says as much during his
pre-battle speech at *Iliad* 16.559–61:

> ἀλλ᾽ εἴ μιν ἀεικισσαίμεθ᾽ ἑλόντες,
> τεύχεά τ᾽ ὤμοιιν ἀφελοίμεθα, καί τιν᾽ ἑταίρων
> αὐτοῦ ἀμυνομένων δαμασαίμεθα νηλέϊ χαλκῷ.

> If only we could take hold of and mutilate him
> and remove the armour from his shoulders, and kill comrades
> trying to protect him with pitiless bronze.

The fate of Sarpedon's corpse is presaged earlier by Sarpedon himself, who
begs Hector to guard his body should he die from a wound he has received
from Tlepolemus (5.684–8). That Hector flees without reply foreshadows
Sarpedon's corpse's fate here and anticipates the uncertain outcome of the
skirmish in book 16. Glaucus voices further concern over the fate of
the corpse when he chides Hector for neglecting to protect Sarpedon and
the Lycian allies from the Myrmidons, whom he fears will despoil
Sarpedon and 'mutilate his corpse' (16.545: ἀεικίσσωσι δὲ νεκρὸν). The

---

[2] On these lines see Garland (1985): 92–3, Kirk (1990): *ad locc.*    [3] Murnaghan (1997): 31.
[4] Segal (1971): 18–19; Janko (1992): *ad* 16.419–683.

verb *aeikizein* appears here for the first time, accompanying the intensification of the corpse abuse theme and the fate of dead heroes.[5]

The two armies battle around Sarpedon's corpse in a destructive fog stirred up by Zeus (16.567–8). The skirmish blankets him in blood, dust, and weapons; he's made unrecognizable (638–40). A simile comparing the armies to flies buzzing about full milk pails hints at the decay awaiting his corpse.[6] After Zeus drives off the Trojans, the Achaeans strip the armour from Sarpedon's body and parade it around the Achaean camp (663–5).

Though here the abuse of Sarpedon's body is largely accidental (a product of the battle waged around and on top of it), this scene anticipates the abuse Achilles attempts to level against Hector's corpse in book 22. After Achilles kills the Trojan prince, the Achaeans circle around Hector and take turns stabbing him, sharing – at least ritually – in his slaughter (22.369–75).[7] Hector's 'imposing beauty' stands out to the Achaeans who compare his once impenetrable frame to its present lifelessness. He was beautiful in life as Achilles approached to kill him (321: χρόα καλόν), and is now beautiful in death (370–1: οἳ καὶ θηήσαντο φυὴν καὶ εἶδος ἀγητὸν | Ἕκτορος, 'they scrutinized the stature and breathtaking beauty of Hector'). They stab him to test the softness of his flesh, but also to corrupt that beauty, to make him ugly. Achilles further disfigures the corpse by dragging Hector on the ground behind his chariot, grinding his face into the dust (397–8). This treatment of Hector's corpse mars the hero's face (402–3: κάρη δ᾽ ἅπαν ἐν κονίῃσι | κεῖτο πάρος χαρίεν, 'and his whole head, formerly so handsome, was lying in the dust'), mirroring the fate of Sarpedon, whom not even a man who knew him well could recognize (16.638–9: οὐδ᾽ ἂν ἔτι φράδμων περ ἀνὴρ Σαρπηδόνα δῖον | ἔγνω), covered head to toe in weapons and dust (639–40: κονίῃσιν).[8]

The initial disfiguring of Hector's corpse is granted by Zeus (403–4) – Achilles' wrath is explicitly associated with Zeus from the prologue (1.5: Διὸς ... βουλή, 'the plan of Zeus') – but Achilles takes this beyond the bounds of battlefield anger by his repeated abuse. Hector is barely even himself anymore, just 'mute earth' and utterly defenceless (*Il.* 24.53–4: μὴ ἀγαθῷ περ ἐόντι νεμεσσηθέωμέν οἱ ἡμεῖς· | κωφὴν γὰρ δὴ γαῖαν ἀεικίζει μενεαίνων, 'though he's a brave man, let him be careful not to anger us; for

---

[5] Segal (1971): 18.      [6] Janko (1992): *ad* 16.633–44; Neal (2006b): 21–2.
[7] Griffin (1980): 47; Vernant (1991): 63; de Jong (2012): *ad* 22.371–5; Lovatt (2013): 262–4.
[8] See Segal (1971): 41–2, Vernant (1991): 70–1, de Jong (2012): *ad* 22.401–4 on the parallel of the disfiguring of Hector's and Sarpedon's corpses. See de Jong (2012): 13–15 for details on the interconnectedness of the deaths of Sarpedon, Patroclus, and Hector.

look, in his rage he mutilates mute earth').[9] Achilles drags Hector's body around Patroclus' pyre, attempting to tear the flesh (23.187; 24.21, 51–2, 416–17). Sarpedon's disfiguring was incidental, but the Achaeans' and Achilles' actions betray a deeper agenda, an attempt at dehumanizing, at blurring the lines between the uniqueness of an individual and the universality of anonymous human or animal flesh (or of dirt, earth), which squares with Adriana Cavarero's ideas of horrorism, of homicidal overkill (she writes at length about the *Iliad*, but largely misses the importance of the fact that Hector is dead while all of this is happening). Achilles is not satisfied with simply killing Hector: he wants to make him less-than-human, to destroy him.[10]

Along with the physical defiling of corpses, the narrative contains threats and fears of corpse mutilation. We have already seen Glaucus' fear of the mutilation of Sarpedon's corpse (16.545). The poem is riddled with threats of corpses being consumed by dogs and birds, instigated by the horrific description from the prologue (1.1–5):

μῆνιν ἄειδε θεὰ Πηληϊάδεω Ἀχιλῆος
οὐλομένην, ἣ μυρί᾽ Ἀχαιοῖς ἄλγε᾽ ἔθηκε,
πολλὰς δ᾽ ἰφθίμους ψυχὰς Ἄϊδι προΐαψεν
ἡρώων, αὐτοὺς δὲ ἑλώρια τεῦχε κύνεσσιν
οἰωνοῖσί τε πᾶσι, Διὸς δ᾽ ἐτελείετο βουλή

Sing, goddess, the destructive wrath of Peleus' son Achilles,
which put countless pains upon the Achaeans,
and sent many great souls of heroes to Hades,
and set them up as prey for dogs
and for all birds, and the will of Zeus was fulfilled.

Examples of threats and fears (direct or narratively implied) of corpses being left to the devices of dogs and/or birds proliferate.[11] Among these,

---

[9]   On Apollo's criticisms (24.46–54), see Segal (1971): 58–60, Macleod (1982): *ad* 33–76, van Wees (1992): 129–30, de Jong (2012): *ad* 22.395, 403–4. See my discussion above pp. 18–21.

[10]  Cavarero (2009): esp. 7–12. Vernant (1991) makes similar points about corpse abuse as dehumanizing. Simone Weil's (2003) famous essay on war and/in the *Iliad* construes the 'force' of war as a nightmarish process of warping humanity into inhumanity; see also Holmes (2010): 33–6. See Segal (1971): 41–7, linking Hector's destruction with the eventual destruction of Troy.

[11]  Kucewicz (2016): 430–2 provides the most comprehensive list. See also Faust (1970) for dogs in particular in *Il.* and *Od.*; Segal (1971); Redfield (1975): 168–9, 200–1; Vermeule (1979): 103–9; Griffin (1980): 115–19; Vernant (1991): 71–2. Phil Klay's *Redeployment* (2014), a fictionalized collection of short stories detailing the experiences of American soldiers in Iraq and Afghanistan and their re-acclimation into civilian society, begins with the account of a soldier in Fallujah charged with defending corpses from scavenging dogs. Klay, a Marine Corps veteran, based the story around the very real 'Operation Scooby' efforts to protect dead bodies from stray dogs. Cf. similarly Michael

Hector aims to throw Patroclus' body to the dogs after severing his head from his corpse (17.126–7). Charles Segal and others argue that the threat of corpse abuse through decapitation takes on a life of its own at this point.[12] Hector's attempt is rephrased by Iris in a dream to Achilles, though the goddess shifts the language slightly to include the impaling of Patroclus' head on a pike (18.175–7). Later Achilles returns the threat of decapitation to Hector (18.333–5). Patroclus' blood-stained helmet rolls in the dust (16.794–6), a moment evocative of decapitation and Hector's subsequent threat. Hector himself will wear that same bloody helmet, sealing his own fate and allusions to (unfulfilled) decapitation at the hands of Achilles. Most savagely, as we have seen,[13] Achilles, becoming the human embodiment of a carrion beast, will threaten to eat Hector's corpse (22.345–7).[14] His threat is echoed by that of Hecuba, who will express the desire to gnaw Achilles' raw liver, in retaliation for his treatment of her son Hector (24.212–14).[15]

Fears of corpse mutilation recur throughout the final third of the poem as well. Achilles fears Patroclus' body will be infested with maggots and worms (19.23–7), Hecuba fears Hector's corpse will lie on the shore as fodder for the dogs (22.88–9), as does Andromache who also invokes scavenging worms (22.508–9). Priam fears his own corpse will be left for his dogs to devour (22.66–71),[16] and further fears Hector has been hacked to pieces and thrown to dogs (24.406–9). Achilles and Priam fear that their loved ones, through mutilation and decomposition, will become unrecognizable and less than human.[17] This is reflected in and inspired by the physical treatment of Sarpedon's and Hector's corpses, who both lose their sense of self and being through the disfiguring abuse they receive.

Despite the energy lavished on the theme of corpse abuse, the acts, threats, and fears are all ultimately unfulfilled or unsuccessful. Everywhere

---

Pitre (another veteran-author) on *This American Life*: 'Once More, with Feeling' (www.thisamer icanlife.org/603/once-more-with-feeling 2 December 2016).

[12] On decapitation in the *Iliad* see Friedrich (2003): 45–51, Fenik (1968): 15 n.11, 84, Segal (1971): 20–3. Besides threats of *post mortem* decapitation, the *Iliad* contains seven examples of actual battlefield decapitation: 10.454–7; 11.146; 11.261; 13.202–5; 14.465–8; 14.496–8; 20.481–2 (I discuss the example at 13.202–5 below pp. 34–41).

[13] See p. 3.

[14] See Redfield (1975): 198–9. Segal (1971): 36–41 notes the proliferation of animal images in book 22, leading to Achilles' animalistic wish to cannibalize Hector. On Achilles' cannibalism generally see Griffin (1980): 20–1; Goldhill (1991): 89–91; Neal (2006b): 30–3.

[15] Zeus elsewhere describes Hera and her wrath as cannibalistic toward Priam and his sons (*Il.* 4.34–6).

[16] Priam fears his corpse will suffer the same treatment that Achilles plans for Hector; see Anderson (1997): 34.

[17] Vernant (1991): 73–4.

the gods intervene: Zeus (sending along Apollo) rescues Sarpedon's corpse, and Sleep and Death deliver the body to his family for proper death rites (16.667–75); Apollo preserves Sarpedon's body from decay with the application of ambrosia (16.670, 680). Thetis assures Achilles that Patroclus' flesh will remain fresh, even if it lies on the ground for a full year (19.33), and she infuses ambrosia and nectar into his nostrils so he remains intact (19.38–9). Aphrodite drives beasts away from Hector's corpse, night and day, and she anoints him with oil (23.184–7), and Apollo blocks the sun from drying out his body with a thick cloud and shields him with his aegis (23.188–91, 24.18–21).[18] Hermes reassures Priam that his son is untouched by maggots, his wounds have been closed up (those delivered *post mortem* by the Greek army); Hector's corpse is under the protection of the gods (24.411–23). And in the end Achilles finally returns Hector's body to Priam (24.599–601).

All threats of corpses being tossed to dogs and birds are also unfulfilled.[19] The closest the poem comes to an example of a corpse being consumed by animals is that of Asteropaeus at 21.201–4. He's one of Achilles' hapless victims tossed into the Scamander; his body is torn and chewed by fish and eels.[20] This actualizes the mafioso 'sleep with the fishes' threat Achilles makes to Lycaon at 21.122–7. The corpse of Asteropaeus is clearly abused, in the unusual context of a watery venue. But even here the abuse is only allowed to go so far. The personified Scamander's retaliatory action constitutes an act of defiance in the face of moral degeneration vis-à-vis the treatment of the dead: the river-god rises up in opposition to Achilles' cruel glutting of the river with corpses and the divine act should be read as a metapoetic marker for our understanding of Homer's disdain for the mistreatment of the dead in the poem.[21] The episode ends with the makeshift cremation of all the Trojan dead killed by Achilles – the corpses in the river are all explicitly tossed upon the bank by Scamander (21.235–7) – after this, importantly, Hephaestus roasts the corpses *first* (343–4) before turning his attention to the river itself, as Hera had commanded; this act restores purity and saves the dead from lasting abuse.[22] Homer provides a catalogue

---

[18] Macleod (1982): *ad* 24.18–21; Richardson (1993): *ad locc.*

[19] Kucewicz (2016) argues that because the motif is so pervasive we must imagine the abuses actually take place; but of course Homer is never explicit. The abuses we might (or perhaps are invited to) envision are in the actual narrative of the poem, in effect, 'sanitized'.

[20] For fish as scavengers of the sea in Homer see Vermeule (1979): 180–6.

[21] See similarly Whitehorne (1983): 133–4.

[22] See Redfield (1975): 250–1 n.15 on the purifying and cleansing properties in the scene of both fire and water, and further on the less horrific nature of the abuses (compared to corpse consumption by birds and dogs), as a result of their occurring under water and thus, 'out of human sight'; cf.

of trees burnt by Hephaestus' fire on the shore (350–2), which burn together with the corpses (and the scavenging fish and eels, 353–5), torching them in a deconstructed tree-felling and pyre-burning ritual. The watery venue for the slaughter itself functions as a further purifying agent. Sarpedon (16.667–9), Patroclus (18.343–51), Hector (24.582), and the anonymous corpses from both sides gathered for cremation (7.425) are all washed with water to cleanse them of impurity before their funeral rites, and here we have ostensibly the same procedure: washing of the corpses before the application of cleansing fire.[23] The waters, once polluted and stained red with blood, again 'flow pure' after Hephaestus' quasi-ritualistic conflagration (21.382).

The *Iliad* also places a great deal of emphasis on proper funeral practice. Andromache reveals the respect Achilles showed to the corpse of her father, Eëtion (6.416–20), which we are meant to remember when he rejects Hector's proposition that the winner of their duel return the body of the slain to his family (22.256–9).[24] Hector offers a similar proposition to the 'best of the Achaeans' whom he challenges in single combat at 7.76–91. Hector repeats the crucial lines concerning the proper respect the victor should pay to the loser's corpse when he is later on his knees at the mercy of Achilles' sword (7.78–9 = 22.342–3). We are meant similarly to juxtapose Hector's words in book 7 with his later threat to leave Ajax's corpse for scavengers to devour (13.824–32), and with his aim to decapitate and impale Patroclus' head, tossing his trunk to the dogs (17.125–7; 18.175–7). Achilles' boast that he will leave Hector's body to be devoured by dogs directly contrasts the funeral the Achaeans will provide for Patroclus (22.335–6).[25] But for all of Achilles' (attempted) mistreatment, Hector's corpse is preserved and eventually handed over to his family in the end. Sarpedon and Patroclus likewise receive the same treatment, though it takes the intervention of Patroclus' unburied ghost in a dream to 'remind' Achilles of the necessity of providing his body obsequies (23.69–92).[26]

Whitehorne (1983): 134, Jones (2005): 23–4. The spreading of the fire is pervasive, expressed in the repetitions of images of burning, from trees to the eels deep in the river-bed; with Richardson (1993): *ad* 21.343–56.
[23] On the process of corpse preparation and cremation in the *Iliad*, see Redfield (1975): 179–82, 185. In the killing of Lycaon and Achilles' subsequent *post mortem* boast over his corpse Neal (2006a): 249–51 and Kelly (2014): 161–2 note sacrificial overtones and the ways in which Achilles here treats his enemy like an animal.
[24] For the contrast between Achilles' actions here and later in his treatment of Hector's corpse, see Segal (1971): 65, de Jong (2012): *ad* 22.256–9. Kelly (2014): 164–5 contrasts Achilles' treatment of Eëtion with his brutal treatment of Eëtion's unarmed sons, noting that Achilles' actions are not uniform, but dictated by his passionate emotions.
[25] Schein (1984): 188.    [26] Burck (1981): 442–3.

The poem ends with the funeral of Hector, and the penultimate book (23) is dedicated almost entirely to the funeral and games in honour of Patroclus. Achilles' seizure of Hector's corpse indicates his understanding of the horror this would cause the Trojan's family and his shade. Achilles himself feared his own body would be lost in the Scamander, unburied and unhonoured at 21.281.[27] Zeus finally indicates just how far beyond the limits of acceptable battlefield behaviour the withholding of funeral rites is as he laments Achilles' 'mad' treatment of Hector (24.114–15): φρεσὶ μαινομένῃσιν | Ἕκτορ' ἔχει παρὰ νηυσὶ κορωνίσιν οὐδ' ἀπέλυσεν, 'in his raging heart he keeps Hector beside the curved ships and did not give him back'.[28] Apollo calls Achilles 'destructive' (24.39: ὀλοῷ Ἀχιλῆϊ) in his treatment of Hector's corpse, bringing us full circle from imagery in the proem (1.1–2: μῆνιν ... Ἀχιλῆος οὐλομένην, 'the destructive wrath of Achilles'). Zeus agrees. This will be the end of that destructiveness that characterized Achilles and the poem as a whole, and the gods agree Hector needs to be honoured like a human, not a *thing*. Whatever uneasiness we as an audience and the characters within the text felt at the accumulation of attempts, threats, and fears of corpse abuse and the withholding of proper funeral rites, ultimately the poet and his heroes learn to respect the bodies of the dead, to restore a proper moral code.[29] *Almost.*

Jasper Griffin and others have demonstrated that among Archaic Greek epics, the *Iliad* stands out for its selective suppression of the fantastic, superstitious, excessively grim, and grotesque,[30] and there is at least some indication that this is the result of a process of subsequent expurgation by later generations of 'Homers' and editors who found these features unbecoming of Homeric heroic expression.[31] Yet the poem retains hints of the sorts of fantastical elements that are more commonly the purview of the Cyclic tradition: Achilles' talking horse Xanthus (19.404–17), his tutelage by the centaur Chiron (11.828–32), an invisibility hat (5.844–5), and so on. So too the *Iliad* at times crosses the boundary between the suggestion of corpse abuse and actual abuse.

The closest the *Iliad* comes to overt corpse mutilation occurs during a rash of revenge killings in the gruesome fighting of book 13.[32] Ajax, son of

---

[27] The line is a double of *Od.* 5.312, where Odysseus expresses his own fear of being lost at sea.

[28] Richardson (1993): *ad* 24.103–19; Hershkowitz (1998a): 150. Hector promises Achilles will face divine wrath if he refuses his corpse proper funeral rites at *Il.* 22.358–60.

[29] Vermeule (1979): 112.     [30] Griffin (1977), Davies (1989): 9, Burgess (2001): 132–71.

[31] E.g. Murray (1961): 120–45.

[32] See McClellan (2017) for a more detailed examination of what follows here, and a discussion of scenes that suggest but do not explicitly foreground *post mortem* mutilation in the poem; see *contra* Kucewicz (2016) who reads abuse into scenes where the evidence is much less clear-cut. The

Oïleus, avenging Hector's killing of Amphimachus, severs the head of
Imbrius' corpse – killed earlier by Ajax, the son of Telamon – and tosses
the head like a ball at the feet of Hector (*Il.* 13.201–5):

ὣς ῥα τὸν ὑψοῦ ἔχοντε δύω Αἴαντε κορυστὰ
τεύχεα συλήτην· κεφαλὴν δ᾿ ἁπαλῆς ἀπὸ δειρῆς
κόψεν Ὀϊλιάδης κεχολωμένος Ἀμφιμάχοιο,
ἦκε δέ μιν σφαιρηδὸν ἑλιξάμενος δι᾿ ὁμίλου·
Ἕκτορι δὲ προπάροιθε ποδῶν πέσεν ἐν κονίῃσι.

So the two warrior Aiantes held Imbrius high
and stripped off his armour. The son of Oïleus chopped the head
from his tender neck, angered by the fate of Amphimachus,
and hurled it spinning like a ball through the crowd of fighters:
it fell in the dust at the feet of Hector.

The decapitation happens in the heat of battle, and thus lacks the pre-
meditation we find in the threats and boasts that are ultimately unfulfilled
elsewhere in the poem. But the brutality of the scene and its blurring of the
lines between battlefield aggression and *post mortem* mutilation deserve
more consideration than scholarship has granted them.

Locrian Ajax is a 'nasty'[33] and 'sadistic'[34] character, who provokes the
wrath of Athena and Poseidon for boastfulness and impiety and is ultimately drowned at sea during his *nostos* (e.g. *Od.* 4.499–510; *Iliou Persis* arg.
3 West). His first appearance in the *Iliad* is signalled by a notice that he's
'far lesser' than his namesake Telamonian Ajax (*Il.* 2.527–9), and his
foolishness is revealed by his meaningless quarrel with Idomeneus during
Patroclus' funeral games (23.473–98). In the subsequent foot-race he falls
face-first in a pile of dung, prompting universal laughter (23.773–84).
Moreover, his attempted rape of Cassandra and defilement of Athena's
temple following the sack of Troy is recounted in the *Iliou Persis* and was
mythic material known to Homer and his audience. Athena's direct intervention against Ajax in the foot-race (causing him to trip and fall: 23.774,
782) anticipates the subsequent conflict between the two in the larger

escalation of revenge or 'retributive' violence is a key theme of the second half of the *Iliad*, but it also
makes its way into the final 'Iliadic' events of the *Odyssey* (in books 22–24) when Odysseus exacts
revenge on the suitors, whose families immediately seek retribution, and Ithaca nearly breaks out
into open warfare. The treatment of the treacherous handmaidens and the goatherd Melanthius is
extreme but still doesn't extend to *post mortem* mutilation. The families of the slain suitors are
allowed to collect the dead for funerals (*Od.* 24.417–19); Melanthius is mutilated (*Od.* 22.474–7) but
left alive to suffer his mutilation as a punishment; see Davies (1994).
[33] Janko (1992): *ad* 13.201–3.    [34] Stanley (1993): 147.

mythic story.[35] The background myth provides context for his character-ization in the *Iliad*.[36] We should not, then, be surprised at Ajax's cruel treatment of Imbrius here. But however we interpret the decapitation, the scene is singularly conspicuous for its brutality.

The scene, I argue, is a nightmarish anticipation of Achilles' abuse of Hector's corpse. Imbrius stands as a surrogate for Hector in the scene itself, as Homer tells us Locrian Ajax decapitates Imbrius in retaliation for Hector's killing of Amphimachus, himself a surrogate for Teucer, whom Hector intended to kill but missed with his spear cast (13.182–85). Ajax can only indirectly take vengeance on Hector (Ajax mutilates Imbrius, not Hector, for Hector's slaying of Amphimachus), since Hector must ulti-mately fall by Achilles' hand, but the beheading represents the exact mutilation with which Achilles will threaten Hector in retaliation for his slaying of Patroclus (18.333–5): νῦν δ᾿ ἐπεὶ οὖν Πάτροκλε σεῦ ὕστερος εἶμ᾿ ὑπὸ γαῖαν, | οὔ σε πρὶν κτεριῶ πρίν γ᾿ Ἕκτορος ἐνθάδ᾿ ἐνεῖκαι | τεύχεα καὶ κεφαλὴν μεγαθύμου σοῖο φονῆος, 'but now, Patroclus, since I will go under the earth after you, I will not bury you until I have brought here the armour and head of great-hearted Hector who killed you'. The formula in the second half of line 203 immediately after the abhorrent description of abuse (κεχολωμένος Ἀμφιμάχοιο) mitigates somewhat the shock of Ajax's act; Homer almost apologizes for what has just occurred. But the participle is telling. Ajax's *cholos* signals implicitly an association with Achilles, the poem's embodiment of human rage (broadly defined).[37] In his prophecy looking ahead to events in the second half of the poem, Zeus assures Hera that Achilles' *cholos* at the death of Patroclus will instigate his slaying of Hector, again a retaliatory murder (15.68): τοῦ δὲ χολωσάμενος κτενεῖ Ἕκτορα δῖος Ἀχιλλεύς, 'angered by the fate of Patroclus, godlike Achilles will kill Hector'. There exists a parallelism – structural, lexical, thematic – linking Ajax and Imbrius with our expectations for Achilles' 'fated' treat-ment of Hector.

There are more links. Imbrius is a Hector-like doublet both in his brief biographical details and in his death scene, which anticipates Hector's near death in book 14. Imbrius lives in Priam's home, husband to the king's illegitimate daughter Medesicaste (the only *nothe* in the poem); Priam 'honoured him like one of his own children' (13.176: ὁ δέ μιν τίεν ἶσα τέκεσσι). His pre-eminence among the Trojans is highlighted (13.175), and

---

[35] Dowden (2004): 202; Kullmann (2015): 120.
[36] Kirk (1990): *ad* 2.527; Janko (1992): *ad* 13.72; Kullmann (2015): 119–20.
[37] See Redfield (1975): 14–18, Walsh (2005): 109.

his fall is likened to the collapse of an ash tree on a high mountain (13.178–
80), indicating his high honour at Troy and prompting Hector's own
response and a skirmish over Imbrius' corpse.[38] He falls, 'and about him
rang his armour inlaid with bronze' (181: ἀμφὶ δέ οἱ βράχε τεύχεα ποικίλα
χαλκῷ). The same pattern of tree simile and clattering fall accompanies
Hector's near-death in the following book (14.409–20). Telamonian Ajax
strikes Hector with a stone, he falls like an oak struck by lightning, and his
bronze-inlaid armour clatters around him (14.420: ἀμφὶ δέ οἱ βράχε τεύχεα
ποικίλα χαλκῷ). Repeated lines are common and usually tell us very little
in Homeric poetry, but this particular line appears elsewhere only at 12.396,
and there it's not joined to a tree-falling simile. Hector's fall here has all the
symptoms of a death-scene,[39] looking back to the parallel scene of Imbrius'
death, and looking forward to his own death in book 22. Hector falls in the
dust (14.418: ἐν κονίῃσι), like Imbrius' head, which rolls to Hector's feet in
the dust (13.205: ἐν κονίῃσι). Imbrius' head is sent rolling 'like a ball'
(13.205: σφαιρηδόν), while Hector is struck and made to spin 'like a top'
(14.413: στρόμβον) before crashing to the ground. The references to playful, unwarlike games add an element of almost whimsical grotesquery to
each scene. In the *Iliad*, a fall in the dust is elsewhere a sure indicator of
death, as it will be for Hector himself (22.330, 402). Hector will eventually
lie in the dust like other dead heroes (22.397–403), but he escapes that fate
in this instance in a scene that is proleptic of his inevitable demise. Still, the
imagery here points explicitly to a death scene. Hector vomits black blood
and black night covers his eyes (14.436–9), and again we sense that his death
is imminent.

The death and decapitation of Imbrius occur just after the poem's midpoint of the close of book 12,[40] a point marked by a shift from the Trojans'
military successes to Poseidon's intervention, Zeus's averting his gaze, and
a sharp reversal of fortunes that builds until the return of Zeus's attention
in book 15, and the devastating loss of Patroclus in 16.[41] That this scene
occurs just after the poem's midpoint has structural and poetic implications.
David Elmer has discussed the importance of a simile at *Iliad* 12.421–3
comparing the struggle between the Achaeans and Trojans around the

---

[38] Janko (1992): *ad* 13.178–80.

[39] Krischer (1971): 72–3; Janko (1992): *ad* 14.414–17; Neal (2006a): 118. All other tree-falling similes accompany a warrior who has died.

[40] See McClellan (2017): 164–6 for issues related to oral performance and performative pauses and divisions.

[41] On the narrative structure of book 13, and its unity with books 14–15, see Stanley (1993): 142–52, Frame (2009): 570–3. Mueller (1984): 86 and Neal (2006a): 195–7 note that with book 13 the *Iliad* becomes more gory and bloody.

Achaean ships to farmers competing for position along the middle point of a
field (like a turf war), which he convincingly posits contains a pointed
reference to the ancient ball game *episkuros/epikoinos*.[42] Elmer argues that
this referent applies to the structure of the poem and the point of 'tense
equilibrium' as the battle vacillates around the Achaean ships, like the ball
game in which two teams contend for position in a common field marked by
a centre line of stones (the *skuros*).[43] He argues that the simile's occurrence at
the poem's midpoint represents both the state of battle and the architecture
of the poem as if 'on the point of a balance beam'.[44] This image finds a
double in the simile immediately following which compares the equilibrium
of battle to equal portions of wool weighed out by a weaver (12.433–6).
That Imbrius' head is thrown and rolling 'like a ball' strengthens the
implicit allusion to the ball game in the simile from book 12 and adds
another layer of the grotesque to the scene as the 'ball' comes to a stop at
Hector's feet at the beginning of the next book. With the Achaeans
gaining the upper hand after Zeus averts his attentions, the ball
(Imbrius' head in simile) seems to fall onto Hector's side of the field, at
the prince's feet, after the Achaeans win the skirmish over the two corpses
(Amphimachus and Imbrius); the Trojans are losing their tactical advan-
tage and the 'game' of battle at this decisive moment in the war and the
poem.

    Zeus's absence as all of this is unfolding paves the way for Hector's death
to potentially take place out of his sight, and the rest of the action up until
he shifts his attention back to the war at the beginning of book 15. At the
opening of book 8, Zeus calls an assembly of the gods. He informs them of
his plan to engineer short-term Trojan success, in accordance with Thetis'
request for a Trojan victory (1.508–10) that will ensure her son Achilles
recompense and respect from the Achaeans once they are required to call
upon his aid (8.5–17). Zeus demands compliance and warns the gods
against interfering. Through book 12, the scenario envisioned by Zeus
has been playing out accordingly, as the Trojans take the upper hand in
battle and Hector establishes himself as the singularly exceptional Trojan
hero whom Achilles will eventually slay, an act which seals Achilles' *kleos*.

    Yet as book 13 opens, Zeus suddenly turns his gaze northward, to the
Thracians, Mysians, and Scythians (13.1–9). The pro-Achaean Poseidon
covertly enters the fray and inspires a string of Achaean military successes,
acting directly against the will of Zeus after the king of the gods diverts his
attention. As the narrator indicates, Poseidon's actions here constitute a

[42] Elmer (2008).   [43] Elmer (2008): 422.   [44] Elmer (2008): 422.

true threat to Zeus's plan to establish a short-term Trojan victory (13.676–8), as Poseidon steers the poem back toward Achaean dominance. The Achaean successes following Poseidon's intervention embolden the pro-Achaean Hera to further action and a further stifling of Zeus's plans. She formulates a hilarious ruse, seducing her husband – this is the so-called *Dios apate*, the 'Beguiling of Zeus' – and again draws his attentions away from the battlefield. Zeus's absence leaves the Trojans and Hector in a state of distress, as book 15 opens as 14 had ended, with Hector gasping for air and spewing black blood. He's apparently about to die.

By Zeus's averting of his directorial gaze, the poem toys with the idea that fate (i.e. poetic tradition) might be derailed, that the story might end too soon or end out of step with Zeus's plan. Throughout Zeus's absence in books 13–15, we are confronted with the possibility of contemplating a mythic alternative to the traditional outlines of the Trojan tale, which dictates that Achilles return to battle and kill Hector himself in retaliation for Hector's slaying of Patroclus.[45] The return of Zeus's focus resets the trajectory of the plot.[46] He revives Hector (with Apollo's help) in a way that suggests a retrieval from death (14.242, 251–2, 15.286–93) and summarizes or prophesies the events that will take place during the rest of the poem up to Achilles' slaying of Hector and even up to the eventual fall of Troy (15.59–71), as if to remind the audience, in metapoetic play, of mythological and narrative necessity.[47] He effectively reminds the audience – the other gods and the poem's real-world listeners (the intra- and extratextual audiences) – of the constraints of fate, which amounts to poetic tradition. The building of a narrative momentum running counter to the expectations dictated by poetic tradition and the metapoetic play of inserting alternative embodiments of the poet to drive the plot (Poseidon and Hera, replacing Zeus) create here in the centre of the poem a carnival-esque moment. In Zeus's absence and with Poseidon and Hera pulling the strings counter to Zeus's and fate's plan, it seems that 'un-Homeric' things manage to seep into a narrative momentarily adrift – not only farce (in the whimsical *Dios apate*) and false endings but also corpse mutilation: else-where Zeus leads the charge in keeping corpses safe from mutilation (cf. esp. 17.268–73; 24.113–16).[48]

---

[45] This narrative technique in the *Iliad* of misdirection and the creation of false or counter expectations in the audience (based on the audience's knowledge of the pre-Iliadic *Faktenkanon*) has been detailed extensively by Morrison (1992).

[46] Elmer (2013): 161.     [47] On the larger metapoetic system in the poem see Elmer (2013): 146–73.

[48] For Poseidon's and Hera's arrogation of Zeus's plan see Stanley (1993): 142–59.

The death and mistreatment of Imbrius in book 13 looks ahead to the death and abuse of Hector, the last victim of the poem, when the focus shifts finally to Hector's corpse and Achilles' repeated attempts to mutilate it. Tellingly, Imbrius' head rolls to a stop at Hector's feet. The unparalleled brutality of this scene in the poem is left entirely unacknowledged by Ajax, Hector, and the poet. Instead, the narrative shifts immediately to Poseidon's anger at the earlier death of his grandson Amphimachus (13.206). Richard Janko attempts to fill the silence by suggesting that the tossing of Imbrius' head at Hector is 'equivalent to a taunting-speech'.[49] It's curious, however, that we do not have a *euchos* over the dead warrior here. Martin Mueller notes that the majority of such gloating speeches occur in books 13 and 14, corresponding to the increased cruelty and grisly injuries which preponderate in these particular books.[50] That the poet pulls back from narrating a gloating speech over Imbrius' corpse after the most frightening scene of violence and cruelty in the poem is all the more conspicuous. The severed head of Imbrius – Hector's surrogate and doublet in the scene – falls at Hector's feet, and the image resonates through book 24 until Hector's own corpse is finally returned to Priam, unmutilated, and given a proper funeral.

Locrian Ajax stands out amongst the 'worst of the Achaeans' (note Idomeneus' telling jab at 23.483–4: ἄλλά τε πάντα | δεύεαι Ἀργείων) and, through his cruel treatment of Imbrius, represents a frightening anticipation of the dark side of Achilles' character in the final books of the *Iliad*. Ajax's decapitation of Imbrius' corpse functions as a surrogate for the consistently threatened, but eventually averted, mutilation of Hector's corpse by Achilles. In his discussion of thematic narrative misdirection, James Morrison argues that the *Iliad*'s narrative prepares us to expect Achilles to carry out the mutilation of Hector's corpse and that the ransoming of Hector's body and the Trojan prince's funeral at the end cut against our expectations.[51] He offers the tantalizing suggestion of J.A.K. Thomson that in the original myth (i.e. the pre-Homeric mythic tradition) Achilles actually decapitated Hector and that our poem has been 'expurgated' of this and other unsavoury content.[52] While this is purely speculative, the suggestion that extra-Homeric mythic alternatives contained the possibility of Hector's (*post mortem?*) decapitation would, if true,

---

[49] Janko (1992): *ad* 13.195–205.    [50] Mueller (1984): 93–5.    [51] Morrison (1992): 85–93.

[52] Murray (1961): 128–9. Cf. (also tantalizingly) early sixth-century black-figure amphorae depicting Achilles tossing the severed head of Troilus at Trojans during the *Leichenkampf* (Florence, Mus. Arch. 70993 = *LIMC* I.1 s.v. Achilleus, sec. VI.c 360; Munich Antikensammlungen 1426 = *LIMC* I.1 s.v. Achilleus, sec. VII.c 364); with Mori (2008): 203 and 203–4 n.43.

add considerable weight to the horror of Imbrius' surrogate mutilation and the anticipation of a similar fate for Hector, which Homer strikingly refuses to narrate. In the end, Hector ultimately escapes the fate of Imbrius thanks to the gods, Priam, and Achilles' return to humanity, but the fear that he too might lose his head has its resonating origins here, making the only clear scene of corpse mutilation in the poem all the more significant.

It is clear that the *Iliad* articulates a definable limit on the imposition of violence in war. We repeatedly see examples of boasts, fears, and attempts aimed at breaking through that limit, only to have the poet pull back from allowing these expressions of violence to reach fruition. This overarching system concerning the appropriate treatment of the dead makes the case of Imbrius singularly conspicuous in the poem. This scene plays a structural and metapoetic role in the *Iliad* that has implications for our reading of the end of the poem and Achilles' attempted yet unfulfilled abuse of Hector's corpse. I argue that these features make the scene meaningful for issues related to the treatment of the dead in the poem, that the scene demands contemplation. If nothing else, I have brought to the forefront a powerful scene in the poem that has been grossly under-analyzed – even in studies that target corpse mistreatment in the poem – in an attempt to test its merits and apply it to the larger themes of abuse in the *Iliad*. However we decide to read and interpret Ajax's treatment of Imbrius' corpse, it is importantly anomalous in the poem, and is an exception to the picture the poet paints of epic violence and cruelty. Homer's heroes kill and are killed and ultimately (*almost* universally) the poet provides for their corpses a peaceful repose.

## The *Aeneid*

My discussion of the *Aeneid* is something of an argument from silence. By that I mean that I intend to coax some meaning from moments in the *Aeneid* that Virgil wilfully writes out of his narrative, that he refuses to narrate. I am interested in scenes of corpse mistreatment and abuse that we know take place during the course of the poem, but which Virgil does not articulate explicitly. Analysis of silence is inherently slippery and little can be offered here in terms of certainty, but it's precisely this uncertainty and confusion that Virgil is exploiting enigmatically as a means of challenging his readers and of eliciting multifaceted readings from *cruces* he leaves unresolved. Our knowledge of the Homeric corpus (especially the *Iliad*) and of references in the *Aeneid* itself provides integral insight into framing

Virgil's silences. We know that the *Aeneid* contains implicit examples of corpse abuse because we repeatedly see the *aftermath* of the abuse: Priam's headless corpse on the shore, the heads of Nisus and Euryalus fixed to pikes, Mezentius' perforated breastplate. But nowhere does the poet include physical detail of *post mortem* violence.

My analysis takes root from a number of studies that address Virgilian silence and narrative gaps, in particular an important article by Robert Edgeworth published posthumously in *Vergilius*, whose methodological framework I will follow in my discussion of Virgil's engagement with Homer: 'I am speaking primarily of occasions when [Virgil's] use of specific elements from the literary tradition creates certain expectations in the minds of the audience, but the poet does not tell us whether these expectations are fulfilled.'[53]

But it's not only the *Aeneid*'s relationship with earlier poetic models that can aid our understanding of the poem's silences. There are powerful political and socio-historical factors at play here as well. It will be useful to begin with a brief review of Roman civil war violence from Marius and Cinna through the proscriptions of Sulla and the second triumvirate, decades of graphic 'spectacularized' violence visited upon the city and vividly recorded in our historical sources. The almost theatrical display of human victims in Rome's most public venues offers a staggering juxtaposition to Virgil's conspicuous poetics of silence in treating corpse abuse in the *Aeneid*. As we shall see, the real-life horrors that Virgil and his audience lived through supplement his already complex engagement with and elaboration of the major Homeric motif of corpse mistreatment.

Corpse mistreatment was emblematic of the civil wars in Rome's and Virgil's own recent history. Both in the 80s BCE and later during the second round of proscriptions by the triumvirate of Antony, Lepidus, and Octavian in 43–42 BCE, Rome, and the forum in particular, became a horrific trophy case for mutilated bodies. Historical records are littered with examples from this time of *post mortem* decapitations, severed heads impaled on pikes and paraded, bodies left unburied to rot or for wild animals to consume, or tossed into the Tiber.[54] Widespread abuse and

---

[53] Edgeworth (2005): 3. Heinze (1993): 165, 187 n.41 on Virgil's silence in articulating death scenes and his leaving explication of the events to the imagination of the reader. See also Quinn (1968): 339–49 on Virgil's use of 'implicit comment'. These analyses presuppose a reader-response model that enlists the active participation of the reader in making meaning from a text through 'filling' provocative *lacunae* with their own interpretations, suppositions, etc. This interpretative principle goes back at least to Theophrastus (fr. 696 Fortenbaugh); see Nünlist (2009): 164–7.

[54] The most thorough treatment of the violence of proscriptions is Hinard (1985). Note also Hinard (1984), which condenses material related to corpse abuse. See Voisin (1984) and Jervis

display of Roman corpses seems to have begun with Cinna and Marius in 87 BCE, though some earlier notable examples of targeted mistreatment set the stage for the large-scale internecine atrocities that followed.

In 133 BCE a senatorial mob slaughtered Tiberius Gracchus and his partisans (a few thousand men) and summarily dumped their corpses in the Tiber (Livy *Per.* 58; Plut. *Ti. Gracch.* 20.2; App. *B Ciu.* 1.16; Val. Max. 1.4.2). A little over a decade later, in 121 BCE, Tiberius' younger brother Gaius was decapitated, his brain removed and replaced with lead – his head was apparently worth its weight in gold – and paraded on a spear-point (Plut. *C. Gracch.* 17.2–5). Gaius' and his supporters' bodies were likewise dumped in the Tiber. In 100 BCE, after being bludgeoned to death by roof tiles in the Curia Hostilia, the tribune and populist L. Appuleius Saturninus was decapitated, his head paraded, and (perhaps) subsequently put on display by Gaius Rabirius at dinner parties (*De uir. ill.* 73.12).

Physical *post mortem* violence, funeral denial (dumping in the Tiber), and public display intertwine in these grisly but relatively isolated historical events. This deadly cocktail was the baseline for the large-scale horrors Marius and Cinna visited upon Rome in 87 BCE. The pair quickly accumulated the severed heads of political enemies and displayed them *en masse* at the rostra. As the traditional venue for the public exhibition of corpses of Roman nobility during a funeral procession (Polyb. 6.53), the rostra seem a targeted site for the perversion of ritual practice. Trunks also lay in the street to rot, devoured by birds and dogs, explicitly forbidden funeral by family members (App. *B Ciu.* 1.73; Flor. 2.9.14; Plut. *Mar.* 44.6). Among countless abuses recorded in our sources is the disruption of Cn. Pompeius Strabo's funeral (the father of Pompeius Magnus – Pompey 'the Great') by a riotous mob. In the middle of the ceremony, the rioters dragged Strabo's corpse from the pyre and hauled his half-cremated corpse through the streets by a hook (Vell. Pat. 2.21.4; Plut. *Pomp.* 1.2).[55]

With Sulla's proscriptions Rome's violence reaches a crescendo. The dead are not only mutilated and put on display in the forum and elsewhere, but abusers are *paid* for their services. As if to demonstrate his 'expansion' of Marius' atrocities, Sulla targeted Marius' own long-dead corpse as a site for a kind of grotesque corporal *amplificatio*: in 82 BCE he exhumed Marius (dead since January 86 BCE), desecrated his tomb, destroyed his funeral monument, and cast his ashes into the Anio (Cic. *Leg.* 2.56–7; Pliny

(2001) on head-hunting; Richlin (1999) on Cicero's decapitation; Kyle (1998) and Hope (2000) contain invaluable discussion of abuse and funeral denial. What follows below is greatly indebted to these studies.

[55] See p. 126 below.

*HN* 7.187; Val. Max. 9.2.1). The tossing of the dead into Rome's rivers was by now *de rigueur* (e.g. App. *B Ciu.* 1.88); the most brutal example occurred after the battle at the Colline Gate when Sulla ordered thousands of dead bodies dumped in the Tiber (Val. Max. 9.2.1; Flor. 2.9.24).

The horrors proliferate. Marius' nephew M. Marius Gratidianus was torn to pieces at Q. Catulus' tomb by Catiline on Sulla's orders (Q. Cicero *Comment. pet.* 10.1–7):

> qui hominem carissimum populo Romano, M. Marium, inspectante populo Romano uitibus per totam urbem ceciderit, ad bustum egerit, ibi omni cruciatu lacerarit, uiuo stanti collum gladio sua dextera secuerit, cum sinistra capillum eius a uertice teneret, caput sua manu tulerit, cum inter digitos eius riui sanguinis fluerent.

> [Catiline], who lashed the Roman peoples' dearest, M. Marius, through the whole city while the Roman people watched, led him to the tomb, mangled him there with every sort of torture, and with him standing alive, slashed his neck with the sword in his right hand, when held the hair of his head in his left, he carried the head in his hand, while streams of blood flowed between his fingers.

That this bodily violence was a visual spectacle is made explicit (cf. Sen. *De ira* 3.18.1–2; Lucan *BC* 2.177–93[56]). And the mutilation at Catulus' tomb weaves perverse human sacrificial ritual into the act. Gratidianus' severed head – along with those of Brutus Damasippus, C. Carrinas, and others – were subsequently sent by Sulla to Praeneste to be paraded around the walls on the tips of spears (Vell. Pat. 2.27.1–3; App. *B Ciu.* 1.93; Dio Cass. 30–35 fr. 109.4; Oros. 5.21.8).

The first triumvirate (Pompey, Caesar, and Crassus) did not follow Sulla's lead in proscribing political enemies. But the influence of earlier abuses was by this point unavoidable. Caesar hung the heads of mutineers on the wall of the Regia in the forum in 46 BCE (Dio Cass. 43.24). Pompey's own severed head was presented to Caesar as a 'gift' in Egypt (App. *B Ciu.* 2.85–7; Luc. *BC* 9.1010–34),[57] aping the earlier commoditized system of head-hunting under Sulla. Pompey's son Gnaeus was decapitated in 45 BCE, his head sent to Caesar's forces in Hispalis who put it on display in their camp (Ps.-Caesar *Bell. Hisp.* 39). A month earlier at Munda, Caesar constructed a rampart facing the city out of the bodies of slain soldiers, each topped with a severed head impaled on sword-point creating a horrific palisade. This, we are told, was both functional (the palisade

---

[56] On Lucan's rendering of the mutilation, see below pp. 117–19.    [57] See pp. 138–40.

enclosed the enemy) and psychological, a form of terrorism (*Bell. Hisp.* 32).[58] Caesar too seems to have been subjected to *post mortem* violence. Nicolaus of Damascus, our earliest source for Caesar's murder in Pompey's senate-house, notes that the conspirators added *post mortem* blows to Caesar's corpse as evidence of their 'sharing in the deed' (*FGrH* 90 F 130.24.90: καὶ οὐδεὶς ἔτι λοιπὸς ἦν ὃς οὐχὶ νεκρὸν κείμενον ἔπαιεν ὅπως ἂν καὶ αὐτὸς δοκοίη τοῦ ἔργου συνῆφθαι, 'and there was no one remaining who did not strike his corpse lying there, so each would seem to have shared in the act'); the scene recalls (perhaps intentionally) the Achaeans' ritual stabbing of Hector's corpse at *Iliad* 22.369–75.

The second triumvirate 'revived' the Sullan tradition of proscriptions, offering rewards for the slaughter of Roman citizens. Again severed heads offered sure proof of services rendered. The most famous head was Cicero's, dashed off (along with his hands) at Antony's order and sent back to decorate the rostra. Livy's account, preserved by the elder Seneca, supplies the details of Cicero's assassination on 7 December 43 BCE (Sen. *Suas.* 6.17):

> prominenti ex lectica praebentique inmotam ceruicem caput praecisum est. nec <id> satis stolidae crudelitati militum fuit: manus quoque scripsisse aliquid in Antonium exprobantes praeciderunt. ita relatum caput ad Antonium iussuque eius inter duas manus in rostris positum, ubi ille consul, ubi saepe consularis, ubi eo ipso anno adversus Antonium quanta nulla umquam humana uox cum admiratione eloquentiae auditus fuerat; uix attollentes lacrimis oculos humentes intueri truncata membra ciuis poterant.

> Leaning forward from the litter and offering his motionless neck, his head was cut off. This was not enough for the senseless cruelty of the soldiers: they cut off his hands too, blaming them for having written against Antony. So the head was brought back to Antony and, by his order, was placed between the two hands on the rostra where that man, as consul and often as ex-consul, and in that same year had been heard railing against Antony, with such admiration for his eloquence comparable to no other human voice. The citizens, lifting their eyes wet with tears, could scarcely look at his severed limbs.

Again the *post mortem* grotesquery is framed through the perspective of an internal audience, here frozen in paralytic stare, scarcely able to look, yet looking nonetheless at Cicero's mutilated limbs. The contrast between Cicero's oratorical performances 'on stage', as it were, in front of an audience, and now Antony's 'staging' of Cicero's fragmented body signals

---

[58] See Osgood (2006): 43–4 on the cold 'matter-of-factness' of the author in describing civil war horrors.

a jarring change in theatrical production. There is of course cruel symbolism in propping Cicero's head and hands at the rostra, but this was also violence and horror on display, intended explicitly for audience consumption.

I will have more to say about Octavian's role in all of this when we look in more detail at Virgil's Aeneas. For now it's worth stressing the pervasiveness of corpse abuse and of the public displays of abuse in Rome in the decades leading up to Virgil's writing. This was a disturbing part of the fabric of Roman 'social life' during extensive periods of internecine upheaval. As we shift to a consideration of the *Aeneid* in light of Homeric themes and motifs, it will become clear that Virgil aims to contrast the amorality of Roman civil war with what amounts to a poetics of decorum in Homer's handling of corpse mistreatment. The *Iliad's* obsession with the treatment of the dead offered Virgil an epic master-theme; his and his audience's visceral experience with the *reality* of this theme supplied Virgil with considerable space for poetic innovation.

Virgil builds on the Iliadic model but goes even further than Homer by allowing the abuse that is nearly entirely denied in the *Iliad* to seep into his poem, while still distancing himself from that abuse by refusing to narrate it. Virgil's reworking of the Iliadic 'Doloneia' is instructive. The scene of Nisus' and Euryalus' night-raid in *Aeneid* 9 is modelled on Diomedes' and Odysseus' sortie into enemy territory in *Iliad* 10. While the Achaean pair provides an obvious initial parallel for our two Trojans, Virgil complicates the Iliadic model by having Nisus and Euryalus die in the Rutulian camp, thus conflating the success of Homer's Diomedes and Odysseus with the failed mission of the Trojan scout, Dolon. Virgil has Nisus and Euryalus play the role of both Greeks and Trojans, but they die (appropriately) as Trojans.[59] The deaths are described in detail (*Aen.* 9.431–45): Euryalus is pierced through the ribs and chest and dies, neck drooping, like poppies wet with rain (434–7); Nisus rushes to avenge the death and dies *confossus* (445: 'pierced'), falling on top of Euryalus' corpse. Virgil's memorable epitaph for the dead heroes (446–9) is followed by the grisly description of their severed heads pierced on pikes and paraded at the front of Turnus' battle line (465–7):

> quin ipsa arrectis (uisu miserabile) in hastis
> praefigunt capita et multo clamore sequuntur
> Euryali et Nisi.

---

[59] Anderson (1990): 247; Fratantuono (2007): 279. See also Knauer (1964): 266–9, 275–7, Hardie (1994): 29–31, Mebane (2009).

And (terrible to see) on raised spear-points
they thrust the heads themselves of Nisus and Euryalus,
and with great cheering they followed.

The image conflates two scenes in Homer: Achilles' attempted mutilation of Hector's corpse at *Iliad* 22.405–515 before the Trojan walls is reframed here as a *post mortem teichoscopy*, 'completing' (almost as a postscript) the abuses Achilles is unable to visit upon Hector; and Iris' report to Achilles in a dream of what Hector 'intended' to do to Patroclus' head (*Il.* 18.176–7: κεφαλὴν δέ ἑ θυμὸς ἄνωγε | πῆξαι ἀνὰ σκολόπεσσι ταμόνθ᾽ ἁπαλῆς ἀπὸ δειρῆς, 'for his anger commands him to cut the head from the tender neck and thrust it on stakes').[60] The latter intertext is especially intriguing since the impaling of decapitated heads in the *Aeneid* actualizes the type of corpse abuse only ever attempted, threatened, and feared in the *Iliad*. Virgil carries out the most brutal threat of abuse uttered in Homer's poem, but the initial act of *post mortem* decapitation is left entirely out of Virgil's narrative. Nisus and Euryalus die in a bloody embrace followed by Virgil's narrative interjection, images of Rutulian mourning, and blood-soaked soil. But then we have a change of scenery: Dawn appears and scatters her light upon the earth, revealing Turnus, his troops, and, now, the heads of Nisus and Euryalus (*Aen.* 9.459–67). What Virgil leaves hidden in the darkness before dawn is the decapitation of the two heroes; it is as if the scene of abuse has been expurgated from the text.

Nisus and Euryalus receive treatment similar to their Iliadic model Dolon, who has his head cut off at *Iliad* 10.457, in one of the more brutally descriptive death scenes in Homeric poetry. Dolon's pleading with Diomedes is literally cut short, and his head hits the dust still mumbling (454–7):

ἦ, καὶ ὃ μέν μιν ἔμελλε γενείου χειρὶ παχείῃ
ἁψάμενος λίσσεσθαι, ὃ δ᾽ αὐχένα μέσσον ἔλασσε
φασγάνῳ ἀΐξας, ἀπὸ δ᾽ ἄμφω κέρσε τένοντε·
φθεγγομένου δ᾽ ἄρα τοῦ γε κάρη κονίῃσιν ἐμίχθη.

He spoke and was trying to touch his chin with his strong hand
and grab it to supplicate him, but Diomedes whacked him mid-neck
with a sword blow, and sliced through each sinew:
still pleading his head fell to the dust.

---

[60] Knauer (1964): 31, 275–7; Hardie (1994): *ad locc.* On decapitation in the *Aeneid* see Heuzé (1985): 78–81.

Virgil's night raid is modelled so pointedly on the Iliadic Doloneia that actions from the model text can and should be read against Virgil's staging in the *Aeneid*. Virgil's audience is expected to have this scene from the Doloneia in mind almost as a 'script' Virgil is repurposing and expanding, so our expectations for violent decapitation might reasonably be met by our knowledge of the decapitation of Dolon in Homer.[61]

But Virgil doesn't typically shy away from brutality,[62] and he may be providing a glimpse of what this scene of corpse abuse might have looked like at *Aeneid* 9.331–3, during the more successful stretch of the night-raid. As he cuts his way through drunk and sleeping Rutulians, Nisus slays three attendants of Turnus' augur Rhamnes by lopping off their 'drooping necks' (331: *pendentia colla*), before he attacks the augur himself (332–3): *tum caput ipsi aufert domino truncumque relinquit | sanguine singultantem*, 'then he chops off the head of their master and leaves the trunk gurgling blood'. The phrase *pendentia colla* prepares us for Euryalus' own drooping neck (434: *ceruix conlapsa*), weighed down like wet poppies, which 'bow their heads when their stems tire' (436–7: *lassoue papauera collo | demisere caput*). He's like a purple flower severed by the plough (435–6),[63] an image which itself suggests decapitation (*OLD* s.v. *collum* 1–4, and *OLD* s.v. *caput* 1–8, 13–14, are resoundingly corporeal words), but veils the repugnance of the future act through a *pathos*-rich floral metaphor. By offering the image 100 lines earlier of the dangling necks of Rhamnes and his acolytes severed with brutal detail, Virgil offers us the opportunity to read in these described decapitations the non-narrated mutilation of Nisus and Euryalus. Moreover, drunk, sleeping, helpless victims are not all that dissimilar to corpses: neither can offer resistance, neither open their eyes. When we couple this with the 'decapitated' flower heads, Virgil offers a further articulation of the details of corpse abuse.

By narrating the decapitations of separate but crucially related 'victims', Virgil is able to provide his audience with the graphic detail they relished,[64] while simultaneously distancing himself from directly describing the abuse of corpses.[65] The narrative silence stimulates reader participation. We have

---

[61] For this type of intertextual *aemulatio* see Barchiesi (2015): Chapter 4.

[62] Farron (1985) and (1986), Heuzé (1985): 116, Harrison (1988), Horsfall (1995): 174, Feeney (1999): 180.

[63] On Virgil's integration of earlier poetic material here see Fowler (1987): 189–90.

[64] Harrison (1988) and (1991): xxi–xxii; Feeney (1999).

[65] Virgil's periphrasis of the details is rounded off in his description of the presentation of the heads on pikes: the interjection *uisu miserabile* (465) betrays his disgust, and the image ends with one of Virgil's most poignant half-lines (467: *Euryali et Nisi*), grimly doubling (inadvertently?) the severing of the pair's heads.

cribs, if we need something to follow, but the actual corpse mutilations are left to the imagination of the reader.

This narrative of silence is not a one-off. At the end of book 10, Aeneas kills Mezentius with a blow to the neck that splatters blood over his breastplate (10.907–8). Mezentius' armour is the focus of the beginning of book 11, as Aeneas sets up a *tropaeum* of the spoils to Mars (11.7–8: *magne ... bellipotens*). But here the breastplate is described as pierced twelve times (9–10: *bis sex thoraca petitum | perfossumque locis*), a feature not mentioned during the fighting by Virgil and thus presumably meted out after Mezentius' death.[66]

What do we make of this? While Virgil casts a silence over the gap separating books 10 and 11, there is much we are obliged or tempted to read into the mutilation. The twelve holes in the breastplate, as Servius first understood it, may represent the twelve allied cities of Etruria, formerly under the sway of the brutal king, sharing in the abuse of Mezentius' corpse.[67] Communal corpse abuse evokes the Achaeans' group-stabbing of Hector's corpse at *Iliad* 22.369–75, as each hesitatingly pierces the flesh while sharing in some aspect of the 'killing'. Mezentius' blood-splattered breastplate and his crests dripping with blood (*Aen.* 11.8: *rorantis sanguine cristas*) recall Hector's 'blood-stained arms' (τεύχε᾽ ... | αἱματόεντ᾽) at *Iliad* 22.368–9. Though Hector's wounds are closed by the gods (*Il.* 24.420–3) and his corpse preserved, Mezentius, the *contemptor diuum*, 'scorner of the gods' (*Aen.* 7.648; cf. 8.7), will not enjoy the same divine treatment. Whatever the fate of Mezentius' actual corpse, he's reduced to a bloody shell of himself, a *truncus* bearing bloody arms (11.16): *manibusque meis Mezentius hic est*, 'here, made by my hands, is Mezentius'.

The fate of Mezentius' corpse is especially intriguing since the themes of funeral rites and treatment of the dead at this point in the epic have been building steadily.[68] Lycian Orontes is thrown overboard, the first casualty of the poem (1.113–17), and he reappears in the underworld among the host of unburied dead, along with the helmsman Palinurus, another casualty of the deep, destined to lie naked on an unknown land (5.871: he's killed on the shore): both are unable to cross the Styx (6.333–9). Sychaeus' appearance to Dido as an unburied ghost occurs midway through book 1 (353–6). Priam's headless corpse, lying on the shore, leaves the issue of the funeral for the fallen king unaddressed (2.550–8). Polydorus' corpse is appeased

[66] See Lyne (1989): 113, Harrison (1991): *ad* 10.906, Anderson (1999): 198–9, Edgeworth (2005): 6, Fulkerson (2008): 22–3.
[67] Serv. *ad Aen.* 11.9. Edgeworth (2005): 6; Fratantuono (2007): 323. See *contra* Horsfall (2003): *ad* 11.9, 16.
[68] See James (1995): 627–33 on the pervasive theme of burial or non-burial in the poem.

and offered fresh funeral rites (3.41–68). Though Hector is buried at Troy, Andromache sets up a cenotaph for him (and Astyanax) at Buthrotum, and calls his spirit to occupy the empty tomb (3.303–4). Aeneas cannot enter the underworld until he has buried Misenus, whose neglected corpse (another lying on the shore, 6.162–3) is polluting the fleet (6.149–52, 171–4). Aeneas goes as far as raising a cenotaph for Deiphobus (6.505–8). He also buries his father, Anchises (followed by funeral games) in book 5, and his nurse Caieta at the beginning of book 7; along with Pallas, these are the only characters in the poem to receive anything resembling a proper funeral.

Nisus had anticipated his own demise and abuse before the night raid and tried to take measures to ensure his body was dealt with properly (9.213–15):

> sit qui me raptum pugna pretioue redemptum
> mandet humo, solita aut si qua id Fortuna uetabit,
> absenti ferat inferias decoretque sepulcro.

> Let there be someone to bury me snatched from battle
> or ransomed; or if Fortune forbids what's customary,
> let someone give me rites and honour me, absent, with a tomb.

The prayer will fall on deaf ears as his and Euryalus' corpses are ultimately mutilated. Euryalus' mother's mourning over her son is expressed largely in terms of unfulfilled funeral rites (9.486–9). She fears his corpse, mangled, dismembered (490–1), is already the property of scavenging dogs and birds (485–6: *heu, terra ignota canibus data praeda Latinis | alitibusque iaces!*, 'alas, you lie in an unknown land feeding the dogs and birds of Latium!'), bringing us within the realm of Homeric fears of corpse mutilation.[69]

The issues related to funeral rites continue into book 10. While Aeneas (with care and pity: 10.821–32) and Turnus (mockingly: 10.491–5) hand over the bodies of Pallas and Lausus, respectively, for funeral rites, Aeneas, in one brutal *euchos*, paraphrases a slew of Homeric typological threats of corpse abuse after ruthlessly decapitating the supplicating Tarquitus mid-speech (*Aen.* 10.554–60):[70]

> tum caput orantis nequiquam et multa parantis
> dicere deturbat terrae, truncumque tepentem
> prouoluens super haec inimico pectore fatur:
> 'istic nunc, metuende, iace. non te optima mater

---

[69] On the scene of Euryalus' mother's lament see Sharrock (2011), McAuley (2016): 82–4.
[70] Harrison (1991): *ad locc.* See Farron (1986): 72–4, 78–9 on Aeneas' actions here in light of Greco-Roman opinions of funeral rites and corpse treatment.

condet humi patrioque onerabit membra sepulcro:
alitibus linquere feris, aut gurgite mersum
unda feret piscesque impasti uulnera lambent'.

Then as the man uselessly begged and tried to keep pleading,
he sliced off his head to the ground, and rolling the warm trunk
over from above, he said this, with his heart full of hatred:
'lie there now, object of fear. Your excellent mother won't
bury you in the earth or load your limbs in the family tomb:
you'll be left for savage birds, or, sunk in the abyss,
a wave will carry you away and hungry fish will lick your wounds'.

Virgil does not tell us the ultimate fate of Tarquitus' corpse, but the taunt/
threat of corpse abuse via scavenging birds, and a mother deprived of the
ability to perform funeral rites echoes the fear of Euryalus' mother in the
previous book. This is combined with a reworking of Achilles' boast to
Lycaon at *Iliad* 21.122–7, and Asteropaeus being consumed by fish at
21.203–4.[71] Aeneas' threat builds upon the theme of mistreatment in the
poem; the *possibility* of abuse is powerful, with or without its ultimate
verification. Moreover, Aeneas kills Tarquitus by decapitating him, which
recalls the corpse abuse of Nisus and Euryalus whose heads, we've seen, are
removed and stuck on pikes. Aeneas' threat is the most brutal in the
poem,[72] and by alluding to the language of Euryalus' mother's fear and
the actual abuse dealt to Nisus' and Euryalus' corpses, the boast becomes
more visceral.

When we arrive at Aeneas' treatment of Mezentius, we have to reconcile
his boasting of corpse abuse with his inversely *pius* treatment of Mezentius'
own son, Lausus, whom Aeneas by contrast allows to keep his armour and
returns for funeral rites (*Aen.* 10.827).[73] Mezentius' final words echo
Hector's request to Achilles to ensure he receives a proper funeral (*Il.*
22.338–43).[74] He fears the Etruscans will mutilate him if he's left unburied
(*Aen.* 10.903–6). Whether Aeneas includes him in the mass funeral at
11.100–19 is unstated, but that Aeneas refuses to grant the wish that his
corpse escape abuse is confirmed by the puncture wounds in Mezentius'
breastplate. This linkage, *pre* and *post mortem*, with Hector in the *Iliad* is
significant for our understanding of the imagery Virgil was evoking implicitly for his audience,[75] and it may go some way toward filling the narrative

---

[71] Dyson (2001): 90–1.
[72] Mazzocchini (2000): 82; Clausen (2002): 196–7; Putnam (2011): 36–7.
[73] Cf. Achilles' return of Andromache's father's corpse at *Il.*6.416–19; Harrison (1991): *ad loc.*
[74] Knauer (1964): 420 *ad* 10.900–6; Harrison (1991): *ad* 10.903–4.
[75] *Pace* Horsfall (2003): *ad* 11.9–10 and *ad* 14–28.

gap Virgil places between Mezentius' death and the *tropaeum* Aeneas sets up. But again, though our recognition of the source adds vividness to Virgil's silence, these 'tracce del modello'[76] do not actually answer anything for us directly. We do not know whether Aeneas treated father like son, and despite our knowledge of Mezentius' corpse abuse, Virgil again distances himself from describing it.

Whatever Aeneas' exact involvement in the treatment of Mezentius, Virgil seems to cast the world of pre-Trojan Italy as a site of violence and barbarity. Cacus, the poem's ogreish 'Bad Guy' embodiment of uncouth, uncivilized savagery (8.194: *semihominis*; 8.267: *semiferi*), has the entrance to his cave decorated with the heads of men on pikes (8.196–7): *foribusque adfixa superbis | ora uirum tristi pendebant pallida tabo*, 'and affixed with pride at the entryway were hanging human heads growing pale with grim putrefaction'. Turnus oversaw the Rutulians' decapitating and impaling of Nisus' and Euryalus' heads, imagery directly recalling the impaled heads lining Cacus' cave: (9.471–2): *simul **ora uirum praefixa** mouebant | nota nimis miseris atroque fluentia **tabo***, 'at the same time the impaled human heads, which they recognized too well, dripping with black putrefaction, moved them to sorrow'.[77] Turnus later careens his chariot over dead bodies, grinding the corpses and splattering their blood like morning dew on the ground (12.326–40) in a scene reminiscent of Tullia's brutal treatment of her father Servius' corpse at Livy 1.48.7 (cf. 1.59.10). Mezentius is castigated by Evander for his cruel, 'subhuman' (*Aen.* 8.484: *effera*) treatment of stitching corpses to living victims as a luridly novel form of both torture and corpse abuse (8.485–8). Later, to vindicate his son's murder, Mezentius hopes to decapitate Aeneas and parade his head (10.862–5):

> aut hodie uictor spolia illa cruenta[78]
> et caput Aeneae referes Lausique dolorum
> ultor eris mecum, aut, aperit si nulla uiam uis,
> occumbes pariter

> Today you will either carry back, victorious, the bloody spoils
> and head of Aeneas and be an avenger of Lausus' sorrows
> with me, or, if no amount of force opens a path for us,
> you will die by my side.

---

[76] From Barchiesi (1984).    [77] Hardie (1994): *ad* 9.471–2.
[78] Mynors prints *cruenti*; *cruenta* is clearly better here. See Barchiesi (2015): 78–9, 155 n.6.

But this form of corpse abuse is not limited to Italic peoples in the poem
nor to the poem's 'Iliadic' second half. The theme begins before Aeneas
and his band of Trojans reach Italian shores, before they leave Troy.[79]
Aeneas recounts the fate of Priam to Dido and her coterie (2.550–8):

> hoc dicens altaria ad ipsa trementem
> traxit et in multo lapsantem sanguine nati,
> implicuitque comam laeua, dextraque coruscum
> extulit ac lateri capulo tenus abdidit ensem.
> haec finis Priami fatorum, hic exitus illum
> sorte tulit Troiam incensam et prolapsa uidentem                555
> Pergama, tot quondam populis terrisque superbum
> regnatorem Asiae. iacet ingens litore truncus,
> auulsumque umeris caput et sine nomine corpus.

> Saying this [Pyrrhus] dragged him, trembling
> and slipping in the copious blood of his son, to the altar itself.
> He grabbed his hair with his left hand and with his right drew his
> glittering sword and buried it up to the hilt in his side.
> This was the limit of Priam's destiny, this death
> took him by lot, seeing Troy in flames and Pergamum's collapse,    555
> a man once the proud ruler for so many people and lands
> of Asia. He lies a huge trunk on the shore,
> a head ripped from his shoulders and a corpse without a name.

Virgil is putting Priam's own fears at *Iliad* 22.59–71 into action.[80] The
horror of the Homeric Priam's death his Virgilian equivalent metapoetically knows,[81] and, as we learn through the imagery of 'headlessness', stands
as synecdoche for the ultimate fall of Troy in the *Aeneid*.[82] Still, Pyrrhus'
actual actions are not very easy to follow. He grabs Priam's hair with his left
hand – presumably to pull the head back and expose the neck – only to
deliver the death blow to the king's ribs.[83] The language sets up a dramatic

[79] Mazzocchini (2000): 282 n.17.
[80] Knauer (1964): 381 *ad* 2.550b–558. See Bowie (1990): 470–2 for a deeper analysis of the links between this scene in the *Aeneid* and books 22 and 24 of the *Iliad*.
[81] See O'Sullivan (2009): 457–61 on the 'narratological play' here between the Priam of the *Iliad* and the *Aeneid*; similarly Smith (1999): 244–8, Dekel (2012): 68–75.
[82] In the *Iliad*, the death of Hector symbolized the death of Troy, proleptically cast outside the confines of Homer's actual poem (see esp. *Il.* 22.410–11, 506–7 with de Jong (2012): *ad locc.*), but here Virgil reframes slightly the angle of synecdochic death by actualizing Priam's fears of being the 'last' (*Il.* 22.66) of his people to die before Troy finally collapses. See Heinze (1993): 23–4 with 58 n.62 on Virgil's innovation in aligning the death of Priam with the fall of Troy. For the monarch's head as the rational/pivotal driving force of the body politic see Ash (1997): 196–200, Cowan (2007a): 21–2, Mebane (2016).
[83] See Horsfall (2008): *ad* 2.552 and (2010): 244.

scene of decapitation only to eschew it awkwardly for a blow to the heart.
We then, in Priam's famous epitaph (*Aen.* 2.554–8), hear of his headless
trunk lying on the shore. Virgil is not averse to narrating scenes of battle
specific decapitation (cf. 9.331–3, 9.770–1, 10.394, 10.552–5, 12.382), so it's
telling that he avoids describing such action here and reserves the beheading for an unnarrated scene of corpse abuse.

The elision in Virgil's depiction of the action is stunning: Priam is killed
by Pyrrhus at the altar in the middle of the palace, and then he's lying on
the shore without a head. How Priam gets to the shore and who does the
*post mortem* decapitating are not specified. Virgil seems to be blending
various accounts of Priam's death into one scene. The Greek tradition
largely agrees that Priam was killed by Neoptolemus (Pyrrhus) at the altar
of Zeus Herceus or near it.[84] But Servius (*ad Aen.* 2.506) refers to another
version of Priam's death, employed by Pacuvius in an unidentified play:[85]

> alii dicunt quod a Pyrrho in domo quidem sua captus est (Priamus), sed ad
> tumulum Achillis tractus occisusque est iuxta Sigeum promunturium: nam in
> Rhoeteo Aiax sepultus est: tunc eius caput conto fixum Pyrrhus circumtulit.

> Some say that Priam was indeed captured in his home by Pyrrhus, but was
> dragged to the tomb of Achilles and killed close to Cape Sigeum, for Ajax is
> buried at Rhoeteum: then Pyrrhus carried around his head stuck on a pike.

The 'some' refers to (at least) Pacuvius, which we know from another
Servian note *ad Aeneid* 2.557.[86] We must assume Pyrrhus is doing the
decapitating and impaling, and the reference to the shore reminds us of
Achilles' tomb at Cape Sigeum. The image in Pacuvius of Priam's head on
a stake reminds us of Hector's (reported) threat to Patroclus in the *Iliad*
(18.176–7). This also marks the actualization of Achilles' threat to decapitate Hector's corpse at *Iliad* 18.333–5 neatly (and gruesomely) completed

---

[84] Cf. Paus. 10.27.2 (citing Lesches *MI* fr. 16 Bernabé); Procl. *Chrest.* (*Iliupersis* argumentum); Pind.
*Pae.* 6.112–15; Eur. *Hec.* 21–4; Eur. *Tro.* 16–17, 481–3; [ps.]Apollod. *Epit.* 5.21, etc. The iconographic
tradition is more disturbing: the killing of Astyanax is linked with Priam's death, first tangentially
(the child is dashed to the ground while his grandparents look on behind the altar), later directly, as
Priam's corpse is beaten by Neoptolemus, who wields Astyanax like a club; Austin (1964): *ad* 2.506–
58; Gantz (1993): 655–7; *LIMC* 7.1.518–21; Anderson (1997): index s.v. 'Astyanax, in art'.

[85] For the Pacuvius source here see Horsfall (2008): *ad* 2.557 and (2010), Delvigo (2013): 29. Scafoglio
(2012) has most recently attempted to assign the events described by Servius to Pacuvius' *Hermiona*.
See my discussion of Lucan's engagement with this material below, pp. 73–6.

[86] Serv. *ad Aen.* 2.557: *IACET INGENS LITORE TRUNCUS Pompei tangit historiam . . . quod autem
dicit LITORE, illud, ut supra diximus, respicit, quod in Pacuuii tragoedia continetur*, '"he lies, a huge
trunk on the shore" touches on the history of Pompey . . . And the fact that he says "on the shore," as
I said above, recalls what is found in Pacuvius' tragedy'. See *contra* Fraenkel (1964): 2.370, Horsfall
(2008): *ad* 2.557 and (2010): 244 n.49.

by the warrior's son, but transferred to the father of the initially intended victim:[87]

νῦν δ᾽ ἐπεὶ οὖν Πάτροκλε σεῦ ὕστερος εἶμ᾽ ὑπὸ γαῖαν,
οὔ σε πρὶν κτεριῶ πρίν γ᾽ Ἕκτορος ἐνθάδ᾽ ἐνεῖκαι
τεύχεα καὶ κεφαλὴν μεγαθύμου σοῖο φονῆος

But now, Patroclus, since I go under the earth after you,
I will not bury you until I bring here the armour
and the head of Hector, your great-hearted killer.

As for allusion within the *Aeneid*, we think of the heads of Nisus and Euryalus cut off and displayed as trophies. If Virgil is alluding to the alternate mythic account in Pacuvius (as seems likely), Priam's headless trunk with head impaled and paraded by Pyrrhus (extrapoetically) is the complement to – and precedent for – the trunkless heads that suffer similar abuse elsewhere in the poem.

Despite the variety of (self-/extra-) referential allusions this scene unveils, the doubling of mythic traditions and the narrative confusion have proved troublesome. The scene, it seems, is a 'neglected oddity in V.'s narrative';[88] it is alleged that the inconsistency would have been fixed during the final edit, though it's nice to have a text that 'manhandles common sense a bit';[89] the device of 'narrative dislocation', not uncommon in *imperial* epic, 'is not a feature of Virgil', and thus stands out here;[90] maybe *litore* should be emended to *limine*, so the body can remain at the palace, and so on.[91] Virgil elsewhere threads conflicting accounts of mythic stories into his narrative in a sort of Hellenistic-style encyclopaedic stockpiling of sources, so the presence of two versions of Priam's death should not strike us as some authorial conflict over which version he wanted to use here, or something he would have edited later.[92] Virgil is famously averse to

[87] See Smith (1999): 247–8 on Pyrrhus completing the work of his father in destroying Troy. See also Putnam (1965): 33–7; Dekel (2012): 68 with 128 n.26.
[88] Horsfall (2008): *ad* 2.552.
[89] Heuzé (1985): 80: 'il faut se féliciter de disposer d'un texte qui malmène un peu le bon sens'.
[90] Bowie (1990): 473. Much of Bowie's piece on the relation between Priam's and Pompey's death here, and Virgil's nod to Pollio's lost account of Pompey's death, is excellent, but the claim that the 'narrative dislocation' (after the main caesura in 557) serves to highlight the allusion to Pompey, that by dramatically changing the location of the scene from palace to shore, we are made to recall the fallen Roman general more profoundly, misses the larger point about Virgil's narrative approach to corpse abuse. While the allusion to Pompey is clear, the argument fails to recognize the function of narrative dislocation that Virgil employs in *all* such scenes of corpse mistreatment in the *Aen.*; this is not a one-off, *pace* Bowie (1990): 473.
[91] Edgeworth (1986): 150.
[92] See Horsfall (2016) *passim* on Virgil's blending of source material. Note also Dyson (2001): 87–9, Clausen (2002): 119–21. See O'Hara (2007): 85–91: his discussion of Virgilian 'inconsistency' is

univocal presentation and argumentation,[93] pedantically adherent to and knowledgeable of literary tradition, and he wanted his audience to know it. R.G. Austin's comment is telling: 'Virgil appears to combine in his own way the two versions of Priam's death.'[94] It's the *in his own way* that has ruffled so many feathers. We might look (as often helpfully) to Seneca for an early informed reading of Virgil's merging of the two mythic traditions into one narrative, in his seamless recapitulation of Priam's demise at *Troades* 140–1: *magno ... Ioui uictima caesus | Sigea premis litora truncus*, 'slaughtered as a victim to great Jove, you press on the Sigean shore, a trunk'. The details of the events are even more 'truncated' here, but again the narrative is hardly compromised.

Virgil's scene is striking because of the cinematic transportation the reader experiences, supplemented by our knowledge of the dual strands of myth the poet is tugging. But it is what Virgil does *not* narrate for us, I argue, that is the most jarring image from the scene: the beheading and impaling. Instead, the poet presents a suddenly headless corpse. The intertext with Pacuvius informs us of the head's location. Far from being an oddity of Virgil's narrative or something requiring emendation, the narrative gap fits perfectly the pattern of Virgilian silence we have seen regarding scenes of corpse abuse. Virgil consistently avoids direct narration of mutilation and instead leaves apertures that we are encouraged to fill with examples from his own or other sources that he guides us toward implicitly through inter- or intratextual cues. Virgil knows the Pacuvius source; he includes it, but again purposefully writes out the precise moment of mutilation. The two mythic accounts are merged into one extended scene, interrupted by Virgil's characteristic silence in treating scenes of corpse abuse.

As a final word on this famously obstreperous scene, I refer again to Servius' commentary *ad Aeneid* 2.558, as his note here has important implications both for our understanding of this passage and the larger issues of narrative 'gaps' we have been analyzing. Servius glosses the sudden image of Priam's headless corpse thus: *auulsumque umeris caput hoc est quod* κατὰ τὸ σιωπώμενον *accipi debet*. The Greek phrase (κατὰ τὸ σιωπώμενον; cf. Serv. *ad Aen.* 2.552) Servius uses is difficult to understand until we recognize

excellent. Yet even here he finds the conflated versions of Priam's death 'clearly challenging': 'In the tradition, Priam was killed in two different places, but in a narrative that often (but perhaps not always) invites us to read it as realistic, should he not be killed in one place?' (86).
[93] See especially Thomas (2000) and (2001), Conte (2007): 150–69, Tarrant (2012): 17–30 on Virgil's wilful ambiguity/ambivalence.
[94] Austin (1964): *ad* 2.557.

that this is a stock phrase among literary critics from at least Zenodotus, Aristarchus, and the *Iliad* scholiasts to articulate story elements left 'in silence' or 'implicit' by the poet and requiring active cooperation on the part of the reader to *fill* the narrative gaps. René Nünlist discusses the literary history of this phrase among the Homeric scholia and beyond (with further examples from Strabo, Ps.-Demetrius, Porphyry, and indeed Servius in his *Aeneid* commentary),[95] noting that what was understood to be the 'deliberate' aim of creating narrative gaps and omissions which necessitates the cooperation of the reader mirrors the *Rezeptionsästhetik* of Wolfgang Iser and others of the Konstanzer Schule.[96] Servius deploys this standard expression to describe the narrative gap separating Priam's death scene and his sudden appearance headless on the shore, the implicit details of which must be 'understood' (*accipi*) through the participation of the reader in the complex process of meaning-making. It's worth stressing Virgil's indebtedness to the Homeric scholia, as Robin Schlunk and others have documented,[97] and it seems not unlikely that the deliberate silences both in scenes of corpse mistreatment and elsewhere in the poem represent a conscious effort on Virgil's part to punctuate his narrative with the kinds of provocative gaps that elicited debate among Homeric literary critics. Reading modern reader-response theory *back* into Virgil here may, in fact, be nothing more than reacting to and reactivating the 'lacunose' narrative techniques that Virgil was engaging through his reading of Homeric (and other) literary criticism on the narrative gaps and omissions in the Homeric corpus.

There are two other issues of silence related to death, burial, and corpse treatment that I shall consider briefly. The first concerns the ultimate fate of Aeneas (anticipated in Dido's curse), the second is the death of Turnus that brings the poem to a close in book 12. Both of these examples reach beyond the end of the poem and are thus qualitatively different from the moments where Virgil omits gruesome details in his presentation of the narrative. Still, the self-effacement in these cases is comparable and instructive.

We have seen the images of bodies lying unburied on the sand or shore (Palinurus, Priam, Misenus, Phegeus, Tarquitus (via threat), Deiphobus (via cenotaph)), and Virgil provides another in the form of Dido's curse directed at Aeneas (*Aen.* 4.612–20):

---

[95] Nünlist (2009): 157–73.   [96] Nünlist (2009): 166.
[97] Schlunk (1974); Schmit-Neuerburg (1999).

si tangere portus
infandum caput ac terris adnare necesse est,
et sic fata Iouis poscunt, hic terminus haeret,
at bello audacis populi uexatus et armis,                                    615
finibus extorris, complexu auulsus Iuli
auxilium imploret uideatque indigna suorum
funera; nec, cum se sub leges pacis iniquae
tradiderit, regno aut optata luce fruatur,
sed cadat ante diem mediaque inhumatus harena.

If the abominable
leader must make it to port or float to shore,
and Jupiter's destiny demands it, this endpoint is fixed,
still, battered by war and weapons of bold people,                           615
driven from his territories, ripped from Iulus' embrace,
let him beg for aid and watch the undeserved slaughter of his
people; and, when he has surrendered himself to laws of an unjust peace,
do not let him enjoy his kingdom or hoped-for light.
Instead, let him die ahead of schedule, unburied in the middle of the sand.

Most of Dido's curse plays out accurately in the course of the poem,[98] but
the narrative ends before Aeneas dies. Her curse coincides generally with
the sum of the myths relating to Aeneas' death: after a battle next to the
Numicus River, Aeneas is gone, after having fallen into the river, or rising
into the heavens, with his body either found in the river or never recovered.[99] The similarity between the language of Aeneas' end in the curse and
the fates of these other victims in the poem has led some to see in these
described deaths a foreshadowing of Aeneas' own demise,[100] as the symbolic prefiguring of an ending beyond the scope of the epic, instigated by
the amalgam of Jupiter's (positive) prophecy (1.258–66) and Dido's (negative) curse. The imagery is picked up by Venus in a moment of weakness,
expressed by her willingness to allow Aeneas to be 'tossed upon the sea', a
victim of fate – and bane of epic heroes[101] – so long as it ensures the
protection of Ascanius (10.48–9), and the proto-Roman line. Virgil again is
teasing different strands of the Aeneas myth to complicate our picture of a
future beyond his poem. Because the *Aeneid* does not cover this episode,
Virgil adds imagery predictive of Aeneas' death in the surrogate deaths of
other characters 'unburied on the shore'.

---

[98] O'Hara (1990): 101; Horsfall (2016): 66–8; Quint (1993): 110.
[99] Outlined at O'Hara (1990): 105–6 n.34, Dyson (2001): 51–2. See Serv. *ad Aen.* 4.620.
[100] O'Hara (1990): 104–11; Quint (1993): 86–93; Dyson (2001): 50–94.
[101] See *Od.* 5.299–312; *Aen.* 1.94–101. Cf. Hes. *Op.* 687. See my discussions below on this motif,
pp. 121–2, 143–8, 256–62.

Similarly the fate of Turnus' corpse is left outside the scope of Virgil's narrative, but predictive imagery elsewhere in the poem and in allusions to the *Iliad* give us some grounds for filling the silence. Mezentius' death and corpse abuse parallel in many ways the death of Hector in the *Iliad*. When Turnus is whisked away to Ardea by Juno, Mezentius represents a surrogate for and an anticipation of Aeneas' eventual slaying of Turnus, also modelled on Achilles' slaying of Hector.[102] So Aeneas' treatment of Mezentius can be read as a deliberate anticipation of what will happen to Turnus.[103] The silence that Virgil casts over the mutilation of Mezentius is expanded into an open-endedness in Turnus' death.[104] Like Mezentius, like Hector, Turnus' dying words concern the treatment of his corpse (*Aen* 12.931–6):

> 'equidem merui nec deprecor' inquit;
> 'utere sorte tua. miseri te si qua parentis
> tangere cura potest, oro (fuit et tibi talis
> Anchises genitor) Dauni miserere senectae
> et me, seu corpus spoliatum lumine mavis,
> redde meis.'

> 'I truly deserve this, nor am I seeking a pardon' he said.
> 'Seize your opportunity. If any love of a wretched parent can
> touch you (and Anchises was such a parent to you),
> I beg, pity the aged Daunus and give me,
> or if you'd rather my body robbed of life,
> back to my people.'

In Homer, Achilles is clear in his response (*Il.* 22.335–6, 345–54). In Virgil, in both cases, Aeneas is silent.[105]

The beauty of the poem's ending is its ambiguity, not only because Virgil doesn't tell us what happens to Turnus' corpse, but because even the traces of literary cues are ambiguous here. Turnus' words evoke both Hector's words to Achilles (*Il.* 22.338–43), and also, through the plea 'by your father', Priam's to Achilles (*Il.* 24.486–506): the one rejected, the other successful.[106] Likewise, within the *Aeneid*'s own narrative framework,

---

[102] Mezentius functions as Jove's surrogate for Turnus like Juno's surrogate apparition of Aeneas (10.689–90); Barchiesi (2015): 38–9, 149 n.4. See also Van Nortwick (1980): 309, James (1995): 630–2.

[103] Fulkerson (2008): 26–8.    [104] James (1995): 632–3.

[105] Aeneas is literally silent in the case of Mezentius, who gets the last word. In response to Turnus' request Aeneas says nothing: Lyne (1990): 336: 'Book 12 ends in an echoing silence'; Fulkerson (2008): 31: 'the silence of [the poem's] ending echoes loudly'; Fratantuono (2007): 396.

[106] Barchiesi (2015): 84–91; Horsfall (1995): 204–5; Tarrant (2012): *ad* 12.931–8.

though Aeneas (either directly, or by handing the body over to the Etruscans) is complicit in the abuse of Mezentius' corpse, his treatment of Mezentius' son Lausus moments before his duel with the father represents an unusual and striking display of battlefield respect and piety:[107] Aeneas pities Lausus (who also invokes the relationship of sons and fathers, *Aen.* 10.827) and hands him over for proper funeral ritual. Lausus, we might recall, is dubbed like Hector 'tamer of horses' (7.651: *equum domitor*; from Homer's *hippodamos*), and Aeneas' treatment of his corpse evokes directly Achilles' handling of Hector's corpse when he finally relinquishes the Trojan prince to his father at *Iliad* 24.589.[108] This doubling of corpse treatment response, spread between Mezentius and Lausus, reflects the extremes of Achilles' treatment of Hector's corpse over the final 3 books of the *Iliad*, and serves as a further comparative paradigm for our expectations of Aeneas' treatment of Turnus.[109] This dichotomy between (Aeneas' treatment of) Mezentius and Lausus further reflects a tension in Virgil's representation of Turnus himself as both bloodthirsty Turnus-*turannos* and sympathetic *iuuenis* destined to die before his time (e.g. *Aen.* 12.149, 220–1, 598).[110]

While Achilles eventually handed the corpse of Hector over to Priam, the new-Achilles, Neoptolemus/Pyrrhus, was less generous than his father in the treatment of Priam's corpse. Michael Putnam and others have noticed a variety of resonances linking Aeneas after the death of Pallas with the Pyrrhus of book 2 at Troy.[111] This idea that Aeneas takes over the more sinister elements of Achilles embodied in/by Pyrrhus is a good one – they are both, as it were, Achilles *rediuiuus*, and so linked – though it's usually employed as a means of casting blanket aspersions on Aeneas' character. The association simply adds another layer to the complexity Virgil has created that blurs our view of the poem's close, particularly with regard to what we imagine Aeneas will do with Turnus' corpse.

The deaths of Priam and Turnus are linked structurally: Priam's death seals the fate of Troy and brings the Trojan War to a close; Turnus' death seals the fate of Italians and Trojans and closes *that* war and poem. Both die 'sacrificially': Priam is dragged through his son's blood to an altar, Turnus is sacrificed to the shade of Pallas (but also in effect *by* Pallas at 12.948–9: *Pallas te . . . Pallas | immolat*, 'Pallas, *Pallas* sacrifices you'). The formulaic

---

[107] Barchiesi (2015): 2–4.     [108] Harrison (1991): *ad* 10.831; Barchiesi (2015): 151 n.19.
[109] See Edgeworth (2005): 5–6.     [110] I owe this last observation to Philip Hardie.
[111] Putnam (1965): 172, 175, 177 and (1995): 204–5. Cf. Boyle (1986): 127–9, 154–6, 172 and Dekel (2012): 112–14.

*hoc dicens* precedes each death-blow.[112] Aeneas as narrator tells us that (in all likelihood) Pyrrhus left Priam headless and unburied. Will Aeneas leave Turnus similarly a *truncus*, as Evander had wishfully hoped Pallas (whom Aeneas channels with his death-blow) would accomplish (11.173–5: *tu quoque nunc stares immanis truncus in armis,*[113] | *esset par aetas et idem si robur ab annis,* | *Turne,* 'you also now would stand a huge trunk in armour, Turnus, if you had an equal age and the same strength of years')? Of course, we can but wonder. But the *mise en abyme* linking the 'ending' of Priam with the death of Turnus and the silence of the poem's close is poignant.[114]

Our recollection of these strings of paired contradictory allusions at the end of the poem creates in the reader a two-fold expectation of what Aeneas' treatment of Turnus' corpse will be, and it is this which makes the poem's end so fundamentally mystifying. Even the verb Virgil chooses to finish off Turnus toys insidiously with this concluding crux he blankets in silence: Aeneas 'buries' his sword in Turnus' breast, but will he bury (or allow to be buried) his victim's corpse (12.949: *condit*)?[115] Virgil conspicuously avoids the narrative resolution book 24 provides for the *Iliad*, and this is finally his greatest silence of all.[116]

In these last two examples, Virgil's narrative silence is compounded to reach beyond the textual confines of his poem, but as elsewhere he employs implicit imagery as a means of filling and/or complicating the narrative aperture. Virgil's silences are provocative. They offer us considerable room to negotiate our own interests in the scenes of abuse and funeral denial that he refuses to engage directly. Homer reveals the possibility of corpse abuse, only to snatch it away as something ultimately outside the rational order of his heroic cosmos: heroes can boast, threaten, and even attempt to mutilate a corpse, but rarely successfully, as the gods and the poet eventually intervene. Virgil is more elusive. While he outstrips Homer in allowing his heroes a larger range of *post mortem* abuse, his silence in revealing the action of that abuse betrays the limits of his willingness to inject overt corpse mistreatment into his narrative. Virgil's allegiance to Homeric poetics only allowed him to go so far: while the *Iliad* expresses a moral horror of carrying out the mutilation of corpses, there is in the *Aeneid* a moral horror of *describing* the abuses that we know have happened, even though Virgil is prepared to concede that corpse abuse actually does occur.

---

[112] Tarrant (2012): *ad* 12.950: 'a formula reserved by V. for life-ending moments'.
[113] See Horsfall (2003): *ad* 11.173 for *armis* preferred to a common but unnecessary emendation of *aruis*.
[114] Fowler (1997b): 264–5.
[115] See James (1995), Rimell (2015): 39–62 on the semantic range of *condere* in the *Aen.*
[116] Though see Jenkyns (1985): 73–7.

It is in this pregnant silence, I suggest, that we find space for Rome's internecine atrocities. Our historical sources for the violence in the last few decades of the Republic are conspicuously late – there is a certain 'silence' here as well. Not until the principate is firmly established do we have full accounts of the abuses committed during the civil wars in the 50 or so years before Virgil began writing the *Aeneid* (in 29 BCE). The relative literary silence, *inter alia*, likely reflects a fear of the mistreatment that people like Cicero most famously incurred for conspicuous dissension from political upheaval via his verbal haymakers aimed at Antony in the *Philippics* (e.g. Plut. *Cic.* 48–9; App. *B Ciu.* 19–20). The political landscape at the time of Virgil's writing made overt references to the brutality that ushered in change complicated, at the very least. That said, Virgil appears to project into the mytho-historic past the hopes and fears of his present, and always with an eye to the uncertain future. The psychological trauma the civil wars caused implanted itself in Rome's collective consciousness, and nods to the historical violence bleed through Virgil's text.[117]

The corpse abuse, funeral denial, threats, and fears of mutilation that Virgil weaves into his narrative all have points of contact with the horrors that helped rip the Republic to pieces, and his contemporary readers would have recognized these allusions in his poem. One cannot help seeing Pompey,[118] Cicero,[119] or Marius Gratidianus[120] in the depiction of Priam's headless mutilated corpse; or the heads of Gratidianus, Damasippus, C. Carrinas, and others paraded on pikes around the walls of Praeneste in the parading of Nisus' and Euryalus' impaled heads;[121] or Caesar's gashed corpse in the tyrant Mezentius' perforated armour; or the proliferation of heads on display in the forum in the heads that line the entrance to Cacus' cave; or corpses floating down the Tiber, or left to rot, or for animals to consume, in Aeneas' taunting over Tarquitus' corpse, and so on. Homer offered Virgil a powerful epic theme in issues related to corpse treatment, but his own and his readers' life experiences added enormous emotional weight to the poetic dialogue. Virgil brings the corpse abuse of Rome into his poetic heroic universe, but he had no need to provide his Roman audience detailed articulation of those abuses since their own witnessing of Rome's kaleidoscopic violence left wounds that had not fully healed. In remaining conspicuously silent, Virgil draws his

---

[117] Much has been written on civil war imagery in the *Aeneid*, esp. in books 7–12: see MacKay (1963); Camps (1969): 96–101; Quint (1993): 76–83; Horsfall (1995): 155–61; Rossi (2004): 165–8, 192–6; Marincola (2010); Tarrant (2012): 6–8.

[118] E.g. Serv. *ad Aen.* 2.557; Bowie (1990).        [119] Richlin (1999): 204.

[120] Austin (1964): *ad loc*; Horsfall (2010): 244; Delvigo (2013): 38–9.        [121] Ahl (2007): 411–15.

audience in more closely to these moments where the narrative stops suddenly and encourages them to fill the silence with the spectacle of horrors he refrains from articulating.[122]

And we can unpack this even further. The *Aeneid* functioned almost immediately as the major poetic monument of what was still an evolving Augustan regime by Virgil's death in 19 BCE. Where it falls in the ideological chronology is debated (was it a formulated product of or an appropriated symbol for the Augustan programme?), but it certainly resonated in roughly the same way that the Mausoleum Augusti, the Temple of Apollo Palatinus, Mars Ultor, Arch of Augustus, Ara Pacis, among many other physical monuments, did, as growing ideological and semiotic emblems of the embryonic principate[123] – not to mention the import of Virgil's own *Georgics* (especially the proem of *G.* 3), Horace's *Odes*, and the litany of public ceremonies, which became part of the validation of the new system. These other monuments, all glorifying and recalling a link to the Republican past but promoting a new imperial future, actively avoided direct memorialization of Rome's, particularly Augustus' own, involvement in the civil wars that led to this socio-political present. Octavian destroyed documents relating to the triumvirs' actions in 36 BCE (App. *B Ciu.* 5.132). He later avoided elaboration of the bloody civil wars in his 'sanitized' *Res Gestae*,[124] and Suetonius tells us that Claudius was schooled by his mother Antonia and grandmother Livia not to offer a 'true and free account' of the time period between Caesar's murder and the end of the civil wars in his history of Augustus' reign (Suet. *Claud.* 41.2).[125] It's only with Caligula's rise to power that various histories from the end of the Republic and early empire – suppressed on account of their criticisms of Julius Caesar and his successors – were stripped of their censorship and granted universal exposure (Suet. *Calig.* 16.1); Tiberian accounts were

---

[122] We might compare Manlius Torquatus' treatment of the corpse of his Gallic adversary at Livy 7.10.11. Livy (Virgil's contemporary) is explicit that Torquatus left the corpse 'intact' (*corpus . . . intactum*) except for a bloody chain which he 'despoiled' (*spoliauit*) from the dead man's neck. No Virgilian silence here, rather *denial* of expected mutilation; 'expected' because Livy's source Quadrigarius (Gell. *NA* 9.13.7–19 = Quadrigarius fr. 10b Peter) tells us Torquatus chopped off his enemy's head to get at the necklace (*caput praecidit*). But the obtruded refusal of decapitation for a foreign enemy makes way for Torquatus' later severing of his own son's head in the next book (Livy 8.7.21). That Livy has Torquatus direct this sort of violence toward his own flesh-and-blood and not an external enemy may hint at (and offer commentary on) the self-defeating abuses of more recent Roman history (8.7.22: *Manlianaque imperia non in praesentia modo horrenda sed exempli etiam tristis in posterum essent*, 'Manlian Commands were not only a source of horror at that time, but also a grim example for the future'). Virgil acknowledges the story with characteristic distancing effects: Torquatus' shade is simply 'savage with his axe' (*Aen.* 6.824: *saeuum . . . secure*).
[123] See Zanker (1988) on the monuments.   [124] Tarrant (2012): 27.   [125] Osgood (2006): 1.

painfully obsequious (e.g. Velleius Paterculus, Valerius Maximus), or snuffed out for 'treason' (Cremutius Cordus).[126] There was clearly a concerted effort to sanitize public *memoria*, to expurgate much unsavoriness.[127]

The *Aeneid* too is calculating, expurgating. The scope of Virgil's poetic project allowed him to eschew direct focus on the current political and institutional structure, only addressing these elements obliquely: we are not bludgeoned with Augustan panegyric here, but so too the elements of civil war in the poem's second half only glance subtly toward the real-life civil wars in Rome's recent past. The mythological narrative and generic epic superstructure, while helping to reveal so much that is hidden in the narrative by way of poetic engagement, simultaneously form something like a shroud through which the political content is purposefully muddled. It is for the audience to negotiate this allusive space between history and *literary* history. Despite this careful distancing, the period's protagonist, Augustus, is everywhere in the *Aeneid*, and he's particularly present in Virgil's *pius Aeneas*. We just have to dig around a bit to find him.

The associations Virgil constructs between his Aeneas and the historical Octavian/Augustus present a number of issues, particularly when read against the silence of the final scene of the poem. We might remember that according to Suetonius, Octavian had famously raged against the corpse of Brutus after Philippi, decapitating him and shipping his head to Rome for public display at the foot of Caesar's statue (Suet. *Aug.* 13; cf. Dio Cass. 47.49.2 for the head lost in transit). He also denied funerals for Brutus' comrades by promising that carrion birds would see to their corpses (Suet. *Aug.* 13: *iam istam uolucrum fore potestatem*), he impaled the mass of masterless slaves deployed under Sextus Pompey (Dio Cass. 49.12), and offered Roman senators and *Equites* up as human sacrifices to the altar of *Diuus Iulius* during the siege at Perusia (Suet. *Aug.* 15; Dio Cass. 48.14.4). This last reference recalls Aeneas' prepared human sacrifices to Pallas' shade at *Aeneid* 10.517–20 and 11.81–2, a proposition also relegated to narrative silence when Virgil refuses to tell us whether the sacrifices were ultimately performed.[128] And we should find it disturbing in light of the second round of proscriptions that the 'gifts of the people' (8.721: *dona . . . populorum*) which Augustus 'pins to proud doorposts' (721–2: *aptatque superbis | postibus*) on Aeneas' futuristic shield recall Cacus' earlier head-

---

[126] Gowing (2010).

[127] See Giusti (2016) reading Arendt's reading of totalitarian ideology into Augustanism and the *Aeneid*'s role in this system; see my discussion on Lucan's engagement with Augustan ideology below, pp. 167–9.

[128] Farron (1985): 26–8; Tarrant (2012): 26; Barchiesi (2015): 62–3.

hunting in the same book (8.196–7: *foribus adfixa superbis | ora uirum*).[129]
Whether or not the details are historical doesn't really matter. The stories
persisted and became part of the life of Octavian that Augustus never could
quite shake, and their influence on Virgil, his audience, and subsequent
audiences cannot have been insignificant (e.g. Sen. *Clem.* 1.11.1: *haec*
*Augustus senex aut iam in senectutem annis uergentibus; in adulescentia caluit,*
*arsit ira, multa fecit, ad quae inuitus oculos retorquebat.* 'such was Augustus
as an old man, or just growing into old age [i.e. kind, restrained, forgiving];
in his youth he was hot tempered and burned with anger, and did many
things which he later did not want to recall'[130]).

These acts and boasts have reasonably been viewed as evocative of
Homeric battle rage, and Appian even records that after Julius Caesar's
death, a furious Octavian claimed he was determined to avenge the
murdered Caesar as Achilles avenged Patroclus (App. *B Ciu.* 3.13). But
that Octavian is said to have actually carried out these abuses makes the acts
decidedly un-Homeric; if anything, Homer sets a clear limit to battle rage
related specifically to corpse treatment, and his heroes are not typically
granted the freedom to debase themselves by crossing too far into
inhumanity, often despite their best efforts. What Octavian evokes is of
course very much *Roman*, and Roman in the very real context of the civil
wars that ultimately brought Octavian into position as Rome's *primus inter*
*pares*, Augustus. Scholarship has tended to view Aeneas as an epic hero who
must break away from 'Iliadic' passion and bloodlust and learn to embrace
Roman self-control. But the amorality and mindlessness of the string of
civil wars that serve as a backdrop for Virgil's composition and Augustus'
ascendancy significantly destabilize this developmental trajectory, particularly when read against the relative decorum of the *Iliad* in its handling of
corpse treatment. Octavian's rage and abuse (however justified or mitigated by the context of revenge and filial piety) tally uncomfortably with
some of the more unsavoury actions of Aeneas, particularly his treatment of
Tarquitus and his involvement in the abuse of Mezentius, and these images
should colour our reading of the end of the poem.[131]

Virgil's Aeneas is not a Homeric epic hero. Indeed, much of Virgil's
innovation in the reconfiguration of Homeric epic is his intricate balancing
and imbricating of mythic, historic, and contemporary time, and the
(deliberately) resulting tensions inherent in this chronological interplay

---

[129] Fowler (1990): 51–2; Thomas (2001): 206–7.
[130] Cf. Sen. *Clem.* 1.9; Dio Cass. 56.44.1; Stat. *Silu.* 4.1.31–2.
[131] Quint (1993): 79–80: the scene of Aeneas' slaying of Turnus 'is unmistakably one of [Roman] civil
war' (80).

create historicizing moments that bubble up to the epic's surface. Where Homer rejected corpse abuse, Virgil retrojects the corpse abuse emblematic of Rome's civil wars into proto-Roman mytho-history, though shielding his audience somewhat from its visceral horrors by refusing to narrate the details: we 'narrate' them by filling these hermeneutic fissures. Virgil is attempting to establish a heroic code based on *pietas* through Aeneas, but it's not clear whether this new code and its hero resemble the amoral horrors of civil war violence, or whether they fall more in line with the prior Homeric heroic value code that placed a limit on abuse. It isn't clear whether we should read Aeneas in the end as a rash young Octavian capable of the overkill he displayed in his abuse of Brutus and his companions, or an older, maturing, composed Augustus averse to such savagery. By 19 BCE, of course, both Aeneas and Augustus are heroes 'unfulfilled'.[132] Virgil's silence is deliberate and significant. It allows his readers to involve themselves as productive participants in the creation of Augustan ideology by permitting them to supplement the poet with whatever memories, emotions, and aspirations they hold.

---

[132]  This is Nisbet's (1978–80: 59) description of *Aeneas imperator*; cf. Tarrant (2012): 27.

# CHAPTER 2

# Decapitation in Lucan, Statius, and Silius Italicus

John Dryden famously aphorized in his 'Dedication' to *Examen Poeticum* that 'Virgil had the gift of expressing much in little, and sometimes in silence'.[1] We've explored some of the implications of this silence in detail, but it is Virgil's imperial successors who provide *materia* for a direct engagement with narrative gaps concerning the treatment of the dead that he leaves tantalizingly and wilfully unexplored in the *Aeneid*. Lucan first takes up the gauntlet; Statius and Silius address Virgilian silence in their own unique ways, but very often (unavoidably) through the lens of Lucan's redefinition of the epic landscape. In all three epics there emerges a pattern of 'filling in' *lacunae* Virgil has insinuated into his narrative in scenes of corpse abuse, constituting a sort of 'anaplerotic' poetics of engagement with Virgilian silence;[2] their epics, in a sense, play out or stage the interpretative dynamics of a reader-response system instigated by Virgil's lacunose narrative techniques.[3] This exegetic explication of Virgilian silence governing the treatment of the dead is violently distorted in all three poems. This chapter analyzes some of the ways in which Lucan, Statius, and Silius appropriate and manipulate their epic models by examining three scenes: Pompey's death and decapitation in the *BC*; Tydeus' cannibalism of Melanippus' severed head and Tydeus' own subsequent abuse by the Thebans in the *Thebaid*; and Theron's mutilation of Asbyte's corpse, followed by his own corpse abuse at the hands of Hannibal and Asbyte's Numidian coterie in the *Punica*. These scenes all involve decapitation and further abuse aimed at a severed head and thus represent the actualization of the most grisly abuses found in earlier martial epic. The similarities hinge on the hyper-intertextuality of these poems, as each poet looks back to earlier generations of model scenes of abuse for material to

---

[1] Hammond and Hopkins (2000): 225–6; and quoted in Quinn (1968): 339.
[2] See Barchiesi (2015): 72 who uses the term to describe the *Odyssey*'s engagement with gaps in the *Iliad*.
[3] That Virgilian complexity, inconsistency, tension (etc.) offered a launch-pad for successive epicists has been well discussed, but see esp. Hardie (1993): 1–3, 58 (programmatically), and 57–87 *passim*.

revive and repurpose; the result is a self-consciously vertiginous textual landscape. The chapter offers a synoptic view of the three epicists' engagement with this particular motif and the ways in which decapitation features in the larger functioning of each poet's epic universe.

## Pompey in Lucan's *Bellum ciuile*

Lucan's *Bellum ciuile* is a poem born of Virgilian silence. Lucan stages, over the course of 10 books, Anchises' elliptical fears of future civil warfare conveyed to Aeneas in the underworld (*Aen.* 6.826–35).[4] While it's obvious to Virgil's readers that Anchises is speaking of the war between Caesar and Pompey, his language is ambiguous and couched in terms of negation (he never mentions Caesar or Pompey by name).[5] Neither Virgil nor Anchises has any desire to openly elaborate the horrors of civil war. Lucan, we are promised, will be 'more than' clear (*plus quam, BC* 1.1–2).[6] His play of joining subject matter with the *horrida bella*, 'grim wars' (*Aen.* 7.41; cf. 6.86–7) of the *Aeneid*'s Iliadic second half, articulated in *BC*'s proem, further magnifies his exploration of Virgil's narrative silences.[7] This macrocosmic treatment in Lucan's epic design, his über-amplification of Virgil's ambiguous silences,[8] is expressed everywhere in the *BC* as the surgical probing of Virgil's texts unlocks for him new and unexamined poetic paths. Lucan's exploitation of Virgil's silence occurs most dramatically at the microscopic level in his handling of the treatment of the dead. What Virgil omitted from his epic is everywhere in the *BC* a point of departure and a source of poetic inspiration.

The masterstroke of epic corpse mutilation in the poem is Lucan's depiction of the tortuous death and abuse of Pompey in *BC* 8. The scene, or more specifically one allusion in the scene (8.698–711), has been championed as the most famous intertextual reference in the poem, as Pompey's headless corpse battered by the waves recalls Virgil's scene of

---

[4] Barnes (1995): 268; Putnam (1995): 224–5; Narducci (2002): 21–2, 223–4; Casali (2011): 85–6. Cf. also the implicit allusion to the internecine struggle voiced by Juno at *Aen.* 7.317: *hac gener atque socer coeant mercede suorum*, 'and may father and son-in-law unite at such a cost to their own people'.

[5] Casali (2011): 86.

[6] See Henderson (1998): 165–211, whose challenging but brilliant piece is in many ways an explication of the potential and implications of Lucan's poetics of *plus quam*. See Ambühl (2015): 4–5 (programmatically) *et passim* on Lucan's *plus quam* as a metapoetic marker for his efforts to surpass *all* literary predecessors.

[7] Casali (2011): 84. On Lucan's appropriation of Virgil's 'middle' see Tesoriero (2004): esp. 212–15.

[8] On Lucan's poetic engagement with Virgilian themes and *topoi*, see esp. Barnes (1995): 268–72, Thomas (2001): 83–92, Narducci (2002), Casali (2011).

Priam's corpse in *Aeneid* 2. The allusion is doubly striking as Virgil's scene had already posited a correspondence between Priam and Pompey, so Lucan is effectively reactivating and rehistoricizing the model by acknowledging Virgil's nod to the corpse of Pompey in his depiction of Priam. It's a rather dazzling play on Virgil's meta-historical moment in the *Aeneid* and has deservedly received scholarly attention.[9] My interest, rather than simply the matching epitaphs of each poem's headless leader, lies in the details Lucan lavishes on the scene that lead to the intertext with Virgil, which function as an explication of Virgil's silence concerning Priam's – and by allusion, Pompey's – corpse abuse.

Let's focus first on the scene itself. In terms of technical action, the Egyptian Achillas stabs Pompey in a small boat off the coast of Egypt (8.618–19), and Septimius, a Roman mercenary, subsequently saws off his head (667–73). Around the simple details of the murder Lucan adds an astonishing amount of 'extra' material that serves to lengthen Pompey's death scene into something almost 'operatic'.[10] The scene is introduced and interrupted by apostrophic asides (scornfully: to the gods 542–50, Ptolemy 550–60, Fortuna 600–4; mournfully: to Pompey 604–8), brief speeches by Pompey (579–82) and his wife Cornelia (584–9), and descriptions of the anguish of Cornelia and Pompey's fleet at his impending doom (589–95). Then the stabbing is followed by Pompey's stoic obmutescence and internal monologue (622–35) and Cornelia's 'pitiable words' (639–61), which introduce further delays. Cornelia's request that Pompey see her face before he dies (646–7) seems to suggest to Septimius a more gruesome way of extending the murder: the actual head that will be the focus of attention is of course Pompey's, which Septimius saws from the dying man's shoulders. This repeated fragmenting of narrative action through authorial asides and intratextual audience reaction mimics the physical mutilation of Pompey, pulling the audience in an array of disparate focalized directions as the leader himself is torn apart.[11]

We are transported from the ever-swooning super-Andromache Cornelia (cf. 5.799, 8.59, 8.662; cf. *Il.* 22.466–7) to Pompey's tiny death-boat, where Septimius grabs his still-breathing head (8.667–73):

---

[9] The seminal analysis is Narducci (1973), reworked in (2002): 111–16. See also valuable discussions in Bowie (1990), Hinds (1998): 8–10, 100, Berno (2004).

[10] Malamud (2003): 33. Cf. Hutchinson (1993): 321–3, Erasmo (2008): 112–14.

[11] See Erasmo (2008): 110–12. On the association between narrative/syntactical fragmentation and bodily dismemberment in Lucan, generally, see Quint (1993): 140–7, Bartsch (1997): 10–47, Dinter (2012): 27–9. For this theme in the Neronian poets see Most (1992).

> nam saeuus in ipso
> Septimius sceleris maius scelus inuenit actu,
> ac retegit sacros scisso uelamine uoltus
> semianimis Magni spirantiaque occupat ora
> collaque in obliquo ponit languentia transtro.
> tunc neruos uenasque secat nodosaque frangit
> ossa diu: nondum artis erat caput ense rotare.

> For savage Septimius
> in the very act of crime enacted an even worse crime:
> he tears the covering and reveals the sacred features
> of half-living Magnus, and he grabs his still-breathing head
> and places the drooping neck on the cross-beam.
> Then he saws sinews and veins, he cracks through knotty
> vertebrae a long while: not yet was whirling heads with a sword an art form.

The winking 'apology' for his description of the lurid crushing of knotty neck bones as a result of a transitional period between decapitation by axe and sword only amplifies the horror of the abuse, which Lucan describes with morbid enthusiasm.[12] Septimius himself is characterized as sub-human, an animal (599–600): *immanis uiolentus atrox nullaque ferarum | mitior in caedes*, 'monstrous, savage, frightful, not meeker than any wild animal in his love of slaughter'.[13] The graphic details continue for another 18 lines, as the head attempts to speak and move its eyes (682–3: *dum uiuunt uoltus atque os in murmura pulsant | singultus animae, dum lumina nuda rigescunt*, 'while features live and breath's gurgles drive the mouth to mumbles, while staring eyes go stiff'),[14] before eventually being thrust on a pike (684: **suffixum caput est**). The image evokes the impaled heads of Nisus and Euryalus (*Aen.* 9.466: **praefigunt capita**). Virgil remained silent on the physical action of the decapitation of his two warriors, the silence (perhaps unintentionally, yet powerfully) symbolized and marked by a rare half-line leaving their names before the gap (467: *Euryali et Nisi . . .*). Lucan takes his cue from this silence, picking up where Virgil left off.

In Lucan's scene the text itself is broken apart syntactically, the spear separated from its function as the head-holding trophy pole by three agonizing lines (*BC* 8.681–4: *Pharioque ueruto . . . suffixum caput est*, 'on a

---

[12] Hutchinson (1993): 323, Quint (1993): 144, Narducci (2002): 443–4, Chiesa (2005): 16–18.

[13] Rieks (1967): 193.

[14] The image of a mumbling decapitated head has an abundant *Fortleben* in imperial Latin poetry: Sen. *Thy.* 727–9, *Ag.* 901–3; Stat. *Theb.* 5.236–8, 10.516–18; Sil. *Pun.* 5.416–18, 15.469–70. The main models are Hom. *Il.* 10.457 = *Od.* 22.329; Enn. *Ann.* 483–4 Skutsch; Verg. *Aen.* 10.554; Ov. *Met.* 5.104–6, 6.557–60, 11.50–3. On automatism of cut-off body parts (including some 'talking-heads'), see Dinter (2012): 37–49; Mayer (1981): *ad* 682–3.

Pharian spear . . . the head is fixed'). Lucan's play on the ridiculousness of this extended death scene finds another syntactical twist with the delayed *diu* in his haptic description of the sawing of Pompey's neck (673).[15] His decapitated head is transfixed like Nisus' and Euryalus' heads, but, as it is cut off, it also sobs blood like the pair's sleeping *victim*, the augur Rhamnes, during the night-raid (*Aen.* 9.332–3: *tum caput ipsi aufert domino truncumque reliquit | sanguine* **singultantem**, 'then [Nisus] chops off the head of their master and leaves the trunk gurgling blood'; with *BC* 8.682–3, above).[16] The image is inverted, however: Rhamnes' trunk gurgles, Pompey's severed head is *singultus*. Virgil's scene of the night-raid victims' decapitation anticipated Nisus and Euryalus' own ending, and here Lucan seems to lump both images into Pompey's extended murder scene.

But Lucan is not finished. Pompey's head is then embalmed in order that 'proof of the guilt' remain for Ptolemy and ultimately Caesar (8.688–91):

> tunc arte nefanda
> summota est capiti tabes, raptoque cerebro
> adsiccata cutis, putrisque effluxit ab alto
> umor, et infuso facies solidata ueneno est.

> Then by criminal art
> the liquid is drawn from the head, and after the brain is torn out,
> the skin is dehydrated, and the festering moisture drained from
> within, and the face was frozen stiff by administering venom.

The embalming continues the corpse mutilation and also places the scene within the realm of the dark and morally suspect arts (*arte nefanda*) of Erichtho, whose treatment of corpses in *BC* 6 finds a counterpart here.[17] The scene of embalming echoes the description of Erichtho's mutilation of a corpse's head (6.566–9). Whatever reference Lucan is making to the burgeoning practice of necromancy and Egyptian-style embalming at Rome,[18] he's more specifically and poignantly pushing epic beyond

---

[15] See Hutchinson (1993): 323, Erasmo (2008): 112, Estèves (2010): 209, Mebane (2016): 206. Cf. the grisly description in Weiss and Hassan (2016): 247–8: 'One suspected ISIS fighter, an Egyptian national, was lynched in front of numerous international journalists by two uniformed Iraqi police officers, as Iraqi intelligence agents and at least one other policeman tried in vain to stop them . . . But the locals and the militias egged them on to exact revenge for the Egyptian's alleged knife murder of a fellow federal police officer. "The killer started to saw through the neck, but it was slow-going. He lifted the blade again and slammed it into the Egyptian's neck another four times. Then he sawed back and forth".'

[16] Moretti (1985): 138.    [17] Korenjak (1996): *ad* 6.566; Erasmo (2008): 116.

[18] See Mayer (1981): *ad* 8.688, Erasmo (2008): 116, Toynbee (1971): 41 for embalming at Rome.

conventional limits.[19] Perhaps there is a sinister play on the Egyptian-style 'embalming' practices in the *Iliad* in the preservation via 'ambrosial oils' of Hector's, Sarpedon's, and Patroclus' corpses by Apollo, Aphrodite, and Thetis.[20] Pompey is definitively the Homeric-style vanquished hero in Lucan's poem, an epic victim. While the *Iliad*'s famous corpses are protected and preserved from abuse by Homer's gods, Pompey's corpse (his *caput*) is preserved *in* its abuse off the shores of Egypt.

It's here that we find the intertext with Virgil's *Aeneid* and the headless corpse of Priam on the shore (*BC* 8.698–9, 708–11):

> **litora** Pompeium feriunt, **truncus**que uadosis
> huc illuc iactatur aquis . . .
>
>                    pulsatur harenis,
> carpitur in scopulis hausto per uolnera fluctu,
> ludibrium pelagi, nullaque manente figura
> una nota est <u>Magno</u> **capitis iactura reuolsi**.

> the shores strike Pompey, and his trunk
> is cast back and forth by shallow waters . . .
>                 He's battered on the sands,
> ripped apart on the rocks, taking in waves through his wounds,
> the plaything of the sea, and with no form remaining
> the one identifiable feature of Magnus is the loss of a severed head.

In the Aeneid passage, Priam, we recall (*Aen.* 2.557–8)

>           iacet <u>ingens</u> litore truncus,
> **auulsum**que umeris **caput** et sine nomine corpus . . .

>           lies a huge trunk on the shore,
> a head ripped from his shoulders and a corpse without a name.

References to this intertext have been building since the *matrona*'s prophecy at *BC* 1.685–6, where she 'recognizes' (*agnosco*: the future Pompey, the past Priam) a headless deformed trunk lying in the sand: *hunc ego, fluminea deformis* **truncus** *harena | qui* ***iacet***, *agnosco*, 'I recognize that man, a misshapen trunk who lies on the river sands'. Later at 2.171–3, the elderly survivor of the earlier civil violence under Marius and Sulla recalls how he struggled to match his brother's decapitated head to the necks of

---

[19] Hutchinson (1993): 324–6; Seo (2013): 87: 'the indignities heaped upon Pompey's mortal flesh prolong the death scene nearly to the point of bathos'.

[20] On this form of preservation in the *Iliad* see Redfield (1975): 179, 255–6 n.48, Garland (1985): 34; Stanley (1993): 192, 195.

countless trunks beaten by waves against the shore (189). He also recalls Roman leaders' heads paraded on pikes and dumped in piles in the forum (160–1).[21] In book 8 alone, Pompey weighs the relative value of his own and Caesar's 'severed necks' (8.8–12); in his polemic against Pompey, Lentulus evokes imagery of mutilated headless Roman generals (436–7); and Pompey demands his wife and son test the faith of Ptolemy by his own (i.e. Pompey's) neck (581–2).[22]

We might expect the allusions to end here, with Virgil's Priam and Lucan's Pompey lying headless on the shore, but Lucan presses on. Virgil allowed Priam's corpse to remain a pathetic symbol of Troy's fall, with the silence of the corpse's final fate (will he be consumed by birds and dogs according to (threatened) Iliadic custom?) ringing emblematic of the smouldering buildings in the scene's backdrop. Lucan, however, devotes another 160 lines to the makeshift funeral for Pompey *truncus* (8.712–872), in a whimsical display of his taste for gore (e.g. 8.777–8, 786–8). Lucan's scene is full of *pathos* as well, but of a wholly new and perverse kind: it's overindulgent and bursting at the seams (here too Lucan cannot contain his apostrophic madness, asides, and delays), in direct engagement with Virgil's *pathos* of silence.

Pompey's trunk represents not simply an allusion to the death of Priam in *Aeneid* 2: the entire scene of Pompey's death and mutilation illuminates Virgil's silence concerning the fate of Priam. Lucan provides explicit and shocking details of the removal of Pompey's head and its further mutilation.[23] Where Virgil described the death of Priam followed suddenly by a headless corpse, Lucan tells us what happened between the lines within the narrative gap in clinical hypertrophic detail.[24] This is an autopsy of Priam's corpse and of Virgil's lacunose *corpus*.

Lucan's text (catching Virgil's allusion) also follows the Pacuvian model of Priam's head, cut off and transfixed by a pike and paraded (Serv. *ad Aen.* 2.557):

---

[21] Fantham (1992a): *ad* 2.160–1; Narducci (2002): 119, 145 n.40. On the scenes from book 2 see below pp. 116–20.

[22] See Estèves (2010) for more on Lucan's development of the theme of decapitation. Ormand (1994): 47 calls Pompey's phrasing at 8.581–2 'oddly proleptic', but Lucan is being ruefully and purposefully heavy-handed.

[23] Mayer's (1981: *ad* 8.663–91) note on the limited brutality in this scene because Lucan does not supply copious blood is difficult to understand. Cf. his introduction to lines 577–711. The horrors (e.g.) of Picasso's *Guernica* or Goya's *Los desastres de la Guerra* are hardly mitigated by their presentation in black and white.

[24] Schnepf (1970): 383–4 identifies Lucan's indulgence in graphic realism to create horror. Lohmar (2013): 136–40 also discusses Lucan's attempt to fill the narrative 'gap' in Virgil's treatment of the death of Priam.

IACET INGENS LITORE TRUNCUS Pompei tangit historiam ... quod
autem dicit LITORE, illud, ut supra diximus, respicit, quod in Pacuuii
tragoedia continetur

'he lies, a huge trunk on the shore' touches on the history of Pompey ...
Moreover the fact that he says 'on the shore', as I said above, recalls what is
found in Pacuvius' tragedy.

A second note completes the image (*ad Aen.* 2.506):

alii dicunt quod a Pyrrho in domo quidem sua captus est (Priamus), sed ad
tumulum Achillis tractus occisusque est iuxta Sigeum promunturium ...
tunc eius caput conto fixum Pyrrhus circumtulit.[25]

Some say that Priam was indeed captured in his home by Pyrrhus, but was
dragged to the tomb of Achilles and killed close to Cape Sigeum ... and
then Pyrrhus carried around his head stuck on a pike.

We see the initial impaling immediately after Pompey's head is removed
(*BC* 8.679–84), but the full reference comes in book 9 when we return to
the scene of the crime, as Pompey's death and mutilation are described
again but this time from the perspective of Pompey's son Sextus (9.133–43):

uidi ego magnanimi lacerantes pectora patris,
nec credens Pharium tantum potuisse tyrannum
litore Niliaco socerum iam stare putaui.                          135
sed me nec sanguis nec tantum uolnera nostri
adfecere senis, quantum gestata per urbem
ora ducis, quae transfixo sublimia pilo
uidimus: haec fama est oculis uictoris iniqui
seruari, scelerisque fidem quaesisse tyrannum.                    140
nam corpus Phariaene canes auidaeque uolucres
distulerint, an furtiuus, quem uidimus, ignis
soluerit, ignoro.

I saw them mangling the chest of our great-hearted father,
and not believing a Pharian tyrant could possess so much power,
I thought his father-in-law stood on the Nile's shore already.     135
But neither the blood nor the wounds of our old man
moved me as much as the leader's head carried through the city
which we saw uplifted with a pike pierced through it;
word is this is kept for the eyes of the hostile victor,
and the tyrant sought evidence of the crime.                       140
But if Pharian dogs or gluttonous birds scattered

[25] See my discussion above, pp. 54–7.

his corpse, or stolen fire, which we saw,
dissolved it, I don't know.

This is Lucan at his finest, bridging the gap completely now between Priam and Pompey (literary/historical) by reactivating the implicit Pacuvian allusion which he had signalled earlier and which Virgil hinted at elliptically. Sextus' description effectively re-stages the horror of the murder, complementing the perspective and reaction of Cornelia in the previous book. By readdressing the scene, Lucan provides a further continuation of Pompey's already exaggerated death through an immediate flashback of a scene narrated only 300 lines earlier.

Sextus' description, however, is full of narrative inconsistency, as Emanuele Narducci stressed.[26] In sum: Sextus could not have seen the head impaled and paraded around Pelusium because, as we know from the account of book 8, the Pompeians' ship flees directly after Achillas stabs Pompey but before Septimius decapitates him (8.661–2); moreover, it's difficult to imagine how Sextus, or any other of Pompey's crew, could have been able to enter the town safely to witness the head being paraded. For Narducci, Lucan sacrificed narrative plausibility for the effect of *enargeia*. This explanation is akin to Richard Heinze's description of Virgil's sacrificing of 'narrative coherence' in Aeneas' depiction of the death of Priam: Virgil eschews the coherence of Aeneas' first-person narrative for 'a higher artistic economy of the work'.[27] The focus on vividness justifies the narrative impossibility of Aeneas viewing Priam's trunk on the shore. This is not coincidental. Lucan is toying with the narrative of Virgil's scene. As Aeneas describes the fate of the *truncus* he could not have seen (from the vantage point of city to shore), Sextus describes the fate of the/its head he too could not have seen (from the perspective of the shore to the city).

Sextus' initial description of Pompey's death (9.133: *uidi ego*) matches the confidence of Aeneas' articulation of the slaughter wrought by Pyrrhus in Priam's palace (2.499: *uidi ipse*, 'I myself saw'; 501: *uidi*, 'I saw'). But Lucan amplifies the play on perspective with a crescendo of optical opacity in the series of verbs Sextus uses to describe the events surrounding his father's death and abuse: *uidi, non credens, putaui, uidimus, haec fama est, ignoro.* Sextus' 'ignorance' of the final fate of his father's headless corpse contradicts Cornelia's confidence that the fire and smoke they see as they sail away represent the pyre of Pompey's 'improper funeral' (9.54, 62–3, 73–7). Sextus'

---

[26] Narducci (2002): 451 n.52.    [27] Heinze (1993): 24.

building uncertainty gives Lucan the space to suggest the possibility that Pompey has been consumed by dogs and birds (141–3), the age-old fear of epic heroes as well as the actual fate of Pompey's soldiers at Pharsalus (7.825–46), and of Curio at 4.809–10, whose death functions largely as an anticipatory surrogate for Pompey in the poem.[28] Pompey's death is recast moments after the narrative of his actual death, and the varying accounts of his corpse's fate allow his mutilation to take multiple forms, all congruent with the worst imaginable abuses in prior epic literature (and coupled with the embalming, perhaps something *recherché*).[29] Lucan kills and mutilates Pompey repeatedly, but from different angles and perspectives, and this repetition magnifies the climactic scene of his death.

The deeper narratorial allusion between the scenes intensifies Lucan's engagement with Virgilian silence through repeated allusion to and redefinition of the *Aeneid*'s poetic programme. Whether narrative possibility 'allowed' it or not, Lucan put into Sextus' account a description of nightmarish corpse abuse, coincident with the account in Pacuvius that Virgil alludes to – by having Priam's headless corpse appear on the Sigean shore – but the details of which he excises from his narrative. Pompey's mutilation actualizes the unfulfilled threat of Hector (via Iris' paraphrasing to Achilles in a dream, *Il.* 18.175–7) to impale Patroclus' severed head on a pike,[30] and the presence of Achillas evokes the *Iliad*'s Achilles, who likewise threatened to decapitate Hector at *Iliad* 18.333–5.[31]

The latter allusion has deeper resonances here since Lucan – along with clear analogical associations – elsewhere aligns Pompey with Hector through their similar expressions of doomed fate before their respective 'duels': Hector's duel with Achilles, and Pompey's with Caesar (*Il.* 22.296–305; *BC* 7.85–6).[32] Lucan also compares Pompey to Hector at the beginning of *BC* 8 when, returning from Pharsalus, he meets Cornelia bearing an unmistakable resemblance to the ghost of Hector who appears to Aeneas in his dream in *Aeneid* 2. Compare *BC* 8.56–7: *deformem pallore ducem uoltusque prementem | canitiem atque* **atro squalentis puluere** *uestes*, 'the leader, misshapen by pallor, white hair concealing his face, and his clothes

---

[28] On the relationship between Curio and Pompey in Lucan see Narducci (2002): 171–3, Radicke (2004): 311–12, Fucecchi (2011b): 240–3.

[29] On the multiplicity of evocations of Pompey's mutilated body see Loupiac (1998): 167–8, Galtier (2010).

[30] Lausberg (1985): 1596 notes the structural correspondence between Patroclus' death (book 16 of 24) and Pompey's death (book 8 of 12), though this depends on our confidence that Lucan planned his epic in 12 books.

[31] Hardie (1993): 38.      [32] Narducci (2002): 303.

stiff with black dust', with *Aeneid* 2.272–3, 277 (of Hector's ghost): *raptatus bigis ut quondam,* **aterque** *cruento* | **puluere** *perque pedes traiectus lora tumentis . . . squalentem barbam et concretos sanguine crinis . . .*, 'as when he was once dragged by the chariot, black with bloody dust, with lashes passed through his swelling feet . . . his beard stiffened and hair caked with blood'. Pompey's eventual death and abuse are assured here via his association with Hector, another 'synecdochic' epic loser,[33] and his continued existence post-Pharsalus is implicitly articulated through the allusion to Hector's ghost as a 'living-death'. While history did not allow Caesar to kill and abuse Pompey as Achilles treats Hector, nevertheless a surrogate, Achillas, in this intertextual game, actualizes Achilles' decapitation threat from *Iliad* 18 against the defeated Hector-Pompey. Pompey resembles the blending of the threatened corpse abuse of both an Achaean (Patroclus) and Trojan (Hector) warrior.

Moreover, Sextus' description of the head being paraded through Pelusium recalls the heads of Nisus and Euryalus and those that line Cacus' cave in the *Aeneid*, trophies meant to be displayed. But where Virgil completely removed the details of *post mortem* decapitation, and Homer left the threats unfulfilled, Lucan is not lacking in clinical specificity. His allusion to Virgil's depiction of Priam's/Pompey's death is not simply allusion for its own sake, but is a central feature of his poetics of excess. Priam's death occupies the same thematically climactic location of Virgil's *Iliou persis* as Pompey's death occupies in the framework of Lucan's whole poem: both symbolic of the destruction of bodily integrity as akin to the decapitation of civic identity, the severing of the *caput orbis/mundi*,[34] as Pompey's son articulates for us after the fact (*BC* 9.123–5): *stat summa caputque* | *orbis, an occidimus Romanaque Magnus ad umbras* | *abstulit?*, 'does the high commander and head of the world stand or have we fallen, and has Magnus carried Rome off to the shadows?' The pun is superlatively tasteless,[35] the epitome of Lucan's *modus operandi*. The Roman State/ Republic as a shattered, mutilated 'body' is a leitmotif in Lucan's poem (e.g. 1.2–3; 2.141–3; 5.36–7, 252; 7.292–4, 579, 721–2; 10.416–17; etc.), and Pompey's *corpus/truncus* is the ultimate 'embodiment' of that State.[36]

---

[33] See Hardie (1993): 4 for the term.
[34] Narducci (1973) 323. See Hardie (1993): 7 on Pompey as a synecdochic hero. Cf. Lucan's own articulation of Rome as the *caput mundi* at *BC* 2.136, 655–6. For more details on Lucan's equation of Pompey's headlessness with Rome's fall, see Ahl (1976): 185–9, 221–2, Dinter (2012): 19–21, 34–5, 47–9, 129, Bexley (2010): 138–40; Calonne (2010): 232 on Lucan's panoply of abandoned *cadauera* in *BC* as symbolic of the corpse of Rome's body politic; Mebane (2016): 205–8 on the decapitation as evocative of the unending self-destruction of Rome's civic body.
[35] *Pace* Bexley (2010): 138.  [36] Though see my discussion below, pp. 167–9.

Where Virgil could evoke this image of the fall of Troy in and as the death and decapitation of Priam in the epitaphic brevity of a few words, Lucan logorrheically rends the 'body politic' piece by piece, word by word.

As well as recapitulating the climax of destruction in *Aeneid* 2, so Pompey's death also echoes the climactic close of Virgil's poem, as Pompey's reaction to his death-blow refashions the vocabulary of the final line of the *Aeneid* (12.952): *uitaque cum gemitu fugit indignata sub umbras*, 'and life flits off indignantly with a groan under the shadows'; with *BC* 8.619: *nullo gemitu consensit ad ictum*, 'he yielded to the blow without a groan'. Coupled with Pompey *indignatus*, 'resentful', at 8.614, Lucan has presented the reader with a Stoic refashioning (*nullo gemitu*) of Turnus' death at the hands of Aeneas, a new 'reading' of the end of the *Aeneid*.[37] Achillas, not Caesar, kills Pompey, but Caesar is omnipresent: no matter his killer, Pompey assures himself he dies only by Caesar's hand (8.627–9).[38] The silence concerning Turnus' possible corpse abuse in Virgil is in Lucan a poetic launching-pad. Pompey's suppression of his groan is only the beginning and what follows is the sort of abuse most feared by heroic losers. In death Pompey recalls Priam and Turnus, Patroclus and Hector, and a host of other abused (or potentially abused) corpses woven together in a web of complex intertextual engagement. But unlike his poetic predecessors, Lucan does not omit the brutal details.

It isn't simply the description of Pompey's death and mutilation that is blown out of proportion, but also the lengths to which Lucan allows the process of death and dying to occur, as I've indicated. And while I examine this Lucanian aesthetic in more detail elsewhere,[39] it deserves mention here. Pompey shows signs of life after he's repeatedly stabbed, and even after his head is removed and placed on the pike (*BC* 8.670–1, 682–4). The process of his quasi-cremation is hurried but its description is granted copious space for grisly detail, and the retelling of his murder through Sextus' variant description allows the scene of death and corpse abuse further narrative life. Most disturbingly, Pompey is granted a further afterlife at the end of book 9, when his head is presented to Caesar by one of Ptolemy's minions (9.1032–4): *opertum | detexit tenuitque caput. iam languida morte | effigies habitum noti mutauerat oris*, 'he revealed and held up the covered head. Already drooping with death, his appearance had warped the state of his well-known face.' The head is decaying, drooping, which, while disgusting, is ultimately not surprising for a severed head. But considering the initial description that the mummification *solidified* his features and, looking to the future, for those who saw the severed head, 'death changed nothing of Pompey's countenance and face' (8.665–7, 691), this further detail of his changed expression adds another sardonic twist in the impossibly extended process of dying.[40] Shades of Ovidian metamorphoses shine through here and elsewhere in *BC* but the change is still more perverse than anything even Ovid might have imagined. In a metaphorical 'death with interruptions',[41] the living body eventually becomes a corpse, but – as we shall see again and again – in the drawn-out process of dying and being dead, Lucan and the other imperial Latin epicists find space for further bizarre transformations.[42]

## Tydeus in Statius' *Thebaid*

Statius' depiction of Tydeus' death and cannibalism of his victim-killer Melanippus' head at *Thebaid* 8.716–66 is the most gruesome scene of corpse abuse in an epic obsessed with the treatment of the dead.[43] The scene and its building narrative encompassing Tydeus' linked *aristeiai* in books 2 and 8 is also a *tour de force* of Statius' vertiginous engagement with his epic predecessors. As in my discussion of Lucan's Pompey, I am interested here mostly in Statius' exploitation of Homeric and Virgilian motifs and the larger effect of this exploitation on his poetic programme. But Statius' borrowings from a larger literary sphere, particularly Ovid's depiction of the Calydonian boar hunt from *Metamorphoses* 8, are clearly present here as well, and they help to further define the bestial nature of Tydeus' character.[44]

At the close of Tydeus' *aristeia* in book 8 he's struck by the spear-cast of Melanippus, who is hesitant to take credit for his actions (*Theb.* 8.716–21). Tydeus responds by striking back at Melanippus, and as a last request, demands his companions bring him the head of his victim-killer (735–44). Capaneus is quick to act. Book 8 closes with a flourish of horror (751–66):

[40] Erasmo (2008): 116, 123.   [41] From José Saramago's (2005) *Death with Interruptions.*

[42] See Bartsch (1997): 17–47 for an excellent discussion of Lucan's blurring of animate and inanimate, bodily/societal/syntactical integrity, and related themes. See Hömke (2010): 98–104 on the aestheticization of the process of dying in Lucan's Scaeva episode; Dinter (2012): 37–49 on the automatism of severed limbs; Estèves (2010): 209–10 on the theme of 'mort-vivant' in the context of severed heads; Mebane (2016): 205–12 on themes of 'irresolution and repetition' in Pompey's death.

[43] On death rites in the poem see Burck (1981): 464–80, Feeney (1991): 341, 359–63, Ripoll (1998): 296–301, Pagán (2000), Pollmann (2001), Erasmo (2008): 140–53, Parkes (2011): 88–92; van der Keur (2013): 333–7.

[44] Lovatt (2010): 71–6 has looked at the scene in light of the cannibalism at Livy 22.51.9, which was also adapted by Silius (6.41–54).

erigitur Tydeus uultuque occurrit et amens
laetitiaque iraque, ut singultantia uidit
ora trucesque[45] oculos seseque agnouit in illo,
imperat abscisum porgi, laeuaque receptum
spectat atrox hostile caput, gliscitque tepentis        755
lumina torua uidens et adhuc dubitantia figi.
infelix contentus erat: plus exigit ultrix
Tisiphone; iamque inflexo Tritonia patre
uenerat et misero decus inmortale ferebat,
atque illum effracti perfusum tabe cerebri        760
aspicit et uiuo scelerantem sanguine fauces
(nec comites auferre ualent): stetit aspera Gorgon
crinibus emissis rectique ante ora cerastae
uelauere deam; fugit auersata iacentem,
nec prius astra subit quam mystica lampas et insons        765
Ilissos multa purgauit lumina lympha.

Tydeus lifts himself up and meets him face to face, mad
with joy and rage as he sees the mouth gurgling,
grim eyes, and recognizes himself in that other man.
He demands his enemy's lopped-off head brought
to him, and taking it in his left hand, gazes savagely and swells,        755
seeing the eyes warm, staring, and still hesitant to stay fixed.
The unlucky man was satisfied, but vindictive Tisiphone demands
more. Now with her father swayed, Tritonia had come
and she was bringing the poor man immortal glory.
And she sees him drenched in the filth of a brain smashed        760
to bits and his jaws polluted with living blood
(his companions can't steal it from him), the Gorgon stood
stiff with rising hair, and crested serpents arrayed before her face
veiled the goddess. She turns and flees the fallen man,
nor does she enter the stars until the mystic lamp and blameless        765
Elisos purged her eyes with copious clear water.

This is a moment of captivating *furor* and *horror* whose combination serves as a microcosm of the thematic thrust of Statius' whole poem.[46] Capaneus removes the head of the still breathing, gurgling Melanippus (*singultantia . . . ora*), eyes hesitating to grow fixed, in an image 'revived' of Pompey's decapitation at *BC* 8.682–3 (*dum uiuunt uoltus atque* **os** *in murmura pulsant* | **singultus** *animae, dum* **lumina** *nuda rigescunt*, 'while features live and breath's gurgles drive the mouth to mumbles, while staring eyes go stiff'). The imagery also recalls

---

[45] Hill (1983) prints *trahique* here, but *trucesque* gives a better sense. See Håkanson (1973): 57–8, Augoustakis (2016): *ad loc.*

[46] E.g. Ganiban (2007) on the 'horrific' effects of *nefas* in the poem; cf. Taisne (1994).

Rhamnes' headless gurgling trunk at *Aeneid* 9.332–3 (*sanguine* **singultantem**), and even more explicitly Venus' Fury-like parading of a severed head in Valerius' blood-soaked depiction of the Lemnian massacre (in the same *sedes*) at VF 2.211–13: **singultantia** *gestans* | *ora manu*, '[Venus] brandishing a gurgling head in her hand'.[47] Melanippus' head still shows signs of life even when Tydeus grabs it as it hesitates to meet his eyes (*Theb.* 8.756). Tydeus is happy simply to gaze at his enemy's head, but Tisiphone wants more: she compels Tydeus to devour the brains of Melanippus, completing Dis's demand at 8.71–2 that someone 'in the manner of a rabid beast munch his enemy's head' (*sit, qui rabidarum more ferarum* | *mandat atrox hostile caput*; cf. 3.544–5).[48]

There are recent historical overtones here too. Tacitus records a spectacular moment in 70 CE when one Curtius Montanus accused the *delator* M. Aquilius Regulus of biting the severed head of Galba's heir Piso Licinianus during the horrors of Rome's post-Neronian civil war in 69 CE (*Hist.* 4.42). Rhiannon Ash argues that Statius is blending this disturbing event with Otho's earlier gazing at Piso Licinianus' head, recorded by Tacitus at *Histories* 1.44. How much of this inspired Statius' scene of Tydeus' own gazing and cannibalism is unknowable, but the poem as a whole is infected with the darkness, violence, and despair of civil wars on par with what plagued Rome after Nero's suicide.[49] It is not unreasonable to imagine that, beyond literary allusions, Statius might have spliced the mythological scene with a similarly famous and frightening historical event that recalled it.[50]

Tydeus' act is deemed so repulsive, such a display of bestial *nefas* that Pallas, who had received divine sanction from Jupiter to bestow immortality on her favourite (*Theb.* 8.758–9), flees the scene to cleanse her eyes, contaminated by what she sees (765–6), and allows Tydeus to die. That the visual spectacle of horror contaminates Pallas' eyes and requires ritual purification is a hallmark of theoretical discourse on 'disgust'. William Ian Miller's description of the reaction to sensory contact – physical, visual, gustatorial, etc. – with things that elicit disgust offers a useful framework for reading Pallas' reaction here: 'when something disgusts us . . . we feel tainted, burdened by the belief that anything that comes into contact with the disgusting thing also acquires the capacity to disgust as a consequence

[47] See below pp. 187–90. [48] Ganiban (2007): 124. [49] See below, Chapter 5.
[50] Williams (1978): 221–2; Ash (2015): 219. Cf. Dio's report of the cannibalism of Caligula's corpse by his murderers (59.29.7).

of that contact. We thus hasten to purify ourselves.'[51] Pallas' reaction is decidedly unsettling. It defines (in case we needed it) the horror of Tydeus' actions, such that they are physically miasmic to viewers and risk spreading further contagion.[52] This has additional extratextual implications. Perhaps we too flee like Pallas from Statius' scene at this point,[53] disgusted by the grotesquery and unable to continue – Mars will avert his gaze at the beginning of the next book as a result of Tydeus' crime (9.4–7), and eventually all the *superi* turn away from Thebes and the war at Jupiter's instigation (11.126–35). But if we read on we betray our own voyeuristic captivation by the horror, we expose *ourselves* to this sensory pollution, and declare allegiance to the infernal gods (Dis and Tisiphone) who have put on the 'show' and continue to watch in spite of – or on account of – the risks. The divine intratextual audience presents contrasting modes of viewership for the reader, creating something like what Kristeva calls a 'vortex of summons and repulsion' as we follow Tydeus' debasement from nearly divine hero to ravenous savage.[54] Statius foregrounds our implicature in the horror-scene he describes, signalled by a juxtaposition of intratextual visual and focal cues we are forced to weigh against one another.[55]

Pallas' first line of defence is another symbol of visual confusion: the snake hairs on the goddess' *gorgoneion* raise up to shield her eyes (8.762–4). The scene as a whole recalls the earlier *ekphrasis* of Perseus carrying Medusa's severed head – eyes still moving, face drooping – on the libation bowl that Adrastus displays to Tydeus and Polynices at *Thebaid* 1.543–7.[56] In a frightening perversion of the earlier scene, Tydeus stares at Melanippus' head with macabre joy (8.752: *laetitia*) as he and we as an audience were earlier invited to ogle the frightening but enjoyable images displayed on the prized bowl. Yet Tydeus' joy is mindless and self-destructive, suffused with disgust at the fragility of his own mortal frame (738–9) reflected in the mirror-image of his victim-killer Melanippus in whom he recognizes his own demise (753: *seseque agnouit in illo*). We approach here the excessiveness of Kantian *Genuss* (or *jouissance*), a nature-defying joy that revels in its own *consumptive* 'unpleasure'. Rather than viewing art as in book 1, with his death scene Tydeus has become a figure in *ekphrasis*, whose horror both rejects viewer

---

[51] Miller (1997): 12; and further: 'disgust puts us to the burden of cleansing and purifying' (p.26).
[52] See Lovatt (2013): 73–7 on pollution and divine gaze in epic with emphasis on the *Thebaid*.
[53] Henderson (1998): 236–7.    [54] Kristeva (1982): 1.
[55] See Bernstein (2004), Ganiban (2007): 176–85 for similar issues of vision and focalization during the brothers' duel in *Theb.* 11; also Gervais (2013) on spectatorship and the gaze more broadly in Statius and Tarantino.
[56] Newlands (2012): 82.

gaze (Pallas and Mars) as well as draws it in (the subterranean gods', the Gorgon's, and our own readerly gaze). The presence of Medusa's severed head here at the climax clinches the impression of an artistic freeze-frame brought about by the paralyzing horror of Tydeus' actions.

Our reminder of Adrastus' libation bowl and Perseus' severing of Medusa's head might also recall for an epic audience Ovid's description in *Metamorphoses* 5 of Perseus' subsequent deployment of this ekphrastic trinket during his and Andromeda's botched wedding-banquet in Ethiopia – one of the only epic-style battle narratives in the poem and an internecine conflict at that. Like Tydeus, Perseus slays an outrageous number of attackers before he's ultimately surrounded and overwhelmed by insurmountable odds (*Met.* 5.177; *Theb.* 8.700–2). But Perseus has a special weapon. The scene is heaped with visual cues. As Perseus bears the severed Gorgon's head he warns his 'friends' to look away from her petrifying gaze (*Met.* 5.179–80: *uultus auertite uestros, | si quis amicus adest!*). There is winking playfulness in this metapoetic protreptic, as Perseus and Ovid speak out to audiences beyond textual confines: of course *we can't* look away (as Pallas does, *Theb.* 8.764: **auersata**) despite our amicable relations with the poet.[57] The hero uses Medusa's head to turn 200 rude wedding guests into palatial statuary (209).[58] Capping the list of victims is the troublemaker Phineus who, moments before being petrified himself, 'recognizes his own' amongst the metamorphic marble fighters (212: *agnoscitque suos*), as Tydeus recognizes his own dismal fate (*Theb.* 8.753: *seseque agnouit*) in the face of Melanippus, which is beginning to turn to stone (756: *adhuc dubitantia figi*). Rather than revealing the Gorgon's head, Tydeus becomes the object of its gaze and is metaphorically frozen by its penetrating stare. The playful gaze of Ovid's scene is destroyed by the horror of Tydeus' anthropophagy, which is monumentalized in its criminality by Pallas' ever-functioning apotropaic emblem. The possibility that Statius is aiming to create a 'still-life' of horror evocative of and as a literary complement to the *physically* petrified monument of this same mythic moment on the Temple A relief at Pyrgi (*c.* 465 BCE) is tantalizing and perhaps not unlikely.[59] Of course we cannot know if Statius ever saw the famous temple in Etruria, but the imagery in the relief shares narrative commonalities with Statius' poetic

---

[57] And the risks are real: even the friendly Aconteus is petrified (*Met.* 5.201–2).
[58] See Lovatt (2013): 347–50 on Perseus, Medusa, and the gaze in Ovid's scene.
[59] For the relief and other visual arts depicting Tydeus' anthropophagy see Augoustakis (2016): xxxiv–xxxvi, with De Grummond (2006): 55. Cf. Braund and Gilbert (2003): 277.

rendering of the myth. On the temple terracottas Pallas is pictured with a small jug containing Tydeus' immortality elixir – a reminder of what he has just lost – while the centrepiece of the image captures his savage feast. Pallas' rejection of her favourite is clinched as she lifts the *gorgoneion* up to her face to shield her eyes from contamination.

Statius' scene as a whole also borrows much from Pompey's famous death-scene in *BC* 8 (which itself borrows extensively from Ovid's depiction of the decapitation of Medusa in *Met.* 4).[60] Both Pompey and Melanippus are mortally wounded and dying as their heads are removed. Pompey is stabbed (*BC* 8.618–19) before his eventual decapitation (667); Melanippus is speared at *Thebaid* 8.727, carried to Tydeus by Capaneus (745–50) and decapitated (753–4). Both men are gasping for air (*BC* 8.670: *spirantia . . . ora*, 682–3: *os . . . singultus*; *Theb.* 8.752–3: *singultantia . . . ora*), and the eyes of each are still staring (*BC* 8.683: *lumina nuda*; *Theb.* 8.756: *lumina torua . . . adhuc dubitantia figi*). As I mentioned above, Statius may be looking back to Lucan's own model here as well in Virgil's description of the decapitations of sleeping men during Nisus' and Euryalus' night-raid at *Aeneid* 9.332–3, itself recalling (probably intentionally) the 'snorting corpses' of decapitated victims described in the messenger speech of Euripides' *Rhesus* (789: κλύω δ᾽ ἐπάρας κρᾶτα μυχθισμὸν νεκρῶν, 'I hear the snorting of corpses as I raise my head').[61] But ultimately this is viewed through a Lucanian lens and his amplification of the scene.

Both heads receive further 'criminal' assault after their separation from the body: Pompey's head is fixed on a pike and embalmed (*BC* 8.688: *arte nefanda*), and Tydeus gnaws on Melanippus' head, breaking the bounds of what is acknowledged as *fas* (his companions 'complained he had broken the laws governing hate': *rupisse queruntur fas odii* at *Theb.* 9.3–4). Tydeus' staring competition with Melanippus' head at *Thebaid* 8.751–6 evokes the confrontation between Caesar and Pompey's head in Egypt (*BC* 9.1032–9). The play of victor eyeing vanquished is compounded by Pompey's earlier imagining of his own death at the hands of Caesar (*BC* 8.628–9: *quacumque feriris, | crede manum soceri*, 'whoever strikes you, believe it's the hand of your father-in-law'), though the authors of his demise are Septimius and Achillas, and in the end Caesar will hold his severed head. Capaneus in Statius' poem orchestrates Melanippus' decapitation, but it is Tydeus who holds and confronts his head. There is in *sese . . . agnouit in illo* a lexical nod

---

[60]  See Augoustakis (2016): xxxix–xl and *ad locc.* for some of these allusions.
[61]  Hardie (1994): *ad* 9.333; cf. Hom. *Il.* 10.521, in the same mythic event, of men 'gasping amid streams of blood', though not in direct reference to decapitations.

to Amphiaraus' earlier prophetic recognition of his own impending doom
(*Theb.* 3.546–7: *illum . . . | qui cadit, agnosco,* 'I recognize that man who
falls') which already engages the matrona's prophecy of Pompey's looming
death at *BC* 1.685–6 (*hunc ego, fluminea deformis truncus harena | qui iacet,
agnosco,* 'I recognize that man, a misshapen trunk who lies on the river
sands'). Tydeus sees in his victim-killer his own approaching fate, as
another epic corpse sprawled out in death (*Theb.* 8.764: *iacentem*; 9.2:
*iacentem*).[62] Statius 'recognizes' all of these past and present (literary)
corpses, and signals his own position in the intertextual gambit by adding
Tydeus to the list of those lying in death (9.17): *et nunc ille iacet,* 'and now
that one lies'. With brimming ingenuity, Statius has channelled the
extended death and abuse of Pompey in Lucan's poem (over 2 books)
into one breathless cinematic/*ekphrastic* shot.

   While there are significant debts to Statius' epic predecessors in Virgil,
Ovid, Lucan, and Valerius Flaccus (and others), actual accounts of Tydeus'
abuse of Melanippus' corpse and his own death are rather scarce in the
extant epic record. In the wake of epic literary tradition, Tydeus' cannibalism is fairly peripheral. Homer alludes to Tydeus' death at *Iliad* 14.114,
but says nothing of his meal (cf. 4.376–400; 5.800–8). Virgil also makes no
reference to the anthropophagy in the *Aeneid*. Statius' source appears to
have been the lost epic-cycle poem the *Thebais* (schol. *ad Iliad* 5.126):

> Τυδεὺς ὁ Οἰωνέως ἐν τῷ Θηβαικῷ πολέμῳ ὑπὸ Μελανίππου τοῦ Ἀστάκου
> ἐτρώθη, Ἀμφιάρεως δὲ κτείνας τὸν Μελάνιππον τὴν κεφαλὴν ἐκόμισε, καὶ
> ἀνοίξας αὐτὴν ὁ Τυδεὺς τὸν ἐγκέφαλον ἐρρόφει ἀπὸ θυμοῦ. Ἀθηνᾶ δὲ
> κομίζουσα Τυδεῖ ἀθανασίαν, ἰδοῦσα τὸ μίασμα, ἀπεστράφη αὐτόν.

> Tydeus, son of Oeneus, was wounded by Melanippus, son of Astacus, in the
> Theban war. Amphiaraus killed Melanippus and brought his head, and
> Tydeus, opening up his skull, greedily gulped down his brain. Athena was
> bringing down immortality for Tydeus; but when she saw the *miasma* she
> turned away from him.

Even here the account is slightly different. Statius has Capaneus retrieve
Melanippus' body and sever his head whereas the *Thebais* attributes this to
Amphiaraus, who is the traditional mortal enemy of Tydeus. The same
details are found in the scholium to Pindar *Nemean* 10.12, Pausanias 9.18.1,
and Apollodorus 3.6.8.[63] While it is Tisiphone who ultimately pushes
Tydeus over the edge to cannibalism (cf. her boast at *Theb.* 11.87–8:

---

[62] Larson (2014): 8: 'We cannot confront another person's head without sharing an understanding:
face to face, we are peering into ourselves.'

[63] On the literary tradition see Beazley (1947), Gantz (1993): 518, McNelis (2007): 132–3.

*miserum insatiabilis edit | me tradente caput*, 'insatiable, he eats the poor man's head which I gave to him'), Statius' rewriting of the myth whereby Tydeus himself demands the head is in line with the general beastliness of his character in the poem.

Oracular and prophetic allusions to Tydeus' cannibalism remind us throughout the epic of his eventual animal savagery (1.41–2, 3.544–5, 8.71–2), as do allusions, from his initial appearance, that he's 'bloodstained with rage' (1.408: *rabiem cruentam*; cf. 8.478–9, 530–1), and his exit makes literal this frightening epithet (9.1–2): *rabies . . . cruenti | Tydeos*.[64] Statius also includes more subtle imagery that anticipates the dehumanizing of his character – the first in a series of heroic downfalls that highlight the descent of the poem and its warriors into animalistic *furor*. His association with animals and beasts anticipates his transition from *uir* to *fera* at the moment of his death, instigating his abuse of Melanippus' corpse.[65]

At the outset of his *aristeia* in book 8, Tydeus alludes to his defeat of the Theban ambush from book 2 in a rather startling way (8.664–71):

> quo terga datis? licet ecce peremptos
> ulcisci socios maestamque rependere noctem.
> ille ego inexpletis solus qui caedibus hausi
> quinquaginta animas: totidem, totidem heia gregatim
> ferte manus! nulline patres, nulline iacentum
> unanimi fratres? quae tanta obliuio luctus?
> quam pudet Inachias contentum abiisse Mycenas!
> hine super Thebis?

> Why do you turn your backs? Look, here's an opportunity
> to avenge your slain friends and pay back that gloomy night.
> I'm the one who alone devoured fifty souls with insatiable
> slaughter: oh yes, send in hoards as many and as many
> corps! No fathers, no like-minded brothers
> of the fallen? How so blind to grief?
> It shames me that I left content for Inachian Mycenae!
> Are these what's left of Thebes?

Tydeus did not merely kill his attackers, he 'devoured' them (*hausi*), with insatiable slaughter (*inexpletis caedibus*) that is ever growing (*hine super*

---

[64] Dewar (1991): *ad* 9.1f; Hershkowitz (1995): 58.

[65] Tydeus' animalistic/monstrous associations in *Theb.* 8 are already anticipated by allusions during the *monomachia* in book 2, as Gervais (2015) has demonstrated. For a general discussion of the mechanism of dehumanization as illustrated by comparison to animals in the *Theb.*, see Franchet d'Espèrey (1999): 171–205. On Tydeus' cannibalism as an act that dehumanizes him see e.g. Rieks (1967): 214–16, Vessey (1973): 225–6, 292–4, Feeney (1991): 360–1, Franchet d'Espèrey (1999): 174–8, Ripoll (1998): 329–32, 336–9.

*Thebis?*). This same imagery of consumption occurs during his *aristeia*
when the Theban army is *consumitur* around him alone (8.700–2):
'expended' or 'used up', but with the implicit echoes of consumption
evoked in his earlier boast.[66] Tydeus had been compared to a ravenous
lion thirsting for a bull's bloody neck (8.593–6), matching a simile at the
end of his *aristeia* in book 2 of a lion who has gorged itself on blood (2.675–
81). Both images underscore this linguistic image of bloodthirstiness, and
also anticipate his literal desire for blood when he eats Melanippus'
brains.[67]

Tydeus' degeneration into animal *furor* is doubled by the verbal animality
of his speech (8.664–71), distorted in syntax, abandoning verbs, anaphoric in
phrasing, and marked by a general rushed incoherence. The language
matches Tydeus' physical exhaustion, but also points to his becoming less
than human. He's further compared to a wolf chasing a wounded steer
(8.691–4) and to a tigress devouring an entire flock (8.474–5). Neil Coffee has
illustrated how Tydeus' evocation of consumption in his boast to the
Thebans also echoes Statius' language in book 2 to describe the insatiable
hunger of the Sphinx for human flesh (the monster's belly is *inexpleta* at
2.518, with 8.666 of Tydeus).[68] During his fight against the 50 Theban
ambushers, Tydeus occupies the old perch of the Sphinx to defend himself
(2.554–6), becoming a stand-in for the ravenous bird-monster. By reactivating the imagery of the Sphinx by verbal allusions in book 8 to each
character's desire for blood (already implied in his initial *aristeia*), Statius
paves the way for Tydeus' *actual* consumption of human flesh, bringing
graphically to life the world of metaphor and simile (lions, tigers, monsters)
when Tydeus eats Melanippus' head.[69]

This jarring transformation from man to *outré* animal hybrid is what
Eteocles latches onto at the opening of the next book (9.12–20):

> quisquamne Pelasgis
> mitis adhuc hominemque gerit? iam morsibus uncis
> (pro furor! usque adeo tela exsatiauimus?) artus
> dilacerant. nonne Hyrcanis bellare putatis                    15
> tigribus, aut saeuos Libyae contra ire leones?
> et nunc ille iacet (pulchra o solacia leti!)
> ore tenens hostile caput, dulcique nefandus
> inmoritur tabo; nos ferrum inmite facesque:
> illis nuda odia, et feritas iam non eget armis.

---

[66] Coffee (2009): 196–7.    [67] Vessey (1973): 225; Franchet d'Espèrey (1999): 175.
[68] Coffee (2009): 195–8; also Gervais (2015): 60, 72–4.    [69] Franchet d'Espèrey (1999): 176.

Is there anyone who still
feels merciful towards the Pelasgi? Now they're tearing at our
limbs with hooked teeth (what madness! have we so gorged their
weapons this way?). Do you not think we are fighting Hyrcanian          15
tigers, or going against savage Libyan lions?
And now that man lies (o sweet solace of death!),
holding the enemy head in his mouth, and he dies, corrupted
by sweet gore. We have harsh swords and firebrands:
for them it's raw hatred and ferocity now needing no weapons.

Tydeus and the Argives are no longer men, they are savage animals (*feritas*), fighting not with swords, but tooth and claw. Eteocles highlights two of the animals Tydeus was compared to in epic simile: a bloodthirsty lion and tiger. It will be to a lion, long sought after (*diu*) again that he's compared when the Thebans eventually capture his corpse at 9.189–95. This perversion of epic simile brings about the fulfilment of Dis's curse at the outset of book 8 when he demanded there be one who takes on the nature of a wild animal (8.71–2). Eteocles' words directly recall Dis's (*hostile caput* in the same *sedes*). Tydeus has become so beastly (*feram*, again: 9.99) that even vultures, *monstra*, and fire dare not devour his corpse (9.102–3).

Tydeus' cannibalism of Melanippus recalls Hecuba's unfulfilled wish that she had the ability to eat Achilles' liver for his treatment of her son (*Il.* 24.212–13): τοῦ ἐγὼ μέσον ἧπαρ ἔχοιμι | ἐσθέμεναι προσφῦσα, 'I wish I could sink my teeth in mid-liver and eat it'. It also recalls her verbal abuse of Achilles as a monstrous 'raw flesh eater', (*Il.* 24.207: ὠμηστής), and accomplishes Achilles' unfulfilled threat to eat Hector after the latter is mortally wounded (22.346–7): αἲ γάρ πως αὐτόν με μένος καὶ θυμὸς ἀνήη | ὤμ' ἀποταμνόμενον κρέα ἔδμεναι, 'I wish that my might and heart would impel me to carve up your flesh and devour it'.[70] The wrath and fury that Achilles wishes to muster are the very essence of Tydeus' being: he's *immodicum irae* | *Tydea*, 'Tydeus, limitless in his rage' (*Theb.* 1.41) from the moment he enters the epic stage, unbounded and limitless in excess. He's a ravenous Polyphemus (*Od.* 9.287–93), a faulty Hercules, who abandons humanity at the cost of his own immortality (or at the cost of a more reputable immortality).[71] And his cannibalism defeats Hesiod's claim that divine dispensation separates humans from beasts as creatures *unable* to consume their own kind (*Op.* 276–80).

---

[70] Henderson (1998): 235 with n.55; Braund and Gilbert (2003): 276–80; Parkes (2011): 91.
[71] See Ripoll (1998): 147–9, 339, Gervais (2015): 72–6 on Tydeus and Hercules.

But he's not simply a gluttonous offensive threat. Tydeus, who wears a bristling boar-skin mantle, is cast from the outset of the epic metaphorically as a boar (*Theb.* 1.397, 488–90), specifically a Calydonian boar,[72] appropriate considering his pedigree as the son of Oeneus from Calydon. This association becomes crucial for the dual *aristeiai* of Tydeus in books 2 and 8. After a failed delegation to Eteocles, Tydeus storms off. Statius compares him to Diana's Calydonian boar hunted by the Pelopean band (2.469–75):

> Oeneae uindex sic ille Dianae
> erectus saetis et aduncae fulmine malae,
> cum premeret Pelopea phalanx, saxa obuia uoluens
> fractaque perfossis arbusta Acheloia ripis,
> iam Telamona solo, iam stratum Ixiona linquens
> te, Meleagre, subit: ibi demum cuspide lata
> haesit et obnixo ferrum laxauit in armo.

> Like that avenger of Oenean Diana
> erect with bristles and the thunderbolt of his hooked jaw,
> when the Pelopean phalanx hems him in, rolling stones in his path
> and shattered the Acheloian trees from the dug-out banks,
> now leaving Telamon stretched out on the dirt, next Ixion,
> he comes at you, Meleager; there finally he stops at
> the wide spear head and slackens the iron on his firm shoulder.

Eteocles immediately sends a troop of 50 men to hunt down Tydeus in a perverse re-enactment of the famous Calydonian boar hunt.[73] Only here the 'boar' wins. Tydeus demolishes his attackers, leaving one (Maeon) to report back to Eteocles news of their failed mission. Statius' borrowings from Ovid's scene of the boar hunt in *Metamorphoses* 8 are clear, as Alison Keith and Kyle Gervais have demonstrated: note in particular the description of Ovid's ferocious boar (*Met.* 8.284–9), 'avenger of Diana' (272: **uindex … Dianae**), and Statius' boar in simile (above), coupled with the description of Tydeus' cloak (*Theb.* 1.488–90), which is the *same* cloak Meleager gifted Atalanta at *Metamorphoses* 8.428–9. The allusions to Ovid's boar-hunt continue during Tydeus' *monomachia*: e.g. the initial ineffectual spear-casts which graze the boar and Tydeus' boar-hide (*Met.* 8.345–55; *Theb.* 2.538–46).[74] Contrastingly, however, while Meleager's band had succeeded in bringing down their quarry, Tydeus lives to fight another day.

---

[72] Keith (2002): 389–92; Gervais (2015): 58–60, 74–6.    [73] See Ahl (1986): 2876.
[74] See Keith (2002): 389–92; Gervais (2015): 58–9 and (2017): *ad locc.*

The 'conclusion' to Statius' re-enactment of Ovid's boar hunt comes during Tydeus' *aristeia* in book 8. At the resumption, the 'boarish Calydonian'[75] will not be as lucky as he was in book 2. Tydeus himself links the two passages in his opening boast to the Theban army in book 8 when he alludes to his 'consumption' of the 50 in book 2 (*Theb.* 8.664–71).[76] Tydeus demands a rematch of his earlier fight with 'as many and as many corps' as he faced in the woods (8.667–8: *totidem, totidem heia gregatim | ferte manus!*). The literal *monomachia*/boar-hunt of book 2 is recast here as the whole Theban army (re-)focuses its efforts on him alone (8.701–2): *unum acies circum consumitur, unum | omnia tela uouent*, 'battle lines are expended upon the one man, every weapon dedicated to him alone'. In book 2 Tydeus had similarly announced his own position as one vs many (2.548–9: *solus, | solus in arma uoco*, 'by myself, by myself I challenge you to fight'). He piles up mounds of corpses and spoils that confine him (700–1), and missiles puncture his boar-skin mantle (705–6). The deictic *ecce* ('look!') at 8.716, directing our attention to an unidentified spear cast (Statius delays mention of Melanippus for effect), replays the same moment in book 2 which instigated the fighting between Tydeus and his ambushers at 2.538 (*ecce autem*). There the weapon grazed Tydeus' boar-skin and fell ineffectually. But in this instance, the weapon brings Tydeus down. This moment completes (or 'corrects') the hunt for Tydeus begun in book 2 in a similar fashion as Meleager's spear finally levels the boar (*Met.* 8.414–19) after the other hunters had failed (345–57).

After Meleager kills the boar, the rest of the troop rejoice, gather around the huge beast, hesitating to touch it, but all join in its ritual stabbing (*Met.* 8.420–4):

> **gaudia testantur** socii clamore secundo
> uictricemque petunt dextrae coniungere dextram
> inmanemque **ferum** multa tellure iacentem
> mirantes spectant neque adhuc contingere tutum
> esse putant, sed **tela** tamen sua quisque <u>cruentat</u>.

> The troop prove their joy with wild shouts of applause
> and seek to join the victor hand in hand and
> they stare marvelling at the huge beast lying stretched
> over so much ground, and still figure it's not safe to touch him.
> But each nevertheless bloodies their spears.

[75] Henderson (1998): 234.

[76] On the connection between the linked *aristeiai* see Vessey (1973): 292, Hutchinson (1993): 176–7, Hershkowitz (1995): 57, Lovatt (2005): 227–30, McNelis (2007): 131.

Precisely the same scenario (with identical verbal cues) plays out in the Theban treatment of Tydeus' corpse in book 9 after winning the *Leichenkampf* (*Theb.* 9.177–8, 183–8):[77]

> et Tyrii iam corpus habent, iam **gaudia** magnae
> **testantur** uoces . . .
>
>        . . . nusquam arma, manusque quiescunt;
> nulla uiri **feritas**: iuuat ora rigentia leto
> et formidatos impune lacessere uultus.                                            185
> hic amor, hoc una timidi fortesque sequuntur
> nobilitare manus, <u>infectaque</u> <u>sanguine</u> **tela**
> coniugibus seruant paruisque ostendere natis.

> Now the Tyrians have the corpse, now their loud cries
> prove their joy . . .
>        . . . no weapons anywhere, his hands are quiet,
> no manly beastliness: it's delightful to see his face stiffen in death
> and to attack his frightening features without punishment.               185
> They love this; in this way timid and brave equally aim
> to make their hands famous, and they keep their spears stained
> with blood to show off to their wives and young children.

The savage boar-man is dead, and the victors (brave and timid alike) share in his killing. Both scenes derive from the depiction of the Achaeans' abuse of Hector's corpse at *Iliad* 22.369–75:[78]

> ἄλλοι δὲ περίδραμον υἷες Ἀχαιῶν,
> οἳ καὶ θηήσαντο φυήν καὶ εἶδος ἀγητὸν
> Ἕκτορος· οὐδ᾽ ἄρα οἵ τις ἀνουτητί γε παρέστη.
> ὧδε δέ τις εἴπεσκεν ἰδὼν ἐς πλησίον ἄλλον·
> 'ὢ πόποι, ἦ μάλα δὴ μαλακώτερος ἀμφαφάασθαι
> Ἕκτωρ ἢ ὅτε νῆας ἐνέπρησεν πυρὶ κηλέῳ'.
> ὣς ἄρα τις εἴπεσκε καὶ οὐτήσασκε παραστάς.

> But the other sons of the Achaeans came running around him,
> and they marvelled at the stature and the wonderful beauty
> of Hector. Not one of them who was present did not stab him.
> And they spoke to each other, each looking at the one next to him:
> 'Well now, Hector is way softer to the touch than he was
> when he set fire to the ships with the burning torch.'
> So each would say standing next to him, stabbing him.

---

[77] Dewar (1991): *ad locc.* notes the verbal parallels.

[78] For Statius' recollection of Hector's corpse abuse see Juhnke (1972): 136 and 358 (index 3 s.v. '*Thebais*'), and 131–7 on Homeric (and Virgilian) allusions in the death of Tydeus and the battle over his body.

Fear attenuates after the huge adversary is brought down, and the warriors ritually bloody their spear points. But while Hector's body was protected and preserved by the gods for eventual funeral ritual at Troy,[79] Tydeus' divine protector Pallas flees and abandons her plan to provide Tydeus with immortality after witnessing his eating of Melanippus' brains (*Theb.* 8.758–66).

The scene has some further epic resonances that similarly serve to heighten the horror of Tydeus' death and corpse abuse.[80] The most obvious antecedent is Turnus at the end of his *aristeia* at *Aeneid* 9.806–14, when, abandoned by Juno, he begins to feel his own strength slipping away. Lexical parallels link this scene with both of Tydeus' *aristeiai* (*Theb.* 2.668–81; 8.700–15). Turnus was ultimately saved by his close proximity to the Tiber: he dives into the waters to escape. Tydeus, in the first instance, survives the fight with the fifty ambushers despite his dwindling strength. In his final battle in book 8 the enemy proliferate and he is immured by a mountain of corpses, exposing himself to Melanippus' spear-cast. Pallas' absence opens the door for Tisiphone, who drives him to cannibalistic madness.

The scene recalls Camilla's death in *Aeneid* 11.[81] Like Tydeus, she too is struck by a spear thrown by an enemy who fears to identify himself (his name is Arruns: *Aen.* 11.806). But the role of divinity separates the scenes. While Pallas abandons Tydeus at the moment of his death, Diana (Camilla's protector) promises proper death rites and a return to her homeland (*Aen.* 11.593–4) as well as vengeance (845–9).

Scholars have also noted Statius' debt to Lucan's description of Scaeva, who is similarly pierced to the bone (cf. *BC* 6.195: *stantis in **summis ossibus** hastas*; *Theb.* 8.702: ***summis** haec **ossibus** haerent*), 'forested' with spears (*BC* 6.205: ***densamque** ferens in pectore <u>siluam</u>*; *Theb.* 8.704–5: ***densis** iam consitus hastis | ferratum quatit umbo <u>nemus</u>*), and singled out as the object of an all vs one attack with the emphatic *illum . . . illum* (*BC* 6.189; *Theb.* 8.694). The piercing of Scaeva's eyeball by an anonymous flying arrow is marked by a deictic '*ecce*' (*BC* 6.214), as Statius had similarly identified the anonymous spear-cast that strikes Tydeus (*Theb.* 8.716: *ecce*).[82] Scaeva offers an interesting comparative model since his *aristeia* ends with what

---

[79] See pp. 20, 32–4.

[80] Gervais (2013): 142–7, (2015) and (2017): *ad locc.* notices many of the same complex multi-layered allusions during Tydeus' *monomachia* in *Theb.* 2, which helps to connect his paired *aristeiai* in books 2 and 8. On Statius' allusiveness in crafting Tydeus' final fight in *Theb.* 8, see esp. Zwierlein (1988): 67–75; also Williams (1978): 203–4, McNelis (2007): 131–2, Augoustakis (2016): *ad locc.*

[81] Zwierlein (1988): 72–3; McNelis (2007): 132 and n.26.       [82] Zwierlein (1988): 71–2.

appears to be his death, as his fellow soldiers carry him on high honouring him as a deity (*BC* 6.250–4) and Lucan *faux*-eulogizes him for criminal *uirtus* (260–2; cf. 147–8: *pronus ad omne nefas et qui nesciret in armis | quam magnum uirtus crimen ciuilibus esset*, 'ready for every evil, he didn't know how great a crime virtue is in civil wars'). This is not the final image of Scaeva's corpse, however, or his last appearance in the poem, as Lucan 'resurrects' him for the closing image in his epic (*BC* 10.542–6). Tydeus too is carried away from the field of battle by his troops at the point of death, but lives just long enough to also debase himself with criminal *uirtus* when he cannibalizes Melanippus' head. He dies yet reappears at the end of the poem kissing with those ravenous lips his mourning wife Deipyle (*Theb.* 12.802–3).

But it is Mezentius, from his *aristeia* and death at the end of *Aeneid* 10 and his unnarrated corpse abuse at the start of book 11, who represents the most intriguing model.[83] Tydeus' *aristeia* shares key resonances with Mezentius', particularly Virgil's opening simile comparing Mezentius to a boar surrounded by hunters (*Aen.* 10.707–18); Virgil also emphasizes the motif of one fighter vs many (*Aen.* 10.689–701).[84] There exists a clear verbal parallel between Virgil's *concurrunt Tyrrhenae acies atque omnibus uni, | uni odiisque uiro telisque frequentibus instant*, 'every Tyrrhenian weapon launches at this one man alone, the whole force of spears, he's the one goal for all their hatred' (10.691–2), and the Statian lines noted above, *Thebaid.* 8.701–2: *unum acies circum consumitur, unum | omnia tela uouent* and 2.548–9: *solus, | solus in arma uoco*. In addition to direct word parallelism, note also the epanalepsis over the line break of *uni, | uni* matched by *solus, | solus* at *Thebaid* 2.548–9.

Mezentius, moreover, explicitly anticipates Tydeus' bestial savagery (*feritas*): he's characterized by the 'savage fierceness of his soul' (*Aen.* 10.898: *effera uis animi*) and by his 'savage deeds' (8.483–4: *facta ... effera*: of his torture method of attaching dead bodies to the living), a stronger association than the *ferocitas* of Turnus or Aeneas, and elsewhere only applied to the monster Cacus in Virgil's poem (8.205: *furiis Caci mens effera*, 'his mind savage with fury') and Dido, in the throes of her divinely

---

[83] As D'Alessandro Behr (2007): 47 has articulated, Lucan borrowed much from Virgil's Mezentius for his depiction of Scaeva, so it seems Statius' rendering of Tydeus here should be viewed through a Lucanian lens; certainly the elements of horror in the scene share a poetic synergy with Lucan. The detailed discussion in Zwierlein (1988) does not mention Statius' debts to Virgil's Mezentius.

[84] See Hardie (1986): 285–91 on the one vs many motif in battle scenes in the *Aen.*, including Mezentius in book 10 and Hardie (1993): 3–10 of the motif more generally. See also Williams (1978): 199–205.

induced madness (4.642: *coeptis immanibus effera Dido*, 'Dido, savage with her frightful undertaking').[85] In a simile likening him to a ravenous lion – bestial and man-devouring, 'foul gore bathes his monstrous face' (*Aen.* 10.727–8: *lauit improba taeter | ora cruor*) – Mezentius prefigures Tydeus' recurring *cruentus* epithet. The simile likening him to a defensive boar shifts to that of an offensive lion (10.723–9) to accommodate Mezentius' altered battle tactics.[86] This doubles Tydeus' own movement – and corresponding similes – from defensive to offensive fighter. Tydeus essentially (with the added feature of cannibalism) completes Mezentius' aim of decapitating his enemy Aeneas and carrying off his 'bloody spoils' (*Aen.* 10.862–3: *aut hodie uictor spolia illa cruenta | et caput Aeneae referes*), but both are themselves ultimately 'bloodied' in death (*Aen.* 10.908: *cruore; Theb.* 9.1: *cruenti*). The heroes are removed from the front lines during their *aristeiai* to tend to battle wounds, surrounded by comrades (*Aen.* 10.833–8; *Theb.* 8.728–33):[87] Tydeus' wounds are fatal, though he manages one last spear-cast; Mezentius will return to battle but is killed almost immediately by Aeneas. These allusions alone might not necessarily lead us to assume Statius was working directly around Virgil's depiction of Mezentius' swan-song – since they share commonalities with a variety of Homeric motifs – but the aftermath of each scene nails the relationship.

   The transition from *Aeneid* 10 to 11 is curious in that, unlike other book endings of the poem, the narrative structure bleeds into the beginning of the next book, which deals further with the aftermath of Mezentius' death and the quasi-narrative of his corpse abuse, juxtaposed with the proper funeral for Pallas and the nameless dead on each side. Statius too typically follows a tightly structured pattern for book endings, but the transition between books 8 and 9, which track the narrative of Tydeus and his corpse, breaks the mould and has resonances with Virgil's treatment of Mezentius' ending.[88] Both heroes die at the close of a book, and early in the next are abused by their captors. We might also stretch Pallas' abandonment of Tydeus at the moment of his death to Mezentius' overt godlessness (*contemptor diuum*):[89] both men are ultimately left to the devices of their captors.

---

[85] Ripoll (1998): 336–7. For Tydeus and *feritas*, cf. *Theb.* 9.20, 184. Harrison (1991): *ad* 10.711 notes the particular (traditional) ferocity of the boar, and the simile is appropriate to each hero.
[86] Basson (1984): 60–1.    [87] Juhnke (1972): 131 n.339.
[88] McNelis (2007): 133 and n.31. Cf. similarly the transition from *Theb.* 7–8 which also follows the odd journey of Amphiaraus' 'corpse'; see below pp. 218–21.
[89] While Capaneus most naturally shares the affinity for atheism with Mezentius (Chaudhuri (2014): 260–2, 271, 274–5), Ahl (1986): 2864 notes that other traditions focus more directly on Tydeus' own

Coupled with the boar imagery and linguistic ties of the one vs many motif, it seems Statius is compounding imagery (perhaps already adopted by Ovid in his own reading of Mezentius' death and aftermath) of Ovid's boar hunt and Mezentius' *aristeia* and abuse. The difference is that Statius fills the narrative gap of the *Aeneid*'s depiction of Mezentius' corpse abuse and anthropomorphizes (while retaining the bestial characteristics of) Ovid's rampaging boar. Statius inserts the traditional Homeric feature of *Leichenkampf*, a motif Virgil does not adopt in his epic, and adds the grim description of enemy soldiers sharing in the mutilation of the captured corpse. Virgil simply described Mezentius' perforated breastplate as a piquant afterthought leaving the space between books 10 and 11 for his audience to guess at the abuse his corpse received; Statius showcases the corpse receiving its wounds. As with Lucan's exploration of Virgilian silence concerning the treatment of Priam's corpse, Statius actualizes both implicit imagery in the *Aeneid* and also the attempted but unfulfilled abuses in the *Iliad* to horrific effect. This imagery is activated through the lens of Ovid's depiction of the killing and ritual abuse of a ferocious animal.

If we consider the death and corpse abuse of Tydeus from an Iliadic perspective alone, the hero seems to embody the most perverse aspects of both Achilles and Hector during the climax of book 22. Tydeus' cannibalism of Melanippus' corpse represents the realization of Achilles' threat to Hector (*Il.* 22.346–7), and Tydeus' own corpse mutilation is ultimately (via allusions to Mezentius and Ovid's Calydonian boar) derived from the Achaeans' ritual stabbing of Hector (22.369–75). In effect, Tydeus is transformed from a more savage Achilles to a more unfortunate Hector, from über-abuser to über-abused, as the focus of mutilation shifts (between the end of book 8 and the beginning of 9) from Melanippus' mutilated and cannibalized body to Tydeus' own mutilated corpse. This double role is anticipated by the paralleling of animal allusions that cast Tydeus as offensive and defensive beast, the captured boar and long-sought-after lion.

Despite Eteocles' disgust at Tydeus' behaviour, the bestial savagery is not simply contained in this one man or his coterie. Much as Hecuba's defamation of Achilles' 'savagery' contaminates her own mind until she too claims to crave human flesh (*Il.* 22.212), the Thebans are swept up in the contagion of bestiality (*Theb.* 9.25–31):

hostility to the gods, which makes him 'something of a double for Capaneus', and, naturally, for Mezentius as well.

> furor omnibus idem
> Tydeos inuisi spoliis raptoque potiri
> corpore. non aliter subtexunt astra cateruae
> incestarum auium, longe quibus aura nocentem
> aera desertasque tulit sine funere mortes;
> illo auidae cum uoce ruunt, sonat arduus aether
> plausibus, et caelo uolucres cessere minores.

> For all there is the same frenzy
> to take hold of hated Tydeus' spoils and his plundered
> corpse. Just as flocks of foul birds blanket the stars
> when a distant breeze has brought noxious air
> and the dead abandoned without funeral rites;
> greedy, with characteristic calls, they fly down, the lofty aether
> echoes with flapping, and smaller birds withdraw from the sky.

In a scene of similes come to life, the Thebans are greedy carrion birds, bane of epic corpses (Achilles had promised Hector that dogs and birds would devour him completely, *Il.* 22.354, recapitulating the image from the proem, *Il.* 1.4). What began as condemnation of Tydeus' and the Argives' unbounded *furor* and *feritas* in Eteocles' speech to inflame his troops, spreads to infect them, as they too become prey to dehumanizing activity (*Theb.* 9.184–5): *iuuat ora rigentia leto | et formidatos impune lacessere uultus. | hic amor*, 'it's delightful to see his face stiffen in death and to attack his frightening features without punishment. They love this.'[90] Like Melanippus, Tydeus' corpse too is mutilated and implicitly cannibalized.

The transformation from man to beast is emblematic of the final third of Statius' poem, following Dis's injunction for monstrous crimes (esp. 8.66–74). The subhuman behaviour of Tydeus is a product of the building animal savagery Statius activates by invoking a *noua Calliope* to assist in his Iliadic war-song (8.373–4). That humans will descend into raging beasts is symbolized immediately after the re-invocation by imagery of horses and their riders woven crudely into ire-filled centaurs (8.392–3): *corpora ceu mixti dominis irasque sedentum | induerint*, 'as if their bodies were mixed with their masters and they donned the rage of their riders'. The same image is evoked again when Tydeus slays Prothous with a spear that pierces both rider and horse, pinning them in death as they tumble to the ground intertwined as one creature (8.536–47).[91] Tydeus is the first in a series of

---

[90] See Dewar (1991): *ad* 9.1–31, 27ff, 177–195, Ganiban (2007): 127 n.46.

[91] The first casualty of the war in book 7 is the Theban Pterelas who is killed by Tydeus. He's similarly pinned by a spear to his horse and is compared, in death, to a centaur (7.636–40). Vessey (1973): 259 n.1 comments that this description signals 'the beginning of the reign of bestiality at Thebes'. Tydeus is

warriors gripped by bestial *furor* that manifests most strikingly in the abuse and mistreatment of corpses, culminating in Creon's refusal of funerals for the dead Argives (11.661–4, 12.94–103), and his own desire to lead beasts and birds to the corpses (12.97–8).[92] The noxious air equating Tydeus' corpse with the fodder of vultures (9.28–9) lingers as a prefiguring of Creon's ban that leaves the fields strewn with foul decay (cf. 11.661–4, 754; 12.247–9, 565–7, 712–14).[93] He's described as behaving inhumanly: only war and arms can compel him to behave 'like a human' again (12.165–6: *bello cogendus et armis | in mores hominemque Creon*, 'Creon must be compelled by war and arms into the ways of humanity').[94] Tydeus' beastly abuse of Melanippus' corpse reverberates to infect the vulture-Thebans who abuse his own body, and the plague spreads to encompass the entire epic.

### Asbyte, Theron, and Hannibal in Silius Italicus' *Punica*

Two of the most graphic scenes of corpse abuse in Silius' *Punica* come in swift succession during the siege of Saguntum in book 2. In the first, Asbyte, an Amazonian *uirgo* modelled on Penthesilea and Camilla, is killed, decapitated, and her head thrust onto a pike by Theron, the Herculean defender-priest of Saguntum (*Pun.* 2.188–207). He in turn is killed by Hannibal as recompense for the murder and abuse of Asbyte, and his body mutilated and left for the birds to devour (208–69). The two scenes are loaded with Homeric and Virgilian allusions but, as in the examples from Lucan and Statius, the implicit or silent staging of corpse mistreatment in the epic models finds its logical and gruesome 'conclusion' in Silius' reworking.

The siege of Saguntum functions as a mini-epic that is at once tangential to the physical war between Rome and Carthage (Rome does not play a part in the siege), but crucial as the battle that ultimately brings Rome directly into conflict with Carthage. Silius is acutely aware of the historical accounts (e.g. Polyb. 3.6; Livy 21.5–6), which offer him the opportunity to establish Hannibal's 'heroic' epic credentials and the very real threat he will

---

compared in simile to the centaur Pholus during the ambush at 2.559–64, an indication of his savagery and bestial nature; with Gervais (2015): 62–5. See Franchet d'Espèrey (1999): 193–7 on Statius' similes comparing Hippomedon and Tydeus to centaurs as a dehumanizing indicator. See Taisne (1994): 88 on horses, their riders, and the 'contagion du *furor* destructeur'. Gervais (2015): 70–1 equates centauromachy with civil war. See also Perutelli (2000): 194–6, Gibson (2008): 100–1, Augoustakis (2016): *ad* 8.392–3 and index s.v.
[92] See below Chapter 5 *passim*.     [93] Joyce (2008): 411 n.27–31.
[94] Rieks (1967): 221–2; Feeney (1991): 360–1.

pose to Rome. The destruction of Saguntum thus serves a dual role of anticipating the fates of both Rome (feared) and Carthage (actualized), while also repeatedly looking back to the fall of Troy, an event that ostensibly was the impetus for the foundation of Rome; the episode is protatic and crucial for our understanding of events and themes that will follow. This imagery of rising and falling is repeatedly evoked in the scenes of death and mutilation of Asbyte and Theron outside the walls of a crumbling achronic every-city,[95] as Silius casts his eyes backward and forward in mytho-historical time.

Asbyte enters the battlefield and, following the role of Virgil's Camilla, her most prominent literary antecedent,[96] immediately begins her offensive onslaught (*Pun.* 2.56–86). But, as with Camilla, her moment of glory is brief. She's hunted down by the aptly named Theron (the 'hunter'),[97] priest and double of Hercules,[98] who upends her chariot by frightening the horses with the open jaws of his lion-skin cloak (192–6). What follows is a scene of escalating brutality (197–205):

> tum saltu Asbyten conantem linquere pugnas
> occupat incussa gemina inter tempora claua
> feruentesque rotas turbataque frena pauore
> disiecto spargit collisa per ossa cerebro                    200
> ac rapta properans caedem ostentare bipenni
> amputat e curru reuolutae uirginis ora.
> necdum irae positae. celsa nam figitur hasta
> spectandum caput; id gestent ante agmina Poenum
> imperat et propere currus ad moenia uertant.

> Then with a leap he seizes Asbyte as she tries to flee the battle,
> his club smashed between both temples
> and he splatters the shining wheels and horses confused by fright
> with bits of brain through her broken skull,                    200
> and, rushing to show off his kill with her stolen axe,
> he lops off the head of the virgin who'd rolled out of the chariot.
> But his rage is not yet sated: for fixed on a tall spear

---

[95] On this feature of cities in the *Punica* blurring and blending, looking backward and forward in time (cities 'indivisible'), see Cowan (2007a) and (2007b).

[96] Much of the scholarship on this scene (2.56–269) has concerned the literary tradition of Asbyte's character as a neo-Amazonian Camilla/Penthesilea: e.g. Albrecht (1964): 172, Küppers (1986): 141–53, Vinchesi (2005): 108–122, Lovatt (2013): 305–6. Uccellini (2006) is more expansive.

[97] Augoustakis (2010): 123; Tipping (2010): 19 with n.23.

[98] Theron is a composite of Hercules and Herculean-style warriors from Homer, Virgil, Valerius, and others: Areithous, *Il.* 7.136–41; Aventinus, *Aen.* 7.655–9; Cisseus and Gyas, *Aen.* 10.317–22; Hercules, VF 3.161–2, etc. See Bernstein (2017): *ad* 2.153–9, with possible allusions also to Statius' Tirynthians (*Theb.* 4.154–6, 11.45–6).

is her head for all to see. He orders his men to brandish it before the Punic line, and turn the chariot back immediately to the city walls.

Theron's splattering of brains with a club befits Hercules,[99] but the subsequent decapitation and, his anger not yet satisfied (203), impaling of her head on a spear as a *spectaculum* for the Carthaginian army is pressing the limits of even Hercules' own inclinations to *ira*. This form of brutal corpse abuse is a favourite of Silius (cf. 5.151–2, 7.704, 15.813–14, 17.308). And all such scenes have the stain of Roman civil war abuses. Of particular importance for Silius and his Flavian audience was the supposed severing, impaling, and parading of Galba's head on a pike after his murder in the forum in January, 69 CE. The account is preserved in Suetonius (*Galb.* 20.2):

> iugulatus est ad lacum Curti ac relictum ita uti erat, donec gregarius miles a frumentatione rediens abiecto onere caput ei amputauit; et quoniam capillo arripere non poterat, in gremium abdidit, mox inserto per os pollice ad Othonem detulit. ille lixis calonibusque donauit, qui hasta suffixum non sine ludibrio circum castra portarunt . . .

> He was killed near Lake Curtius, left there where he was, until a common soldier returning from grain distribution, put down his load and decapitated him. And since he couldn't take him by the hair, he hid it in his robes. Eventually he brought it to Otho with his finger in its mouth. He gifted it to his attendants and staff-servants, who stuck it onto a pike and carried it around the camp like a toy.

The historical context everywhere casts a shadow over the poetic expressions of corporal violence. Virgil wove features of Rome's intestine violence into his depictions of abuse in the *Aeneid*, as we have seen. But these allusions are elliptical and vague.[100] Statius and Silius have no hesitations evoking the violence of their own recent civil wars following the death of Nero and, in most cases, exploit this sort of graphic scenery as focal points for narrative action.

Theron's savage act elicits his abandonment by divine favour (*Pun.* 2.206) and Hannibal's own boundless anger (208–10: *namque aderat toto ore ferens iramque minasque* | *Hannibal et caesam Asbyten fixique tropaeum* | *infandum capitis furiata mente dolebat*, 'for Hannibal came up wearing rage and menace across his face, and in his seething heart he pained to see

---

[99] Cf. Ov. *Fast.* 1.575–6; VF 3.165–9; [Sen.] *HO* 1449–51, *HF* 1006–7, 1024–6; see Bernstein (2017): *ad* 2.197–205, 198.
[100] See pp. 41–66.

Asbyte killed and the unspeakable trophy of her spitted head'; cf. 239, 242). The Saguntines flee in terror at Hannibal's approach and barricade themselves inside the city walls, leaving Theron alone to defend the gates while his people watch in horror from the heights. Silius constructs the scene as a spectacle. Theron yells to his comrades to play the role of spectacular audience (230–1: *spectacula tantum | ferte, uiri*). The action is evocative of the *teichoscopia* of *Iliad* 3.146–53, as Priam and his people prepare to watch from the walls the duel between Menelaus and Paris. But more relevant contextually are the extended final duels that end the warring in both the *Iliad* (Achilles vs Hector) and the *Aeneid* (Aeneas vs Turnus), particularly since, as in the literary models, Theron (the eventual victim) flees from his more powerful attacker (Hannibal) after ineffectually hurling his weapon (*Pun.* 2.248–50; cf. *Il.* 22.137–66, *Aen.* 12.742–65).[101] The outcome is the same: Hannibal catches Theron and after framing the immolation as retributive and offering his death to the shade of Asbyte (*Pun.* 2.258: *i, miseram Asbyten leto solare propinquo*, 'go, comfort miserable Asbyte with your death in quick succession'), he buries (260: *condit*) his sword in Theron's neck. Achilles had directly recalled Patroclus after stabbing Hector (*Il.* 22.331–5),[102] and Aeneas channelled Pallas, who will take retribution through Aeneas' sacrificial death-blow (12.950: *condit*). Silius' lone usage of *condere* in the Virgilian coinage of 'bury a sword' (*OLD* s.v. *condo* 7b) occurs here, echoing explicitly the close of the *Aeneid*.

The scene ends with the contrasting treatment of Asbyte's and Theron's corpses (*Pun.* 2.264–9):

> at Nomadum furibunda cohors miserabile humandi
> deproperat munus tumulique adiungit honorem
> et rapto cineres ter circum corpore lustrat.
> hinc letale uiri robur tegimenque tremendum
> in flammas iaciunt ambustoque ore genisque
> deforme alitibus liquere cadauer Hiberis.

> But the raging Numidian troop rushes to carry out the sad
> task of her burial and they add the honour of a tomb
> and drag the captured body three times around her ashes.
> Then the man's deadly club and frightening head covering
> they toss into the flames and, when his face and beard were scorched,
> they left his mutilated corpse to the Spanish birds.

---

[101] Juhnke (1972): 191; Küppers (1986): 147–8; Spaltenstein (1986); *ad* 2.247; Vinchesi (2005): 122; Bernstein (2017): xxiv–xxv and *ad locc.*

[102] Juhnke (1972): 191; note Achilles' words at 22.271–2.

Asbyte's body is burned on the pyre, along with Theron's club and lion-skin cape. But the corpse (*cadauer*[103]) of Theron is abused (266: cf. *Il.* 23.13, 24.16) and further mutilated by having only his beard and face burned, matching symbolically the abuse he dealt to Asbyte.[104] His corpse is then left to the birds, accomplishing the most brutal threats and fears of Homer's and Virgil's heroes. Theron had scolded his army, who fled at the sight of Hannibal, for being 'disgraceful' or 'unsightly' (232: *heu deforme!*), a feature he now shares with them (269: *deforme ... cadauer*).[105]

Scholars have noted the scene's appropriation of Iliadic material and character doubling: Hannibal's revenge slaying of Theron mirrors Achilles' slaying of Hector; and as the roles suggest, as Hector killed Patroclus, so Theron kills Asbyte.[106] Hannibal's approach to Theron in bright glimmering armour, causing fear and the flight of the Saguntine warriors into their city (2.211–14, 222), matches Achilles at the outset of his duel with Hector, whose flashing armour causes the latter to flee in terror (*Il.* 22.131–7). Hannibal assumes Achilles' famous epithet 'swift-footed' at *Punica* 2.212 (*membris uelocibus*). The Saguntine matrons' fear that if they allow Theron entry into the city walls Hannibal might be granted entry as well, replays Priam's fear that Achilles might gain access to Troy at *Iliad* 21.531–6, and so on.

Along with these narrative connections are more graphic allusions to threatened and attempted acts of corpse abuse in Homer, which Silius draws out in his recasting of the scene. Theron's role as 'new-Hector' in this mini-drama of larger Iliadic motifs finds a grisly complement in Hector's attempted abuse of Patroclus in Homer's poem. After slaying Patroclus, Homer tells us Hector was dragging away his corpse with the express intent of decapitating him and throwing his trunk to the Trojan dogs (*Il.* 17.126–7). Later, Iris relays to Achilles that Hector wants to decapitate Patroclus and fix his head on a stake, displaying it on the

---

[103] See Bernstein (2017): *ad loc.* Silius' use of *cadauer* is jarring, un-Virgilian (one appearance in the *Aen.*, one in VF, three in Statius' *Theb.*, 17 in the *Pun.*), and is a clear sign of Lucanian influence (36 appearances in *BC*: see Mayer (1981): 14 and *ad* 8.438; generally Chiesa (2005): 24–9, Calonne (2010)). It's a word of plague in Lucretius and Ovid. (e.g. Lucr. 6.1155, 1273–4; Ov. *Met.* 7.602). Virgil reserves it only for the corpse of his monster Cacus at *Aen.* 8.264, and at *G.* 3.556–7 of animals in a plague. In his *Ibis*, Ovid uses *cadauer* three times (168, 338, 515) in the context of maledictions he hopes to heap on the unnamed recipient of his curse. By way of comparison, Silius employs the more common poetic usage *corpus* for a dead body only eight times of the forty-seven appearances of the word in the *Pun.* as it applies to humans (thirty-nine instances), animals (seven instances), and the State anthropomorphized (one instance). All seventeen examples of *cadauer* in the *Pun.* refer to dead human bodies: this is, as for Lucan, his preferred word for 'corpse'.

[104] Augoustakis (2010): 128.    [105] Bernstein (2017): *ad* 2.269.

[106] Juhnke (1972): 189–91; Bernstein (2017): *ad locc.*

city's walls (18.175–7), and these words spur Achilles to action. Silius has Theron, in the role of a new Hector, actually carry out these mutilations of Asbyte. Hannibal retaliates, focusing specifically on the abuse levelled at her head and corpse (*Pun.* 2.208–10). Theron's corpse abuse mirrors Achilles' attempted abuse of Hector: dragging the body in the dirt around the tomb of Asbyte-Patroclus (*Pun.* 2.266; cf. *Il.* 23.187, 24.14–16, 51–2, 416–17, 755–6).[107] The fate of his corpse as fodder for birds comparative to Asbyte's proper treatment represents Achilles' boast to Hector that he will glut birds and dogs while Patroclus receives the customary funeral pyre (*Pun.* 2.264–9; *Il.* 22.335–6, cf. 22.354). The juxtaposition between Patroclus' funeral and Hector's unhonoured corpse in *Iliad* 23 is jarring.

Though the abuse dealt to Hector's corpse is brutal, he has the constant protection of the gods who ultimately preserve his body until Achilles hands him over to Priam (*Il.* 23.184–7; 23.190–1, 24.20–1).[108] Theron will have no such luck as the gods abandon him after his overt mutilation of Asbyte (*Pun.* 2.206). The specific emphasis on the facial mutilation of Theron also recalls Achilles' treatment of Hector, whom he drags face first in the dirt (*Il.* 22.397–8), marring his features (402–3). This act is symbolic of the threat of decapitation Achilles utters at 18.333–5, but which Homer does not allow to unfold in the poem. Like Achilles, Hannibal aims to dehumanize his victim by literally 'effacing' him, disfiguring him, by rendering him indistinguishable on the field of battle among the heaps of corpses. The *Punica* scene effectively stages in microcosm the action of Homer's narrative combined with points of unfulfilled threats and boasts of corpse mutilation.

Iliadic intertextual cues are only part of the picture. Silius interlaces the Homeric models with scenes from the *Aeneid* that themselves have an integrated poetic engagement with the relevant Iliadic material, creating an allusive imbroglio of 'double imitation' in classical poetics.[109] Asbyte's abuse by Theron, as noted, stages a gruesome recapitulation of Camilla's death in *Aeneid* 11 that combines elements of abuse elsewhere in Virgil's poem. But whereas Camilla dies rather peacefully, surrounded by her coterie and avenged by Diana (via Opis: *Aen.* 11.818–67), Silius forgoes the *pathos* of the model scene and weaves imagery of Nisus' and Euryalus' corpse abuse into the narrative of Asbyte's death (*Aen.* 9.465–72).[110] As in

---

[107] Spaltenstein (1986): *ad* 2.266; Vinchesi (2005): 122; Bernstein (2017): *ad* 2.266.
[108] See pp. 20, 32–4.   [109] See Hardie (1989): 3–4 for the general outline.
[110] Spaltenstein (1986): *ad* 2.203; Vinchesi (2005): 121 n.98; Bernstein (2017): *ad* 2.197–205, 209–10. Uccellini (2006): 252–3 on the juxtaposition between Camilla's death and Asbyte's. Lovatt (2013): 306 mentions Nisus and Euryalus and Hopleus and Dymas from *Theb.* 10.

the Virgilian example, Asbyte's head is impaled and put on display (*Pun.* 2.201: *properans caedem ostentare*, 'rushing to show off his kill'; 203–4: *celsa nam figitur hasta | spectandum* **caput**, 'for fixed on a tall spear is her head for all to see'; cf. *Aen.* 9.465–6: *quin ipsa arrectis ... in* **hastis** | *praefigunt* **capita**, 'on raised spear-points they thrust their heads'); she's made a trophy (*Pun.* 2.209: *tropaeum*) that incites Hannibal's wrath.

Virgil's silence in actually describing the physical corpse abuse is in Silius a point of departure. The description of mutilation is not here expanded to the lengths of Lucan's description of Pompey's decapitation and abuse – nothing in extant epic is – but it is no less hideous an example of bestial savagery that defies the scale of appropriate human(e) behaviour in Silian epic combat. The scene itself reworks Lucan's description of Pompey's decapitation and head-impaling at *BC* 8.681–4: *Phario ... ueruto* | ... **suffixum caput est**,[111] coupled with Sextus Pompey's *aperçu* of the parading of his father's impaled head as a spectacle in Egypt (9.136–9), both of which are already in dialogue with the scene of decapitation from the *Aeneid*. Lucan had set the stage to allow vivid description of this form of corpse abuse into epic poetry, and Silius follows suit.

Theron appropriately embodies the duality of man-beast typical of his double, Hercules, and even 'transforms' into the beast whose skin he wears when he brandishes the head of the lion to frighten Asbyte's horses (*Pun.* 2.192–4).[112] His overstepping of the bounds of acceptable epic battlefield *ira* (by abusing an enemy corpse) results in his immediate abandonment by the gods (206), akin to the fate of Tydeus, whose animal savagery triggered the evaporation of his impending immortality when Pallas fled at the sight of his brain-stained jaws (*Theb.* 8.760–6).[113] Both heroes degenerate into a more monstrous Hercules character, and for their bestiality (both transform into the animals whose skins they wear) they lose a chance at the divinely granted *apotheosis* Jupiter's son enjoyed. This is perhaps best articulated by Silius' description of Theron's corpse as a *deforme cadauer* (*Pun.* 2.269), which recalls directly Virgil's description of the monster Cacus' corpse after he's slain by Hercules at *Aeneid.* 8.264: *informe cadauer*, Virgil's only use of the prosaic *cadauer* in the poem. Theron shares the fate of an earlier epic monster, the intertextual victim of the hero in whose massive footsteps he follows.

---

[111] Silius exploits the scene of Pompey's death and abuse elsewhere in the *Pun.*, see Bassett (1959): 14, Marpicati (1999).
[112] Tipping (2010): 19.    [113] Tipping (2010): 19 n.24.

After Hannibal kills Theron, Asbyte's Numidian band drag his corpse three times around her ashes (*Pun.* 2.266: *et rapto cineres **ter circum corpore** lustrat*) mimicking the *Aeneid*'s description (on Dido's temple at Carthage) of Achilles' dragging of Hector's corpse around the walls of Troy (*Aen.* 1.483–4: ***ter circum** Iliacos raptauerat Hectora muros, | exanimumque auro **corpus** uendebat Achilles*).[114] The game of referential association with prior epic role-playing becomes muddled when we delve into the intertextual characterizations more closely. Hannibal's swift response to Asbyte's death casts him in the role of Virgil's Turnus, who seeks vengeance for Camilla's death, as does his association elsewhere more cosmically with Juno, both leaders' divine protector.[115] But the allusion to Nisus and Euryalus who suffer the same *post mortem* abuse as Asbyte, link *Theron* with Turnus (who oversaw the impaling of Nisus' and Euryalus' heads) and portray Hannibal as an avenging Aeneas, specifically as the focus on the abuse dealt to Asbyte's corpse, is highlighted as the impetus for Hannibal's retaliatory attack (*Pun.* 2.209–10).

The transition between Asbyte's death and Theron's own demise further amplifies this parallelism of Virgilian role-jockeying, as Silius' aside concerning Theron's ignorance of his own impending doom demonstrates (206–7): *haec caecus fati diuumque abeunte fauore | uicino Theron edebat proelia leto*, 'blind to his doom absent divine favour, Theron was fighting on with death encroaching'. This echoes Virgil's aside about Turnus' fate after he has killed Pallas (*Aen.* 10.500–5):[116]

> quo nunc Turnus ouat spolio gaudetque potitus.
> nescia mens hominum fati sortisque futurae
> et seruare modum rebus sublata secundis!
> Turno tempus erit magno cum optauerit emptum
> intactum Pallanta, et cum spolia ista diemque
> oderit[117]

> Now Turnus rejoices in the spoils and delights having obtained it.
> The mind of humans, ignorant of fate or future chance,
> and unable to stick to limits, exalted in good fortune!
> A time will come for great Turnus when he'll wish he'd paid a price
> for an untouched Pallas, and when he will hate these spoils
> and this day.

---

[114] Spaltenstein (1986): *ad* 2.266; Bernstein (2017): *ad* 2.266.
[115] On the correspondence between Hannibal and Turnus in the *Pun.* see Albrecht (1964): 168–73, Kißel (1979): 108–11, Ripoll (1998): 244–7, 333–4, Klaassen (2009): 99–106, Tipping (2010): index s.v. 'Hannibal, and Turnus'.
[116] Bernstein (2017): *ad* 2.206.
[117] Cf. Hom. *Il.* 17.201–8: Zeus's reaction to Hector wearing Patroclus' armour.

Theron's obsession with winning Asbyte's *spolia* (her glittering chariot and armour, *Pun.* 2.166–8) links him to Turnus, whose despoiling of Pallas' baldric ultimately eradicates any hope of *clementia* Aeneas might have mustered. Hannibal, as an avenging Aeneas, hunts down the 'fleeing-hunter' (*Pun.* 2.247–50, with *Aen.* 12.742–65) and kills him, replaying Aeneas' words and death-blow in his killing of Turnus (*Pun.* 2.258–60; *Aen.* 12.947–51). By condemning Theron's corpse to be fodder for birds (*Pun.* 2.269), Hannibal again assumes the role of Aeneas, who, in the lone Iliadic-style threat of animal corpse consumption in the *Aeneid*, promised the same fate over the (decapitated) corpse of Tarquitus (*Aen.* 10.557–60).[118] And by alluding to Aeneas' *euchos* of corpse abuse along with imagery reflective of the end of the *Aeneid*, Silius here stages a 'version' of the end of Virgil's poem – with further refracted cues from Virgil's own model, Achilles' slaying of Hector in the *Iliad* – which plays out the abuse of Turnus' corpse that is left unstated in the original.[119]

The multiplicity of intertextual allusions pointedly and wilfully complicates our reading of the text and the implications of the scene as a whole. In interlacing imagery from the main duels in the *Iliad* and *Aeneid* with allusions to corpse abuse elsewhere in these predecessor poems, Silius has created a composite of antagonistic models for Hannibal: he's at once an Achilles-Aeneas and a Hector-Turnus. This technique of imitation, whereby an author posits alternative contrasting models for specific characters is a device typical of Virgil's own engagement with his Homeric (Iliadic) model, as Aeneas and Turnus take turns 'competing' for the roles of Achilles and Hector.[120] Silius continues the poetic game, but with the added element of weaving Virgil's own epic heroes into his text, adding another layer of association.[121] This is not simply Silius' attempt at stockpiling allusions to Homer and Virgil. There is deeper narratological significance to the references during this Asbyte–Theron scene.

---

[118] Bernstein (2017): *ad* 2.269. On Aeneas' boast, see pp. 50–1 above.

[119] Re-presentations and (per)versions of the end of the *Aeneid* function as early 'readings' of Virgil's climax. Silius toys with alternate endings throughout the *Punica:* cf. Hannibal's slaying of Murrus at *Pun.* 1.456–517, the Elder Scipio's slaying of Crixus (4.289–97), Pedianus' revenge killing of Cinyps who was gifted Paulus' helmet by Hannibal (12.212–58), the two thwarted duels between Hannibal and Scipio at Cannae (9.434–85) and later at Zama (17.385–405, 509–21), Nero's slaying of Hasdrubal at Metaurus at 15.794–823, Hasdrubal's dying words granting Nero the power to 'use what battle gives you' (15.801: *utere Marte tuo*) echoing the dying Turnus' words to Aeneas (*Aen.* 12.932: *utere sorte tua*), etc.

[120] Anderson (1990) is the classic study. See Van Nortwick (1980), King (1982).

[121] On Silian 'role-doubling', particularly in terms of Hannibal's character: e.g. Klaassen (2009): 99–106, Tipping (2010): 83–92, Fucecchi (2011a): 312–18, Stocks (2014): 53–75.

Crucial to our understanding of Silius' intertextual gymnastics is the role of Saguntum as a city under siege.[122] As the initial target of Hannibal's wrath in the poem, the city functions as a prefiguring of what (potentially) Hannibal will do to Rome.[123] But the siege and eventual sack also function as a recapitulation of Troy's fall, and so look forward ultimately to the fall of Carthage.[124] All of these allusions to fallen and threatened cities, past and future, are poignantly reflected in the literary models Silius uses to help frame his scene.

Theron's role as the lone defender of his city (*Pun.* 2.228–32), whose death will throw open the Saguntine walls to destruction (240–1), casts him as the embodiment of his city's fortunes. This symbolism is strengthened through his role as a human equivalent of the city's mythical founder and builder of her walls, Hercules. Theron's death instigates Saguntum's fall, and his burnt beard and face (268–9) stand as synecdoche for the mass conflagration that destroys the city.[125] This association of the death of a leader with the fall of his city has an epic parallel with the death of Hector in the *Iliad*, whose death is seen as symbolic and proleptic of the burning of Troy itself, projected beyond the scope of Homer's poem (esp. *Il.* 22.410–11; cf. *Ilias Latina* 1019–20, 1140, 1053–6). The idea is picked up by Virgil, who equates Priam's death with the fall of Troy in *Aeneid* 2, and by Lucan, who stages the fall of the Republic through Pompey's murder off the shore of Egypt in *BC* 8. By framing his scene around Achilles' slaying of Hector, Silius equates the fall of Saguntum with that of Troy, previewed and symbolized by the death of each city's heroic gate-keeper. Hannibal here is the Achillean sacker of cities, and Theron the ill-starred would-be saviour of his homeland, a Hector analogue. Theron's death and/as the city's destruction is echoed in the divine realm, as Juno (through her minion Tisiphone) defeats Hercules' attempt (through the personified Fides) to encourage the suffering Saguntines to bravely resist the Carthaginian assault (*Pun.* 2.475–649), a rekindling of their age-old animosity.[126] Both godly and human figures of Hercules fail and Saguntum crumbles as a result.

[122] The Saguntum episode as a whole has received considerable attention: see Augoustakis (2010): 113–36 and notes for additional bibliography; also Schettino (2011), Stocks (2014): index s.v. 'Saguntum', and Bernstein's (2017) commentary.
[123] Albrecht (1964): 24–7; Dominik (2003): 474–80.
[124] Hardie (1993): 81–2 summarizes neatly. Cf. Livy 21.10.10 (Hanno's speech), positing a correlation between the fall of Saguntum and the fall of Carthage.
[125] Augoustakis (2010): 128.   [126] Augoustakis (2010): 114.

Even in victory, however, comes a premonition of Hannibal's ultimate defeat. The lasting image of the sack of Saguntum – the final lines of book 2 in fact – is not one of promise and joy for the Carthaginian leader, but an epilogue of defeat and death (2.699–707):

> cui uero non aequa dedit uictoria nomen
> (audite, o gentes, neu rumpite foedera pacis                700
> nec regnis postferte fidem!), uagus exul in orbe
> errabit toto patriis proiectus ab oris,
> tergaque uertentem trepidans Carthago uidebit.
> saepe Saguntinis somnos exterritus umbris
> optabit cecidisse manu, ferroque negato                705
> inuictus quondam Stygias bellator ad undas
> **deformata** feret liuenti **membra** ueneno.

> But in truth for him, an unjust victory brought renown
> (hear it, o nations, don't break pacts of peace                700
> nor consider loyalty less than power!), a roaming exile
> he will wander the whole world expelled from his native shores,
> and trembling Carthage will see him turning his back.
> Often, frightened in his sleep by Saguntine ghosts,
> he will wish he had died by his own hand; and when the steel has
>          been refused,                705
> the warrior once invincible to the Stygian waters
> will carry down limbs deformed by blackened poison.

Here it's an image of Hannibal's deformed corpse, not that of Theron or the other Saguntines, that ends the narrative of the siege. Yet Hannibal's *deformata membra* do directly recall Theron's *deforme cadauer*[127] (2.269), as well as the hideous sight of the emaciated Saguntines just before they commit mass societal suicide (466–8: *iam lurida sola | tecta cute et uenis male iuncta trementibus ossa | extant consumptis uisu **deformia membris**, 'now covered only by sallow skin and poorly joined by quivering veins, the bones protrude, disgusting to see with the limbs eaten away'). At the end of the episode, Silius presents us with his own poetic prefigured disfiguring of Hannibal's corpse (by poison), evoking and blending the fates of both Theron and the suicidal Saguntines, whose paired demise stands for the destruction of their city.

---

[127] The word *membra* is standard poetic synecdoche for *corpus* (*OLD* s.v. *membrum* 2) and, by extension, *cadauer*, Silius' preferred term for a dead human (see p. 101 n.103 above).

Although his death is outside the framework of Silius' poem,[128] we come
back to this scene at the end of the *Punica*, as Hannibal sees the finish line
and defeat and contemplates the suicide we are told will not yet be granted
to him. Scipio has gained the upper hand in the war, the Carthaginians
have lost a string of battles, and Hannibal is forced back to Carthage to try
to prevent Scipio and the invading Roman army from obliterating home-
base. After he is led away from the field of battle (Zama) by a ruse
orchestrated by Juno, and as he watches his army's destruction from a
short distance away, Hannibal looks to his sword and considers suicide
(17.561–6):

> 'mea signa secuti,
> quis pugnae auspicium dedimus, caeduntur, et absens
> accipio gemitus uocesque ac uerba uocantum
> Hannibalem. quis nostra satis delicta piabit
> Tartareus torrens?' simul haec fundebat et una                    565
> spectabat dextram ac leti feruebat amore.

> 'Those who followed my standards,
> whom I urged on to war are being slaughtered, and absent,
> I hear their groans and their cries and the words of those calling
> "Hannibal". What Tartarean river will ever expiate
> my crimes?' As he poured out these words, at the same time          565
> he looked at his right hand and raged with a desire for death.

As here, Hannibal's attempted suicide mentioned at 2.705 looks ahead to
his *actual* suicide beyond the confines of the poem, and is the closest Silius
can come to illustrating his demise without breaking historical strictures.
Concomitant with Hannibal's fall climaxing in book 17 is the dismemberment of Carthage itself, described as being held together by the one man
alone, one name alone, even (17.149–51): *stabat Carthago truncatis undique
membris | uni innixa uiro, tantoque fragore ruentem | Hannibal absenti
retinebat nomine molem*, 'with all her limbs severed, Carthage stood leaning
on one man alone, and Hannibal held up her mass from falling with a
massive crash with his name, even *in absentia*'. Carthage's complete reli-
ance on Hannibal alone posits a synecdochic relationship between the city
and its leader,[129] in the same way we observed with Hector (in the *Iliad*)

---

[128] Hannibal's death is also anticipated by the Sibyl at *Pun.* 13.892–3, the last lines of her prophecy to
Scipio: *pocula furtiuo rapiet properata ueneno | ac tandem terras longa formidine soluet*, 'he will
secretly snatch a cup in haste full of poison and finally loose the world from long-lasting terror'.

[129] On the synecdochic relationship between Hannibal and Carthage, see e.g. Kißel (1979): 33–4, 62–4;
Hardie (1993): 51; Marks (2008): 76–85; Cowan (2007a): 21–2; Tipping (2010): 66 n.41, 75, 181–2.

and Priam (in the *Aeneid*) for Troy, Pompey for the Roman Republic (in Lucan), and Theron for Saguntum. The security of Carthage depends entirely on that of its leader, as Scipio understands, prompting his challenge of Hannibal at Zama (17.512–18):

> Hannibal unus
> dum restet, non, si muris Carthaginis ignis
> subdatur caesique cadant exercitus omnis,
> profectum Latio. contra, si concidat unus,      515
> nequiquam fore Agenoreis cuncta arma uirosque.
> illum igitur lustrans circumfert lumina campo
> rimaturque ducem.

> While Hannibal alone
> stood firm, not even if fire brought down Carthage's walls
> or if the entire army fell slaughtered,
> would Rome make headway. Conversely, if he alone should fall,      515
> all Carthage's arms and men would be utterly useless.
> Therefore he casts his eyes all over the field, surveying,
> and he searches for that leader.

Carthage's 'arms and men' (516: *arma uirosque*) are nothing when weighed against Hannibal's singular importance.[130] Hannibal subsumes his own nation, he outbids the *Aeneid*'s famous credo. The contrast between one and many is hammered home. Without its leader, Carthage will fall to pieces, and we see this at the close of the epic (17.616–24): as Hannibal flees, Carthage opens her gates to Scipio, surrenders her war elephants, money, and has her fleet burned.[131]

Raymond Marks fruitfully compares Hannibal's demise in the final books of the *Punica* and his forfeiture of military prowess for a 'shadow of a great name' to Pompey's demise in Lucan's *BC*, with further allusions to the long-sought-after 'head' (*caput*) of each leader.[132] Just like the dismemberment of Carthage, Hannibal's downfall is implicitly articulated as the severing of a head from its body.[133] Hannibal's *caput* is directly sought out as an object of desire by Romans (*Pun.* 1.483–4, 2.26–7, 3.126–7, 5.151–3, 10.51–3, 11.318–20).[134]

---

[130] Tipping (2010): 181–2. On Silius' repurposing of the *incipit* of Virgil's *Aeneid* see Cowan (2007b): 26 n.91, Landrey (2014).

[131] See below pp. 256–71 for more on these and other scenes in *Pun.* 17.      [132] Marks (2008).

[133] Cf. Livy's description of Hannibal as the head (*caput*) and citadel (*arx*) not just of Carthage, but the whole of the Second Punic War (28.42).

[134] Marks (2008): 67; Bernstein (2017): *ad.* 2.26–7.

Particularly piquant (and gruesome) is the decapitation of Hannibal's brother and 'double' Hasdrubal (15.805–8), whose murder and corpse abuse function as a surrogate slaying of Hannibal himself.[135] Like Asbyte, Hasdrubal's head is thrust onto a pike and paraded before the Carthaginian leader (15.813–23). The orchestrator of this act, the (hyper-historical?) consul Gaius Claudius Nero, defines the decapitation of Hasdrubal as full retribution for Hannibal's victories earlier in the war (814–16), reworking the consul Flaminius' earlier claim at Trasimene that Hannibal's head alone, severed and paraded on a pike, could 'expiate' Rome's mass slain (5.151–3). Livy's Hannibal saw his and Carthage's future defeat in the death and decapitation of Hasdrubal (27.51.11–12: *Hannibal tanto simul publico familiarique ictus luctu, agnoscere se fortunam Carthaginis fertur dixisse*, 'Hannibal, struck simultaneously by public and private affliction, is said to have stated he recognized the fate of Carthage'),[136] and Silius prepares us for the symbolic dismemberment of Carthage and Hannibal through the surrogate mutilation of Hannibal's brother. Hannibal acted immediately and ragefully at the parading of Asbyte's head at Saguntum, but here, enfeebled, he resigns himself to defeat and removes his camp to avoid the dangers of battle.

Interest in the scene of Hasdrubal's abuse has typically focused on the possible allusions Silius is making between the ruthlessness of the emperor Nero and his historical namesake.[137] As Ben Tipping notes, the intertext with Virgil's scene of the parading of Nisus and Euryalus' heads in the *Aeneid* and Virgil's interjected disgust (9.465: *uisu miserabile*) should probably be read into Silius' scene, despite the poet's silence concerning the overt brutality of Gaius Claudius Nero's act.[138] Whether this reflects back on the emperor Nero is unclear, but probably not unlikely; emperor Nero had a penchant for severed heads (Tac. *Ann.* 14.57–64; [Sen.] *Oct.* 437–8).[139] Livy (27.51.11) says that Gaius Claudius Nero ordered Hasdrubal's head to be cast into Hannibal's camp, and Frontinus (*Str.* 2.9.2) tells us that Nero did this himself. As elsewhere, it's also hard not to see in this scene of corpse abuse the brutality of Rome's civil wars, in particular the abuse visited upon the emperor Galba and his adopted heir Piso.[140]

[135] Augoustakis (2003); Marks (2008): 78–9.    [136] Spaltenstein (1990): *ad* 15.813.
[137] E.g. Ahl, Davis, and Pomeroy (1986): 2540–2; McGuire (1997): 80, 143; Marks (2005a): 264–5; Tipping (2010): 43–4.
[138] Tipping (2010): 44, with Ahl, Davis, and Pomperoy (1986): 2541, *contra* Marks (2005a): 264 n.78.
[139] McGuire (1997): 143; Tipping (2010): 44.
[140] Ahl, Davis, and Pomeroy (1986): 2541; Tipping (2010): 44.

The anticipatory image of Hannibal's death at the end of book 2 also contains imagery linking Hannibal's itinerancy after Zama and Carthage's subjugation (*Pun.* 2.701–2: *uagus exul in orbe* | *errabit toto*, 'a roaming exile, he will wander the whole world') to Aeneas' (and Odysseus') wandering after the fall of Troy.[141] This is echoed again at 17.211–17 when Hannibal looks back in tears at Italy, as Silius compares him to an exile driven to distant shores leaving his homeland behind. Hannibal has spent so much of his adult life in Italy that it has become his home. Silius exploits this in a simile that recalls directly Aeneas' abandoning of Troy at *Aeneid* 3.10–12.[142] Whereas Aeneas looks back at his own devastated city, Hannibal looks back at the city he had hoped to destroy, the city that Aeneas' wanderings would eventually produce. He is, in this sense, a 'malfunctioning Aeneas',[143] trying to destroy the world Aeneas created. But by losing, he will essentially accomplish the same goal as Aeneas of forming and strengthening Roman identity.[144] He thus also accomplishes Jupiter's aim of testing the sluggish Romans with character-building warfare (*Pun.* 3.573–83).[145]

Lucan had repurposed these lines of Aeneas' flight from Troy for his own depiction of Pompey's flight from Rome at *BC* 3.3–7, as he looks back (like Aeneas) at the home he will never see again. Silius has neatly blended both passages for his description of Hannibal's flight from Italy, both of which play on his associative, competing roles of epic victor and victim.[146] Hannibal aims at victory from defeat like Aeneas, but like Pompey his flight from Rome will only guarantee his ultimate failure and death, Carthage crumbling concomitantly with him like the Republic's collapse with Pompey.[147] Both will leave deformed corpses lying far from the field of battle and far from home.

By presenting this anticipatory imagery of defeat and destruction at the end of Hannibal's successful conquest of Saguntum in *Punica* 2, Silius cleverly combines Saguntum's collapse with Troy's as the impetus for the

---

[141] Klaassen (2009): 103. See Bernstein (2017): *ad* 2.701–2 for additional poetic allusions.

[142] Marks (2003): 138–43 for this and other connections between Hannibal and Aeneas at the end of the *Punica*.

[143] Albrecht (1964): 173–7. See Ahl, Davis, and Pomeroy (1986): 2511–19, Fowler (2000): 93–107, Pomeroy (2000): 158–61, Klaassen (2009), Stocks (2014): 61–4. On Hannibal's distortion of epic heroism generally see Marks (2005a): 89–90, Ripoll (1998): 49–53, 128–30, Bernstein (2010): 279–81.

[144] Ahl, Davis, and Pomeroy (1986): 2516; Klaassen (2009): 105.

[145] On Jupiter's prophecy in Silius see Marks (2005a): 211–22, Jacobs (2010): 126–30, Fucecchi (2012).

[146] Mills (2009): 53–5. I discuss this feature of Hannibal's characterization in more detail in Chapter 6.

[147] On Silius' use of Lucan's Pompey from *BC* 3, see Ahl, Davis, and Pompery (1986): 2516–18, Fucecchi (1990): 159–60 and (2011a): 316–17, Stocks (2014): 69–70.

rising of Roman power. Just as Troy's fall in the *Aeneid* was necessary for providing the momentum which brought about the founding of Rome, so Saguntum's sacking facilitates (and functions as surrogate for) Rome's transition from city to imperial world power. Rome's pre-ordained rise comes at the expense of Hannibal and Carthage, whose loss is essentially collateral damage to Rome's continued ascent.

Thus at the outset of the war, following a siege that is supposed to foreshadow the fall of Rome,[148] Silius presents us with the image of Hannibal's deformed corpse (*Pun.* 2.707), symbolic of his failure and the destruction of his city. Saguntum in fact represents the only successful siege in the poem, setting a standard that will not be matched for the rest of the war: the poem effectively follows Hannibal from victory to defeat.[149] In his first major victory is an immediate anticipation of his ultimate failure,[150] and this tension between his role as victor and vanquished is captured in the splitting of his character's intertextual models between epic winners and losers. His *deformata membra* (2.707) recall Theron's *deforme cadauer* (2.269) moments after the latter has accomplished his greatest victory in slaying Asbyte, as well the bodies of the suicidal Saguntines (468: *deformia membris*), blending images of his own eventual defeat and suicide. As Hannibal will learn, in the *Punica* victory is never far from defeat.

## Conclusions

This chapter has explored Lucan's, Statius', and Silius' engagement with the normative features of corpse treatment represented by the most extreme example of abuse in Homer's *Iliad* and Virgil's *Aeneid*: the mutilation of an enemy head. These imperial epicists in every way pervert their poetic models through a similar engaged and disruptive *imitatio*, wrenching cracks in Homer's and Virgil's narrative frameworks. Earlier epic scenes of corpse violence are 'revived' and given new literary life, only to be savaged with even more detail and clinical specificity this time around. What's clear is the driving interplay and intertextuality between

---

[148] E.g. Venus' lines connecting the fall of Saguntum with the expected/feared fall of Rome, and linking these directly back to Troy (3.559–69). See Kißel (1979): 39–42, Jacobs (2010): 126–8 for valuable examinations of these lines.

[149] McGuire (1997): 208–9. Ripoll (1998): 421 n.206 and Marks (2005a): 91 with n.78 both juxtapose the trajectories of Hannibal and Scipio in the epic.

[150] Hannibal's surmounting of the Alps in *Pun.* 3 is similarly followed by Jupiter's prophecy of his inevitable defeat; see Vessey (1982): 333–4. On the theme of victory in defeat and defeat in victory in the *Punica* (for both Rome and Carthage) see now Dominik (2006): 119–23, Jacobs (2010). For the theme of Roman victory from defeat in the Republic generally, see Clark (2014).

these authors who compete to be different both from their epic predecessors and from each other.

My focus on corpse mistreatment as a way of approaching this poetic engagement is strategic in that it represents for the previous epic tradition a largely taboo subject. Homer presents corpse mutilation as something imagined in the heat of wrathful or vindictive fury, but these threats are rarely allowed to manifest, as this would carry his heroes beyond the limits of proper heroic conduct. In Virgil, we have more evidence of abuse taking place, yet at the final moment the poet shifts focus away from the act and leaves the audience to imagine a scene of horror that he pointedly refuses to narrate for us. What the post-Augustan epicists have done is place the focus directly on these scenes of horror, opening up and exploring the imagined or attempted threats and narrative silences, filling these gaps in a reactionary narrative engagement. There is an attempt in these imperial epics to make explicit tensions and silences that already aim at implicit suggestion. By referring allusively to the material of prior epic and transforming it, they implode the moral (and structural) compass that guides those poems through their inclusion of gruesome versions of threatened or implied scenes of corpse abuse. These scenes 'attack' the earlier models in Homer and Virgil, and explode the limits those poets imposed on expressions of corporal violence and anger.

While I suggest that the post-Augustan epicists all in a sense 're-stage' scenes from the earlier poems that touch elusively on *post mortem* decapitation and further *caput*-abuses, this supposition requires further unpacking. There is much socio-historical context at play in this intertextual dialogue (as I've hinted at), and I discuss this in more detail in the following chapters. But for now it will be useful to set out some general observations about poetics that are crucial for our understanding of intertextual engagement in these poems.

As an audience, we experience this poetic re-staging through a variety of referential effects that take us to a prior moment in epic poetic history.[151] This occurs most broadly through *Szenentypen* that invite us to read back to an earlier scene in an earlier epic poem as a narrative guide, which will then be inflected and transformed. When the foreign invader Hannibal meets Theron alone on the battlefield in a duel beneath the walls of his

---

[151] What follows in many ways combines the intertextual model of Barchiesi (2015) on Virgil's appropriation of Iliadic material (see also Barchiesi (2001): 141–54 more generally), with the practice of what has been called 'double allusion/imitation' or 'window reference', where one author imitates and repurposes two models, 'one of which is at the same time the model for the other', Hardie (1989): 4. Cf. Hinds (1998): 25–47.

opponent's home city with his fellow citizens looking on in horror, slays him, and abuses his corpse, we can be expected to read this as formulaically or analogically recasting the duel between Achilles and Hector in *Iliad* 22, but with an altered 'conclusion' in which the victor successfully mutilates his victim's corpse without the gods' intervention. Along with 'type-scenes' are more precise lexical cues that point to an earlier model, as when Hannibal 'buries' his sword in Theron's neck to close the duel (*Pun.* 2.260: *condit*), unmistakably repurposing Virgil's coinage of *condere* in this sense for Aeneas' death-blow to Turnus which famously closes their own duel and Virgil's poem (*Aen.* 12.951: *condit*). Silius contrastingly fills the narrative silence concerning the issue of Turnus' corpse treatment left unresolved in Virgil's poem by showing us what happens to the corpse of the defeated enemy, almost as a coda to his reading of the end of the *Aeneid*.

As the example here illustrates, these types of allusive cues point the reader to a model which itself has very often been given extra interpretive weight through an intermediary re-interpretation. In the above case, Virgil's duel between Aeneas and Turnus is already generated (and skilfully transformed) from the duel between Achilles and Hector in Homer. Silius uses both models, but repurposes them into a new whole. Similarly Statius' elaboration of the abuse dealt to Mezentius' corpse in the silence between *Aeneid* 10 and 11 for his scene of Tydeus' abuse by the Thebans in *Thebaid* 9, has already been modelled by Virgil on the Achaeans' ritual stabbing of Hector's corpse in *Iliad* 22. This is mediated again through Ovid's staging of the Calydonian boar hunt and the ritual stabbing of the beast by the famous band of hunters in *Metamorphoses* 8, which itself looks back to the earlier scenes in the *Aeneid* and the *Iliad* (among others).

This form of complex imitation is not simply poetic window-dressing. All of these reference points help in our analysis of Statius' scene, his characterization of Tydeus and the Theban warriors who mutilate him, and provide some sense of the poet's own interest in and interpretation of his models. Each model is identifiable in isolation but Statius has intricately woven them all together into a seamless coexistent whole. I do not mean to suggest that this kind of intertextual reading is the only way readers are able to gain understanding from these texts (far from it); rather, and simply, the hyper-sensitivity to earlier scenes and motifs forms a basic poetics of epic engagement that these poets take as a baseline for generic and generative composition (cf. Sen. *Ep.* 79.6, 84.2–5; Longinus 13.2–4). By tracing the literary cues we are able to follow the development of a particular motif stretched through multiple connected redefinitions of the epic landscape.

# CHAPTER 3

# Unburied Past: Lucan's Bellum ciuile

In the opening paragraph of his monumental book *The Roman Revolution*, Ronald Syme offers a striking corporeal metaphor for the state of Rome's *res publica* following the death of Augustus: 'The greatest of the Roman historians began his *Annals* with the accession to the Principate of Tiberius, stepson and son by adoption of Augustus, consort in his powers. Not until that day was the funeral of the Free State consummated in solemn and legal ceremony. The corpse had long been dead.'[1] The analogy would have resonated with Romans, not least Lucan. On a macroscopic and metapoetic level Lucan's epic reads rather like a funeral monument or epitaph for the death of Rome's *res publica*. But his view of the 'funeral' for the Republican state body is not as clear-cut as Syme's. What becomes immediately apparent is that – like the poem itself – there is little in Lucan's treatment of death rites (for physical bodies and/or bodies of state) that is traditional or typical. This is at least in part a consequence of the oddity of Lucan's approach to death: despite the almost overwhelming emphasis in the *Bellum ciuile* on shattered and fractured 'bodies', Lucan everywhere delays, avoids, or even reverses the final death-blow. The poem is heaped with figures continually on the *verge* of death, at the point of expiration. And when bodies do finally expire, they have an odd way of coming back to life. It's hard, it seems, to bury something that refuses to die. This chapter treats Lucan's obsession with distorted death rites largely through a close analysis of three 'deadly' characters: Pompey, Caesar, and Erichtho. The elderly survivor's recollection of civil strife under Marius and Sulla in *BC* 2 offers an *entrée* to this material, as the themes illustrated therein set the stage for the more expansive readings that follow.

---

[1] Syme (1939): 1.

## PTSD

The first extended scene in Lucan's *BC* that engages with issues of funeral rites forms the bulk of the anonymous old man's agonizing spoken narrative from 2.67–233.[2] With the civil war between Pompey and Caesar beginning to take shape, Lucan looks back to the earlier Roman civil war through the voice of an elderly survivor who takes over the role of narrator and recounts the violence Marius and Sulla visited upon Rome from 87–82 BCE. His tale is an anamnestic horror show of atrocities. He recalls cases of slaughter, mutilation, decapitation, suicides, piles of corpses decaying, and bodies blocking the flow of the Tiber. The scene functions as a prelude – historically and narratively – to the atrocities of the 'current' civil war between Caesar and Pompey, and as a baseline of brutality and cruelty that Lucan's narrator and his characters will aim to eclipse.[3] The scene ends with Lucan's description of the elders almost prophetically looking ahead to what they know will be a war *worse than* the civil war they remember (2.231–3). This earlier narrative (the survivor's 'poem') is terrible, but Lucan's will be much worse (*BC* 1.1: *bella . . . plus quam ciuilia*).

The survivor's story is punctuated by descriptions of funeral perversion. 'Tombs', we are told, 'were stuffed with fugitives, the living intermingled with buried bodies' (2.152–3: *busta repleta fuga, permixtaque uiua sepultis | corpora*), the mass packed tombs evocative of Roman collective 'stench-pits' (*puticuli*).[4] But here the lines between the living and the dead are blurred. The imagery recalls Virgil's description of Mezentius' method of torture in the *Aeneid*, whereby he would fasten rotting corpses to living bodies and wait for them to die (*Aen.* 8.485–8). But now, the living seek out the dead voluntarily, and breach their tombs to do so.[5] There is here a whiff of Erichtho's tomb-raiding and living among the dead in Thessaly (e.g. 6.511–12: *desertaque busta | incolit et tumulos expulsis obtinet umbris*, 'she lives in abandoned tombs and occupies graves after driving out their ghosts').[6] The witch's presence stains the epic, particularly in scenes related to funeral rites. As often, Lucan aims to paint civil wars (past, present, future) as boundary-breaching or dissolving, and this includes the boundaries separating life and death: civil war is like a wa(l)king death.[7]

---

[2] On these lines see esp. Conte (1968), Fantham (1992a): 90–121, Fratantuono (2012): 59–66, Ambühl (2015): 309–36.

[3] See Henderson (1998): 177–81, Ambühl (2015): 335, Gowing (2005): 85–6 on the failure here of memory to inspire aversion to a renewal of civil wars.

[4] On *puticuli* see Hopkins (1983): 207–10.      [5] Arweiler (2006); Fratantuono (2012): 63.

[6] On Erichtho and her witchcraft see below pp. 158–67.

[7] See pp. 167–9 for more on this feature of Lucan's poetics.

A series of suicides climaxes with a man constructing his own pyre and immolating himself Hercules-like (2.159: *desilit in flammas et, dum licet, occupat ignes,* 'he leaps into the flames and, while he can, he takes the fires'). This is the only way to ensure his corpse will be 'properly' handled. Subsequently, to drive the point home, we see just how difficult it is for the survivors to cremate the dead.[8] The piles of corpses lie rotting, the decay blurring their features so family members cannot distinguish one from another (166–8). The speaker recalls his own personal experience trying to provide funeral rites for his brother (169–73):

> meque ipsum memini, caesi deformia fratris
> ora rogo cupidum uetitisque inponere flammis,
> omnia Sullanae lustrasse cadauera pacis
> perque omnis truncos, cum qua ceruice recisum
> conueniat, quaesisse, caput.

> I remember how I myself yearned to put my slaughtered brother's
> deformed face on the pyre and impermissible flames,
> how I surveyed all the corpses of 'Sulla's peace'
> and through all the trunks sought out a neck
> to fit his severed head.

The syntax of the final clause is chopped up to recall the body's mutilation, and the confusion reflects the speaker's inability to locate the fragmented pieces of his brother – we're looking for the *caput* (delayed until verse 173), he's looking for the *truncus*. He doesn't tell us whether he was ultimately able to attach the disfigured head to its body and burn the entire corpse of his brother.[9] Much of the imagery in the speaker's story, and particularly this scene, anticipates Pompey's death.[10] Pompey's son, without direct knowledge of the location of his father's *truncus*, which was burned separately on the Egyptian shore, will declare his intention to provide flames for his father's severed head (9.158–61), but this wish goes unfulfilled.[11] Ultimately the task falls to Caesar to provide burial for Pompey's head in Egypt (9.1089–93).[12]

Elsewhere, the tomb of Catulus is propitiated with blood offerings, but it is *human* blood, that of Marius Gratidianus,[13] and the shade rejects the

---

[8] Fantham (1992a): *ad* 2.157–9.

[9] See Thorne (2011): 372–4 on the 'crisis of memory' of prior civil war vis-à-vis proper funeral rites here.

[10] Fantham (1992a): *ad* 2.160–1, 166–7, 172.    [11] See p. 138.    [12] See pp. 139–41.

[13] See Conte (1968): 234–6, Fantham (1992a): *ad* 2.173–93 and *ad locc.*, Chiesa (2005): 13–14, Dinter (2012): 46–7, Ambühl (2015): 314–20. Cf. Q. Cicero *Comment. pet.* 10.1–7, Sall. *Hist* 1 fr. 44 Maurenbrecher, Sen. *De ira* 3.18. See also above p. 44.

offering (174–6): *cum uictima tristes | inferias Marius forsan nolentibus umbris | pendit inexpleto non fanda piacula busto*, 'when Marius, as victim, with the shades perhaps denying the grim offerings, paid out a wicked sacrifice to an unsatisfied tomb'. Elaine Fantham notes the confusion here of *inexpleto busto*: 'Either L[ucan] contrasts the insatiable thirst of the burial ground with the undemanding shade, or *inexpletus* . . . means rather "unsatisfied by this wrong kind of atonement".'[14] Take your pick; in either case, the funereal context is totally distorted, as are the implicit links to epic predecessor scenes like Achilles' offering of prisoners to Patroclus' shade (*Il.* 21.26–32, 23.175–6), Achilles' (shade's) own demand for the sacrifice of Polyxena at his tomb (Ov. *Met.* 13.439–82), and Aeneas' (silent) sacrifice of prisoners to Pallas' shade (*Aen.* 10.517–20, 11.81–2). In the previous epics, the brutality of this offering is clear, but each poet excises any specific detail about the sacrifice of the living victims. Ovid's narrative is the most explicit, but emphasis is on Polyxena's courage and poise in facing death. More frightening is Catullus' depiction in his epyllion (64.368–70): *alta Polyxenia madefient caede sepulcra; | quae, uelut ancipiti succumbens uictima ferro, | proiciet truncum summisso poplite corpus*, 'the high tomb will drip with Polyxena's slaughter, who, like a victim falling beneath the double-edged sword, kneeling, will toss down her body, her trunk'. The allusion to the propitiating of Achilles' shade is clear (362). Catullus handles the scene with brutal realism, but this is still miles from Lucan's torture scene.[15] Lucan has made a point of focusing directly on the description of the sacrifice in grisly specificity (*BC* 2.177–93). The poet lavishes detail on the torture of Marius Gratidianus, who is slaughtered to the point of death but not *beyond* it (178–80): *uidimus et toto quamuis in corpore caeso | nil animae letale datum, moremque nefandae | dirum saeuitiae, pereuntis parcere morti*, 'and although his whole body was slashed nothing fatal was administered, and we saw the horrible practice of unspeakable savagery: to keep death from the dying man'. As he hovers somewhere between living and dying, his body feeds an 'unsatisfied tomb' while he lacks the honour of one.[16]

The elderly survivor closes with the only real funeral in this story, Sulla's own (2.221–2): *hisne salus rerum, felix his Sulla uocari, | his meruit tumulum medio sibi tollere Campo?*, 'for this did Sulla deserve to be called "Saviour of the State," or "Lucky," or to raise a tomb for himself in the middle of the Campus?' Sulla is given a public funeral and buried on the Campus

[14] Fantham (1992a): *ad* 2.174–5.
[15] For these and other poetic sacrificial allusions, see esp. Ambühl (2015): 314–20.
[16] Hinard (1984): 303–7 and (1985): 377–80 argues that the stylistic (historical) mutilation of Marius Gratidianus functioned as a perverse reversal of an aristocratic funeral.

Martius,[17] the site of his executions of the Samnites captured after the
battle of the Colline Gate. Lucan lumps this together with the massacre of
Marian soldiers after Praeneste to heighten the effects of civil war horror, in
defiance, it seems, of historical accuracy.[18] Following a lengthy description
of the unburied bodies piled high on the Campus (196–220), the description of Sulla's *tumulus* at the same location is a gruesome juxtaposition.[19]
Sulla's tomb is presented in the poem in contrast to and at the (literally,
public[20]) expense of the funeral perversions and 'unburials' of his civil war.
His single tomb comes with the denial of proper burial for the countless
multitude of civil war victims.[21]

The specific focus on Sulla's funeral and on the abuse and funeral denial
of 'a Marius' might allow us to infer a deeper subtext here. Earlier Lucan
had alluded elliptically to the *post mortem* fate of Gaius Marius, the uncle of
Marius Gratidianus, with a further mention of the unburied ghosts of
Sulla's slaughter on the Campus (1.580–3):

> e medio uisi consurgere Campo
> tristia Sullani cecinere oracula manes,
> tollentemque caput gelidas Anienis ad undas
> agricolae fracto Marium fugere sepulchro.
>
> From the middle of the Campus are seen to rise
> the shades of Sulla, singing dreadful oracles,
> and while Marius was lifting his head toward Anio's cool waters
> the farmers fled from the shattered his tomb.

The shades of Sulla's victims,[22] consigned to death without funerals, whom
he watched die without disturbance or care (2.207–9),[23] rise from the
Campus here as a foreshadowing of the plethoric details Lucan will invest
in their corporeal dissolving *into* the field in book 2. The 'shattered tomb'
and waters of the Anio hint at Sulla's Erichthonian raiding of Marius' tomb

---

[17] Cf. Cic. *Leg.* 2.57; App. *B Ciu.* 1.105–6; Plut. *Sull.* 38    [18] Braund (1992): 240 n.197.
[19] Henderson (1998): 179.
[20] Sulla's funeral (to add insult to injury) was paid for at public expense, a day of holiday was declared, and the rites constituted one of the most ostentatious funeral celebrations Rome had ever seen; see Flower (1996): 123–4.
[21] On Lucan's inversion of the Virgilian theme of 'one for the many' see Hardie (1993): 7–8, 10–11, 30–2, 53–6.
[22] See Bagnani (1955), rightly, for *Sullani manes* as the ghosts of those killed by Sulla as opposed to Sulla's *own* ghost.
[23] Sulla's voyeuristic madness and rejection of funerals for the dead here anticipates Caesar's viewing of the corpses of those slain at Pharsalus the morning after the major battle, also deprived of funeral rites (7.786–99); see below pp. 148–52. See further Fantham (1992a): *ad* 2.207–8, Leigh (1997): 30, 289, Narducci (2002): 119.

and the scattering of his decaying remains in that river in 82 BCE.[24] Pliny
notes that Sulla, recognizing that his mistreatment of Marius' interred
corpse might come back to haunt him, made arrangements to have his own
corpse cremated.[25] By alluding back narratively and forward chronologically to the description of Sulla the tomb-raider and the ghosts of his victims
still unpacified, the inclusion of Sulla's own tomb at the end of the
survivor's tale is all the more unsettling: the most bloodthirsty character
in this earlier civil war is the only one to emerge physically unscathed,
gifted with a place in Elysium (6.787).[26]

## Pompey's Rest, in Pieces

I have devoted some space to Pompey's death in *BC* 8.[27] Here I shall look
more closely at his funeral and the extended rites that accompany it. The
description of Pompey's physical funeral occupies very little narrative space
in the poem, but the scene is a stunning perversion of traditional Roman
practice which follows naturally from Pompey's perverse murder and
mutilation. Lucan wastes no time parroting epic conventions to heighten
the shock and outrage at the miserable end to his hero of the Republican
cause.

From the outset, Pompey's funeral is farce, as Lucan describes Fortuna
rushing to throw together a grave for Pompey out of pity or, more sinisterly,
so as to deny him the chance of a better one (8.713–14). In death Pompey
mirrored Virgil's Priam (*Aen.* 2.550–8), and it takes the efforts of a devotee to
fashion something resembling a funeral, which Priam seems to have lacked.[28]
A follower of Pompey called Cordus emerges from the woods to retrieve the
body. The presence of a solitary mortal charged with caring for an epic hero's
corpse sharply juxtaposes the divine treatment Sarpedon, Patroclus, and
Hector receive in the *Iliad*.[29] Cordus engages the sea in something of a
warped *Leichenkampf* (*BC* 8.723–4, 753–4), like those over the dead Patroclus

---

[24] Pliny *HN* 7.187. Cf. Cic. *Leg.* 2.56–7; Val. Max. 9.2.1, and my earlier discussion pp. 43–4. See Roche
(2009): *ad* 1.582–3. Whether we are to imagine the tomb as being shattered by Sulla or by Marius'
shade (Roche (2009): *ad* 1.583 with Sil. *Pun.* 8.642) is incidental, considering the fate of Marius'
corpse at Sulla's hands, as Lucan's audience will have known.

[25] Hinard (1985): 47; Kyle (1998): 220 and 234 n.50; Hope (2000): 114–15.

[26] Ahl (1976): 139 with n.19 notes that in the *BC* the adjective *Sullanus* evokes bloodthirstiness and
ferocity.

[27] See pp. 68–79.

[28] Priam unburied: Man. 4.64–5; Sen. *Tro.* 55–6, 140–1. Pompey unburied: Vell. Pat. 2.53.3; App. *B
Ciu.* 2.86 (fragmentary rites); Narducci (2002): 113–14.

[29] Galtier (2010): 195.

and Sarpedon.[30] In the end, however, the sea relents and even aids Cordus in heaving Pompey's body to shore. Cordus pilfers half-baked embers from a neighbouring pyre and constructs a tiny cremation pit in the sand (756: *exigua . . . scrobe*), the size of which is set in sharp contrast to the 'Mr Big' it's meant to contain.[31] As Annemarie Ambühl has argued most extensively, Lucan likely has in mind here the story of Eteocles and Polynices whose mingled remains on a pyre outside Thebes brought a *post mortem* reigniting of their own personal civil war. The Theban myth and its Greek tragedies were not foreign to Lucan's conception of internecine horrors, as he mentions explicitly the fractured flames of the Theban pyre housing the remains of the ever-duelling brothers Polynices and Eteocles at *BC* 1.549–52 as mythic context for his poem.[32] Whether or not Lucan is reactivating this imagery here (and I'm convinced he is), the fact that it requires stolen fire and contaminated embers to kindle Pompey's own pyre is in itself pathetic and pointedly grotesque.

There is further play on epic tropes as Cordus takes broken fragments of a small boat to place in the pit (755: *lacerae fragmenta carinae*). The contrast here between the major tree-felling scenes in Homer, Ennius, and Virgil for the construction of a funeral pyre is typically shocking and underscores the pathos of Pompey's funeral.[33] The image borrows from Manilius (4.54–5: *ut corpus sepeliret naufragus ignis | eiectaeque rogum facerent **fragmenta carinae**?*, '[who could believe] that shipwreck fire would burn your corpse and scraps of a shattered boat would form a pyre?'),[34] who likewise contrasts Pompey's magnificent deeds with the exiguous nature of his death rites. The Manilian image is spliced with Alcyone's fear that her sea-bound husband Ceyx will end up a shipwreck victim lost in the waves at Ovid's *Metamorphoses* 11.428–9: *et laceras nuper tabulas in litore uidi | et saepe in tumulis sine corpore nomina legi*, 'I saw recently wrecked ship beams on the shore, and I've often read names on tombs lacking bodies'.[35] Ovid is already 'reading' (*legi; tabulas* also has literary overtones) Virgil's earlier

---

[30] Fucecchi (2011b): 254.

[31] Mayer (1981): *ad* 8.756, 771. On the juxtaposition generally see Rimell (2015): 243–4.

[32] Ambühl (2015): 78–83, 276–85. Burck (1981): 481–2 and Lovatt (1999): 143–4 have shown that Statius borrowed from Lucan's depiction of Pompey's death for his own description of the cremation of Polynices in *Theb.* 12. No doubt he was reaffirming Lucan's own allusion to the Greek myth. On Statius' scene, see below pp. 229–32.

[33] Mayer (1981): 169; Erasmo (2008): 117. Major epic tree-felling scenes: Hom. *Il.* 23.108–26, Enn. *Ann.* 175–9 Skutsch, Verg. *Aen.* 6.176–82, 11.133–8.

[34] Mayer (1981): *ad* 8.755.

[35] Bruère (1951) examines connections between Pompey-Cornelia and Ceyx-Alcyone throughout the *BC*.

description of Priam's death in *Aeneid* 2 – e.g. 2.558: *sine nomine corpus* –
which, as I've noted, is the major model for Lucan's construction of
Pompey's death-scene.[36] Like Pompey's (and Priam's) *truncus*, Ceyx's
wave-battered body is washed ashore (*Met.* 11.723–30), but his metamorphosis into a halcyon bird saves him the ignominy of the cursory funeral
Pompey is forced to receive. Lucan articulates that Cordus cannot even free
enough space for embers to be placed beneath Pompey's corpse, so he's
kindled with flames at his side (*BC* 8.756–8): *nobile corpus | robora nulla
premunt, nulla strue membra recumbunt: | admotus Magnum, non subditus,
accipit ignis*, 'no wood presses upon the well-known corpse, the limbs lie on
no heap: the fire receives Magnus not from below, but at his side'. The
emphasis here is on negation (*nulla, nulla, non*),[37] and, as we shall see, this
forms the basis of Lucan's extended narrative of Pompey's funeral.

Cordus then provides a lament over Pompey's corpse which again
highlights absence (759–75):

> ille sedens iuxta flammas 'o maxime' dixit
> 'ductor et Hesperii maiestas nominis una,                                    760
> si tibi iactatu pelagi, si funere nullo
> tristior iste rogus, manes animamque potentem
> officiis auerte meis: iniuria fati
> hoc fas esse iubet; ne ponti belua quicquam,
> ne fera, ne uolucres, ne saeui Caesaris ira                                   765
> audeat, exiguam, quantum potes, accipe flammam
> Romana succense manu. fortuna recursus
> si det in Hesperiam, non hac in sede quiescent
> tam sacri cineres, sed te Cornelia, Magne,
> accipiet nostraque manu transfundet in urnam.                                 770
> interea paruo signemus litora saxo,
> ut nota sit busti; siquis placare peremptum
> forte uolet plenos et reddere mortis honores,
> inueniat trunci cineres et norit harenas
> ad quas, Magne, tuum referat caput'.                                          775

> Sitting close to the flames, he said: 'O mightiest
> leader and singular splendour of the Hesperian name,                          760
> if this pyre is worse for you than both being jostled by the sea,
> or lacking a tomb, then avert your shade and strong spirit
> from my services. The inequity of Fate
> orders this to be right, lest any sea-monster,
> or beast, or birds, or the wrath of savage Caesar                             765

yearn for you; accept as much as you can, a tiny flame,
lit by a Roman hand. If Fortune grants a homecoming
to Hesperia, not in this spot will rest
such sacred ashes, but, Magnus, Cornelia
will accept you, and pour you into the urn from my hand.          770
Meanwhile let me mark the shore with a small rock
to mark your grave; if anyone might want to appease you in death
by chance and offer full honours of death,
let him happen upon your trunk's ashes and recognize the sands
to which, Magnus, he should restore your head.'                  775

Most apparent is the absence of Pompey's wife Cornelia, who is imagined
as receiving the ashes in Italy and not at the site of cremation in Egypt.
Cordus had earlier expressed reserved joy that Cornelia was not present at
this sham funeral to provide the torch for the pyre and the traditional
lament (739–42). This will instead be his task, as he assumes the role
typically reserved for the widow or eldest son,[38] as well as acting as an
'ill-equipped corpse-burner' (738: *sordidus ustor*). The funeral is lowly and
on foreign soil (hence the focus on the ashes' hopeful return to Italy at 767–
70), in sharp contrast to the funeral Pompey should have received. Cordus
ends his lament, the last word in fact, with a chilling reminder of the most
obvious absence in the scene: Pompey's severed head (774–5). The focus of
Pompey's murder had been squarely his head: its severing, continued
functioning, impaling, and embalming. But with the head *en route* to
Ptolemy – and ultimately Caesar – Lucan shifts focus to the headless
corpse. For the first time in seventy lines we are reminded that this funeral
is being conducted over a *truncus*. Cordus hopes someone will eventually
reunite the head with its torso, but his prayer for reunion only serves to
recall the scene of dismemberment, and so the lament ends on a grisly note.

Again Lucan contrasts here the discrepancy between the 'greatness' of
Pompey and his paltry funeral ritual (670: *Magne*; 771: *paruo*). The
juxtaposition and the funereal context recall Ovid's requiem for Achilles
at the close of *Metamorphoses* 12, one of the handful of examples in the
poem of a body bypassing metamorphosis for death and burial (*Met.*
12.612–18):[39]

---

[38] Keith (2008): 245–8.

[39] Ovid is partial to funereal surrogates and cenotaphs: see Hardie (2002): 84–91. For 'traditional' (I'm
being generous) burials/funerals in the *Metamorphoses*: 2.325–8 (Phaethon); 2.619–30 (Coronis);
4.166 (Pyramus and Thisbe); 8.234–6 (Icarus); 9.229–72 (Hercules); 11.332 (Chione); 13.423–8 (sons
of Hecuba); 13.523–35 (Polyxena: half-completed?); 13.583–4 (Memnon); 14.441–4 (Caieta); 14.744–
53 (Iphis).

iam timor ille Phrygum, decus et tutela Pelasgi
**nominis**, Aeacides, **caput** insuperabile bello,
arserat: armarat deus idem idemque cremarat;
iam **cinis** est, et de tam **magno** restat Achille                    615
nescio quid **paruam**, quod non bene **conpleat urnam**,
at uiuit totum quae gloria **conpleat** orbem

Now that terror of the Phrygians, glory and protection of the Pelasgian
name, Achilles, head-honcho, unconquerable in war,
had burned: the same god had armed him and cremated him.
Now he's ash, and from so great Achilles there remains                   615
something that would not even sufficiently fill a small urn.
But his fame lives on to fill the whole world.

Like Pompey, Achilles is too big (*magno . . . Achille*) to justify the scanty
funeral ash he produces, barely able to fill a small urn (*paruam . . . urnam*).
Ovid sets Achilles' pitiful funeral ash and tomb against the boundlessness
of the hero's fame, which fills the whole world. As Hardie notes, this
variation of the *topos* 'the world as a tomb' resonates with Lucan's contrasting presentation of Pompey's pitiful grave on the Egyptian shore and
his eternal *tumulus* bounded only by the limits of the earth (*BC* 8.798–9):
*Romanum nomen et omne | imperium Magno tumuli est modus*, 'the name of
Rome and all its empire are the limits of Magnus' tomb'.[40] Pompey too
will have an immortal fame that fills the world and transcends his physically deficient grave which is in no way able to mar his *fama* (858–9): *nil ista
nocebunt | famae busta tuae.*

For now at least it is Pompey's physical body, not his reputation, that
preoccupies Cordus and Lucan. Cordus is compelled by duty to perform
rites over Pompey's corpse (763: *officiis . . . meis*),[41] but the more practical
reason is to prevent the corpse being outraged by beasts (764–6): *ne ponti
belua quicquam, | ne fera, ne uolucres, ne saeui Caesaris ira | audeat, exiguam,
quantum potes, accipe flammam*, 'lest any sea-monster, or beast, or birds, or
the wrath of savage Caesar yearn for you; accept as much as you can, a tiny
flame'. I have detailed earlier the standard epic fear of corpse mutilation by
animals, instigated by the *Iliad*'s proem (1.4–5),[42] and Cordus here is
attempting to spare Pompey that fate and the fate of his own soldiers at
Pharsalus, whose corpses glut all forms of Thessalian beast (cf. *BC* 7.825–
46). Yet it's Caesar's presence capping this list of scavengers that is most

---

[40] Hardie (2002): 86 n.52.
[41] Coffee (2009): 154 notes that this is the only act in the poem described as an *officium*.
[42] See Chapter 1 on Homer and Virgil.

shocking and might be a more pointed comment on Lucan's description of Caesar after the battle at Pharsalus breakfasting atop dead Pompeian soldiers (7.792–4): *epulisque patur | ille locus, uoltus ex quo faciesque iacentum | agnoscat*, 'a place for eating is set up from where he can spy the faces and the features of the dead'. As was the case at Pharsalus there is the suggestion of cannibalism in these lines as Caesar's savagery uncomfortably straddles the line between man and beast.[43] After that battle, birds drop (propitiatory?) blood and severed human limbs from the sky onto Caesar's face (838–40). When we next see him, Caesar is described as 'satiated with the slaughter of Emathia' (9.950: *Emathia satiatus clade*; cf. 10.74: *sanguine Thessalicae cladis perfusus*, '[Caesar] drenched with blood of Thessalian slaughter'); earlier his wrath had been '*un*satiated with slaughter' (7.802: *nondum satiata caedibus ira*).[44] There are traces of Erichtho's battlefield grazing here (cf. 6.543–53, 577–88), and her work in concert with beasts, tearing human flesh, seems to be echoed in this description of Caesar as an animal scavenger.

The small funeral flame is at least hot enough to provide Lucan space to indulge his taste for gore (8.777–8): *carpitur et lentum Magnus destillat in ignem | tabe fouens bustum*, 'Magnus is consumed and melts into the sluggish fire, stoking the pyre with slime'. The detail is 'realistic if macabre',[45] and the image of Pompey distilling into the fire creates a gruesome contrast with the more sombre description of Pompey's ashes being poured from Cordus' hand to Cornelia's funerary urn in the lines quoted above (770: *transfundet in urnam*).

Cordus breaks off the ceremony and hides, but devotion and Lucan's apostrophic reproaches compel him to complete his task (785–6). He removes the half-burnt bones (786–7: *semusta . . . ossa*) from the pyre, not yet separated from their muscles, and quenches them in the sea. The remains are heaped up and sprinkled with a bit of dirt, covered with a rock which he inscribes with an epitaph (793): *hic situs est Magnus*, 'here lies Magnus'.[46] The juxtaposition between the funeral rites for Patroclus in the *Iliad* (*Il.* 23.236–57) and Pallas in the *Aeneid* (esp. *Aen.* 9.59–99) is pointedly jarring. In particular, the special care given to Patroclus' bones and the

[43] Ambühl (2015): 177.
[44] Ambühl (2015): 338–9. See Ahl (1976): 213–14, Petrone (1996): 143–4, Pagán (2000): 431, Narducci (2002): 229, Chaudhuri (2014): 178–80 on allusions to cannibalism in Caesar's dining on the battlefield in *BC* 7. See Ambühl (2015): 273–6 for possible allusions to sacrificial perversion in Soph. *Ant.*
[45] Noy (2000): 190.    [46] See Malamud (1995): 178, Spencer (2005): 61–2, Day (2013): 224–5.

enormous size of his burial mound stand in dramatic opposition to Magnus' half-burnt bones and speck of dirt.[47]

Alison Keith has argued that Cordus' disposal of Pompey's corpse is 'ritually correct', considering he burns the corpse on a pyre, quenches the remains in liquid, and collects the ashes.[48] While technically true, all of these actions are distorted in ways that highlight ritual corruption:[49] traditional liquids like fresh water or wine are replaced by sea water; Cordus covers the ashes with a rock to prevent even a light breeze from carrying them away. Most striking, the remains themselves are half-burnt, with muscles and bone marrow still largely intact. For Romans, who were entirely preoccupied with funeral rites, the idea of a half-burnt body was explicitly a source of horror for the living and an affront to the dead.[50] Lucan's description of Pompey's half-cremation and abuse has some disturbing resonances with the evidence of the mistreatment of the corpse of Pompey's father (Pompeius Strabo) after his death in 87 BCE. The elder Pompey was ripped from his pyre, half-cremated, and his corpse was abused and dragged through the streets (e.g. Vell. Pat. 2.21.4; Plut. *Pomp.* 1.2).[51] While Pompeius Magnus' own death and abuse provided sufficient material for elaboration, Lucan will also have had in mind the cremation disruption of his father here. Lucan's scene of Pompey's half-completed cremation was meant to shock and appal his audience, and the fact that Cordus attempts to adhere to the traditional framework of funerary rites but fails so spectacularly makes the scene all the more disturbing.

The focus on ritual corruption has everywhere the stain of the ritually corrupt Erichtho, whom Lucan fashions raiding funerals and snatching half-burnt corpses from funeral pyres in the service of her dark arts. Consider her manner of thievery (*BC* 6.533–7):

> fumantis iuuenum cineres ardentiaque ossa
> e mediis rapit illa rogis ipsamque parentes
> quam tenuere facem, nigroque uolantia fumo
> feralis fragmenta tori uestesque fluentis
> colligit in cineres et olentis membra fauillas.

> Smoking ashes of the young and burning bones
> she snatches from the middle of the pyre and the very torch

---

[47] Lausberg (1985): 1596 n.117.   [48] Keith (2008): 247–8, with Toynbee (1971): 50.

[49] Galtier (2010): 196 argues that Cordus cannot compensate for Cornelia's presence not only because he's ill-equipped to play the part of a mourning widow, but also because of his lower social rank. See also Loupiac (1998): 169. Keith (2008): 251 notes that Cordus carries out the obligation owed to the *patronus* by his social inferiors.

[50] Kyle (1998): 222; Noy (2000); Erasmo (2008): 211 n.18.   [51] See p. 43.

which the parents hold. And she collects fragments of the funeral
bed flying around in black smoke, and robes dissolving
into ashes and embers smelling of limbs.

I have noted how the embalming of Pompey's head resembles Erichtho's
mutilation of a head during Lucan's description of the witch's atrocities
(6.566–9).[52] Just as she was present symbolically in this earlier scene, so too
she is recalled as Cordus hastily removes Pompey's half-burnt limbs from
the pyre.

Erichtho casts spells to ensure the war remains in Thessaly so she will
have fodder – in the form of fields of corpses – for more witchcraft. She had
expressed the 'hope to dismember the corpses of slaughtered kings' (6.584:
*caesorum truncare cadauera regum | sperat*) and steal Hesperian ashes and
the bones of noblemen (6.585–6). The image of truncated, 'chopped up
kings' and noblemen's bones looks ahead to Pompey's death and mutilation and the events of book 8 that leave him a literal *truncus*. We may even
be tempted to read 'Caesar(s)' into *caesorum regum*,[53] in which case
Erichtho has both a telescopic future-view toward the Ides and Caesar's
own shredded corpse, and a keen eye for Ovid's wordplay at *Metamorphoses*
15.840 of Caesar's sliced-up body: *caeso de corpore*. Her main concern,
however, eschews all implicit allusion: she wants to see what she can steal
from the bodies of Pompey and Caesar at Pharsalus (*BC* 6.587–8). While
this desire is not directly granted to her, Pompey's stolen embalmed head
and half-burnt torso actualize the kind of demonic witchcraft Erichtho
champions. She's outwardly the embodiment of the anti-funeral, and the
epic – and its climax of Pompey's death and funeral – is saturated with her
spells and allegorical presence.[54]

These then are the physical funeral rites for Pompey in the poem. They
are hurried, half-complete, distorted, and ritually corrupt. But they represent only a small part of a larger picture of Lucan's extended requiem for
Pompey. Just as Lucan refashions Pompey's death scene and mutilation in
a variety of forms before and after the actual scene of the crime, he also
scatters elements of Pompey's death rites throughout the epic as bizarre
supplements to the funeral Cordus provides on the Egyptian shore.[55] Many

---

[52] See p. 71.

[53] For Lucan's play on Caesar and 'slaughter/sever' (*caedere*) see Henderson (1998): 204 with n.136,
Korenjak (1996): *ad* 6.584, Narducci (2002): 223.

[54] As we shall see shortly, however, the situation is more complicated than this, as ultimately Erichtho
provides the only 'successful' funeral in the poem, in a typical Lucanian paradox; outwardly her
many atrocities include abuses aimed at the dead and buried (see pp. 158–67).

[55] What follows here is an expansion and elaboration of material in Loupiac (1998): 167–72.

of these are in the form of negative enumeration,[56] in which Lucan as narrator and other characters imagine a better set of circumstances for Pompey's end. Coupled with these are scenes of mock or substitute funerals, a eulogy *in absentia*, imagined parades, and other funereal features which, taken together, create a full picture of the grand spectacle Lucan imagines Pompey *would have* received at Rome.

The disparate funeral elements Lucan presents here square with what we know of Roman aristocratic funeral procedure as set out by Polybius (6.53–4; cf. Dion. Hal. *Ant. Rom.* 7.72). This included a procession of the corpse accompanied by family and friends, actors wearing masks (*imagines*) of deceased relatives, professional mourners, and musicians. The corpse was brought to the forum, whereupon the eldest son (or another family member) delivered a funeral oration praising his father and recalling his exploits (*laudatio funebris*). The corpse was buried or cremated, and a death-mask (*imago*) was made to recreate exactly the features of the deceased. All of these elements appear in Lucan's re-imagining of Pompey's death rites, but they are importantly scattered, distorted, or unfulfilled. Lucan creates a multiplicity of funerals or funeral contexts for Pompey, all of which fly in the face of his actual funeral. In their fragmented state, these rites feign propriety and recall the fragmentation of Pompey's own body and the body of the Republican cause he represents.

The first example of this extended funeral for Pompey occurs in book 3. Lucan has included the standard epic *topos* of a catalogue of troops; all the people are listed who will fight for Pompey and the Republican cause against Caesar (*BC* 3.169–297). The catalogue already distorts the features of a typical epic catalogue of troops,[57] but Lucan's summary of peoples warps distortion further into perversion (290–2):

> tot inmensae comites missura ruinae
> exciuit populos et dignas funere Magni
> exequias Fortuna dedit.

> Fortune, about to send companions for his massive downfall,
> called on so many people and provided obsequies worthy
> of Magnus' funeral.

The mass of troops, outnumbering the host of Cyrus, Xerxes, and Agamemnon (284–90), are dramatically articulated as participants in Pompey's funeral pomp, arrayed not for battle but for the last rites of the man for whom they have not yet begun fighting. The catalogue is built up

---

[56] Bramble (1983): 52–3.    [57] Masters (1992): 11–13.

monumentally in anticipation of war only to be toppled, as Lucan reminds us of Pompey's inevitable failure and death alone on the sand: this is not a war, it's a death-march for the leader.[58]

Book 7 opens with Pompey's dream as he imagines being cheered and celebrated by the Roman populace in his own theatre the night before the battle of Pharsalus (7.7–19).[59] The happy dream, an 'empty apparition' (8: *uana . . . imagine*), which casts Pompey back to his youthful exploits, shifts in Lucan's own reminder of the realities of the present campaign (24–8),[60] which precipitates a movement from joy to sorrow. Rome personified, cast as Pompey's lover (29–32),[61] will not be able to tend his grave, since he will be buried on foreign soil (35–6) – this scene anticipates Cornelia's fate as she mourns her inability to carry out proper funeral procedure for her husband.[62] The adulatory applause at Pompey's triumph turns into envisioned public lamentation, which represents the first negative enumeration of Pompey's funeral rites (37–44):

> te mixto flesset luctu iuuenisque senexque
> iniussusque puer; lacerasset crine soluto
> pectora femineum ceu Bruti funere uolgus.
> nunc quoque, tela licet paueant uictoris iniqui,          40
> nuntiet ipse licet Caesar tua funera, flebunt,
> sed dum tura ferunt, dum laurea serta Tonanti.
> o miseri, quorum gemitus edere dolorem,
> qui te non pleno pariter planxere theatro.

> In mingled grief, young man and old would have wept for you,
> unbidden boy too; with loosened hair the crowd would have torn
> their chests, a female crowd similar to those at Brutus' funeral.
> Now also, although they fear the weapons of the unjust conqueror,    40
> even if Caesar himself reports your death, they will weep,
> but while they carry incense and woven laurel to the Thunderer.
> O dysphoric people, whose groans gnaw at your grief,
> who did not lament for you side by side in full theatre.

The theatre of applause (9: *theatri*) becomes a theatre of silent mourning (44: *theatro*).[63] The Roman people, multiplying the grief of Rome herself in

---

[58] Hunink (1992): *ad* 3.291; Masters (1992): 13; Fratantuono (2012): 107.

[59] See Radicke (2004): 376–8, with 376 n.5. Note additionally Perutelli (2000): 150–3, Dinter (2012): 30, Fratantuono (2012): 270–1.

[60] On the blurring of temporality in this dream sequence see Narducci (2002): 293. Note that Pompey dreams of past triumphs, while Caesar rejects future triumphs owed to him (3.73–9).

[61] See Ahl (1976): 178–81, Perutelli (2000): 152, Narducci (2002): 292–3, Dinter (2012): 30, Fratantuono (2012): 270.

[62] Dinter (2012): 30.    [63] Perutelli (2000): 153; Penwill (2009): 85.

the earlier image,[64] are imagined publicly mourning their dead leader in a figurative *funus publicum*, with ritual lamentation (weeping men, women, and children; women with loosened hair 'tearing their breasts').[65] Sulla received a grandiose *funus publicum* similar to what is portrayed here (App. *B Ciu.* 1.105–6), and Pompey oversaw the proper cremation of his body (Plut. *Sull.* 38). The contrast – 'master' (Sulla) to protégé (Pompey) – may have been on Lucan's mind, as it surely was during the description of Sulla's tomb at the close of the survivor's Boschian nightmare in book 2.

The transitional juxtaposition between theatrical applause and mourning is doubled by Lucan's odd description of the Roman people stifling their anguish over Pompey's death while simultaneously celebrating Caesar's triumph (*BC* 7.40–4). This movement from a publicly honoured, triumphant Pompey to his death and public funeral, which is effectively silenced by Caesar's triumph and its own mass celebration, closes the dream sequence with a manifestly disturbing twist.[66] At the outset of the major battle of the poem (and the war), Lucan focuses on the public funeral for Pompey that will not take place (7.37: '[the people] *would have* wept for you'), positioning the reader chronologically after the battle and Pompey's defeat, and undercutting the momentum he has built for the militaristic climax. The war is a lost cause, and Lucan's focus is already on Pompey's solitary death and funeral. As in the example from book 3, the vast size of the imagined audience for the public ceremony highlights the actuality of Pompey's funerary isolation.

Around the physical rites in book 8 Lucan has added a series of negative enumerations which further add to the funeral procession Pompey will not receive. The first comes from Cordus himself, who delivers a speech over Pompey's body before cremation (8.729–35):

> non pretiosa petit cumulato ture sepulchra
> Pompeius, Fortuna, tuus, non pinguis ad astra                    730
> ut ferat e membris Eoos fumus odores,
> ut Romana suum gestent pia colla parentem,
> praeferat ut ueteres feralis pompa triumphos,
> ut resonent tristi cantu fora, totus ut ignes
> proiectis maerens exercitus ambiat armis.

> Not a pricey pyre piled up with incense does your
> Pompey seek, Fortune; or that up to the stars should dense        730
> smoke bear eastern perfumes from his limbs;

[64] Dinter (2012): 30.    [65] On the rite see Toynbee (1971): 55–6.
[66] See D'Alessandro Behr (2007): 69–70 for similar points.

or that pious Roman necks should carry their parent;
or that his funeral pomp should depict his old triumphs;
or that the Fora should echo with sorrowful song; or that all the army,
in mourning, weapons thrown down, should march around the flames.

Under normal circumstances, Pompey would have received precisely this
sort of lavish display at a grand funeral in Rome,[67] and by including the
image of this rite, Lucan has created a further substitute funeral for Pompey
along the lines of the *funus publicum* from book 7. The contrast here
between what Pompey should have received and his actual fate still elicits
*pathos* and a further reminder of the perversion of Lucan's epic world, the
price of wars 'worse than civil'.[68] Pompey does not ask for all of this lofty
pomp (729: *non ... petit*), he only requires the lowly tomb of a plebeian
funeral and a flame (736–7), and this is naturally all Cordus can offer.
Cordus (/Lucan), rhetorically, gives Pompey a 'voice' here. He presents
Pompey as someone uninterested in fancy funeral rites. While acknowledging the funeral Pompey did *not* have, Cordus simultaneously paints a
flattering picture of Pompey having mastered that concern and satisfied
with the rites he receives.

Next Cordus imagines Cornelia's lament over her husband's corpse and
her (impossible) performance of the traditional rites reserved for a widow
(739–42):

> sit satis, o superi, quod non Cornelia fuso
> crine iacet subicique facem conplexa maritum
> imperat, extremo sed abest a munere busti
> infelix coniunx nec adhuc a litore longe est.

> Let it be sufficient, O gods, that Cornelia, with loosened
> hair, doesn't lie down and, embracing her husband, command the torch
> be placed under him, but that she's absent from pyre's last duty,
> unlucky wife, still not very far from the shore.

In reality, Cordus is 'acting' as the lamenting wife; *Cordus*, the 'heart' or
'dear one' whose name speaks out as a substitute for Cornelia, Pompey's
wife, his 'sweetheart' *in absentia*.[69] As in the previous examples, the
imagined funeral rites are distorted, as Cordus seems to describe
Cornelia immolating herself on the pyre with Pompey (739–41). If Lucan
had in mind the cremation of Polynices as he was constructing the scene,
the image of a wife burning herself on a pyre with her husband would keep

[67] Loupiac (1998): 169; Galtier (2010): 196–7.    [68] Braund (1992): xlix; Keith (2008): 246.
[69] See Keith (2008): 246–8 for Cordus' appropriation of the role of lamenting widow.

us in a Theban context by recalling Evadne's self-immolation on the pyre
of her husband Capaneus.[70] Hence Cordus holds Cornelia's absence as
being the only (relative) good to come from Pompey's lowly isolated
funeral.

The final negative enumeration from book 8 comes after Cordus
inscribes Pompey's pithy epitaph on a stone (793), which elicits Lucan's
wrath. His apostrophe of Cordus morphs into a list of Pompey's achievements, which deserve commemoration (806–15):

> quod si tam sacro dignaris nomine saxum
> adde actus tantos monimentaque maxuma rerum,
> adde trucis Lepidi motus Alpinaque bella
> armaque Sertori reuocato consule uicta
> et currus quos egit eques, commercia tuta            810
> gentibus et pauidos Cilicas maris, adde subactam
> barbariem gentesque uagas et quidquid in Euro
> regnorum Boreaque iacet. dic semper ab armis
> ciuilem repetisse togam, ter curribus actis
> contentum multos patriae donasse triumphos.          815

> But if you deem the rock worthy of so sacred a name,
> add his countless exploits and greatest memorials of his acts,
> add the uprisings of fierce Lepidus and the Alpine war,
> and the defeated army of Sertorius after the consul was called back,
> and the chariots which he drove as a knight, trade safe            810
> for the nations and Cilicians terrified of the sea. Add the taming
> of the barbarian and vagrant nations, and whatever kingdoms
> lie east and north. Say that always from war
> he returned to the civilian's toga; after driving chariots three times
> he contentedly put aside many triumphs for his fatherland.         815

These and the following lines (816–22) serve as Lucan's *laudatio funebris*
over Pompey.[71] Here are his great achievements in life which deserve – or
demand: note the fervent anaphora of *adde*[72] – to be recorded in death. Yet
not simply recorded, but rather 'monumentalized'. Lucan is constructing
an epitaphic funeral monument for Pompey, a poetic tomb of impossible
size to house a record of his immense deeds (816: *quis capit haec tumulus?*,

---

[70] Mayer (1981): *ad* 8.740.

[71] Burck (1981): 482; Mayer (1981): *ad* 8.793. Galtier (2010): 201 argues that Lucan's narrative imposition here is a further indication of the problem of Cordus' funeral, since the poet supplies the
*laudatio funebris* that his character is unable to. For specifics on the *laudatio funebris* see Kierdorf
(1980).

[72] Day (2013): 223.

'what grave can capture all of this?').[73] Appian records that Pompey's grave read simply: τῷ ναοῖς βρίθοντι πόσῃ σπάνις ἔπλετο τύμβου, 'for one so rich in temples, what a pitiful tomb this is' (*B Ciu.* 2.86). The juxtaposition between Pompey's monumental fame in life and his pauper funeral is at the heart of Lucan's passage, as we have seen.[74] The 'virtual monument' further enumerates Lucan's broadening portrait of Pompey's imaginary funeral in reaction to his *actual* funeral on the Egyptian shore. The monument, however, is quickly destroyed as Lucan reverses field in favour of the subtle grandeur of Cordus' perishable tomb, which, unlike a more lasting physical monument, will never offer sure proof even of Pompey's death (*BC* 8.865–9).[75] This emblem of Pompey's idealized funeral is recorded, only to be cast aside as impermissible, and Lucan's own words – his poem – become a more lasting monument of Pompey's life and death.

The allusions to Horace's *Odes* 3.30 are unavoidable here.[76] There too the power of poetic monumentality, in a strongly funerary context, eclipses the perishable value of monuments which in time will waste away (*Carm.* 3.30.1: *exegi monumentum aere perennius*, 'I have raised a monument more lasting than bronze'). Lucan erects a virtual monument, only to reject it in favour of the more lasting monument championed by Horace.[77] Lucan's narratorial confusion, his changes of opinion concerning the appropriate way to treat Pompey's corpse, manifest in re-writings of the actual funeral scene. He first imagines Pompey will remain unhonoured, then castigates Cordus for his hasty funeral, and then imagines an enormous future-tomb, before finally settling on a future in which there exists no tomb at all, equating Pompey with a Jupiter-like omnipresence and mythic immortality. Somewhat paradoxically, Pompey's very 'vitality' is tied to features of decrepitude, ruination, absence (the hollow oak, the headless corpse, quasi-funerals, imaginary eulogies); there is, as Henry Day has illustrated, a certain sublimity in Lucan's multi-layered construction of Pompey's seismic collapse that offers its own monumentality.[78]

The same juxtaposition of imagined funeral rites for Pompey continues in book 9. Lucan halts the momentum of his text in order to retrace

---

[73] On these lines see Day (2013): 222–4, Lovatt (2013): 366.    [74] See pp. 123–4.

[75] Mayer (1981): 185. On the transitory value of the tomb Cordus provides for Pompey, see Hübner (1987): 57–8, Spencer (2005): 61–3, Day (2013): 223–31, Chaudhuri (2014): 186–8.

[76] Lucan will solidify his own place in the tradition of poetic monument-making with Caesar amidst the ruins of Troy (9.980–6); see below pp. 153–5. On poetic immortality in *BC* see Narducci (2002): 171–80.

[77] Gowing (2005): 88; Loupiac (1998): 168. Thorne (2011): 372–4 considers the *BC* as a literary funeral monument which recognizes the danger of monumentalizing *memoria*.

[78] See Day (2013): Chapter 4 on the 'Pompeian sublime'.

elements of Pompey's demise and as a means of creating even more re-
imaginings of his death and funeral. Lucan is known for his delay tactics
(*mora*),[79] but these narrative tricks are normally deployed as a means of
halting the progress of his narrative as it grinds toward the 'unspeakable'
Pharsalus. Here, conversely, Lucan lingers on his tragic hero's ending,
which resulted from the post-battle horror of Pharsalus. In other words,
Lucan is rewinding the film to replay it, slightly differently.

After a series of allusions to Cornelia's absence during Cordus' funeral
for Pompey, Lucan *finally* gives Cornelia a voice of her own (*BC* 9.55–62):

> 'ergo indigna fui', dixit 'Fortuna, marito
> accendisse rogum gelidosque effusa per artus
> **incubuisse** uiro, laceros exurere crines
> **membra**que dispersi pelago conponere Magni,
> **uolneribus** <u>cunctis</u> largos **infundere** fletus,
> ossibus et tepida **uestes inplere fauilla**,                    60
> quidquid ab exstincto licuisset tollere busto
> in templis sparsura deum'.

> 'Fortune', she said, 'I guess I wasn't worthy of lighting
> my husband's pyre and lying upon him, having poured
> myself on his cold limbs, of scorching my torn hair
> and arranging the limbs of Magnus scattered by the sea,
> of pouring floods of tears on his many wounds,
> of loading my robes with bones and warm embers,              60
> of taking whatever I could from his extinguished tomb
> to scatter in the temples of the gods.'

The negative enumeration of her ritual lament echoes directly Cordus' funeral
rites as he adopted Cornelia's role of a mourning widow: both address (and
condemn) Fortuna (cf. 8.730); *incubuisse uiro* (9.57) matches Cordus' act upon
retrieving Pompey's body (8.727: *incubuit Magno*, 'he leaned over Magnus');[80]
she *would have* poured tears into Pompey's wounds, as Cordus does (8.727–8:
*lacrimas . . . **effudit in omne** | **uolnus**, 'he poured tears into all the wounds'; 9.59:
**uolneribus** <u>cunctis</u> largos **infundere** <u>fletus</u>).[81] More striking are the allusions to
the less pious elements of the funeral scene from book 8. Cornelia's wish to
gather up and fill her robes with the ashes and bones from the pyre site recalls
Cordus' collection of the remains from the anonymous pyre which he too
carries in his robes (8.752–3: *sic fatus **plenusque** sinus ardente **fauilla** | peruolat ad*

---

[79] Masters (1992): index s.v. 'delay (*mora*) of narrative'. See also Henderson (1998): 183–6, McNelis
(2004): 268–9.
[80] Wick (2004): *ad loc.*      [81] Wick (2004): *ad loc.*

*truncum,* 'thus he speaks, filling up his robes with burning embers, and hurries back to the trunk'; 9.60: ***inplere fauilla***). Cordus' act is ritually suspect, since he defiles another man's pyre, and Cornelia's implicit allusion to this scene adds an element of perversion to her sentiments. Both ultimately recall Erichtho's theft of corpse-infused embers, adding another unsavoury layer to the mix (6.537): ***uestesque fluentis | colligit in cineres et olentis membra fauillas,*** 'she collects robes dissolving into ashes and embers smelling of limbs'.

Cornelia's lament continues and, as a counter to Cordus' own funeral rites, she performs a surrogate funeral for Pompey using his garments, medals, and armour (9.174–9):

> ut primum in sociae peruenit litora terrae,
> collegit uestes miserique insignia Magni          175
> armaque et inpressas auro, quas gesserat olim.
> exuuias pictasque togas, uelamina summo
> ter conspecta Ioui, funestoque intulit igni.
> ille fuit miserae Magni cinis.

> When she first arrived at the shores of kindred land,
> she collected poor Magnus' garments, accoutrement,          175
> and his armour, stamped with gold, which he had worn in the past;
> and the embroidered toga, clothing highest
> Jupiter saw three times, and she threw them on the funeral fire.
> In her state of grief, those were Magnus' ashes.

Aeneas led surrogate/symbolic funerals for Polydorus (*Aen.* 3.62–8) and Deiphobus (6.505–8); Procne constructed a false sepulchre for Philomela (*Met.* 6.566–70), as did Priam and Hector for Aesacus (*Met.* 12.2–4). Scholars additionally have seen in this a reference to Dido's substitute funeral for Aeneas (*Aen.* 4.494–7, 507–8, 648–51).[82] Lucan will also no doubt have in mind Andromache's substitute funeral for Hector, the original epic model for a quasi- or surrogate cremation (*Il.* 22.508–15):

> 'νῦν δὲ σὲ μὲν παρὰ νηυσὶ κορωνίσι νόσφι τοκήων
> αἰόλαι εὐλαὶ ἔδονται, ἐπεί κε κύνες κορέσωνται
> γυμνόν· ἀτάρ τοι εἵματ᾽ ἐνὶ μεγάροισι κέονται          510
> λεπτά τε καὶ χαρίεντα τετυγμένα χερσὶ γυναικῶν.
> ἀλλ᾽ ἤτοι τάδε πάντα καταφλέξω πυρὶ κηλέῳ
> οὐδὲν σοί γ᾽ ὄφελος, ἐπεὶ οὐκ ἐγκείσεαι αὐτοῖς,
> ἀλλὰ πρὸς Τρώων καὶ Τρωϊάδων κλέος εἶναι'.
> ὣς ἔφατο κλαίουσ᾽, ἐπὶ δὲ στενάχοντο γυναῖκες.

82 Kubiak (1990); Wick (2004): ad 9.176; Erasmo (2008): 121; Augoustakis (2011): 186, 193 n.21.

'But now, along the curving ships and far from your parents,
the nimble worms will eat (when the dogs have had their fill)
your naked corpse, though there is clothing stored in the palace,      510
delicate and beautiful, well-made by women's hands.
But I will burn all of this in a crackling fire,
since they are useless to you, now that you'll never be wrapped in them;
but as your glory, from the men and women of Troy.'
So she spoke weeping, and the women wailed with her.

Andromache watches the chariot carry her husband away to the Achaean
camp on the shore and she faints (*Il.* 22.466–7), as does Cornelia witnessing Pompey's death along the Egyptian shore (*BC* 8.661–2). They scold
their husbands for leaving them alone to cruel fate (*Il.* 22.477–84; *BC*
8.583–9). Andromache's focus on the abuse of Hector's corpse by beasts
and maggots (*Il.* 22.508–9) finds its counterpart in Sextus and the younger
Magnus' concerns for their father's corpse at the hand of scavengers just
before Cornelia's substitute funeral (*BC* 9.141–2). For both women the
focus is on the burning of finely woven garments, and the actions of each
prompt general lamentation (*Il.* 22.515, 23.1; *BC* 9.179–81, 186–8). But
whereas Andromache dissolves in grief (*Il.* 24.725–45), Cornelia transfers
her own sorrow to anger and aggression, as she discharges Pompey's final
orders to her sons and Cato to renew the war, and thus the poem (*BC* 9.84–
97).[83]

Antony Augoustakis sees Cornelia's act (relative to its association with
Dido's substitute funeral aimed at erasing her memory of Aeneas) as an
attempt to move the epic beyond the shadow of Pompey, to bring closure
to his death and move the war/poem forward.[84] Certainly historical parameters dictate this change of focus. From here the epic is entrusted to Cato,
who relieves Pompey as the 'head' of the Republican cause – this is also
symbolically adduced by Pompey's metempsychosis, which transfers his
soul into Cato's head/mind and the breast of Brutus (9.1–18).

But Lucan must never get over Pompey. Aside from further funereal
features, Pompey's ghost continues to haunt the narrative. His soul lives on
in Brutus and Cato (9.17–18), and, further, Cornelia claims Pompey's soul
lives in her own breast (9.70–1). Pompey prevents Caesar's death occurring
prematurely in Egypt (10.6–8); he possesses Pothinus (10.333–7); his shade

---

[83] Keith (2008): 248–9; Augoustakis (2011): 189–90. Hutchinson (2013): 331 (hesitantly) posits a
number of analogical and intertextual connections between Hector/Andromache and Pompey/
Cornelia throughout the poem.
[84] Augoustakis (2011): 193–4, with Keith (2008): 248; cf. Wick (2004): 67.

receives Achillas as a sacrifice (10.524); and *Magnus* in fact closes the epic as it stands (10.543–6).[85]

Pompey's haunting presence continues through additional funeral rites. Cato delivers a eulogy *in absentia* for Pompey (9.190–214), an odd epideixis full of ambivalence and skewed praise,[86] which, far from pushing us past the shadow of Pompey, adds another piece to his never-ending funeral. Cato's is now the second *laudatio funebris* for Pompey, after a string of funerary laments. Cato counters Cordus' initial lament, which calls on Pompey as the greatest leader (8.759–60: *o maxime . . .* | *ductor*), by announcing Pompey as simply a dead citizen (9.190: *ciuis obit*),[87] recalling Pompey's imagined desire for a pauper's funeral at 8.736–8; the speech in general undercuts what has already been said in the other laments.[88] Cato aims more generally at identifying the antitheses in Pompey's character that Lucan's poem everywhere advances (no hagiography this). Cato might be looking towards the future, but in doing so he also takes us back: to book 2, to Marius and Sulla, to a Republic long since crippled, with freedom (*libertas*) a myth only Pompey had been foolish enough to entertain (9.204–7).[89] Cato concludes his speech with a view to his own death, but even here he imagines an ahistorical decapitation for himself that recalls directly Pompey's ending (9.212–14):

> et mihi, si fatis aliena in iura uenimus,
> fac talem, Fortuna, Iubam; non deprecor hosti
> seruari, dum me seruet ceruice recisa.

> And if by fate I come under another's control,
>   make Juba like this to me, Fortune; I don't aim to avoid being kept
> for the enemy, as long as he keeps me with a severed head.

---

[85] 10.543–6: *respexit in agmine denso | Scaeuam perpetuae meritum iam nomina famae | ad campos, Epidamne, tuos, ubi solus apertis | obsedit muris calcantem moenia* **Magnum**, '[Caesar] looked back in the packed crowd at Scaeva, worthy already of the fame of eternal glory on your fields, Epidamnus, where alone, after the walls were opened, he hemmed in Magnus as he stomped upon the bulwarks'. Both Scaeva, the dead soldier who is not really dead, and the headless Pompey are brought back from the dead, so to speak, at the poem's 'death'.

[86] Most scholarship on Cato's speech concerns the ambiguities and antitheses in his description of Pompey's character/life: e.g. Morford (1967): 6–7; Kierdorf (1979); Johnson (1987): 71–2; Bartsch (1997): 84; Narducci (2002): 350–3.

[87] Wick (2004): *ad* 9.190; Seo (2013): 88.      [88] Morford (1967): 6 with n.1.

[89] Johnson (1987): 71–2. A main driving force of Lucan's poem is the damaged state of *libertas* (the symbol of the Roman *res publica*) during this time period and Lucan's own: e.g. *BC* 1.669–72, 3.112–14, 145–7, 4.221–7, 7.641–6; see Ahl (1976): index s.v. 'libertas', Quint (1993): 147–57, Rudich (1997): 125–7. For the 'ruination' of the Republic long before Pharsalus, cf. Cicero writing to Atticus in January 60 (*Att.* 1.18.6): *amissa re publica*, 'with the Republic lost'; in 59 (*Att.* 2.21): *de re publica quid ego tibi subtiliter? tota periit*, 'what can I say to you about the Republic, simply? It's totally ruined'. See below pp. 167–9 for more on Lucan's poeticizing of the loss of *libertas* in his narrative of the Republic's fall and in Neronian Rome.

Lucan eschews the *exemplum* of Cato's famous suicide and replaces the image of *hara-kiri* with Pompey's (equally famous?) decapitation.[90] J. Mira Seo has argued convincingly that Lucan imports features of Cato's Stoic suicide into Pompey's death in book 8, transforming the assassination into a Catonian *mors uoluntaria*.[91] The reverse seems to be at play in Cato's own imagining of his death in book 9. Earlier at *BC* 2.306–19 Cato had anticipated his death again framed around Pompey-like punishments imposed on his head: e.g. *o utinam caelique deis Erebique liceret | hoc caput in cunctas damnatum exponere poenas!*, 'O would that this head, rejected by gods of sky and Hell, could be abandoned to every punishment!' (306–7). It is Cato (not Cicero) who is imagined as the next headless victim of the Senatorial party. While Pompey's death is coloured by Catonian brush strokes, Cato wishes for himself the death Pompey has already received, a stunning *contaminatio*.

Before Cornelia's substitute funeral and Cato's eulogy, Pompey's son swears to locate and bury his father's severed head and exhume the bodies of Alexander the Great, Amasis, Isis, and Osiris, using their remains as fuel for the pyre (9.148–64). The grotesque plan to burn the head using the remains of the dead (there is a hesitation to label them 'gods') as fuel recalls Cordus' theft of the cremation embers from the anonymous pyre, which he used to burn Pompey's *truncus*. Though he cannot know it, this is a darkly poetic attempt at the 'unification' of his father's body (which was also burnt with tainted embers) and head in death. Cato checks the 'worthy wrath' of the youth (9.166), rendering the vow a non-event. But the scene is a chilling reminder that some of Pompey is still out there awaiting Caesar's gaze. Lucan is not finished with Pompey.

We are left wondering about Pompey's head through book 9. And as Martha Malamud and others have shown, the Medusa excursus containing the myth of Perseus' decapitation of Medusa (9.619–99), which is loaded symbolically with allusion to Pompey's decapitation, only serves to heighten our expectations for Pompey's head's eventual confrontation with Caesar.[92] Finally a satellite of Ptolemy gifts Pompey's severed head to Caesar as an indication of allegiance (9.1032–6). Before its arrival, we know that the head was solidified by Egyptian poison (8.687–91) and, according to Pompey's son Sextus, 'paraded' through the streets (9.136–9). There is perhaps a dark allusion – given the context of funeral distortion

[90] On Cato's suicide see Edwards (2007): index s.v. 'Cato, Marcus Porcius (Younger)'.
[91] Seo (2013): 83–8; cf. Malamud (2003): 34.
[92] Fantham (1992b): 110; Malamud (2003); Papaioannou (2005).

throughout Pompey's extended requiem – to the spectacle of funereal ancestor masks (*imagines*) and the paraded solidified 'heads' adorning funeral *pompa* in Roman ritual. Pompey's *caput*, concretized like a death-mask by Egyptian dark arts, yet *imperfect* (it's 'drooping' when Caesar spies it, 1033), recalls the masks used to preserve the faces of dead ancestors.[93] Having lost access to a proper funeral, at which *imagines* would accompany the corpse of the dead man (Polyb. 6.53), Pompey's own preserved *imago* offered a hideous indicator of his death. Cornelia seals implicitly Pompey's head's association with funereal *imagines* when she laments not being able to offer proper rites over his corpse, yet strikingly his '*imago* clings to her guts' (*BC* 9.71–2): *non imis haeret imago | uisceribus?*[94]

The Egyptian satellite shows this Pompeian *imago* to Caesar, who sheds crocodile tears and hurls abuses at the satellite and Ptolemy for the crime (1037–89). Then Caesar demands a burial for the head (1089–1104):

> uos condite busto
> tanti colla ducis, sed non ut crimina solum          1090
> uestra tegat tellus: iusto date tura sepulchro
> et placate caput cineresque in litore fusos
> colligite atque unam sparsis date manibus urnam.
> sentiat aduentum soceri uocesque querentis
> audiat umbra pias. dum nobis omnia praefert,          1095
> dum uitam Phario mauolt debere clienti,
> laeta dies rapta est populis, concordia mundo
> nostra perit. caruere deis mea uota secundis,
> ut te conplexus positis felicibus armis
> adfectus a te ueteres uitamque rogarem,          1100
> Magne, tuam dignaque satis mercede laborum
> contentus par esse tibi. tunc pace fideli
> fecissem ut uictus posses ignoscere diuis,
> fecisses ut Roma mihi.

> You, bury in a tomb
> the great leader's head, but not such that alone the earth          1090
> conceals your crimes: give incense to his rightful sepulchre;
> and appease the head and collect the ashes scattered
> along the shore, and give one urn to the fragmented shade.
> Let him sense the arrival of his father-in-law, let his shade hear

[93] Erasmo (2008): 114–15 hints at this as well considering the description of Pompey's severed head as *sacrum caput* (8.677).
[94] See Hope (2000): 114, Jervis (2001): 136–9 on the display of severed heads as a perversion of funereal *imagines*.

these pious complaints. While he favours everything over me,          1095
while he'd rather owe his life to his Pharian client,
a joyous day has been snatched away from the people, our union
has perished to the world. My prayers lack approving gods,
that I might embrace you, with fortunate arms cast down,
and beg your old friendship from you, beg your life,                 1100
Magnus, and content with a payment well-worth my troubles,
to be on equal terms with you. Then with trusting peace
I might have made you able to forgive the gods after being defeated;
you might have made Rome able to forgive me.

There is an implicit allusion to Cordus' hope that someone might find
Pompey's (*truncus*) ashes on the shore and provide 'full honours' (8.773:
*plenos ... honores*) to the dead man by restoring Pompey's head to the
initial place of cremation (8.772–5).[95] But Caesar's burial, the third funeral
for Pompey in the poem, will usurp Cordus'. His will be a 'rightful
sepulchre' (1091: *iusto ... sepulchro*), combining at last Pompey's head
with what remains of his dispersed torso (1092: *cineres ... fusos*), uniting
scattered body and 'fragmented shade' (1093: *sparsis ... manibus*) in a single
urn, and erasing Cordus' funeral entirely.[96] Here then is an attempt at
some semblance of bodily integrity against which Lucan's whole poem has
been fighting: *Civil War* is a disruption and violation of boundaries, most
viscerally elucidated by Lucan in terms of corporeal dismemberment, with
Pompey's decapitation as its centrepiece.[97] Caesar is the poem's ultimate
boundary violator,[98] so it's rather jarring that Lucan would include his
wilful efforts to unify Pompey's dismembered corpse here.[99] The unity of
Pompey's body is symbolically doubled in Caesar's obituary by his claims
for reconciliation with his nemesis (1097–8), by his desire to 'embrace'
Pompey (1099), to be 'equals' (1102). But these pleas for unification fool no
one and his 'generosity' is undercut by the reaction of his followers who
inwardly deride his feigned *clementia* (1104–8).[100]

False tears and words should leave us with at least the intimation of false
claims, and the book ends on a note of unease and insecurity about whether

---

[95] Wick (2004): *ad* 9.1091; Ambühl (2015): 278 n.239.     [96] Erasmo (2008): 124.
[97] Narducci (1973): 323; Masters (1992): 162 with n.38; Most (1992); Bartsch (1997): 10–47; Mebane
    (2016). On boundary violation/disruption more generally in Lucan, see Henderson (1998): 191–2,
    205–6, Myers (2011), Dinter (2012).
[98] Myers (2011); Spentzou (2018).
[99] Note the analogical allusion here to Seneca's *Phaedra* 1247–79 – suggested to me by Francesca
    D'Alessando Behr – where a father (Theseus) weeps over the fractured body of his son (Hippolytus)
    whom he attempts to reassemble for proper funeral rites.
[100] D'Alessandro Behr (2007): 62–5; Coffee (2009): 145. See Dinter (2012): 105: 'Caesar's *clementia*
    degenerates into farce.' Cf. Dio Cass. 42.8.1–3.

Caesar will actually implement his plan to bury Pompey.[101] Allusions to
Pompey's funeral continue into book 10, most dramatically in Pothinus'
speech arguing for the murder of Caesar (10.378–81):

> aspice litus,
> spem nostri sceleris; pollutos consule fluctus
> quid liceat nobis, tumulumque e puluere paruo
> aspice Pompei non omnia membra tegentem

> Look at the shore,
> hope for our wickedness; ask the polluted waves
> what's licensed to us, and look at his grave, from a pinch of dust,
> not even covering all of Pompey's limbs.

Rhetorical appeals aside, it does at least appear that Pompey's remains are
still lying on the shore, the tiny speck of dust still not covering all of his
'great' limbs (*paruus* again contrasting Pompeius *Magnus*). Pothinus' comment offers a further reminder that not all of Pompey is actually there.[102]
Our unease about Caesar's claims is outwardly confirmed, and Pompey
still remains, at the poem's close, half-buried and fragmented.

This list of features relating to Pompey's funeral in the poem points directly
to Lucan's obsession with the scene of Pompey's ending, its aftermath, and its
implications. Lucan does not simply offer the same funereal features over and
over, he varies elements of Pompey's (real or imagined) funeral in a multiplicity of forms which bombard the audience with an endless series of refashionings of the epic's climax. Lucan does the same thing with Pompey's
actual murder and corpse abuse: we see his death and abuse re-presented
repeatedly in the poem (both anticipated and re-imagined after the fact).[103] All
these fragmentary repetitions,[104] slightly altered, create a tangled patchwork of
one elaborate death and funeral for Pompey, but their imagined, disparate,

---

[101] Erasmo (2008): 124. Lucan elsewhere highlights the schism between Caesar's words and deeds: e.g. the crossing of the Rubicon and defiance of personified Rome (1.190–203) and his fallacious promise to rebuild Troy (9.998–9: cf. Suet. *Iul.* 79.3, Nic. Dam. *Caes.* 20 for rumours of Caesar's supposed desire to move the capital to Alexandria or Troy); see e.g. Bernstein (2011): 266–7. Caesar's sham *clementia* is doubled by his sham *pietas* here: he lacks 'true piety' (9.1056: *uera pietas*: with the irony of 1094–5 and Caesar's *uoces piae* to Pompey's shade). He's a faulty *pius Aeneas*.
[102] Berti (2000): *ad* 10.381.    [103] See pp. 68–79 above.
[104] Erasmo (2008): 124, 127 argues that the repetitions of Pompey's funeral scenes are aimed at confounding and renewing audience mourning. This may be a by-product of Lucan's repetition, but the aim is to swamp the audience with the destruction wrought by civil war and the repetitiveness of civil war itself. Galtier (2010) notes the repetitiveness of Pompey's death and funeral, but his study looks more at Lucan's attempt to rebuild Pompey's image through the destruction of his physical body, leaving ultimately a celebration of his famous name. Loupiac (1998): 167–75 is the most thorough examination of the repetition of Pompey's funeral rites, though there are some gaps here as well.

and unfulfilled state function only as a further recapitulation and reminder of Pompey's brutal decapitation and half-finished funeral.

David Quint and others have argued that repetition in Lucan serves as a constant rehashing of the 'negative cycles' of civil war.[105] Most obviously, this repetition appears in the survivor's tale from book 2, which anticipates the atrocities of the impending war. We also see a view to the future repetition of death and war in the zombie-corpse's prophecy (*BC* 6.802–20), in Mark Antony's premature plotting of Actium (5.478–9), and in the narrator's view of Pharsalus as a battle seemingly always on the horizon (7.207–13). But it is with Pompey that these themes are most poignantly exploited. As the *corpus* which stands for the body of the Republic, Lucan's repeated recycling of Pompey's fragmentary death and funeral functions as a supplementation of the endlessly fragmented, bludgeoned death and funeral for the Republic at the hands of civil war. There is no Virgilian (or perhaps better, Augustan) promise of future prosperity, where present (Virgil's own) readers are invited to view the past as aiming teleologically at Augustan Rome and their own better 'future-perfect' world. Lucan's view of the future is only ever more of this cruel past.

The final image of Pompey's 'tomb' in the poem is the one mentioned above during Pothinus' speech (10.378–81). But Lucan as narrator provides the most chronologically current comment (8.843–6, 849–50):

> satis o nimiumque beatus,
> si mihi contingat manes transferre reuolsos
> Ausoniam, si tale ducis uiolare sepulchrum.                      845
> forsitan . . .

> transibis in urbem,
> Magne, tuam, summusque feret tua busta sacerdos.                 850

> enough and oh too perfect,
> if it fell to me to transfer the torn-up remains
> to Ausonia, if I could violate such a 'tomb' of the leader.      845
> Perhaps . . .
> you will come into your city,
> Magnus, and the highest priest will carry your tomb.             850

---

[105] Quint (1993): 131–57. See also Dinter (2012): 138–43; Mebane (2016); Masters (1992): 6: 'in writing the poem [Lucan] is allowing the civil war to be re-enacted, he *is* re-enacting the war'.

This is a perverse wish. Poet-as-tomb-raider has shades of Sullan madness and puts Lucan on par with Erichtho and later Caesar at Alexandria.[106] Yet this wish fits seamlessly into Lucan's narrative of Pompey's endless funeral(s) and of the cyclical carnage of his *Civil War*. Pompey's very name has inscribed within it the solemn procession (*pompa*) from which Lucan refuses to extricate him.[107] The narrator's final wish replays his poem's agenda: if only he could dig Pompey up one last time, in order to bury him again.

## omnia Caesar erat

Caesar's order to perform rites over Pompey's severed head at the end of *BC* 9 is resoundingly suspicious not only given its own context, but also considering Caesar's aversion to funeral rites elsewhere in the poem. In Book 5, stationed in Epirus with only part of his army and furious with Mark Antony for hesitating to ship the rest of his forces over to Epirus from Italy, Caesar decides to return to Italy by himself in the middle of the night. He enlists the aid of an elderly boatman (Amyclas) and both men attempt to cross the Adriatic in the midst of a massive sea-storm (5.504–677). As they are battered by winds, rain, and sea-swells, Caesar confronts the possibility of his own death at sea with little interest in the fate of his corpse or funeral rites (668–71):

> mihi funere nullo
> est opus, o superi: lacerum retinete cadauer
> fluctibus in mediis, desint mihi busta rogusque,
> dum metuar semper terraque expecter ab omni.

> No funeral for me
> is necessary, o gods; keep my mutilated corpse
> mid-waves; let me lack a tomb and pyre,
> as long as I am always feared and anticipated by every land.

The scene and Caesar's words openly flout the epic models of Aeneas (*Aen.* 1.94–101), Ceyx and his crew (*Met.* 11.539–42, 564–5), and, more directly, Odysseus (*Od.* 5.299–312) and Achilles (*Il.* 21.273–83, with the response of the river-god Scamander at 318–23), who lament the idea of dying at sea (or for Achilles, in a river) and the consequent likelihood of non-burial.[108] Far

[106] See pp. 43–4, 119–20, 155–61.  [107] From Gk. *pompe*; see Feeney (2010): 354 n.16.
[108] Hübner (1987): 53; Narducci (2002): 257; Matthews (2008): *ad* 5.653–71, 668–71l; Hutchinson (2013): 330–1. See Smith (1999): 230–2 on Aeneas' lament at sea blending the laments of Odysseus and Achilles in the Homeric poems. Lucan seems to be intermeshing images from all three: the scenario at sea of Odysseus and Aeneas, and the theomachic context of Achilles' battle with the

from praying for divine intervention to save him from this fate, Caesar embraces the gods' onslaught at the close of his theomachic madness.[109] Achilles, Odysseus, and Aeneas had mourned their inability to die on the battlefield – as proper heroic warriors – but Caesar, in his battle with the (presumed) gods, realizes they are more worthy adversaries than mere mortals and embraces the possibility of death at their hands. He puts himself above (or at least on par with) the gods; he expects to defeat the sea (*BC* 5.503: *sperat superare*), and relishes the fact that such a mighty storm is needed to challenge him in his tiny boat (654–6): '*quantusne euertere' dixit | 'me superis labor est, parua quem puppe sedentem | tam magno petiere mari!*', "how great" he said "is the effort of the gods to destroy me, whom they attack with the powerful sea as I sit in a small boat!'" He fails the gods, rather than the gods failing him (499). Safety is assured, Caesar promises Amyclas, by his presence alone (580–6). He even claims to control the weather (586–8).[110] His megalomania is nowhere more apparent than in this scene from book 5.

Emanuele Narducci notes that Caesar resembles Virgil's Mezentius as a *contemptor diuum*, a scorner of the gods, but whereas Mezentius was made to pay for his godlessness, Caesar's impiety and 'titanic contempt' are in Lucan's poem valorous qualities: the monstrous are rewarded, those seeking a just cause (Pompey/Cato) are paradoxically destined for defeat.[111] Another feature that separates Mezentius and Caesar is that Mezentius never rejected his own funeral rites. His dying words in fact concern the treatment of his corpse (*Aen.* 10.903–6). Caesar's insouciance is emblematic of his presumed superiority both to his epic predecessors, whose concerns are for him trivial,[112] and to the gods, to whom most men pray for a surer outcome in similar moments of desperation.[113] The word *cadauer*, a favourite of Lucan's,[114] is cold and animalistic: Caesar's corpse is mere organic matter to him. He's set his sights higher than corporeal limitations. The tenth wave, the largest (and traditionally the most dangerous: e.g. Lucil. 1152; Ov. *Met.* 11.530, *Tr.* 1.2.49–50; Sen. *Ag.* 502; VF 2.54), rises and casts Caesar back to shore, back where this crazed, warped *aristeia* began, and he emerges alive and unscathed.

---

river-god. Note also AR 4.1251–8, wherein Jason and his crew, stranded on the Libyan coast, bemoan that they had not died attempting some 'mighty deed' (1255: βέλτερον . . . μέγα).

[109] On Caesar as a theomachic or 'god-fighting' figure in *BC* see Chaudhuri (2014): 156–94, though he doesn't discuss the storm scene.

[110] Narducci (2002): 254; Matthews (2008): 150–1 and *ad locc.*; Dinter (2012): 85–6.

[111] Narducci (2002): 254.    [112] Matthews (2008): 227.    [113] Hutchinson (2013): 331.

[114] See esp. Chiesa (2005): 24–9, Calonne (2010), and p. 101 n.103.

As well as rewriting a well-known epic *topos*, the scene also has reso-nances with Pompey's own murder later in the poem. Caesar, in fact, contemplates suffering the same fate that will come to Pompey in book 8: to be an unburied corpse battered by the waves.[115] Caesar's near-death at sea anticipates the setting of Pompey's actual death scene. That Cordus uses fragments of a boat for Pompey's cremation pit calls to mind the nature of Pompey's 'death at sea' in a small boat off the Egyptian shore. The epitaph Cordus inscribes on a stone (*BC* 8.793: *hic situs est Magnus*, 'here lies Magnus') recalls the tradition of Hellenistic shipwreck epigrams, and Pompey should be understood as a quasi-shipwreck victim,[116] like Ovid's Ceyx. At the outset of the battle at Pharsalus, Pompey is described as a sailor letting loose his sails, overcome by violent winds (7.125–7: *ut **uictus** uiolento **nauita** Coro* | *dat regimen uentis ignauumque arte relicta* | *puppis onus trahitur*, 'like the sailor, defeated by turbulent Corus, yields rein to the winds (his skill relinquished) and is dragged along, the ship's dead weight'; cf. Ov. *Met.* 11.492–4). The battle and its aftermath are, by extension, his death at sea.

Both leaders are in a small boat (Caesar, *BC* 5.503: ***exigua* . . . *carina***; Pompey, 8.541: ***exiguam* . . . *carinam***), both call on the gods (5.669: ***o superi***; 8.630: ***o superi***), and they anticipate their mangled and scattered corpses (5.669–70, above, cf. 5.684: *inuitis **spargenda** dabas tua membra procellis?*, 'you gave your limbs to be strewn about by reluctant waves?'; 8.629: ***spargant** lacerentque*, 'they rip and mutilate', cf. 8.751: ***sparsis** Pompei manibus*, 'Pompey's limbs are scattered', 9.58: ***dispersi***, 9.1093: ***sparsis***; 8.667 and 737: ***lacerum***). Caesar considers the gods largely power-less against him (5.579–85), while Pompey claims no god has the power to deprive him of his fortune (8.630–1: *felix*). While we might question the validity of this claim for the quasi-shipwrecked Pompey, it is Caesar who will emerge from the sea as the 'fortunate shipwreck victim' (5.699: *felix naufragus*).[117] While Pompey's death at sea reactivates the epic theme of the sacrifice of one for the many of Palinurus' (unwitting) sacrifice at *Aeneid* 5.814–15 – though still warping Virgil's idea by having Pompey die together with the Republic, instead of for it – Caesar, the embodiment of the new

---

[115] Feeney (2010): 351–2: Hübner (1987): 57–8; Matthews (2008): *ad* 5.668–71, 669; Dinter (2012): 86.

[116] Fratantuono (2012): 342. See Johnson (1987): 81–2 on the anonymous pyre as reminiscent of 'the somber world of the anonymous dead in the *Anthology*, the outcast, the shipwrecked, whom humble piety rescues and pities'.

[117] Amyclas confuses Caesar with a shipwreck victim at the outset of the storm scene as well (5.521: *naufragus*). Hershkowitz (1998a): 228–30 points to the shipwreck simile that anticipates the fall of the Republic at *BC* 1.498–504 in her discussion of the storm scene in book 5.

imperialism, the *caput* (*BC* 5.686) of his burgeoning State, becomes a victorious anti-Palinurus incapable of being sacrificed. Pompey's was the body of the Republic, both dead and torn to pieces, but Caesar(ism) is and was *everything* of this New Rome (3.105–9: senate, consuls, praetors, curules): *omnia Caesar erat* (108).[118]

Caesar's claim to need no tomb and pyre as long as he's feared and awaited by every land (5.670–1) achieves the same boundless 'supernatural omnipresence', to borrow a phrase from Martin Dinter, which Lucan sought for Pompey through the erasure of his funeral monument.[119] The universality of *memoria* or *fama* is the aim of each as he faces death, but Caesar's is more sinister: he demands to be feared, not loved. Lucan here and at the close of book 8, when he rejects the idea of Pompey's physical monument, warps the traditional epic idea that a funeral and physical tomb honoured and preserved the glory of the dead by claiming conversely that the absence of these provides more lasting fame.[120] The brutality of the river-god Scamander's boast to Achilles at *Iliad* 21.318–23 derives from his ability to bury the hero's immortal fame along with his body beneath the sand and silt of his river: Achilles' bones will be unrecoverable and no tomb will be needed to honour him or immortalize him.[121] Lucan rejects this tradition and the idea of a physical monument having any value for immortality. Poetic immortality lasts much longer.[122]

Caesar commands so much control in this presumed death scene at sea that he even provides his own brief *laudatio funebris* (*BC* 5.661–8):[123]

> Arctoas domui gentes, inimica subegi
> arma metu, uidit Magnum mihi Roma secundum,
> iussa plebe tuli fasces per bella negatos;
> nulla meis aberit titulis Romana potestas,
> nec sciet hoc quisquam nisi tu, quae sola meorum					665
> conscia uotorum es, me, quamuis plenus honorum
> et dictator eam Stygias et consul ad umbras,
> priuatum, Fortuna, mori.

> I conquered the northern nations, I broke the hostile
> arms by fear, Rome saw Magnus second place to me,

---

[118] Cf. Ovid's designation (perhaps resignation) of Augustus Caesar as the embodiment of the *res publica* at *Tr.* 4.4.15: *res est publica Caesar*.

[119] Dinter (2012): 86.

[120] See Day (2013): 151–2, 223–31, Chaudhuri (2014): 187–8 for similar points.

[121] Chaudhuri (2014): 188, 203–4.

[122] See pp. 132–3 on Pompey and poetic immortality and pp. 234–40 on Maeon in Statius.

[123] Suet. *Iul.* 84 tells us that Caesar did not receive a proper *laudatio*, and Lucan may be toying with this as Caesar looks forward and the poet looks back in historical time.

with the plebs ordered, I held the Fasces denied by wars;
no position of Roman power will be lacking in my inscription,
and no one except you will know this, Fortune, you who alone          665
are conscious of my prayers, though full of honours –
both dictator and consul – Let me go to the Stygian shades
to die a private citizen.

Pompey will passively require the aid of his loved ones to provide some
semblance of funerary observance, whereas Caesar pre-empts all of this,
denying the importance of his own funeral but (for kicks) offering material
for his tombstone or monument anyway (664: *meis . . . titulis*). Dinter sees
in this scene Caesar's metaliterary/metahistorical self-consciousness of his
eventual divinity, his assurance of apotheosis – he was a fixture in the
Roman pantheon by the time of Lucan's writing[124] – and this may go some
way toward understanding his rejection of mortal funeral rites. The self-
*laudatio* and rejection of rites may also point to the actual circumstances of
Caesar's impromptu cremation in the forum, where he was burned on a
makeshift pyre by a frenzied mob instead of in the Campus Martius where
a traditional pyre had been set up (e.g. Cic. *Phil.* 1.5; Suet. *Iul.* 84.1–5; App.
*B Ciu.* 2.148). Cicero explicitly calls this a 'burial that was no burial' (*Phil.*
1.5: *insepultam sepulturam*). Further, he tells us a tomb (*bustum*) was set up
by Caesar's supporters at the cremation site, but that this too was removed
a few weeks later by Dolabella. And it was not until 29 BCE that a temple
to Diuus Iulius was dedicated to Caesar at the *ustrinum*, immortalizing him
(Dio Cass. 51.22.). Lucan's Caesar rejects proper funeral rites in a way that
largely points to his impending historical funeral perversion.

   This future-view to divinity helps contextualize Caesar's confidence in
challenging the gods to war during Lucan's storm scene. There is something of Diomedes' self-confidence in confronting gods in *Iliad* 5 in
Caesar's theomachy in *BC* 5. Descriptions of sailing have a tendency to
shift to battlefield language (e.g. *BC* 5.583: *medias perrumpe procellas*, 'break
through the middle of the storm'),[125] and the storm passage began with
Caesar's manic desire for battle (476–7). But Caesar, in his prodding
encouragement of Amyclas here, also resembles the goddess Athena moti-
vating Diomedes in battle, leading him as his charioteer against men and
gods (esp. *Il.* 5.120–32). In this way Caesar appropriates the role of epic
divinity: he will become a god regardless and establish a principate of
future-gods, his greatest challenge to the established divine order. In the
absence of traditional divine machinery in the poem, Caesar assumes the

---

[124] Dinter (2012): 85–6.    [125] Matthews (2008): *ad loc.*

role of the gods throughout the extended storm scene: of Athena in the
*Iliad*, of Virgil's Jupiter in *Aeneid* 4,[126] of Ovid's Jupiter and Mercury in
*Metamorphoses* 8.[127]

We should not be surprised then when a pseudo-divine Caesar who
denies potential funeral rites to his *own* corpse during his odd theomachy,
finds no reason to provide funerals for the Pompeian dead after his victory
at Pharsalus. Pompey flees Pharsalus, Caesar and his troops are victorious,
and Caesar takes in the glory of his win and the carnage in the aftermath of
the battle (*BC* 7.786–99):

> tamen omnia passo,
> postquam clara dies Pharsalica damna retexit,
> nulla loci facies reuocat feralibus aruis
> haerentis oculos. cernit propulsa cruore
> flumina et excelsos cumulis aequantia colles                               790
> corpora, sidentis in tabem spectat aceruos
> et Magni numerat populos, epulisque paratur
> ille locus, uoltus ex quo faciesque **iacentum**
> **agnoscat**. iuuat Emathiam non cernere terram
> et lustrare oculis campos sub clade latentes.                              795
> fortunam superosque suos in sanguine cernit.
> ac, ne laeta furens scelerum spectacula perdat,
> inuidet igne rogi miseris, caeloque nocenti
> ingerit Emathiam.

> Nevertheless he endured all of this,
> but after the bright day revealed the Pharsalian massacre,
> no feature of the place turns his eyes away from clinging to
> the deadly fields. He spies rivers driven
> by blood and, equal in size to high hills,                                 790
> are corpses; he sees heaps slipping into decay
> and adds-up Magnus' people. That place is prepared
> for a feast, from where he can scrutinize the faces and features
> of the dead. He delights that he can't perceive the Emathian land,
> that with his eyes he surveys fields blanketed by slaughter.               795
> He perceives his fortune and his own gods in the blood.
> And lest the happy spectacle of his wickedness perish, in his frenzy
> he denies the pyre's flame to the miserable dead, and to the guilty sky
> he lavishes Emathia.

---

[126] Caesar's desire to avoid delay mirrors Jupiter's annoyance that Aeneas is delaying/denying fate by
lingering too long with Dido in Carthage; see Thompson and Bruère (1968): 11.

[127] Caesar enters Amyclas' hut as a storm-tossed traveller, like Jupiter and Mercury entering the home
of Baucis and Philemon in *Met.* 8; Narducci (2002): 251. For more on Caesar's 'divinity' in the
storm scene, see Matthews (2008): index s.v. 'Caesar: god-like behaviour', Day (2013): 149–52.

The mass of troops compiled by Pompey as witness to his presumptive proto-funeral (3.169–297) all rot here on the battlefield at Pharsalus while their leader flees the scene. In the end, though, Pompey's death will match the deaths of his army as they similarly lie unburied and receive substitute rites from afar (9.179–81).[128] There is in *iacentum . . . agnoscat* (7.793–4) an allusion to the raving matron's recognition of Pompey's corpse lying on the shore at 1.685–6: *hunc ego, fluminea deformis truncus harena | qui iacet, agnosco*, 'I recognize that man, a misshapen trunk who lies on the river sands'. Pompey himself equates his own body with the body of his troops, their deaths with his (7.652–3). At 7.117–19 Pompey anticipates his death being mirrored by the death of the Republic. And the dead at Pharsalus are described as *magnis nominibus* (7.209–10), minions of Lucan's description of Pompey as a (shadow of a) great name (1.135: *stat magni nominis umbra*).[129] But with his flight from Pharsalus, the 'head' of the Republic (Pompey) has gone, and its *truncus*, much like Pompey's own on the Egyptian shore in book 8, and *uiscera* are strewn upon the Pharsalian fields. The viscera of the dead which Caesar tramples double as the viscera of Rome and the Senate (7.721–2): *tu, Caesar, in alto | caedis adhuc cumulo patriae per uiscera uadis*, 'you, Caesar, are even now wading through a hefty heap of slaughter, through the viscera of your fatherland'; and further (7.578–80): *monstratque senatum: | scit cruor imperii qui sit, quae uiscera rerum, | unde petat Romam*, 'Caesar points out the Senate: he knows which is the blood of empire, which the viscera of the state, he aims for Rome at its source' (cf. 7.293–4, 491).[130] This all picks up on the *uiscera* on which Lucan founds his suicidal poem in the proem (1.3), and forms a recurrent motif that expands upon Anchises' fears in his address to the future Caesar and Pompey at *Aeneid* 6.832–3: *ne, pueri, ne tanta animis adsuescite bella | neu patriae ualidas in uiscera uertite uiris*, 'no, my boys, don't habituate your spirits to *this* kind of warfare; don't turn your strength and vigour against the viscera of your own country'. Pompey hopes the gods will guide his cause through Caesar's *uiscera* (*BC* 7.349–51, cf. 10.528–9), but it's his own guts that will be heinously probed (8.521, 556–7, 644–5).[131]

There is significant blame to go around here at Pharsalus. First, in terms of the epic tradition, the scene destroys the typical agreement to ensure proper funerals for the dead following a requisite truce (a poeticized proto-*anairesis: Il.* 7.421–32, 24.659–70; *Aen.* 11.100–21, 182–212; cf. 11.22–6),[132]

---

[128] Dinter (2012): 35.    [129] Leigh (1997): 152–7.
[130] Petrone (1996): 142–5; Dinter (2012): 29–37.
[131] On Lucan's use of *uiscera* generally, see Chiesa (2005): 22–3.
[132] Gioseffi (1995). See also Leigh (1997): 292–306, Pagán (2000), Perutelli (2004).

and casts Caesar as a monster for denying these basic rites.[133] Additionally, Caesar takes to its perverse conclusion Achilles' attempts at denying Hector's funeral rites in the *Iliad*,[134] but amplifies this to include an entire unburied army, reminiscent of Creon's funeral ban of the Argive dead that drives the plot of Euripides' *Suppliants* and the end of Statius' *Thebaid*.[135] He resembles Sulla from earlier in the poem, whom Lucan describes denying funerals for the previous civil war's dead (cf. *BC* 2.139–224).[136]

Scholarship has been universally harsh toward Caesar. There are, however, notable complications. Pompey's flight from the battlefield has destroyed any possibility of striking a truce aimed at the collection of the dead (*anairesis*). More troubling, it's clear that the responsibility for provision of obsequies by Greco-Roman custom fell upon the individual commander to collect *his own* dead. Note Onasander *Strategikos* 36.1–2 (mid first-century CE):

> προνοείσθω δὲ τῆς τῶν νεκρῶν κηδείας, μήτε καιρὸν μήθ' ὥραν μήτε τόπον μήτε φόβον προφασιζόμενος, ἄν τε τύχῃ νικῶν, ἄν τε ἡττώμενος· ὁσία μὲν γὰρ καὶ ἡ πρὸς τοὺς ἀποιχομένους εὐσέβεια, ἀναγκαία δὲ καὶ ἡ πρὸς τοὺς ζῶντας ἀπόδειξις. ἕκαστος γὰρ τῶν στρατιωτῶν ὡς αὐτὸς ἀμελούμενος, εἰ πεσὼν ἔτυχεν, παρ' ὀφθαλμοῖς ὁρῶν τὴν τύχην καὶ ὑπὲρ τοῦ μέλλοντος καταμαντευόμενος, ὡς οὐδ' αὐτός, εἰ τεθναίη, ταφησόμενος ἐπαχθῶς φέρει τὴν ἀτύμβευτον ὕβριν.

> The general should provide for the burial of the dead and not offer as a pretext for delay either circumstance or time or place or fear – whether he happens to win or lose. For this is both a holy act of reverence toward the dead and a necessary example for the living. If the dead are unburied, each soldier thinks that his body will not be cared for if, by chance, he falls, seeing what happens with his own eyes and looking to the future. He feels that if he should die, he too will be left unburied and becomes angry at this outrageous lack of burial.

Pompey's flight from the battle and the corpses of his men is a direct dereliction of duty. That the failure to provide funeral rites to the dead

---

[133] See Rieks (1967): 188–9 on Caesar's inhumanity here.    [134] Radicke (2004): 429.

[135] Lovatt (1999): 129–36 argues that Lucan has in mind the tragic/mythic model of Creon for his description of Caesar here. Ambühl (2015): 259–76 looks in more detail at a variety of Greek tragic models. On Creon in Statius, see esp. pp. 203–11 below.

[136] Leigh (1997): 289–90. See Narducci (2002): 228–9, 268 n.125 for a further possible connection to Sulla, who was said to have dined with the severed heads of the proscribed on his dinner table (Val. Max. 9.2.1; Luc. 2.122). Caesar dines among the corpses of slain Pompeians, suggesting cannibalism, as similarly Voisin (1984): 277 discusses in connection with Marius and Sulla dining amidst the severed heads of their victims. Larson (2014): esp. 61–9 examines many American World War Two soldiers' attempts at 'domesticating' the trophy skulls of severed heads of Japanese soldiers.

soldiers will affect the living is made plain after Pompey's own death, when the surviving troops lament the funeral rites *in absentia* for Pompey and the mass dead left to rot at Pharsalus. One soldier (who it seems speaks for all) begs Cato: 'let death proceed to safety; let our old age look forward to lawful flames; civil war scarcely is able to promise burial for its leaders' (*BC* 9.234–6: *mors eat in tutum; iustas sibi nostra senectus | prospiciat flammas: bellum ciuile sepulchra | uix ducibus praestare potest*). The issue is of course precisely what the anonymous soldier pinpoints: civil war complicates things. While Caesar strictly speaking may not have had a militaristic obligation to provide funerals for the enemy dead (this fell to Pompey), the enemy here is still *Roman*, and deserving of rites traditionally and legally owed to Roman soldiers by other Romans.[137] Again – to harp on Lucan's master theme – in civil war, there are no winners, no right or wrong.[138]

However we choose to assign blame, Lucan directs the majority of his apostrophic wrath at Caesar. Though he aims to discern the faces and features of the dead (7.793–4),[139] Caesar dehumanizes his countrymen by reducing the bodies to statistics (792: *Magni numerat populos*, 'he adds-up Magnus' people'),[140] and geographical features (rivers of blood, 789–90; corpses as hills, 790–1; unspecified 'heaps', 791, land inseparable from the bodies covering it, 794–5). The corpses are a measurement of statistical success and a sign of pride. While Pompey tore his gaze away from the horrific scenery (698–9: *nonne iuuat pulsum bellis cessisse nec istud | perspectasse nefas?*), Caesar rejoices in the visual spectacle of carnage (794: *iuuat*; 797: *laeta . . . scelerum spectacula*). This 'spectacular' dialectic, as Matthew Leigh has articulated, draws the reader uncomfortably into a position of channelling Pompey's defeatism or Caesar's voyeurism.[141] The situation, here split between our two heroes, recalls Cornelia's dilemma when faced with Pompey's gruesome murder and mutilation in the next book (8.589–92).[142] In each case, our perspective alignment is focalized

---

[137] E.g. Carrié (1993): 113. See Pagán (2000): 437, commenting on 'aftermath' scenes of battlefield slaughter, generally: 'Proper burial is always the first, most pressing concern of the survivors. It is the duty of the defeated as well as the victorious generals, and it is surely the duty of the grieving family.'

[138] See Ambühl (2015): 263–9 for an excellent discussion of these issues in terms of tragic models Lucan activates. See my discussion below pp. 207–10 for similar concerns in Statius' *Theb*.

[139] Petrone (1996): 144 argues that Caesar's viewing of the faces of the dead distorts Virgil's scene in the underworld when Anchises shows Aeneas the faces of his future descendants (6.755); Narducci (2002): 228; see Thompson and Bruère (1968): 19.

[140] Lovatt (1999): 131. The counting of the dead is a feature of Greco-Roman historiography and military writing and indeed of Caesar's own accounts of the aftermath of battle e.g. *B Ciu.* 1.46, 3.71, 3.99 (of Pharsalus).

[141] Leigh (1997): 291.      [142] See pp. 7–9.

disturbingly through the conflicted gaze of the inset intratextual audience (Noël Carroll's 'horror paradox'[143]). That we read on with Caesar implicates us in his guilty pleasures; we look away and we miss the show.

Caesar's delectation in the field-strewn corpses echoes the god-fighting Erichtho (e.g. 6.526, 540–1, 604), though his breakfast among the dead contrasts her midnight marauding.[144] His victory is equally hers, since her potions, spells, and incantations ensured the battle would be fought at Pharsalus, that the corpses left there would be hers to employ (6.570–88). Pharsalus is their dual Thessalian *aristeia*.[145]

In the end Caesar does not see faces and features of the dead at all, only 'his fortune and his gods in the blood' (7.796: *fortunam superosque suos in sanguine cernit*). Pompey saw himself dying in the blood of the same battle (7.652: *se tam multo pereuntem sanguine uidit*), his own and the Republic's mass defeat. Caesar sees the rise of Caesarism. These dead do not merit funerals, they only serve to validate Caesar's victory and villainy.[146] They are dehumanized, appropriately, because they are a collective 'body' of the Roman *res publica*, as Pompey had implicitly articulated. Caesar thus not only denies funeral rites to dead Romans, he denies a funeral for the dead Republic. This act of *nefas* is heaped upon the gods (798–9), continuing the godlessness, or godlikeness,[147] of Caesar's theomachic actions during the sea storm. As in that instance, there is no divine (re)action. Caesar's (assured) future divinity trivializes, for him, the fate of the dead citizens at Pharsalus. He is incapable of the sort of mortal moralizing we see (e.g.) with Antigone in Sophocles' funereal masterpiece. She *must* bury her brother Polynices because, in her words, she owes a greater allegiance to the dead, with whom she will ultimately reside forever, than the living (*Ant.* 74–6). Caesar awaits a very different sort of eternity. But for now, with the dead beginning to decompose, the mephitic remains prove too much and Caesar flees (*BC* 7.820–2).

Framing the scene of Caesar's bizarre confrontation with Pompey's severed head and his specious request for its burial (9.1035–1108) are Caesar's sightseeing of the ruins of Troy (9.950–99) and his visit to the

---

[143] Carroll (1990); see pp. 8–9.

[144] For the connection between Caesar and Erichtho here see Ahl (1976): 213–14, Johnson (1987): 102, Tesoriero (2004): 204–6, Arweiler (2006), Fratantuono (2012): 302–3. For a general comparison of Caesar and Erichtho see Tesoriero (2004): 201–7.

[145] Johnson (1987): 102, with Thierfelder (1970): 63–7. See also Tesoriero (2004): 205.

[146] Lovatt (2013): 120.

[147] On Caesar's godlike qualities generally in the poem see Henderson (1998): 195–9, Feeney (1991): 295–8, Putnam (1995): 223–40, Nix (2008), Lovatt (2013): 118–20, Chaudhuri (2014): 176–81. On his *supra*-human enigmatic 'inexplicability' see Spentzou (2018).

tomb of Alexander the Great in Alexandria (10.1–52). Alexander is omnipresent here, both in book 10, and since Caesar's visit to Troy imitates the Macedonian king's earlier visit to the sight of Troy (Cic. *Arch.* 24; Plut. *Alex.* 15.4). These episodes play with issues of interment and intimate further allusions to Pompey's extended funeral on the Egyptian shore and beyond. I look first at Caesar's trip to Troy, as he stumbles around the ruins of the once-great city with a local tour guide who points out famous dilapidated monuments.

The site of Troy, with its shadows and once great name, its rotting oaks (*BC* 9.964–9), recalls directly Lucan's description of Pompey as a rotting oak and shadow of a great name at 1.135–43.[148] Beyond this, scholars have noted that the dilapidated Troy resembles Lucan's description of Rome devastated by civil wars, especially after the bloodbath of Pharsalus (7.391–408, cf. 1.21–32).[149] Lucan has cast Pompey as synecdoche for the destruction of the Republic, as the symbol of its fall. This plays on earlier epic symbols: Homer's casting of Hector as the embodiment of Troy's fate in the *Iliad*; Virgil assigning Priam in the same synecdochic role in *Aeneid* 2. Both symbols – symbols of epic defeat – are present in Lucan's depiction of the ruins of Troy (9.976–9):

> Phryx incola manes
> Hectoreos calcare uetat. discussa iacebant
> saxa nec ullius faciem seruantia sacri:
> 'Herceas' monstrator ait 'non respicis aras?'

> The Phrygian local forbids his
> stomping Hector's shade. Scattered stones were lying about,
> not guarding the appearance of anything holy:
> 'Do you have no regard' the guide says, 'for Hercean altars?'

We have seen how Lucan recalls the death of Priam in *Aeneid* 2 for his own depiction of Pompey's death and decapitation in *BC* 8, so it should not surprise us that Priam's death scene and its implications of ruin are noted here, positing a further tie between Troy's fall and the fall of Rome via the death of each city's leader.[150] But Lucan also cleverly links Pompey's tomb with Hector's here at Troy. The aphorism *nullum est sine nomine saxum*, 'there is no stone without a name' (9.973), in the context of dilapidated monuments is evocative of the stone Cordus inscribes with Pompey's

---

[148] Ahl (1976): 214–15; Bartsch (1997): 134–5.
[149] See Ahl (1976): 215–18, Zwierlein (2010): 428–9, Rossi (2001): 321–3, Gowing (2005): 91–4, Spencer (2005).
[150] Rossi (2001): 322–3.

*nomen* to mark the location of his haphazard grave in book 8.[151] The burial site is so lowly that a passer-by would fail to notice Pompey's grave if it were not pointed out (8.820–2). Caesar, oblivious to Hector's tomb, is reprimanded by the Trojan tour-guide for his carelessness in trampling it.[152] Pompey's death and funeral encompass, as a stand in for the fall of the Republic, his dual role as Hector and Priam, the defeated heroes of prior epics, the last bastions of Troy's power as envisioned by Homer and Virgil, respectively. By including these symbolic pointers at the site of a ruined Troy, Lucan offers an homage to his epic predecessors through the lens of defeat, proleptic of his vision of present/future Rome similarly crumbling and dying.

But Lucan's – typically – is an aggressive homage. Caesar's trampling on the Hercean altar recalls Pyrrhus' slaughter of Priam and the desecration of the same sacred site.[153] Achilles and his son had 'ruined' Troy,[154] just as Caesar is making new ruins of his Rome; theirs brought the destruction of a foreign enemy in Troy and the Trojans,[155] Caesar's victories are suicidal by nature of the internecine conflict he wages. Whether we believe that Caesar is cognizant of what he sees at Troy or not,[156] Lucan tells us that he goes out of his way to honour the tombs of Ajax and Achilles, the great Achaean heroes (9.961–3). In this way Caesar aligns himself with the epic winners *contra* his own genealogical connection with the epic losers, whom he stomps underfoot.[157] Lucan's *sphragis* (9.980–6), his monumentalizing of his own poetic achievement and his muse, Caesar, is a monument to Caesar's destructive wickedness and the poet's own implication in that wickedness (by narrating Caesar's villainy).[158] Caesar in the *Bellum ciuile* only ever creates ruins, he tramples (*calcare*),[159] in stark contrast to Aeneas

---

[151] Ormand (1994): 50 n.36.
[152] Ormand (1994): 51–2; Hardie (2008): 316; Galtier (2010): 201.
[153] Hardie (2008): 315; Fratantuono (2012): 385–6.
[154] Putnam (1965): 33–7; Smith (1999): 247–8; Dekel (2012): 68–9.
[155] It's noteworthy that Achilles' wrath was also destructive to his own Achaean cohort, signalled at the poem's *incipit*, as well as to the Trojans (*Il.* 1.1–2): μῆνιν . . . οὐλομένην, 'destructive wrath' diffusely. Caesar similarly in *BC* spreads death and destruction indiscriminately.
[156] Is his sightseeing aimless or attentive: and thus, does he 'stumble' onto Hector's tomb and the altar or does he seek them out for defilement? See Ormand (1994), Rossi (2001), Tesoriero (2005), Ambühl (2015): 347–9.
[157] Tesoriero (2005): 205–6.
[158] Zwierlein (2010): 431–2; Johnson (1987): 120–1; Narducci (2002): 179.
[159] E.g. 7.292–4, 748–9; 9.977, 1043–4; 10.2; Zwierlein (2010): 422; Wick (2004): *ad* 977sq; Day (2013): 177–8. From *calx*, the back of the heel (*OLD* s.v. *calx*[1] 1). Lucan uses the verb of trampling bodies and objects (*OLD* s.v. *calco* 6 a, b). Petronius, catching the refrain, will have his own Caesar in Eumolpus' *Bellum ciuile* 'trample the heights' in his crossing of the Alps (*BC* 152: *haec ubi* **calcauit** *Caesar iuga milite laeto*).

the incessant city-builder. Lucan had feared that Pompey's tomb might be trampled as a result of its inconspicuousness (8.804–5): *erremus populi cinerumque tuorum,* | *Magne, metu nullas Nili calcemus harenas,* 'let us, the people, stray and trample no sands of the Nile in fear, Magnus, of your ashes'.[160] Here symbolically Caesar tramples Pompey's tomb through his desecration of the epic models for this tomb, as he wanders victorious through a graveyard of epics past.

At the opening of the final book of the poem, Caesar stomps into Alexandria (10.2: *calcauit*), and, ignoring all other sites, immediately seeks out the tomb of Alexander the Great. Scholarship has tended, appropriately, to view the scene as Lucan's comparison of Caesar with Alexander, and of the subsequent polemic against Alexander as more obliquely an attack on tyrannical Caesar(s).[161] What has not been adequately acknowledged is the connection that Lucan is making here between Alexander and Pompey and the implications of Caesar's implicit tomb-raiding.

The allusion is subtle but loaded (10.19): *effossum tumulis cupide descendit in antrum,* '[Caesar] descends gleefully into the cave dug out for a tomb'. Lucan everywhere plays with epic *topoi,* and here Caesar's descent into the hollowed-out *antrum* functions as a *katabasis*.[162] Caesar, however, needs no Sibylline guide, he's like Hercules breaching the world of the dead without fear or compunction. But this is not quite the Tartarean cave he enters (e.g. 6.712: *Tartareo . . . antro*), it's one shaped into a *tumulus,* and so Caesar again takes on the guise of an Erichtho or a Sulla gleefully (*cupide*) entering tombs to exhume the dead.

Lucan does not detail exactly what Caesar is doing here. Later emperors are said to have explicitly disrupted Alexander's tomb. Suetonius claims that Octavian, after his victory at Actium in 31 BCE, removed Alexander's sarcophagus, placed a golden diadem on the mummy's head, and sprinkled the corpse with flowers (Suet. *Aug.* 18).[163] More sinisterly, Dio says Octavian broke off part of Alexander' nose in the process (Dio Cass. 51.16.5).[164] Later still, Caligula is alleged to have pilfered a breastplate from the tomb which he then wore on parade across the Bay of Baiae

---

[160] Day (2013): 177 n.178.

[161] See Ahl (1976): 222–30, Zwierlein (2010): 419–20, Quint (1993): 4–6, 155, Auhagen (2001), Narducci (2002): 240–7, Rossi (2005).

[162] Fratantuono (2012): 400; *descendere* is the verb of *katabasis*: e.g. Verg. *Aen.* 6.126, 404; Ov. *Met.* 10.13, 21; Luc. *BC* 6.653; Sil. *Pun.* 13.573, 759; Stat. *Silu.* 5.5.41, etc.

[163] Hope (2000): 123; Erskine (2002): 163.     [164] Erskine (2002): 163.

(Suet. *Calig.* 52; Dio Cass. 59.17.3).[165] Perhaps we are invited to retroject these 'imperial' tomb-raidings into Lucan's silence concerning Caesar's strange descent.

The imagery of tomb-raiding continues as Alexander and his remains are equated with Pompey's scattered corpse from book 8. Alexander's limbs should have been dispersed throughout the world (10.22–3): *sacratis totum spargenda per orbem | membra uiri posuere adytis*, 'they placed the limbs of the man in a sacred shrine, limbs which should have been scattered through the whole world'. This is the corporal punishment Caesar belittles during the storm scene in book 5, but Pompey actually suffers after his own death (cf. 8.629: *spargant lacerentque*, cf. 8.751: *sparsis Pompei manibus*, 9.58: *dispersi*, 9.1093: *sparsis*).[166] Alexander should have been a source of mockery (10.26: *ludibrio*), as Pompey's corpse becomes (8.710): *ludibrium pelagi*, 'plaything of the sea'; 9.14: *risitque sui ludibria trunci*, '[Pompey's ghost] laughed at the insults to its trunk'.[167] Pompey had feared before Pharsalus that he would become the 'plaything' of his father-in-law Caesar (7.380: *ludibrium soceri*); while his trunk becomes a toy of the sea his head comes as a gruesome trinket at which Caesar feigns disgust. Caesar's tomb-raiding brings him into direct contact with the corpse of another Magnus (Alexander), another toy.

Beyond these are more general correspondences between Pompey and Alexander that Lucan has been building throughout the poem and which climax here in the description of each in death. The first mention of Alexander comes during the catalogue of Pompey's troops (3.233–4): *hic ubi Pellaeus post Tethyos aequora ductor | constitit et magno uinci se fassus ab orbe est*, 'here where the Pellaean leader stopped after Tethys' waters and admitted he was conquered by the vastness of the world'. The comparison is meant to champion the might of Pompey's resources in the East, but it doubles as a prelude to his demise: like Alexander, this world conquering will not end well for Pompey.

The same image of Pompey's ill-fated Eastern connections with the Macedonian ruler appears in his message to enlist the aid of the Parthians after his defeat at Pharsalus, containing a catalogue of his exploits in Alexander's old haunts (8.218–38).[168] Lucan frames the battle between Caesar and Pompey as a competition for the right to be the next Alexander (5.1–3): *sic alterna duces bellorum uolnera passos | in Macetum*

[165] Hope (2000): 123; Erskine (2002): 178.　　[166] Berti (2000): *ad* 10.22–3.
[167] Quint (1993): 155; Berti (2000): *ad* 10.26.
[168] Mayer (1981): *ad* 8.227, 237; Tracy (2014): 28–9.

*terras miscens aduersa secundis | seruauit fortuna pares*, 'thus Fortune, mixing failure with success, preserved the leaders for the Macedonians' land, having suffered equally alternate wounds of war'. The *Macetum terras* are meant to recall Alexander, the original world ruler, as each leader balances victory with defeat in pursuit of the Macedonian's legacy of despotism.[169]

Lucan hinted at Pompey's connection to Alexander at the beginning of book 8, but the parallel is clinched at 8.692–9. Here he contrasts Alexander's burial with Pompey's lack of one.[170] Alexander is housed in a vault (694: *sacrato Macedon seruatur in **antro***, 'the Macedonian is kept in a sacred cave'), while Pompey is scattered and tossed in the waves. This scene is the direct precursor to Lucan's description of Caesar visiting the vault of Alexander at the beginning of the final book (10.19: ***antrum***), where he laments the fact that Alexander's remains are not 'scattered' throughout the world as Pompey's have been. There is a sense that while one Magnus is buried, the other must be denied burial. This is implicit in book 8, but clearer at 9.153–4, when the younger Pompey promises to provide a funeral for his father at the expense of exhuming Alexander: *non ego Pellaeas arces adytisque retectum | corpus Alexandri pigra Mareotide mergam?*, 'should I not plunge the Pellaean corpse of Alexander, uncovered from its inner tomb, in the lazy Mareotis?' As David Quint argues, Alexander's body should resemble the fate of his empire: lacerated and broken to pieces after his death.[171] His body should, further, stand for the dismemberment (the *sparagmos*) of his empire just as Lucan has (de)constructed Pompey's body as a stand in for the scattered, dismembered state of Rome's Republic after Pharsalus.

Pompey had styled himself as Alexander: he was, after all, Pompeius 'Magnus'.[172] Alexander-*imitatio* was common among Roman generals, but Pompey it seems appropriated this connection more intensely than other imitators. Plutarch tells us he was nicknamed Alexander in his youth for a physical resemblance between the two – he later modelled his appearance after Alexander – and the trajectory of his youthfully successful career in the East mimicked Alexander's conquests. He even went as far as to wear a cloak said to have belonged to Alexander during his triumph celebrating the Eastern victories (App. *Mith.* 117).[173] Their ends were both catastrophic,

---

[169] Fratantuono (2012): 179.    [170] See Galtier (2010): 198–9.

[171] Quint (1993): 155. Dinter (2012): 17 notes the 'painfully obvious' correspondences between Alexander and Caesar here, but says nothing of the associations between Alexander and Pompey.

[172] Green (2010): 154 n.6: 'We know that Pompey compared *himself* to Alexander; we also know there is not a trace of this in Lucan.' I'm aiming to adjust this second claim.

[173] See Plut. *Pomp.* 2.1–2, 46.1. Cf. Sall. *Hist.* 3 fr. 88 Maurenbrecher; Pliny *HN* 7.95–6; see Rossi (2005): 248.

and both were ultimately embalmed (Alexander's body, Pompey's head). Lucan seems to be toying with this as his description of Pompey's embalming is immediately followed by his frustration that Alexander's (embalmed) body is allowed a final resting place (*BC* 8.692–700).

If Pompey has been more directly associated with Alexander in the poem up to book 10, it is here that Caesar will claim sole succession. After preliminary associations between dead Pompey and dead Alexander during Lucan's polemic against the Macedonian ruler, Alexander's connection with the lightning bolt and star (10.34–5), Caesar's tokens, seals the deal.[174] Caesar has wrested sole claim to Alexander-*imitatio* in Lucan's poem, and this is the ultimate prize of his raiding of Alexander's tomb,[175] the tomb Pompey should have had instead. This association, however, is the kiss of death for Caesar – as it was for Pompey – who exits the epic as it stands perplexed, dismayed, at the point of defeat surrounded by Egyptian troops (10.534–46), while Pompey, in a stunning role reversal, usurps Caesar's deific trampling (10.2: *calcauit Caesar*) in the final image of the poem (10.546): **calcantem moenia Magnum**, ' . . . Magnus stomping upon the ramparts'.[176]

### Re-Animator

No discussion of funeral rites in the *Bellum ciuile* is complete without a comment on Lucan's magnificent witch Erichtho. She appears in book 6, on the eve of the battle of Pharsalus, as Pompey's son Sextus seeks her aid in unveiling the future events of war, his own fate, and the fate of his father, Pompey the Great. Erichtho has generally been, for good reason, an analytical lodestone, but I shall try to place equal emphasis on the corpse-soldier she resurrects and demands to prophesy for Sextus.

Erichtho is the über-witch of Thessaly, so vile and sinister that she scorns the 'too pious' actions of her witchy brood (6.507–8).[177] It is her specialization as a night-witch,[178] dealing exclusively in the dead and rites associated with death, that set her above – and morally below – the others. Lucan

---

[174] Ahl (1976): 224; Berti (2000): *ad locc.*; Auhagen (2001): 136; Narducci (2002): 245; Rossi (2005): 244.

[175] Hardie (2008): 314. Cf. Galtier (2010): 199.

[176] Penwill (2009): 93–5 argues that Caesar's vulnerability and isolation at the end of the poem symbolize his assassination, and the presence of *Magnus* in the final line alludes to his death in Pompey's senate-house before Pompey's statue. The framing and juxtaposing presence of *calcare* at the open and close of book 10 have not been cited as evidence for the 'planned ending' of Lucan's poem, but this does seem to nail the feeling of closure; Rimell (2015): 250 hints at this.

[177] Finiello (2005): 160.

[178] See Gordon (1987): 239–40, Tomassi Moreschini (2005): 149–50, Finiello (2005): 160–3.

provides a list of her many atrocities aimed at corpses (6.529–69). Among these: she buries the living and revives the dead (529–32), she robs funeral pyres of half-burnt corpses (532–7), cannibalizes crucifixion victims (541–9), performs Caesarean sections and hurls the foetuses on burning altars (558–9), and mutilates the heads and cannibalizes corpses at funerals (564–9). She's also able to kill if need be (554–61), but her 'joy' comes from repurposing the dead for her dark arts (541–2 cf. 526, 604). In short (561): *hominum mors omnis in usu est,* 'every human death is put to use'.

Lucan describes all of this as a preamble for the necromancy Erichtho performs for Pompey's son Sextus, who wishes to know the future on the eve of the battle at Pharsalus. While Aeneas and the Sibyl in *Aeneid 6* descend to Hell for the purposes of consulting the ghost of Anchises for future knowledge (the main model scene for Lucan's episode), Erichtho brings Hell to earth by summoning the ghost of a fallen soldier to prophesy. But she doesn't simply seek an *umbra*. True to form, Erichtho reanimates the corpse of a fallen soldier as a vessel for its soul, creating a 'zombie' from a body denied a grave (*BC* 6.626).

The process of her necromancy is arguably the most outlandish example of corpse abuse in the poem. After rummaging through the fields of the dead, Erichtho selects a corpse and drags the body to her workplace by a hook (*uncus*). Here Lucan distorts the role of a public executioner who was charged with dragging corpses with a hook to be dumped into the Tiber (often after an extended period of public exposure and mutilation).[179] Erichtho will not drag this particular corpse to be disposed of, but rather 'to live' (*BC* 6.638–40: *inserto laqueis feralibus unco | per scopulos miserum trahitur per saxa cadauer | uicturum,* 'with a hook thrust into the corpse's noose, the pitiful cadaver is dragged through rocks and through stones *to live*'). The enjambed catachrestic *uicturum* spills into the next line, delaying and perverting the standard trope that the corpse will be dumped like others dragged by a hook.

Next she prepares the corpse, slicing open its chest and pouring boiling blood and lunar poison into newly created wounds (667–9). This scene is essentially a reverse-sacrifice that inverts the Sibyl's animal sacrifice in the

---

[179] Many ancient sources note the dragging of corpses by a hook e.g. Juv. 10.66–7 of Sejanus: *Seianus ducitur unco | spectandus, gaudent omnes,* 'all rejoice as Sejanus is seen dragged by a hook'; Ov. *Ib.* 165–6. In 31 CE Sejanus' corpse was left on the *Scalae Gemoniae* for three days before being dragged to the Tiber (Suet. *Tib.* 61; Dio Cass. 58.11; Sid. Apoll. *Epist.* 1.7.12). The famous scene may have been on Lucan's mind here. See *OLD* s.v. *uncus*² b, Mayor (1979): *ad* Juv. 10.66–7, Hinard (1984): 301, Kyle (1998): index s.v. 'hooks, dragging by'. Note the breathtaking senatorial decree fantasized by SHA *Comm.* 18.3–20.5, demanding the *post mortem* abuse of Commodus with the repeated refrain of dragging by the hook.

*Aeneid* (6.248–9: cf. Ov. *Met.* 7.264–87; Sen. *Med.* 705–38).[180] Into the
corpse she heaps every assortment of execrable substance: rabid dog foam,
lynx viscera, hyena hump, the marrow of a snake-fed doe, and so on (*BC*
6.671–80). Along with these named substances, she adds 'leaves drenched
in spells unspeakable' (682) and venoms of her own creation (684).[181]
Erichtho then unleashes a torrent of cacophonic noises incompatible
with human speech (688–93). When the ghost hesitates to re-enter its
body, she beats the corpse with a live snake like a disgruntled *paedagogus*
lashing an apprehensive student (725–9; cf. Quint. *Inst.* 1.3.13–17) and
threatens the infernal gods (730–49). The scene is wonderfully outrageous.

It's characteristic of Lucan to provide the sardonic twist that this surgically
exacting corpse abuse – along with Pompey's mistreatment the grisliest scene
of *post mortem* mutilation in the epic – manages not further bodily dissolution
but actually to revivify the dead man, creating life from rotting flesh. But this
life is largely signified by its liminality and its grotesque warping of actual life
(755–62): the corpse is more dead than alive (758–9: *nondum facies uiuentis in
illo,* | *iam morientis erat,* 'there was in him the appearance of someone not yet
living, already dying').[182] Erichtho had promised Sextus that new, true, genu-
ine life would be restored to prophesy for him (660: *iam noua, iam uera
reddetur uita figura*). *noua* (metapoetically) anticipates the strange novelty of
Erichtho's/Lucan's creation, undercutting the claims that this will be 'real life',
and setting us up for something much more strange. No surprise then that a
witch whose *métier* is death and dying would create a perversion of actual life.
Death is all Erichtho – like Lucan[183] – knows.

Liminality is a key feature of Lucan's necromancy scene. Erichtho's dealings
with the dead are so entrenched that outwardly there is little separating her
from a walking corpse herself. Her cave too is a liminal place, somewhere
between Hell and the upper world, and resembles the entrance to the underworld in the classic description at *Aeneid* 6.236–41.[184] Erichtho's cave, like the
Sibyl's, represents a marginal area between both worlds, where the boundaries
have been so blurred that her abode might as well be in Hell (*BC* 6.649–53).[185]

[180]  Masters (1992): 192.
[181]  Erichtho's mad-science recalls Sulla's metaphorical venturing too far into the human frame to
       remove the disease in Rome's rotten corpse (2.141–3).
[182]  Housman (1927): *ad loc.*; Tesoriero (2004): 191–2. Note Zissos (1993): *ad* 6.754, 759.
[183]  On Erichtho as *uates* and a metapoetic signifier for the poet Lucan, see O'Higgins (1988), Masters
       (1992): 205–215, Finiello (2005): 178–82.
[184]  Feeney (1986); Masters (1992): 179–95; Hardie (1993): 76–7, 107–9.
[185]  Masters (1992): 190; Hardie (1993): 77. See also Korenjak (1996): *ad* 6.649f., Arweiler (2006) of
       Thessaly subsuming elements of Hell, Dinter (2012): 69.

The witch spends her time navigating this middle space. She rejects civil society and, like a corpse, lives in abandoned tombs (511–12: *deserta . . . busta | incolit*). She's *grata* to the nether gods (513) and intrinsic to that element of Hell that has drifted into the upper world.[186] Erichtho is corpse-like in appearance. Her skin is gaunt with decay and corrupted by hellish pallor (515–18). Virgil had indicated the approaching deaths of Lausus and Turnus by highlighting their pallor (*Aen.* 10.822: *ora . . . pallentia*; 12.221: *iuuenali in corpore pallor*, 'pallor in his youthful body'). Erichtho has the complexion of someone about to die, but lives in a limbo where the brief moment of death pallor is infinitely extended. Virgil describes 'phantoms' as etiolated at *Georgics* 1.477: *simulacra modis pallentia miris*, among the indicators that civil war was about to be unleashed; this is an appropriate reference here in Lucan's lead-up to the climax of his *Civil War*, and his own depiction of troops before battle finds them similarly tinged with deathly *pallor* (*BC* 7.129–30, see below). Erichtho eerily resembles the corpse she will raise from the dead to prophesy for Sextus (6.750–60): both are 'grim' (*maestus, -a, -um*: Erichtho, 625; corpse, 776, 821) and marked with *pallor* (Erichtho, 517; corpse, 759). The living-dead corpse (758–9) similarly hovers caught between two worlds,[187] and this state of liminality is precisely what Erichtho had requested for her necromancy (cf. 6.712–15, 777–9).

The Thessalian stain of death is infectious and Sextus Pompey too comes to resemble a corpse (657–8). He has lost the spark of life: *trementem . . . exanimi defixum lumina uoltu*, 'trembling, eyes frozen, with lifeless face'.[188] Like Erichtho, he takes on the appearance of the reanimated corpse: the ghost-soldier the witch summons will hesitate to enter its old, dead body, the lifeless confines (721–2: *exanimis . . . carceris*) of its prior home. The word *exanimis* is in Lucan only used in the context of corpses, real or metaphorical (the two examples in book 6, plus 2.26, 2.302). As Dolores O'Higgins notes, even the soldiers pre-Pharsalus have faces tinged with death; they *are* death (7.129–30: *multorum pallor in ore | mortis uenturae faciesque simillima fato*, 'the pallor of impending death is on the faces of many, the appearance mirroring their fate').[189]

This plays well with the distorted sequencing of events here, where dead soldiers litter the Thessalian plain before any actual fighting has taken place. The detail is often bemoaned by scholars as evidence of Lucan's

[186] Lovatt (2013): 155.    [187] Korenjak (1996): *ad* 6.750–62.
[188] O'Higgins (1988): 222 with n.43; Korenjak (1996): *ad* 6.658.
[189] Note the pale faces of Cacus' decapitated victims, pierced on pikes (*Aen.* 8.196–7): *foribusque adfixa superbis | **ora uirum tristi pendebant pallida** tabo.*

'carelessness',[190] but is better understood as a nod to the power of witch-craft to manipulate time (e.g. 6.461–5); book 6 in fact ends with Erichtho holding back the approaching day in a fog of night (830).[191] The battle of Pharsalus is bookended by descriptions of fields full of those slain surpris-ingly *at* Pharsalus (6.619–41; 7.786–845). They are in effect dead before the depiction of their *physical* deaths, a frightful sense of *fait accompli*. This is also a pointed comment on the hopelessness of the war and the withered Republican cause. The corpses stand for the already realized death of the Republic, while the Imperial victors (Caesar and Erichtho) rummage through its/their *uiscera*.

Charles Tesoriero compiled an extensive list of comparisons between Erichtho and Caesar, including their impiety toward the gods, state, and family, their consumption by *ira*, the pleasure they derive from their crimes, the desecration of the bodies of the living and dead, tyranny, invocation of infernal powers, and so on. In short: 'Erichtho is Caesar unmasked: pure wickedness, selfish excess, a figure who views the civil war as a means to acquire personal power.'[192] Not surprisingly many of these comparisons concern, in one way or another, the mistreatment of corpses both encounter on the fields of Thessaly.[193] The image that capped Caesar's malevolence after Pharsalus was his denial of funeral rites to the dead soldiers. Yet strangely Erichtho follows a different path here. While we might be skeptical of her promise to offer proper death rites to the reanimated corpse in exchange for the delivery of his prophecy (6.763–70), the final lines of book 6 close with the only 'successful' funeral in Lucan's poem, administered by a witch championed for her abuse of the dead and disruption of traditional rites (820–8):[194]

> sic postquam fata peregit,
> stat uoltu maestus tacito mortemque reposcit.
> carminibus magicis opus est herbisque, cadauer
> ut cadat, et nequeunt animam sibi reddere fata
> consumpto iam iure semel. tunc robore multo
> extruit illa rogum; uenit defunctus ad ignes.                 825
> accensa iuuenem positum strue liquit Erictho
> tandem passa mori, Sextoque ad castra parentis
> it comes

---

[190] E.g. Francken (1896–7): *ad* 6.619, Duff (1928): 348 n.1, Håkanson (1979): 31, Narducci (2002): 147 n.82. See *contra* O'Higgins (1988): 218–19, 225–6, Arweiler (2006), Finiello (2005): 180, Fratantuono (2012): 249–50.

[191] See Arweiler (2006) for Thessaly as a place removed from time and space.

[192] Tesoriero (2004): 201–7; the quote is from p. 203.       [193] Cf. Arweiler (2006).

[194] Zissos (1993): *ad* 6.820–27.

> Thus after delivering the prophecy,
> he stands, face silent, grim, and begs for death again.
> There is need for magic charms and herbs so that the cadaver
> can die, the Fates can't take back his soul,
> their jurisdiction over him spent already the first time. Then loaded
>     with wood
> she erects a pyre; the dead man comes up to the fire.                    825
> Erichtho left the youth, placed on the burning heap,
> at last allowing him to die, and to the camp of his father with Sextus
> she goes as his companion.

Neil Coffee argues that Erichtho ignores basic codes of reciprocal behaviour here since she deprives the corpse of the gift (6.724: *munus*) of not dying a second time, and offers a 'great payment' (762–3: *magna ... mercede*) to the corpse from whom she had pilfered the gift of death.[195] But this is to ignore the fact that the corpse was initially, and otherwise would have remained, *unburied* (626). The greatest disappointment of the corpse's prophecy is that, because he was not buried, he could not descend far enough into the underworld to have seen anything noteworthy to report back (777–9).[196] Lucan's poem fights intensely against the traditional form of epic *katabasis*. Erichtho brings Hell to earth instead of allowing Sextus a chance to descend, and the poet hesitates to ascribe literal descent to Erichtho herself (6.651–3). We have seen how Caesar's descent into Alexander's tomb plays with the *katabasis* theme. And here even the ghosts of the dead fail to cross the Styx. We might weigh the relative value of a proper funeral with the misery of revivification, but Erichtho's corpse, at least, will receive the more lasting funeral rites denied to his fellow countrymen who remain unburied and rotting in Thessaly's fields.

The cremation is bizarre. Spells and potions, like those which brought the corpse back to life, are required to 'kill' it again (822–3: *cadauer ... ut cadat* is wickedly paradoxical[197]), while the spent-man (825: *defunctus*) eerily walks up to his own pyre. But around the absurdity is proper protocol. Erichtho gathers wood for the construction of a large pyre and she leaves only after the corpse has been engulfed in flames. Lucan's bravura display of corpse abuse and necromantic perversity ends with the *dénouement* of a sombre funeral for a dead soldier.

---

[195] Coffee (2009): 125.

[196] Ahl (1976): 138; Masters (1992): 198–9; Zissos (1993): *ad* 6.778. The corpse-soldier is like a painfully ill-informed Er, a slain soldier similarly 'revivified' on a battlefield, who shares his detailed vision of a wraithish underworld (Pl. *Resp.* 10.614b–621b).

[197] Martindale (1976): 47, 53 n.7; Zissos (1993): *ad* 6.755, 6.822; Chiesa (2005): 24–5. Cf. *BC* 2.134: *cecidere cadauera*, with Konenjak (1996): *ad loc.*

Erichtho's treatment here and at 763–70 is 'almost motherly',[198] as she, in the role of a mourning woman, provides the last rites over the 'youth' (826: *iuuenem*). Here the corpse is humanized for the first time (he's elsewhere variously a *corpus, cadauer, umbra, anima*[199]). This touch adds a gentle *pathos* to the funeral and plays up the association of Erichtho as a grieving mother. Erichtho's humanity is for the first time apparent here too; she leaves with Sextus as his *comes* (828: 'companion'), overturning her earlier rejection of civil society. The entire episode has played with marginal and liminal spaces, blurring the distinctions between Hell and the upper world, life and death, humanity and inhumanity, but the final image is one of proper human decency and kindness. Despite their many points of contact in the poem, the mad witch Erichtho offers and oversees the funeral Caesar denied to his fellow Romans and their embodiment as Rome's Republic, and this is perhaps Lucan's most shocking denunciation of the ills and inhumanity of Caesarism.

Scholars have argued that with Erichtho's corpse-soldier Lucan is asking his audience to recall the story about the 'undying' prophetic Gabienus, a Caesarian soldier captured and executed by Sextus Pompey in Sicily (recorded in Pliny *HN* 7.52.178–9).[200] Gabienus is beheaded, but his head hangs on by a thread (*iussu eius incisa ceruice et uix cohaerente, iacuit in litore toto die*), and he somehow manages to deliver a message to Sextus that the cause against Caesar is worth fighting. This allusion provides wonderful texture for the scene looking beyond the confines of Lucan's poem to Sextus' death in Asia and the end of the Pompeian family line. But we should consider briefly another corpse Lucan is recalling here in Erichtho's corpse-zombie: Sextus' father, Pompey the Great.

On an analogical level the link between Anchises (deliverer of prophecy) and Aeneas (receiver) in the model prophetic scene from the underworld in *Aeneid* 6 posits a parallel familial correspondence between the prophetic corpse and his addressee, Sextus Pompey (who, I should add, styled himself *Pius*[201]). Lucan plays with this familial association by calling the corpse *Pompeiana umbra* (*BC* 6.717),[202] essentially translating the famous tag-line of Pompey as *M/magni nominis umbra*, 'shadow of a great name' or

---

[198] Johnson (1987): 27.

[199] Zissos (1993): *ad* 6.826. Korenjak (1996): 28–9 notes the active dehumanizing of the corpse throughout the episode but makes no mention of Lucan's stunning use of *iuuenem* here.

[200] See Grenade (1950): 37–40, Ahl (1976): 133–7, Masters (1992): 197 n.41, 203, Korenjak (1996): 26, Narducci (2002): 127, Fratantuono (2012): 254.

[201] See examples of coinage containing this cognomen in Sydenham (1952): nos. 1041–5; *ILS* 8891; Syme (1939): 157; Grenade (1950): 42 n.2.

[202] Hardie (1993): 109.

'shadow of the name of Magnus' (1.135).[203] This signifier comes during Erichtho's promise to deliver an accurate prophecy – (716–17): *ducis* **omnia** *nato | Pompeiana* **canat** *nostri modo militis umbra*, 'let the Pompeian ghost just recently among our soldiery foretell the future to the son of the leader'[204] – that proves to be less helpful than expected. The corpse itself echoes Erichtho's words when it promises an additional prophecy to come (813–14): *tibi certior* **omnia** *uates | ipse* **canet** *Siculis genitor Pompeius in aruis*, 'a more certain profit will prophesy all to you in Sicily's fields, Pompey himself, your father'. Even then this future *certior uates* will be unable to articulate anything specific to Sextus about his fate.[205] The inexactness of each prophecy (the corpse's and father Pompey's *in futuro*) links them, as do the clear verbal cues: **omnia ... canet** with **omnia ... canat**; the Pompeian shade (6.617) with Pompey's (future) shade. Ultimately it's difficult to differentiate much between the poorly prophetic corpse and the ghost of Pompey who will poorly prophesy for his son in some future beyond Lucan's poem. Aeneas had met his father's shade in the underworld; Sextus, in a scene removed from chronological structures, time and space, meets the zombie of the 'shadow of Pompey' in Thessaly's Hell on earth.

Like Pompey, who is a shade before the moment of his actual death, the corpse is both alive and dead, a zombie who, by the wiles of witchcraft, has died in a battle that has not yet happened. Commentators cite the rather fraught line about the corpse's slit throat (637: *traiecto gutture*[206]) as a key feature linking this corpse to Gabienus,[207] but it also looks ahead to Pompey's demise and his death and mutilation through decapitation off

---

[203] For Lucan's play on Pompey's famous nickname, see esp. Feeney (2010).

[204] The textual issues here have been discussed by Ahl (1976): 136, though *omnia* is surely preferable to *omina*, both stylistically and in light of the same phrasing 100 lines later of another prophecy to come (813–14): *omnia ... canet* in the same metrical position; see Housman (1927): ad 6.716. The other sticking point is the function of *Pompeiana*: does it agree with *omnia* or *umbra*? Again lines 813–14 can help, where *Pompeius* is the subject of *canet*, and *Pompeius* (the man himself as a ghost) can be seen to play off the earlier *Pompeiana umbra*.

[205] I.e. where he will die, when, etc. (815–16). Masters (1992): 196–204 expands on these points in more detail.

[206] Housman (1927): *ad loc.* prints *gutture*. Håkanson (1979): 32–4, Shackleton Bailey (1988): *ad loc.*, and Braund (1992): lv, posit *pectore* for *gutture*, translating 'one with pierced breast', in a reasonable attempt to avoid the issues posed by *gutture* altogether (as well a connection to verses 722–3). But *gutture* plays with the Gabienus and Pompey slit-throat allusions, and issues of 'bad prophecy'. Cf. *Aen.* 10.348 of one Dryops, who has his throat slashed as he's speaking, 'robbing him of life and voice at the same time' (10.345–8): *Clausus | aduenit et rigida Dryopem ferit eminus hasta | sub mentum grauiter pressa, pariterque loquentis | uocem animamque rapit* **traiecto gutture**. The syleptic snatching of life and voice together resonates with the corpse-soldier who was just previously dead, but also unable to speak upon initial request (*BC* 6.760–2).

[207] E.g. Grenade (1950): 38–9.

the Egyptian shore. Martin Korenjak notes that the odd combination of a slit throat with the ability to speak and indeed prophesy recalls (beyond the historical Gabienus model) Homer's dying prophetic Hector (*Iliad* 22.324–9, 356–60).[208] His throat is slashed by Achilles but the windpipe remains intact, and he's able to deliver a prophecy that looks ahead to Achilles' fall at the hands of Paris and Apollo. While Erichtho's ability to make a corpse with a slit throat speak is certainly a sign of her skill at witchcraft, a subtle gesture towards Hector here strengthens the corpse's association with Pompey, whom Lucan repeatedly models on the Trojan prince as the poem's heroic victim.

The corpse's bizarre continuation of life is patently clear, but so too is Lucan's treatment of Pompey's extended death. Even after decapitation Pompey tries to speak (*BC* 8.682–3). His *truncus* and especially his *caput* become their own characters throughout the poem as Lucan repeatedly *revives* Pompey in a cyclical rehashing of his death, abuse, and warped funeral. Most striking are the lexical cues that tie Pompey's half-death with the corpse's strange rebirth.[209] Consider Pompey's sputtering death at 8.682–3: *dum **uiuunt** uultus atque **os** in **murmura** pulsant | singultus animae, dum **lumina nuda** rigescunt*, 'while features live and breath's gurgles drive the mouth to mumbles, while open eyes grow stiff'. Now recall again the revivification of Erichtho's corpse-soldier (6.757–62): *distento **lumina** rictu | **nudantur**. nondum facies **uiuentis** in illo, | iam morientis erat ... | sed **murmure** nullo | **ora** astricta sonant*, 'his eyes lay open with hollow stare. There was in him the appearance of someone not yet living, already dying ... But his closed mouth speaks not a murmur.' This is a haunting reworking which threads together the major scene of death in Lucan's poem with the equally famous zombie rebirth scene. Fortune strikes Pompey down all at one go (8.707–8: ***semel** inpulit illum | dilata Fortuna manu*), while the corpse-soldier is thrust awkwardly at one go from the earth, again in a mirror-image (6.756–7: *terraque **repulsum** est | erectumque **semel***). In the end, in the narrative present (excluding the earlier example of Sulla's tomb in book 2) Erichtho's corpse-soldier and Pompey's are the only corpses to receive anything resembling a funeral before/after Pharsalus, at the oddly tender hands of characters (Cordus and Erichtho) acting out the role of a grieving wife or mother. But through the bizarre circumstances of Lucan's staging of their deaths, both Pompey and Erichtho's zombie have an afterlife, or better, an extension of the process of

---

[208] Korenjak (1996): *ad* 6.637.
[209] Housman (1927): *ad* 6.757–8; Korenjak (1996): 29 and *ad* 6.757–62.

dying, and by linking them in this and other ways Lucan further articulates the nightmarish repetitive cycle of death in and as civil war.

## Conclusions

I linger on these last points about repetitions and the extension of the process of dying for their powerful implications for Lucan's conception of the symbolic death of Rome's *res publica*, and his devious engagement with Augustan rhetoric championing monarchal rule as a restoration, a 'rebirth' of the Republican system and its intimate association with notions of *libertas*. I have written elsewhere about this feature of Lucan's socio-political poetics,[210] so I will not devote too much space to a discussion here. But let me summarize briefly in closing.

Seen through the eyes of contemporary rhetoricians, philosophers, and poets, the end of Rome's Republic – the state battered and shredded by decades of civil war – was cast metaphorically as a process of corporeal mutilation and murder.[211] By its own hand, the republican body politic had symbolically torn itself to pieces (Verg. *Aen.* 6.832–3); what remained was its corpse (e.g. Cic. *Att.* 2.21, 4.18.2). Octavian's eventual victory, solidified after Actium in 31 BCE, ushered in both a seismic reshaping of Rome's political landscape and a contradictory but strategic reframing of this earlier metaphorical language: Augustan propagandizing aimed to 'correct' the imagery of self-destruction by championing a party-line of the Republic's 'rebirth' (*res publica resti-tuta*) and with it the restoration of *libertas*, inseparable from republican aristocratic ideology. Control was supposedly handed back to the senate (Aug. *RG* 34.1; Vell. Pat. 2.89.3). The principate was simply the old Republic born anew from the corpse of the slaughtered state.[212] This illusory but powerful imagery lasts well into the early imperial period, as Alain Gowing has demonstrated.[213] But the fiction of the Republic's 'restoration' was not lost on some.

Lucan's poem, I suggest, consciously blends these two corporeal meta-phors, dramatizing the self-evisceration of the Republic via republican imagery, signalled from the *incipit* (*BC* 1.1–2: *canimus populumque poten-tem | in sua uictrici conuersum uiscera dextra*, 'we sing of a powerful people turning its victorious hand against its own viscera'), while simultaneously

---

[210] McClellan (2018): 63–6; McClellan (forthcoming), more extensively.   [211] See Walters (2011).

[212] See Gowing (2005): 4–6 for some of the political imagery of 'restoration' in the Augustan period and later.

[213] Gowing (2005): esp. 28–66 on Velleius and Valerius Maximus, *et passim*.

retrojecting into his portrait of the republican civil wars a perversion of the
later Augustan and Julio-Claudian ideology of *res publica restituta*. The
result of this conflation and contamination of body-of-state metaphors is
played out through a muddying of the distinction between life and death in
Lucan's epic characters; the poem is populated with humans existing at the
point of expiry, living *beyond* the moment of death, or coming back from
the dead altogether.[214]

The most exquisite symbol for Lucan's exploitation of this political
metaphorizing is Erichtho's zombie-corpse-soldier. In a brilliant discussion, Charles Tesoriero suggested that the corpse-soldier stands for the
republican 'body politic', mangled and misshapen by Erichtho in a micro-
cosmic reflection of Caesar's more pervasive treatment of Pompey's republican forces at Pharsalus (a collective symbol for the slaughtered Roman
state body).[215] The Pompeian soldier is killed in Thessaly, only to be
reanimated into something uncomfortably blurring the lines between life
and death, as we have seen (6.758–9): *nondum facies uiuentis in illo | iam
morientis erat*, 'there was in him the appearance of someone not yet living,
already dying'.[216] If the principate is simply a 'revivified' *res publica libera*,
as Augustus and later Julio-Claudian emperors claimed, then like the
corpse-soldier it exists as a grotesque perversion of actual life, something
caught between living and dying. The corpse-soldier plays out, in effect,
Lucan's sardonic warping of the series of political body-metaphors articulating the Republic's death and 'rebirth'.

What's worse, Lucan's narrator insists that this zombified world *still
exists* (7.638–41):[217]

> maius ab hac acie quam quod sua saecula ferrent
> uolnus habent populi; plus est quam uita salusque
> quod perit: in totum mundi prosternimur aeuum.
> uincitur his gladiis omnis quae seruiet aetas.
>
> From this battle the people suffer a wound greater
> than their own time could bear; it is more than just life and safety
> that perished: we are cast down for the whole of eternity.
> Every age which will be enslaved is defeated by these swords.

The death of the Republic at Pharsalus sealed the death of *libertas* into
Lucan's present; an exhumed zombie-Republic subservient to 'necromantic'

---

[214] Bartsch (1997): esp. 17–29 and Hömke (2010): 103–4 examine Lucan's interest in the extension of
the process of dying, but as a product of aesthetics, not socio-politics.
[215] Tesoriero (2004): 191–2.      [216] See pp. 160, 166.
[217] Quint (1993): 148–51; Leigh (1997): 80–1; Bartsch (2010): 28.

Caesars brought with it an umbratic *libertas* emblematized by the persistence of traditional aristocratic positions and titles now devoid of power and influence. The loss of freedom, violently juxtaposed to Caesarism (7.695–6: *par quod semper habemus,* | *libertas et Caesar, erit,* 'there will be that matched pair which we always have, freedom vs Caesar'[218]) necessitates slavery, and, as Seneca and Ulpian tell us bluntly, Romans compared slavery with death (Sen. *Epist.* 77.18; Ulp. *Dig.* 50.17.209: *seruitutem mortalitati fere comparamus*). Upper-class citizens in Nero's Rome, Lucan suggests, robbed of freedom, are like walking corpses[219] in a 'death-world' dominated by an all-powerful *princeps*. Lucan even savages the conceit that the principate at least brought peace and an end to civil war by lumping *pax* explicitly with subjugation (*BC* 1.670: *cum domino pax ista uenit,* 'peace came with a master'). By collapsing the temporal distance between his poetic subject and his contemporary audience, Lucan is able to superimpose his view of Neronian Rome's slave-state onto a recasting of the *origin* of the present state of affairs.[220] Like his poetic creations, Lucan and his audience similarly struggle to negotiate a space somewhere between life and death.

---

[218] The clashing of verb tenses really hammers home Lucan's point; see Quint (1993): 151.
[219] Similarly O'Higgins (1988): 225.
[220] See esp. Leigh (1997): 77–109 for Lucan's 'merging' of past and present time in *BC* 7.

# CHAPTER 4

# Argonautic Abuses: Valerius Flaccus' (and Apollonius') Argonautica

As in Homeric epic, Valerius Flaccus relegates corpse mistreatment largely to threats and boasts whose outcome is ultimately unelaborated in the poem. Additional evidence of abuse is either left implicit, requiring some effort on the part of the reader to read between the lines, or is offered *ex post facto*, as it were, following a Virgilian poetics of 'silencing' physical details of abusive acts that we know have occurred. The influence of Lucan's generic *Blitzkrieg* is pervasive in Valerius' *Argonautica*, particularly on his innovative infusion of internecine conflict in the myth.[1] But there seems to be an active distancing from Lucan's obsessive poetics of grotesquery.[2] While Valerius is not averse to physical violence and horror, as we will see especially in the account of the Bebrycian tyrant Amycus' treatment of the dead (VF 4.177–85), there is less adherence to Lucanian aesthetics than we will find in Statius and Silius (Chapters 5 and 6). As always, Valerius' treatment of the myth is mediated by Apollonius' Hellenistic epic which also has some interesting things to say vis-à-vis Homer's handling of the motif of corpse mistreatment. This chapter explores corpse mistreatment in both *Argonautica* poems, though the weight of analysis will fall on the Flavian poem and its sophisticated interaction with earlier epic concerning death rites and corporeal violence.

## Elliptical Abuse

Though Valerius' *Argonautica* is not a martial epic *per se*, the poem does display an interest in violence and war and the impact of each on the dead human body. Evidence comes immediately when the tyrannical king Pelias orders Jason to fetch the Golden Fleece from Colchis. Pelias promises that

---

[1] See Schenk (1999): 275–8, 407–9, Zissos (2004), Buckley (2010), Stover (2012) and (2014), Heerink (2016).

[2] Zissos (2004): 22.

were he not slowed by old age Jason would see in the Haemonian court already the 'head and armour' of the Colchian king Aeetes (VF 1.51–2: *si mihi quae quondam uires, et pendere poenas | Colchida iam et regis caput hic atque arma uideres*). The speech is a showy lie (39: *fictis ... dictis*), but Pelias' savagery makes the threat believable. For Pelias, the severed head and armour of an enemy king represent the ultimate spoils of war. Book 1 closes with another threat of corpse violence, this time aimed *at* Pelias, creating a chiastic bookending of the motif. Moments before his suicide, and with the Argonautic crew at sea, Jason's father Aeson curses Pelias, who has sent troops to murder Aeson, his wife Alcimede, and their son Promachus (1.812–14): *quae fida manus, quae cara suorum | diripiat laceretque senem nec membra sepulchro | contegat*, 'let his faithful band, his own dear ones tear apart and mutilate the old man, nor let them bury his limbs in a tomb'. The combination of physical violence and exposure is particularly fierce. Though he cannot know it, the threat will come to pass extratextually when Pelias' own daughters chop up the aged king as a result of Medea's ruse (e.g. Ov. *Met.* 7.297–349). The pre-suicide threat and curse recall Dido's death-bed curse that Aeneas lie dead and unburied soon after reaching Italy (Verg. *Aen.* 4.620);[3] in both Virgil and Valerius the curse will reach fruition outside the confines of the poem. While the poet consigns the actual dismemberment of Pelias to a verbal jab, the murder of Aeson's son Promachus moments later by the royal guard provides an in-text referent for the abuse awaiting Pelias in the future (VF 1.824–5): *te, puer, et uisa pallentem morte parentum | diripiunt adduntque tuis*, 'you, boy, pale at seeing the death of your parents, they mutilate and add you to your family'.[4] Promachus' treatment, when compared with Aeson's curse, is less obviously *post mortem*. While *diripiunt* 'indicates violent dismemberment',[5] it is not clear from the text whether he's hacked to death or hacked apart *after* death. And while the guards 'add' Promachus to the bodies of his parents, we are given no information about the ultimate fate of these corpses.[6]

[3] Hutchinson (1993): 297–8; Kleywegt (2005): *ad* 1.803a–806b; Zissos (2008): xxxv–xxxvi and *ad locc.*
[4] Hutchinson (1993): 300 n.23; Hershkowitz (1998b): 16 n.54, 135; Kleywegt (2005): *ad* 1.820–6; Zissos (2008): *ad* 1.812–13. On these lines generally see McGuire (1997): 189–97.
[5] Zissos *ad* 1.823–5.
[6] McGuire (1997): 195 suggests the scene is coloured by Virgil's apostrophe to Nisus and Euryalus (*Aen.* 9.446–9), given the poetic memorializing and focus on Promachus' youth. I might add both scenes focus explicitly on *mutilation* and the miserable reaction of a parent (Aeson: VF 1.825; Euryalus' mother: *Aen.* 9.481–97). If Valerius has Virgil in mind here, perhaps the association would invite us to read *diripiunt* as *post mortem* abuse.

The examples above are extra-military threats of – or vague allusions to – corpse abuse. The battle at Colchis in *Argonautica* 6 offers Valerius a more traditionally epic venue for verbal jousting and other forms of corpse-related violence. Apollonius has nothing comparable to the martial material here and Valerius' emphasis on the internecine nature of the Colchian conflict (between the brothers Aeetes and Perses) suits the Flavian context of Valerius' writing just after the civil war of 69 CE.[7] During his *aristeia* Perses' ally Gesander slays an elderly priest named Aquites (he has grey hair, 6.306) who had begged to be spared along with his son, Cyrnus, whom the priest had been hoping to extricate from the fighting. As he drives his sword home Gesander boasts over the dying man (6.313–14): *praeda future canum. iuueni sors pulchrior omnis:* | *et certasse manu decet et caruisse sepulchro*, 'you will be prey to dogs. The fate of a young man is in every way more beautiful: both to fight hand-to-hand and to lack a tomb is fitting.' The boast offers an odd mixture of threat and heroic resignation. The old Aquites, he claims, will glut scavenging dogs, a grim fate which matches Priam's fear of becoming prey to his own palace-hounds at *Iliad* 22.66–71.[8] Priam juxtaposes the inherent ugliness of this potential fate with what is, in effect, *dulce et decorum* about a young warrior's war-torn corpse (71–3: νέῳ δέ τε πάντ᾽ ἐπέοικεν | ἀρηῒ κταμένῳ δεδαϊγμένῳ ὀξέϊ χαλκῷ | κεῖσθαι· πάντα δὲ καλὰ θανόντι περ ὅττι φανήῃ, 'for a young man it's in every way fitting to lie torn by the sharp bronze after being killed in war: he's seen as completely beautiful in death'). When dogs tear apart the corpse of an old 'grey-haired' man (74: πολιόν τε κάρη πολιόν τε γένειον), *that*, Priam concludes, is the 'most pitiable fate wretched mortals can incur' (76: τοῦτο δὴ οἴκτιστον πέλεται δειλοῖσι βροτοῖσιν). Homer underscores the point later in the book when Priam's son Hector is ogled by the Achaean soldiery after Achilles has killed him: as the soldiers tentatively approach, 'they scrutinized the stature and breath-taking beauty of Hector' (370–1: οἳ καὶ θηήσαντο φυὴν καὶ εἶδος ἀγητὸν | Ἕκτορος) while each one pierces his flesh with a spear (375).[9]

Aquites' prayer that Gesander spare his son might instigate the second half of the boast: i.e. 'you will feed the dogs, your *son* will be denied a tomb,

---

[7] On civil war in the poem see McGuire (1997): 103–13, Schenk (1999): 169–89, 272–89, Bernstein (2008): 50–4, Buckley (2010), Stover (2012): 113–50; see below pp. 178–9. The dating of the poem is complex and fraught, but it's clearly Flavian. See Stover (2012): 7–26 for a convincing argument that the poem is exclusively a product of the 70s CE.

[8] Wijsman (2000): *ad* 6.313; Spaltenstein (2005): *ad* 6.311–16; Fucecchi (2006): *ad* 6.294–316, 313s; Buckley (2010): 448–9.

[9] See above p. 29.

as is fitting, when I find him'. But Gesander's own cultural customs confuse the situation. He is leader of the Iazygians who, we are told (VF 6.122–8), require their sons to kill them when they become too old and slow to fight. Gesander has just recently 'euthanized' his own father, Voraptus, whom he invokes before slaying the grey-haired priest Aquites (288–91). He castigates his Iazygian cohort for sluggishness which he equates with a sudden bout of 'shameful old age' (283–4: *quae uos subito tam foeda senectus | corripuit*). Aquites' attempt to elicit sympathy from Gesander through appeals to his own father and a father–son bond (305–7: '*te*' que '*per hanc, genitor*', inquit '*tibi si manet, oro | canitiem, compesce minas et sicubi nato | parce meo!*', 'I beg you, by this grey hair, if you have a father of your own, hold back your threats, and if you have a son, spare mine!'), again reworking appeals from Homer's Priam (*Il.* 24.486–506; cf. *Aen.* 10.521–2 of the priest Mago's pleas), fall on particularly deaf ears. Aquites has no business on the battlefield and will die a death – and suffer *post mortem* abuses – worthy of his advanced age. War, it seems, is the stage for young men like Gesander and Aquites' son Cyrnus. Even if death brings about a denial of funeral rites (VF 6.314: *caruisse sepulchro*) this is fitting (314: *decet*), it's *beautiful* (313: *pulchrior*). The idiosyncratic Iazygian custom allows Valerius space to explore the intricacies of Homer's powerful articulation of what constitutes a 'beautiful death' in war.[10] Again, however, nowhere in the text does Valerius confirm that the boasts reach fruition.

Gesander is promptly killed after losing a tug-of-war over the corpse of the Argonaut Canthus (VF 6.350–85) in a scene modelled on the *Leichenkampf* over Patroclus' corpse at *Iliad* 17.123–761 – an epic *topos* ignored by Virgil and Lucan but revived here. Jason's subsequent *aristeia* (VF 6.602–56, 681–9) occurs at the high-point of battle. Like a lion (613–14) he rages ferociously (615: *ferox*; 616: *furit*), slashing through the enemy somewhat randomly with savage sword (616–17: *saeuo ense*) and hostile spear (617: *infesta . . . cuspide*). The brutality of the imagery precipitates an appropriately brutal death-blow (619–20): *caput eripit Auchi | †bracchiaque† et uastis uoluendum mittit harenis*, 'he rips off the head of Auchus and his arms and sends him rolling on the empty sands'.[11] The *harenae* put us symbolically on the sands of the Flavian gladiatorial arena and the scene is 'spectacularized' by the presence of the teichoscopic Medea watching attentively from the city walls (575–601).[12] This is by a sizeable margin

---

[10] For the Homeric 'beautiful death' see Vernant (1991).
[11] The reading of *bracchia* is perfectly sound; see Wijsman (2000): *ad* 6.620.
[12] On the *teichoscopia* here see Fucecchi (1996): 142–65 and (1997), Stover (2012): 207–16, Lovatt (2013): 236–42.

the most violent murder in the poem,[13] and while not explicit it at least hints at corpse abuse.[14]

As the commentaries all note, this scene draws from Agamemnon's slaying of Hippolochus during the former's *aristeia* at *Iliad* 11.145–7: Ἱππόλοχος δ' ἀπόρουσε, τὸν αὖ χαμαὶ ἐξενάριξε | χεῖρας ἀπὸ ξίφεϊ τμήξας ἀπό τ' αὐχένα κόψας, | ὅλμον δ' ὣς ἔσσευε κυλίνδεσθαι δι' ὁμίλου, 'Hippolochus darted out and Agamemnon killed him on the ground, hewing his arms with a sword and lopping off his head, and sent him rolling like a stone through the crowd'. Agamemnon is among the most savage and uncompromising Achaean heroes at Troy, infamous for a war strategy tantamount to prenatal genocide (*Il.* 6.55–60). The allusion here is not wholly flattering to Jason at the beginning of his own *aristeia*. There is unquestionable violence in Agamemnon's act but the details of the killing do not clearly foreground corpse abuse: Hippolochus is not obviously *dead* when Agamemnon truncates him. Valerius' subtle reworking of the Homeric scene toys with this ambiguity. Agamemnon slashes off Hippolochus' arms first, then his head, the more obvious and immediate kill-shot. Jason decapitates Auchus first before subsequently severing his arms. Henri Wijsman calls the inversion 'odd' and less realistic than Homer,[15] but by making Jason decapitate his victim first, the subsequent bodily violence allows us to read Auchus' truncation as *post mortem*, amplifying the ferociousness of Jason's act, even if Valerius is not explicit. It seems reasonable to assume the inversion of the Homeric image is deliberate and therefore not particularly odd and the invocation of realism also doesn't help flesh out our understanding of Valerius' intricate engagement with his model.

My translation above skates over a troublesome bit of Latin. *What* exactly does Jason 'send rolling' (VF 6.620: *uoluendum mittit*) after he truncates Auchus? Like J.H. Mozley,[16] I have supplied an object (*eum*, vel. sim.) to complete the sense, and if Valerius has the scene from *Iliad* 11 in mind, what goes rolling is Auchus' truncated torso.[17] Homer provides a grotesque simile likening Hippolochus's trunk to a tumbling stone; Valerius lets the image speak for itself. But the removal of the simile

---

[13] The back-to-back chariot 'meat-grinder' scenes (6.413–16, 423–6) are grotesque and gory but these are accidental deaths and abuses and not wilful acts of violence aimed at dead bodies.

[14] See Baier (2001): *ad* 6.619–20 for a similar impression.     [15] Wijsman (2000): *ad* 6.620.

[16] Mozley (1934): 347: 'he slashes off Auchus' head and arms, and sends him rolling on the desolate plain'; also Baier (2001): *ad* 6.619–20: 'Er reißt Kopf und Arme des Auchus ab und läßt ihn [den verstrümmelten Auchus] durch den Sand rollen.'

[17] Aeneas similarly kicks over Tarquitus' corpse after decapitating him at *Aeneid* 10.555–6: *truncumque tepentem | prouoluens*. Baier (2001): *ad* 6.619–20 notes the Virgilian allusion but is confused by Valerius' grammatical construction.

obfuscates the picture. Auchus is no longer 'whole', the Latin singular gerundive (and the English object 'him') creates something of a metaphysical dilemma. This is the trouble with dismemberment, it 'fractures' identity and self. There is, of course, a singular object in the sentence that could agree with *uoluendum*: Auchus' severed head (*caput*).[18] Again we have a Homeric antecedent for a head 'sent rolling' on the battlefield (*Il.* 13.202–5):

κεφαλὴν δ' ἁπαλῆς ἀπὸ δειρῆς
κόψεν Ὀϊλιάδης κεχολωμένος Ἀμφιμάχοιο,
ἧκε δέ μιν σφαιρηδὸν ἑλιξάμενος δι' ὁμίλου·
Ἕκτορι δὲ προπάροιθε ποδῶν πέσεν ἐν κονίῃσι.

The son of Oïleus chopped the head
from his tender neck, angered by the fate of Amphimachus,
and hurled it spinning like a ball through the crowd of fighters:
it fell in the dust at the feet of Hector.[19]

As we've seen, this is the only explicit example of corpse abuse in the *Iliad*, perpetrated by one of the poem's nastiest characters.[20] Imbrius' head falls 'in the dust' while (on this reading) Auchus' head falls 'on the empty sands'. Again the avoidance of a vivid Homeric simile obscures things. But an allusion to Homer's Ajax 'the Lesser' here in a clear display of corpse abuse would ratchet up Jason's already thorny association with that poem's Agamemnon. Lucan similarly caps the scene of transgressive outrages at Pharsalus with the hurling of a severed head (*BC* 7.628: *abscisum longe mittat caput*).[21] Given the context of civil war here in Colchis,[22] an allusion to the climax of battlefield violence in Lucan's poem seems intentional. The subtlety and vagueness created by intricating and warping earlier epic scenes of intense bodily violence and the amphibolic obscuring of lexical understanding seem a form of what Andrew Zissos calls 'calculated obfuscation', a common feature of Valerian poetics.[23]

Next up is Jupiter's son Colaxes, destined to die like Sarpedon whose doom Zeus had similarly mourned in the Homeric poem (*Il.* 16.426–507; VF 6.621–56). Oblivious to his fate, Colaxes taunts Jason and his comrades (6.647–8): *uos Scythiae saturare canes Scythiaeque uolucres | huc miseri uenis<tis>?*, 'have you come here, miserable men, to glut Scythian dogs and Scythian birds?' The

---

[18] Fucecchi (1997): *ad* 6.620. *Contra* Spaltenstein (2005): *ad* 6.618–20.
[19] Fucecchi (1997): *ad* 6.620; Baier (2001): *ad* 6.619–20.   [20] See pp. 34–41; McClellan (2017).
[21] Fucecchi (1997): *ad* 6.620, with additional allusions.   [22] More on this below, pp. 178–9.
[23] Zissos (2004): 23 and (2008): xliv–xlvi.

threat is typically Homeric and typically unfulfilled.[24] Colaxes hurls a boulder
which Juno parries aside and Jason pierces his heart with a spear (648–54).
What follows is again somewhat vague and merits comment (654–5): *lapsoque
cruentus | aduolat Aesonides mortemque cadentis acerbat*, 'the bloodthirsty son of
Aeson rushes over to him where he's collapsed and makes bitter the dead man's
death'. How exactly are we to understand Jason's ability to 'embitter' (*acerbat*)
Colaxes' death? What might be implied is a *post mortem* rebuttal to Colaxes'
own unfulfilled taunt that Minyae corpses will become fodder for scavenging
Scythian beasts.[25] Statius will later deploy the rare *acerbare* in this sense at
*Thebaid* 9.302 at the height of Hippomedon's *aristeia*. After a volley of verbal
taunts, the youthful hero 'presses down on his enemies and embitters wounds
with words' (*permit aduersos et acerbat uulnera dictis*). Statius' phrasing makes
more explicit that Hippomedon's verbal taunts are what 'augment' the
physical violence he's administering. And it seems this is how Statius inter-
preted the scene in Valerius since the subsequent image of Hippomedon
'raging with his sword' (*Theb.* 9.303: *ense furit*) picks up Jason's earlier
ferocious entry into battle during his own *aristeia* at VF 6.615–16 (*furit ense*).

But this hardly makes the *Argonautica* scene any clearer. We miss in the
description of Jason's action an indication that it is in fact 'words' that
make Colaxes' death *worse*. And the verb *aduolare* implies physicality:
Jason 'rushed over' to Colaxes in order to somehow exacerbate his
demise.[26] Moreover Valerius' use of the adjective *cruentus* to describe
Jason betrays, potentially, a more sinister motive. This is a frightening
epic word.[27] Valerius elsewhere uses it to describe the monstrous serpen-
tine Typhoeus at 2.27 in his battle with Neptune, Fama ruefully describes
the Dahae as 'bloodthirsty' (2.156–7) in an attempt to inspire madness
among the Lemnian women, and, appropriately, post-massacre Lemnos is
a 'blood-stained land' (2.303) as a result of the divinely induced atrocities
committed there.[28] Earlier epic is hesitant to apply the epithet to heroic
characters. In a less menacing sense, Virgil describes Diomedes as *cruentus*

[24] Fucecchi (1997): *ad* 6.647.
[25] E.g. Spaltenstein (2005): *ad* 6.655–6: '*Mortem acerbat* est certes elliptique, mais Val. renvoie à un
motif bien attesté : le vainqueur insulte sa victime'; see already Langen (1896): *ad loc.*
[26] Wijsman (2000): *ad* 6.655 cites *Aen.* 10.897–8 where Aeneas 'rushes over' (*aduolat Aeneas*) to
Mezentius whom he subsequently calls *acer* in a taunt. This seems to bear out Statius' interpretation
of *acerbare*.
[27] Hershkowitz (1998b): 93 n.222 claims that because the scene is 'focalized' through Jupiter – whose
son Jason has just killed – the adjective is overly harsh. This is unnecessarily deflective of the
brutality we must read here. Baier (2001): *ad loc.*: '"Blutrünstig" ist ein eindeutig negativ belegter
Ausdruck.'
[28] The sea (8.346) and Mars/war (8.395) are also 'bloody'.

from the night-raid slaughter depicted on Juno's temple in Carthage at *Aeneid* 1.471 – the implied 'redness' of the bloody epithet is meant to contrast the 'snow-white canvas tents' (469: *niueis tentoria uelis*) in the visual image more so than to indicate Diomedes' savagery.[29] Later, gore (*cruor*) stains Mezentius' face via the lion simile at *Aeneid* 10.728. This allusion resonates here given Valerius' simile likening Jason to a lion slaughtering penned animals (VF 6.614: *mutat . . . cruores*), an image picked up in adjectival form as Jason hurries over to Colaxes' corpse (654–5).[30] Like Agamemnon and Locrian Ajax, Mezentius is not an ideal heroic model for Jason. Lucan, not surprisingly, brings the epithet to the fore. Mars (*BC* 4.24), Antaeus (4.609), Hannibal (4.789), Cinna (4.822), and Caesar (5.758, 9.15) are all *cruentus* with varying levels of perfidy. As we have seen,[31] Statius will later memorably apply the epithet (repeatedly) to Tydeus (*Theb.* 1.408, 8.478–9, 530–1, 9.1–2), whose savagery manifests in his gruesome *post mortem* consumption of Melanippus' brains (8.760–1). These last two are civil war poems like the war in Colchis into which the Argonauts have insinuated themselves; the internecine conflict at Colchis represents one of Valerius' major innovations on the Argonautic tale and the context for 'bloodthirstiness' is definitively *à propos* here. In sum, this is not good company, nor is the attribution a glowing one for Jason.

The verb *acerbat* at the line end (VF 6.655) is followed immediately after the break by *spargitur hinc* (656). The sense is that Jason 'spreads out from there' (*OLD* s.v. *spargo* 5 c) to attack other enemies (the Alani, in particular).[32] But if we hesitate over the passive verb after learning of bloodthirsty Jason's *post mortem* engagement with Colaxes – whatever his intentions – we can't be blamed for raising an eyebrow. Though Valerius' use of the verb is diffuse, its poignant 'sparagmatic' function (from *sparagmos*, dismemberment) in Lucan might subtly creep in here in a moment of civil war battlefield violence.[33] This is telling given the use of *spargere* at 614 to describe, again, the vicious lion sating its hunger on fattened stable animals in the simile that introduces Jason's *aristeia* (*spargit . . . famem*, 'he scatters his voracity'). As elsewhere Valerius is not explicit and insinuates possible abuses he refrains from narrating in any obvious way.

---

[29] Conte (1999): 283.

[30] Stover (2012): 214–15 rightly notes that the simile also reworks the non-martial simile of Odysseus' initial interaction with Nausicaa at *Od.* 6.130–4. The pseudo-amatory context here, and Valerius' combining of erotic and martial elements in the simile describing Jason, generate 'a great deal of generic tension' (p. 214).

[31] See p. 86.     [32] Baier (2001): *ad loc.*; Fucecchi (1997): *ad loc.* on Jason's 'omnipresence'.

[33] E.g. *BC* 5.684; 8.629, 751; 9.58, 1093; 10.22, etc; see Braund (1992): xlvi.

Though this is Jason's *aristeia* we must not lose sight of the fact that it occurs during a civil war in which the Argonauts have consciously involved themselves,[34] a civil war described as 'honourless' (6.736: *sine honore labores*) and whose outcome is utterly pointless to Jason's mission of acquiring the Golden Fleece (429–30). The battle itself will prove useless since, though routed here, Perses will defeat and depose Aeetes after the Argonauts leave Colchis. Jason's military prowess serves only to accomplish the goals of the 'savage tyrant' Aeetes (7.78: *trucis ... tyranni*). And the *uirtus* his *aristeia* wins him is arrogant and *uncivil* (6.735: *uirtute superbum*).[35] Pelias contrasted Jason's *uirtus* and his own tyranny as incompatible at 1.30 (*uirtusque haud laeta tyranno*); here these 'antitheses' combine uncomfortably at Colchis as Jason does a tyrant's dirty-work. Medea's *teichoscopia* frames Jason's *aristeia* in Iliadic terms (e.g. *Il.* 3.121–394), but the war's internecine nature perverts the heroic quality of individual achievements with the stain of Lucanesque 'negative epic'.[36] Valerius signals this bridge to Lucanian civil war explicitly at 6.402–9 via a simile comparing the Colchian war to *Roman* civil war, reworking the programmatic opening of Lucan's epic (*BC* 1.3–7).[37] The civil wars of 69 CE provide an even more visceral homegrown reference point for Valerius' Flavian audience. This is Roman civil war draped in Homeric colours. The civil war context complicates the possibility Valerius had set up for traditional 'Homeric' *kleos*; and the troubling allusions to Iliadic characters who treat their victims disdainfully already degenerates from the model.

Jason's involvement in the battle serves one major purpose: to put him on display for Medea who, through Juno and Venus' nefarious intervention, will fall desperately in love with him.[38] There is thus an amatory function to Jason's *aristeia*, a blending of *amor* and *arma*.[39] As we shall see

---

[34] Cowan (2014): 245: 'the Argonauts are fully implicated in the internecine quality of this civil war, not morally detached auxiliaries or mercenaries, but as guilty of blurring battle lines as any Colchian stabbing his fellow citizen'.

[35] I read *superbus* here – a loaded and ambiguous word since at least Virgil: see Fowler (1990): 47–52 – pejoratively, *pace* Stover (2012): 212 and (2014): 304, Castelletti (2014): 182. Cf. Baier (2001): *ad* 6.733–6: *uirtus* has become 'stale' (*schal*), robbed of ethical content; Fucecchi (1997): *ad loc.* On Jason's *uirtus* see further Ferenczi (1995), Hershkowitz (1998b): 105–28, Ripoll (1998): 89–94, all generally positive readings.

[36] See esp. Buckley (2010) on the presence of Lucanian civil war in VF 6; note also Zissos (2004): 24–5: the Argonauts' involvement in the 'Lucanesque conflict' in Colchis is 'dubious'.

[37] Strand (1972): 25; Wijsman (2000): *ad* 6.402–9; Buckley (2010): 440–1; Stover (2014): 302. Strand argues that Valerius is alluding either to the civil war of 69 CE or to Lucan's intestine Republican subject matter; see Fucecchi (2006): *ad* 6.402–9 for the civil war reference as 'generica'; cf. McGuire (1997): 58–60; Schenk (1999): 184–5 n.226, 278 n.389.

[38] E.g. Feeney (1991): 325–6, Fucecchi (1996): 143, Schenk (1999): 60, Lovatt (2013): 241.

[39] Stover (2012): 215.

shortly,[40] in Valerius' earlier Lemnian excursus this combination in the poem is decidedly deadly. Jason's *aristeia* is indeed impressive and heroic,[41] but it's not *unproblematic* in an epic landscape suffused with Roman-style tyrants and Roman-style *bella ciuilia*.

## 'Sparagmatic' Abuse

Valerius is generally clear, however, about the importance of obsequies for the dead. The *Argonautica* is punctuated by a few major funerals or funereal rituals: Cyzicus is given full honours after he's killed during the disastrous and accidental 'civil war' between the Argonauts and Doliones in book 3; book 5 opens with back-to-back funerals for Idmon and Tiphys (5.1–62), the appeasement of Sthenelus' ghost (89–100), and a visit to Phrixus' tomb (184–6) and the cenotaph of his now nymph-sister Helle (198–9). Even in the context of civil war Valerius is quick to mention that each army set aside multiple days for the collection of and funerals for their dead (5.275–6): *datus et sociis utrimque cremandis | ille dies alterque dies*, 'that day and the next day were dedicated to the cremation of dead on both sides'. This form of proto-*anairesis* practice mirrors examples at *Iliad* 7.421–32, 24.659–70 and *Aeneid* 11.100–21, 182–212.[42]

Valerius follows Apollonius fairly faithfully and when his account departs it is in order to weave in allusions to other epic funeral scenes (especially from Hector's funeral in *Il.* 24 and Pallas' funeral in *Aen.* 11).[43] Equal effort is spent in the Greek *Argonautica* highlighting the importance of proper funeral ritual. Obsequies are definitively *themis*, 'right', 'law' (AR 1.692, 1061, 2.840) with all of the inherent divine precepts therein. In the case of Cyzicus' funeral, both Apollonius and Valerius march the armed Argonauts three times around Cyzicus' corpse (AR 1.1058–60; VF 3.347–9), Cyzicus' widow Clite interrupts each funeral (AR 1.1063–5; VF 3.313–31: her suicide in AR becomes a dirge in VF), and the seer Mopsus mandates expiatory rituals in order to allow the Argonauts to leave Cyzicus (AR 1.1080–1102; VF 3.377–458). Valerius also follows Apollonius in pairing the funerals for Idmon and Tiphys (AR 2.835–57; VF 5.1–62), followed by the appeasement of Sthenelus' ghost (AR 2.911–29; VF 5.89–100). Apollonius includes funerals for Canthus (AR 4.1499–1501) and Mopsus (4.1532–6) which do not appear in Valerius' poem: Canthus' corpse is whisked away from battle by the Amazon Euryale (VF 6.369–71) and we hear nothing

---

[40] p. 188.    [41] Hershkowitz (1998b): 123–5; Stover (2012): 207–16.

[42] See pp. 28, 51, also 150, 209–10.

[43] E.g. on Cyzicus' funeral scene (VF 3.274–361) see Burck (1981): 455–9, Manuwald (2015): *ad locc.*

about it afterwards; Mopsus is, of course, still alive at the close of Valerius' poem.

The incompleteness of Valerius' epic leaves one massive hole in the full picture of corpse mistreatment in the Argonautic myth: Medea's brother Absyrtus is still alive – and thus *intact* – at the end of the Flavian poem. Apollonius' treatment of Absyrtus' mutilation in his *Argonautica* 4 is far and away the most brutal scene of corpse abuse in the Hellenistic poem. Although we cannot know how Valerius would have handled this famous mythic scene, it's worth exploring Apollonius' version considering its striking departure from Homeric features of corpse treatment and the influence of sparagmatic violence in subsequent Latin epic, including echoes elsewhere in Valerius' poem.

After procuring the Golden Fleece, Jason, Medea, and the Argonauts flee Colchis. Medea's brother Absyrtus and his fleet blockade the entrance to the Adriatic (AR 4.323–37), leaving the Argonauts in a precarious situation: access to the sea from the Ister has been denied and, having now disembarked at the Brygean Islands, the poet and Jason both tell us they would have been defeated had they engaged the Colchians in battle (338–9, 401–2). Jason and Medea hatch a plot, a 'great treachery' (421: μέγαν δόλον) to lure Absyrtus into a private meeting with his sister under the pretence of contriving a counter-plot against the Argonauts.[44] In the *pronaos* of the Brygean temple of Artemis, Jason emerges from his hiding place and strikes Absyrtus with his sword 'like a butcher hacks a large strong-horned bull' (468: βουτύπος ὥς τε μέγαν κερεαλκέα ταῦρον). As he dies Absyrtus stains Medea's silvery garment red with his blood (471–4) – a physical stain to match the *miasma* of the treacherous murder[45] – and she averts her gaze to avoid witnessing the deadly act (465–7). While Medea looks away, the Erinys zooms in, casting a hostile side-eyed glance at the pernicious deed (475–6). The two levels of focalization here implicate the reader in the act of violence: by shifting focus to two internal audiences at the moment of the murder, one who looks away (Medea) and one who looks (the Fury), the poet asks us to choose sides. The reader's choice of alignment is purposefully unsettling.

The Fury's presence indicates that the murder will require expiation. Before this, however, murder suddenly turns to mutilation as Jason dismembers Absyrtus' still-warm corpse (477–81):

---

[44] The details here are elliptical and somewhat confusing; see Byre (1996).
[45] Fränkel (1968): *ad* 4.464–74.

ἥρως δ' Αἰσονίδης ἐξάργματα τάμνε θανόντος,
τρὶς δ' ἀπέλειξε φόνου, τρὶς δ' ἐξ ἄγος ἔπτυσ' ὀδόντων,
ᾗ θέμις αὐθέντῃσι δολοκτασίας ἱλάεσθαι.
ὑγρὸν δ' ἐν γαίῃ κρύψεν νέκυν, ἔνθ' ἔτι νῦν περ
κείαται ὀστέα κεῖνα μετ' ἀνδράσιν Ἀψυρτεῦσιν.

The hero son of Aeson chopped off the extremities of the dead man,
three times he licked the gore, three times spat out the pollution
    through his teeth,
as is right for killers to conciliate those murdered by treachery.
He hid the limp corpse in the ground where, even now,
those bones lie among the Absyrtian people.

This is one of the more horrific examples of corpse abuse in Greco-Roman epic, despite being somewhat 'impersonal' and emotionally detached.[46] It's a combination of physical mistreatment and perversion of funeral rites that far outstrips the sole example of *post mortem* violence in Homer (*Il.* 13.202–5). Because we have already learned about Colchian funerary practice for men and women at the beginning of book 3 (I discuss the scene below[47]), the details of Jason's disposal of Absyrtus cut directly against religious and cultural procedure.[48] He 'hides' (κρύψεν) the corpse in the ground – this is not a burial[49] – matching the secrecy of the ruse and his lying in ambush. The Colchian custom of binding and securing male corpses before they are hoisted into trees is also undone through the bodily *rending* of *maschalismos*, even if we are meant to imagine the extremities were then strung around the mutilated trunk (schol. AR 4.477–9; Ar. Byz. fr. 412 Slater).[50] The language itself here recalls and perverts the procedural funereal description in book 3: ἄγος (3.203; 4.478); θέμις (3.205; 4.479); ἐνὶ γαίῃ (3.204), ἐν γαίῃ (4.480); εἰσέτι νῦν γὰρ (3.203), ἔτι νῦν περ (4.480).[51] As in the earlier aside, the phrase ἔτι νῦν περ momentarily fractures the narrative and we are reminded chillingly that Absyrtus is *still there*, unburied, unhonoured, his supple (or moist?[52]) corpse decomposed to bones.

---

[46] Byre (1996): 13; Mori (2008): 206.    [47] See pp. 195–7.    [48] Ceulemans (2007): 111.
[49] Hunter (2015): *ad loc.*
[50] Our understanding of the brutal ritual (*maschalismos*) that Apollonius seems to be alluding to here is hopelessly unclear. Two examples of the verb μασχαλίζειν ('to put under the arm pits') appear in Greek tragedy (Aesch. *Cho.* 439–43; Soph. *El.* 444–6; cf. Soph. fr. 623 Radt), in both cases to describe Clytemnestra's treatment of Agamemnon's corpse. The tragic material treating the Oresteia myth weighs heavily on Apollonius' rendering of Absyrtus' abuse, as Griffiths (1990) and Hunter (2015): 2–6 and *ad locc.* have shown. In both tragic examples the evidence for the ritual described by Aristophanes Byzantius is unelaborated. Perhaps the verb simply refers to basic corpse mutilation, with Dunn (2018).
[51] Campbell (1994): *ad* 3.200–9.
[52] Livrea (1973): *ad loc.*; Hunter (2015): *ad loc.* Does the word hint at traditions where Absyrtus' corpse will actually end up in the sea?

The murder and dismemberment are swiftly narrated and the details of physical violence occluded somewhat by aetiological asides, antiquarian glosses, and an avoidance of physical details.[53] Apollonius was more explicit in the first book when he described the butchering of bulls by Heracles and Ancaeus at the embarkation of the Argonautic journey.[54] There Jason invokes Apollo at a makeshift altar on the shore, praying for a safe voyage (1.402–24), whereupon Heracles and Ancaeus strike down two sacrificial bulls and dismember them, one for each of Apollo's epithets (*Actius; Embasius*) or perhaps on account of the magnitude of the voyage concomitant with the importance of pre-seafaring propitiation (433):[55] κόπτον, δαίτρευόν τε, καὶ ἱερὰ μῆρ' ἐτάμοντο, 'they cut them up, portioned them, and chopped-off the sacred thigh pieces'. Three verbs in one line indicate the physical violence performed on the sacrificial animals. This is more descriptive than in Absyrtus' dismemberment, but there are a variety of cues that necessitate reading these scenes in concert. The capping ἐτάμοντο – a word with clear sacrificial overtones: *LSJ* s.v. τέμνω II b (especially *Il.* 1.460; *Od.* 3.456) – is the same verb used to describe Jason's dismemberment of Absyrtus at AR 4.477 (τάμνε), and the context of ritual animal slaughter is linked through the simile describing Jason's killing of Absyrtus to a *boutupos* striking a bull (4.468).[56] The *boutupos* was the priest charged with killing the sacrificial bull at the Bouphonia. Like Jason in the *Argonautica*, the priest would sneak up behind the victim and strike it down with one mighty blow.[57] The verb Apollonius deploys to signify the completion of Jason and Medea's act of slaughter (4.475: ἔρεξαν) often has the technical meaning of 'complete a sacrifice' (*LSJ* s.v. ῥέζω II).[58] Moreover Absyrtus, who willingly goes to meet Medea, is comparable to the 'willing' sacrificial victim so important for Greek animal sacrifice;[59] he similarly 'falls to his knees', evoking a sacrificial animal, when Jason strikes him (471: γνὺξ ἤριπε).[60] This takes place in the forecourt of Artemis' temple (469–71), adding another layer of religious and sacrificial overtones. And as Francis Dunn

[53] See Mori (2008): 206, 216–17.
[54] On the ritual and sacrificial activity at Pagasae see Knight (1995): 49–62. See Mori (2008): 156–66 on sacrifice in the poem, generally.
[55] Knight (1995): 50. On the importance of sacrificial rites before sea voyages in ancient Greek culture see Wachsmuth (1967).
[56] Fränkel (1968): *ad* 464–74 makes passing parenthetical reference to the sacrificial slaughter in book 1; cf. Livrea (1973): *ad* 4.469: 'Il sacrificio di Absirto richiama, per la brutalità della descrizione, 1.427-8', followed by Vian (1981): 90 n.4, Knight (1995): 52 n.12. None of these has explored a deeper significance between the two passages.
[57] Porter (1990): 266, 276; Green (1997): 312–13; Ceulemans (2007): 106–7; Mori (2008): 218–19.
[58] Goldhill (1991): 332.    [59] Hunter (1993): 61 n.69.    [60] Hunter (2015): *ad loc.*

has demonstrated through examination of lexicographic and inscriptional evidence, *maschalismos* itself has a secondary or dual association with animal sacrifice.[61] The more visceral description of the butchering in book 1 provides a disturbing intratextual 'guide' for our reading of the brutal, yet elliptical, dismemberment of Absyrtus in the warped sacrificial murder in book 4.

When read against the sacrificial activities at the outset of the Argo's voyage, the ritual slaughter of Absyrtus that initiates the journey home (from the Black Sea and west to Greece) functions as an inversion and perversion of the inaugural rites. This kind of 'reworking' of events from earlier in the poem is a larger feature of book 4.[62] Apollo, whose invocation opens the epic (1.1: ἀρχόμενος σέο, Φοῖβε), is replaced by his sister Artemis – no stranger to human sacrifice[63] – in the forecourt of whose temple the murder occurs; the Argonautic voyage will soon end with the crew navigating past Aulis (4.1779–80), to drive the point of divine familial contrast and human sacrificial overtones home. The prophetic Idmon's confirmation that Apollo has favoured their undertaking (1.436–47) becomes in the *nostos* a side-eyed glare from the Fury (4.475–6), the wrath of Zeus (4.557–8, 577, 585), and a miasmic stain that will require expiation (4.557–61, 584–8, 712–17). Jason's licking and spitting of Absyrtus' blood distorts the consumptive context of ritual slaughter and banquet where wine flows freely, leading to Idas' drunken (and theomachic) outburst at Jason and Idmon (1.463–95). Idas casts a side-eyed glare like the Fury who spies Jason and Medea (1.486). And Heracles' role in the slaughter and butchering of the animals reminds us of his excision from the narrative and his replacement by a Jason who could never live up to his super-sized heroic standards.[64]

It's strange, given the dangers of sea-travel and the obsessive adherence to sacrificial obeisance to the gods for safe voyage,[65] that in their haste to flee Colchis, Jason and Medea forego ritual acts for seafaring. This journey is the beginning of the *nostos* proper (from 4.241),[66] and we expect some form of propitiatory act especially considering the focus on embarkation

[61] Dunn (2018). The word *exargmata* (4.477) also has obvious sacrificial associations and overtones; Ceulemans (2007): 105–6.

[62] Hutchinson (1988): 121–42; Hunter (1993): 61.

[63] E.g. Hdt. 4.103; Eur. *IA* 1524–5: θύμασιν βροτησίοις | χαρεῖσα, '[Artemis] rejoicing in human sacrifices', *IT* 380–4, 1458–61; Paus. 7.19.4.

[64] On the complexities of heroism in the poem, especially in the portrayals of Jason and Heracles, see Adamietz (1970), through comparison with Jason/Hercules in VF, Hunter (1993): 8–41, Clauss (1993): 33–4, 176–211. For a useful survey see Glei (2008): 6–12.

[65] See Wachsmuth's (1967) well-documented compilation of source material.

[66] Livrea (1973): *ad* 4.241; Green (1997): 301 *ad* 241.

and safe-landing sacrifices elsewhere in the poem (e.g. 1.966–7 and 1186: thanks to Apollo Ekbasius for safe landing at Cyzicus and Cius, respectively; 2.531–3: embarkation sacrifices to 'Twelve Blessed Ones' (μακάρεσσι δυώδεκα) at Thynia; 2.686–713: thanks to Apollo of the Dawn for safe landing on Thynias Island; 2.927–9: embarkation sacrifices and dedication to Apollo Protector of Ships at Lyra; 2.1169–70: thanks to Ares for safe landing at Ares Island, etc.).[67] Stranger still, despite eschewing explicit rites of embarkation, the Argonauts offer sacrifices to the Dioscuri for safe arrival at the Stoechades Islands (4.651–3), not to their customary dedicatee Apollo, who plays no direct role in the homeward voyage until its end (4.1706–18).[68] What we get instead of sacrifices congruent with embarkation are propitiatory rites in honour of Medea's special goddess, Hecate – Medea is her priestess – presumably for her role in helping to anaesthetize the serpent guarding the Golden Fleece (4.246–52); these are, it would appear, 'dread rites',[69] since Apollonius piously refuses to articulate them (250: ἄζομαι αὐδῆσαι, 'I shrink in fear from speaking'). What follows the shrouded and vague rites for Hecate is the 'sacrificial' slaughter of Absyrtus at the Temple of Brygean Artemis (459–81), a goddess long identified as functionally identical to Hecate (e.g. Hes. fr. 23a.26, 23b (= Paus. 1.43) Merkelbach-West; Aesch. *Supp.* 676–7).[70] The Hecate-Artemis syncrisis invites us to read the odd ritual behaviour at the beginning of the *nostos* – the conspicuously unnarrated rites for Hecate and the sacrificially suffused slaughter of Absyrtus – together, in tandem, structurally and functionally juxtaposing the ritually correct inaugural rites in book 1. In Hesiod, Hecate is associated with assisting sea-voyagers (*Theog.* 440–7), and Artemis' connections with human sacrifice in the context of sea-travel go back to Agamemnon's sacrifice of Iphigenia at Aulis. Artemis (like Hecate) is goddess of boundaries, borders, transitions; she controls 'highways and harbours' (Callim. *Hymn* 3.38–9), and navigation by sea of bounded and treacherous areas necessitated her protection. She is, as Susan Cole explains, 'a god of turning points'.[71] What's more: 'Artemis's sanctuaries, whether on land at border crossings or on sea at places of embarkation, recognized the sites of emotional challenge, to which, once passed, there was no turning back.'[72] Artemis, we should not forget, is patron goddess of Iolchis, the *telos* of the Argonautic voyage. Her presence at the beginning of the *nostos* indicates the physical and emotional

---

[67] Mori (2008): 157–60 has a helpful table of sacrifices and implied sacrifices in the poem.
[68] Mori (2008): 162; cf. Clare (2002): 161–3.    [69] Hunter (2015): *ad* 4.248–50.
[70] Nelis (1991): 101–3; Mori (2008): 219 with n.99.
[71] Cole (2004): 187; see Cole (2004): 178–97 for more details.    [72] Cole (2004): 188.

transition under way. Whether it's their intention or not, Medea and Jason's murder of Absyrtus functions, both circumstantially and in the architecture of the poem, as an implicit distorted propemptic 'offering' to Artemis-Hecate, the perversion of which paves the way for the familial atrocities awaiting the pair's arrival in Greece projected beyond the boundary of the poem. This is in tune with the assortment of infanticidal imagery in the epic's second half (and especially in book 4) proleptic of the events which will ultimately play out in Euripides' *Medea*.[73]

Medea earlier in book 4 wished the sea had 'torn Jason to pieces' rather than allow him access to Colchis (4.32–3); Jason wished Pelias had 'cruelly torn him limb from limb' before his voyage (2.624–6).[74] Both conspire here to fulfill the violence of these displaced contrafactuals (Medea does the planning, Jason the 'butchering'). In the two earlier literary accounts of the murder, Medea, not Jason, kills her brother. In one account she dismembers the child Absyrtus and leaves his scattered limbs as grim crumbs for her father to collect floating in the sea as the Argo tries to outpace the pursuing Colchians (Pherec. *FGrH* 3 F 32a; cf. Ov. *Met.* 7.54). Euripides, like Apollonius, gave the scene sacrificial overtones, as Jason tells us Medea killed Absyrtus at the hearth before boarding the Argo (*Med.* 1334; cf. Soph. *Colch.* fr. 343 Radt).[75] Apollonius' version is a combination of these elements, the *sparagmos* reworked (and evoked) in Jason's truncation of Absyrtus' corpse, and the hearth expanded into a temple proper. But by shifting the physical violence to Jason, Apollonius amplifies his role in the brutal act and focuses attention on the complexities of his heroic status – the 'disfigurements' of Homeric heroic behaviour – in the final book of the epic.

Apollonius' aside that Jason's licking and spitting of his victim's blood is *themis* (4.479) is odd. The rituals he performs are 'customary' of *maschalismos* but it's difficult to see in them much that is 'right' or 'lawful'; perhaps Apollonius toys with the mixed-meaning 'to question the moral

---

[73] E.g. 3.835–7, 1128–36; 4.1–5, 62–5, 383–7, 411–13, 537–41, 716–17, 1139–41. See Hunter (1993): 123: 'The action of Euripides' tragedy hangs over the epic like a cloud about to burst, so that the later poem becomes almost an explanatory commentary on the terrible events of the drama'; Fusillo (1985): 107–10 on Medea and Euripidean prolepses. The stain of human sacrificial imagery associated with Artemis-Hecate in book 4 might be anticipated by the presence of Iphias, the priestess of Artemis, whom Jason (immediately following a simile likening him to Apollo: 1.307–11; contrast Medea's 'Hecatean' Artemis simile at 3.876–85) ignores at Iolchis before embarking (1.311–16). Her silence is darkly pregnant; see Nelis (1991), Clauss (1993): 53 n.25, Sansone (2000).

[74] Jason's speech is a means of testing the resolve of the Argonauts (2.638) but the violence of his (feigned) dejection nonetheless looks ahead to the dismemberment of Absyrtus two books later; see Hunter (1993): 21.

[75] Hutchinson (1988): 125 with n.66; Bremmer (1997): 85–6.

status of the hero's actions here'.[76] This is in stride with the ironical Homeric usage of *heros* to describe both Absyrtus (471) and Jason (477) in a scene so far removed from Homeric heroism.[77] The mutilation is meant to maim and thus ward off or hamper Absyrtus' vengeful spirit, which might seek retaliation for the deceitfulness and stealth of the murder.[78] It has an apotropaic function. But the act itself is an epic *topos* of vengefulness and violence aimed at the dead rendered (almost) impermissible in Homeric epic. This is what Achilles *wants* to do to Hector but can never really accomplish. The corporeal abuse recalls the humiliating severing of Melanthius' extremities (hands, feet, nose, genitals) at *Odyssey* 22.474–7,[79] but Melanthius is crucially not *dead* when he's mutilated.[80] There's nothing quite like this in the Homeric poems. Apollonius is breaking epic 'rules', even with his (parodic?) justification of the act as ritually *themis*. Despite its apparent apotropaic purpose, *maschalismos* is still corpse abuse, and the desire to humiliate and deny a 'beautiful death' to an enemy cannot be separated from the act.[81]

Again, Absyrtus is still alive at the end of Valerius' poem. But he's Medea's 'ill-fated brother' (VF 8.136: *infelix*[82] *frater*); Medea hopes she has already carried out all acts of *nefas* after her magical arts win Jason the Golden Fleece, looking proleptically to Absyrtus' death and many additional extratextual crimes to come (8.108: *iamque omne nefas, iam, spero, peregi*, 'I hope now, now, I've accomplished all wicked deeds').[83] And her frightening dream anticipates the chase at sea that occurs at the end of the poem (5.337–8; cf. also 7.339–40). How Valerius would have handled the murder, however, must remain a mystery, though he does seem to rule out the Apollonian ruse when Absyrtus declares 'I don't want the fleece, nor do I take you, sister, though offered, nor will there be hope at all of a treaty' (270–2: *nec quaero uellera nec te | accipio, germana, datam nec foederis ulla | spes erit*). It's tempting to see ring composition in the 'mutilation' of Jason's brother, Promachus, at the end of book 1 framed (potentially) by Jason's mutilation of Medea's brother at the end of book 8.[84] Jason is not averse to dismembering

[76]   Goldhill (1991): 331.

[77]   See Hutchinson (1988): 127; Porter (1990): 267 n.35; Green (1997): 313. *Contra* Mori (2008): 205–9.

[78]   Parker (1983): 108; Bremmer (1997): 84; Ceulemans (2007).     [79] Johnston (1999): 158–9.

[80]   See Davies (1994) for Melanthius' mutilation.

[81]   See Vermeule (1979): 236 n.30; Johnston (1999): 159; Ceulemans (2007): 103, 111.

[82]   *infelix* is Schenkl's conjecture replacing *inflexit* in the manuscripts, and followed almost universally by editors (though see Pellucchi (2012): *ad loc.*).

[83]   Pellucchi (2012): *ad* 8.108.

[84]   Hershkowitz (1998b): 9, 16. Ripoll (2008): 180–2 proposes the poem likely would have ended with a duel between Jason and Absyrtus modelled on the Aeneas–Turnus duel from *Aen.* 12. Stover (2011): 195–6 suggests Valerius provides hints that Medea, not Jason, would have killed Absyrtus. On 'endings' generally see Hershkowitz (1998b): 1–34.

opponents as we saw with his slaying of Auchus in book 6 – Valerius follows Apollonius in depicting Jason's violent truncation of an opponent, in a scene that plays with the motif of corpse abuse. This earlier scene of graphic battlefield violence at Colchis might then have anticipated Jason's abuse of Absyrtus, however we are to imagine this scene playing out. Ovid excised the murder of Absyrtus from his *Metamorphoses* 7 (Medea slays and dismembers the *infant* Absyrtus at Ov. *Her.* 12.113–16; cf. *Tr.* 3.9.34–5); Seneca implies Medea chopped up Absyrtus herself at *Medea* 130–4. We can only guess how Valerius might have proceeded.

Still, the theme of sparagmatic corpse abuse is not lost on the Flavian poet. As the Argonauts approach Lemnos, Valerius flashes back to the atrocities that have just recently occurred there in vivid detail. Venus' anger at the disclosure of her affair with Mars and the subsequent scornful neglect of her worship on the island precipitates the punishment of the entire male population (VF 2.98–102). Fama fires the Lemnian women to jealous rage (135–73), whereupon Venus herself, in disguise and accompanied by personified forces of Hell (204–8), bursts in and rouses the women to war (209–14):

> hic aliud Venus et multo magis ipsa tremendum
> orsa nefas gemitus fingit vocesque cadentum                   210
> inrupitque domos et singultantia gestans
> ora manu taboque sinus perfusa recenti
> arrectasque comas: 'meritos en prima reuertor
> ulta toros, permit ecce dies'.

> Now Venus herself commenced another and far greater
> crime: she manufactured the groaning and cries of dying men;   210
> and she burst into homes brandishing a still-gasping
> head in her hand, and stained on her chest with fresh gore
> and her hair standing on end: 'Behold, I return first,
> having avenged my deserving bed. Look, daylight approaches'.

The echoing but false sounds of slaughter are intended to inspire collective mob-violence, and Venus feigns striking the first blow (213–14). She brings evidence of her vicious intentions and the unidentified severed head indicates her expectations for the level of brutality the Lemnian women will administer. The head is still gasping for air (*singultantia . . . ora*), an image recalling similar gruesome scenes in Virgil (night-raid victims: *Aen.* 9.332–3, though here the headless *trunk* is 'gurgling') and Lucan (Pompey: *BC* 8.682–3).[85] Apollonius' quick sketch of the massacre has nothing close

---

[85] Harper Smith (1987): *ad* 2.211 and Poortvliet (1991): *ad* 2.211f note the inversion of the Virgilian image. See pp. 48, 70–1 for the earlier epic scenes.

to this level of violence or specificity (AR 1.609–32).[86] It must shock us that the Love goddess herself is perpetrating such horrid acts. Venus' hellish attendants (Pavor, Discordia, Ira, Dolus, Rabies, Letum, VF 2.204–6) are typical companions of her consort Mars,[87] as Valerius signals when he caps the list by calling Venus *Mauortia coniunx* (208). As in the Colchian civil war discussed above, Love and War come together in a frightening display of corporeal violence.[88]

But whose severed head is this? Is it even *real?* Venus had earlier taken the form of a Lemnian woman named Dryope (174), but many hours have passed by the time she 'hops' back down to Lemnos to lead the women in the slaughter of male citizens in the middle of the night (198: *desilit in Lemnon*; cf. 134 (to Fama): *mox ipsa adero ducamque paratas*, 'soon I myself will come and lead them once they're prepared'). It's possible she deploys the same guise here and that the unnamed husband whom Venus-Dryope lambastes at 180–4 is her unfortunate victim.[89] Or perhaps the head is simply a prop. Venus *is* acting and the scene is loaded with nods to stagecraft: Venus jumps on and off the Lemnian 'stage'; she has various 'costumes' (as Dryope, as a Fury, 102–6,[90] as Bellona, 196–7 – she 'girds' herself for battle (197: *pugnae . . . accincta*) in a way that implies a wardrobe-change; as Mars, 204–8); Fama assumes the role of Neaera (141); the fake off-stage screams of dying men are functionally 'sound-effects' (210; cf. 200–3);[91] the Lemnian women themselves become Furies (162–7, 191–5, 227–8),[92] and are 'acting' when they feign joy at seeing their returning husbands (187–9; they 'play the chorus' at 188: *simulant . . . choros*).[93] Valerius leaves us in the dark. All details of physical action (real or not) are excised, following a Virgilian 'poetics of silence' in depicting corpse abuse. As in Virgil the aftershocks of abuse are on full display but the act itself is expurgated, leaving a narrative ellipsis. If Venus *did* chop off someone's head, we don't see it 'on stage' (nor do we get a 'messenger speech' articulating the atrocity behind the scenes); if the head is a prop, it's a deft – and cynical – mime of the type of grotesquery faddish in Latin poetry's early imperial period, which Valerius generally avoids in his poem.

---

[86] See Vessey (1985).
[87] Vessey (1985): 327; Harper Smith (1987): *ad locc*; Spaltenstein (2002): *ad locc.*
[88] Fucecchi (2014): 120.    [89] Poortvliet (1991): *ad* 211f; Spaltenstein (2002): *ad* 2.209–12.
[90] Vessey (1985): 327, Hardie (1993): 43–4, Hershkowitz (1998b): 178–9 on Furies and other Virgilian character role-playing here; also Buckley (2013): 82–3.
[91] Poortvliet (1991): *ad* 2.209f: 'we are probably not supposed to ask how Venus did the trick'.
[92] Hardie (1993): 44; Schenk (1999): 345–6.
[93] See Buckley (2013): 81–9 for some similar observations. Schenk (1999): 346–7 implies this is a ruse by Venus.

While the anonymity of the severed head links nicely with Lucan's conception of nameless/faceless civil violence, the surgical, haptic corpse abuse we see in the *Bellum ciuile* is not present in the Flavian *Argonautica*.

The theatrical feel of the scene is reinforced by the clear Bacchic overtones. Venus' brandishing of a severed familial head should remind us of Agave's 'proud' display of her son Pentheus' head during a similar exhibition of divinely induced familial slaughter in Euripides' *Bacchae* (1165–1258).[94] Venus claims 'first place' in the slaughter (VF 2.213: *prima reuertor*) as Euripides' Agave claims to outmatch and outpace her fellow Theban 'huntresses' (*Bacch.* 1179: πρῶτον ἐμὸν τὸ γέρας, 'first honour is mine'; 1183: μετ᾽ ἐμὲ μετ᾽ ἐμὲ, 'after me, after me!'). The Lemnian women, fully infected by Venus' frenzy, 'tear apart' the Thracian slaves their husbands brought back as war spoils (VF 2.240: *diripiunt*), evoking the *sparagmos* at *Bacchae* 1125–36 and Ovid *Metamorphoses* 3.731 (*sunt membra uiri manibus direpta nefandis*, 'the man's limbs are torn apart by wicked hands'). This mass mutilation trumps Aeson's curse of Pelias (VF 1.813: *diripiat et laceretque senem*) and the murder of Promachus (1.825: *diripiunt*) in the previous book. What began as a performance-piece by Venus and Fama has suddenly become painfully real. Actual howls and groans have replaced the earlier 'staged' sounds of slaughter Venus had manufactured (VF 2.240–1: *mixti gemitus clamorque precantum | barbarus ignotaeque implebant aethera uoces*, 'a cacophony of groans, barbarous pleading shouts and unintelligible cries filled the air'; 210: *gemitus fingit uocesque cadentum*).[95] Venus has unleashed civil war.

In the next book, Valerius will recall the scene of Pentheus' *sparagmos* via simile to articulate the Argonauts' shocked horror at the realization that they have accidentally (again, in the middle of the night) just battled their guest-friends and *socii* (3.245, 261) the Doliones (263–6):

> tenet exsangues rigor horridus artus
> ceu pauet ad crines et tristia Pentheos ora
> Thyias, ubi impulsae iam se deus agmine matris
> abstulit et caesi uanescunt cornua tauri.

> Horrid paralysis binds their bloodless limbs
> just as the Thyiad pales at the hair and grim face of Pentheus,
> when the god removed himself from the crowd of agitated mothers
> and the horns of the slaughtered bull vanish.

---

[94] Buckley (2013): 89.  [95] Poortvliet (1991): *ad* 2.209f, 240f.

The bull-horn reference brings Euripides back into focus as does the earlier notion that daylight yields clarity (VF 3.257–8; Eur. *Bacch.* 1264–70).[96] The image completes, in effect, the scene from book 2: there Venus-Agave bears a severed family member's head proudly; in the later simile the Argonauts-Agave feel the full-force of paralytic sobriety at the realization of the crime (there is no *anagnorisis* articulated at Lemnos). The context for each Theban image is civil/familial war, one at the outset of hostilities (Lemnos), the other the 'mourning after' (Cyzicus).[97] Lucan bookended his Thessalian/Pharsalian excursus and the climactic battle of his *Civil War* with allusions to Pentheus' *sparagmos* (*BC* 6.357–9, 7.780) as a mythological indicator of the scope of internecine conflict. The stain of Lucan's poem is omnipresent here.[98] Moments after he describes Venus parading the severed head, Valerius halts his narrative and delivers an aside begging some higher power to bring his song to an end (VF 2.218–19): *o qui me uera canentem | sistat et hac nostras exsoluat imagine noctes!*, 'oh who might stop me as I sing the truth and free my nights from this vision!' He cannot record all the 'endless scenes of wickedness' (216: *tot scelerum facies*) that occurred in the dead of night (216–19). This *praeteritio* reworks Lucan's narrative-halting plea before his account of the horrors of Pharsalus (*BC* 7.552–6). Valerius – having reinserted epic's divine machinery – seeks a higher source to relegate his poem to darkness; Lucan invoked his own 'mind' to be silent (552: *hanc fuge, mens, partem belli tenebrisque relinque*, 'mind, flee from this part of the war and cast it to shadows').[99] Both invocations prove futile. Valerius' pre-narrative 'nightmares' (*hac nostras ... imagine noctes*) of the midnight slaughter in Lemnos mirror the nightmares Caesar and his army experience *after* the battle that saw them tear apart the Roman Republican army in the scene that instigated the Theban *sparagmos* simile (*BC* 7.771–6). Through pointed Lucanian echoes, mythology collapses into 'historical' epic in a scene that recalls the *furor* of Roman civil war violence (e.g. VF 2.226–8, 239).[100] Familial violence, civil war, and now *Roman* civil war coalesce here in a song the *uates* should not – but will – sing (VF 2.217): *heu uatem monstris quibus intulit ordo*, 'alas, to what horrors the story has brought the poet'.

[96] Fitch (1976): 117; Hershkowitz (1998a): 39–41.     [97] To purloin a pun from Pagán (2000).

[98] See Schenk (1999): 252–3 n.348.

[99] Harper Smith (1987): *ad* 2.219; Spaltenstein (2002): *ad* 2.216–19; Bernstein (2014): 161.

[100] McGuire (1997): 104–7. See also Bernstein (2008): 50–1 on the Lemnian conflict and Roman civil war.

## Tyrannical Abuse

This is not the only head on display in the *Argonautica*. I noted that Pelias, in an unfulfilled boast, claims he would like to showcase Aeetes' severed head as a trophy of war (1.52). On two other occasions Valerius offers actual evidence of this tyrannical activity. One can be glossed fairly quickly. Again in 'costume' (this time as Circe) Venus implores Medea to aid Jason in his quest to win the Golden Fleece. Her speech ends with examples of other women who scorned their fathers to assist lovers. Among these is Hippodamia who helped Pelops defeat her father Oenomaus in the famous chariot race. Venus says Hippodamia was motivated by her horror at viewing the heads of defeated suitors Oenomaus collected and put on display (7.277–8): *totque ora simul uulgata procorum | respiciens tandem patrios exhorruit axes*, 'and seeing so many heads of suitors displayed together, finally Hippodamia shuddered at her father's chariot'. Venus' deployment of this graphic imagery in a speech meant to persuade Medea is in stride with her physical brandishing of a severed head in the coercive Lemnian episode. The detail of corpse abuse seems gratuitous but it's likely Valerius has Sophocles in mind who in his *Oenomaus* apparently depicts the king using defeated suitors' heads as roof-tiles (fr. 473, 473a Radt = Schol. BD *ad* Pind. *Isthm.* 4.92a). The detail is the mark of tyranny: tyrants collect heads (cf. Sen. *Clem.* 1.26.3).

Venus' aim is to elicit horror, matching Hippodamia's horror at the sight of truncated heads (*exhorruit*). Will Jason suffer the same abuse from Medea's own tyrannical father Aeetes[101] when he flunks his impossible task? Medea *is* horrified (VF 7.295): *horror molles inuaserat annos*, 'horror had invaded her delicate youth'. There follows immediately another allusion via simile to Euripides' Pentheus heading toward his doom (300–6):

> illa sequi iubet et portis exspectat in ipsis
> saeuus Echionia ceu Penthea Bacchus in aula
> deserit infectis per roscida cornua uittis,
> cum tenet ille deum pudibundaque tegmina matris
> tympanaque et mollem subito miser accipit hastam.
> haud aliter deserta pauet perque omnia circum                    305
> fert oculos tectisque negat procedere uirgo.[102]

[Venus] orders her to follow and waits in the doorway itself
just like savage Bacchus leaves Pentheus in the Echionian hall,

---

[101] Aeetes *tyrannus*: 5.264, 319, 387, 470, 547, 659; 6.16; 7.78, 87, 93, 491; see Ripoll (2003–4): 3 n.2; Cowan (2014): 232 n.8. On Aeetes' tyranny in VF and AR generally, see Ripoll (2003–4).

[102] See Buckley (2013): 91–3 for a sophisticated reading of these lines.

his headband suffused by the dew-moistened horns,
when that one has the god in him and his mother's shameful cloak
and suddenly takes up drum and delicate spear, poor guy.
Just so the girl, abandoned, shudders and all around                    305
darts her eyes and refuses to leave the building.

Here it is now applied to Medea and not, as we might have expected, to Jason. Medea is emotionally 'torn' between her loyalty to her father and the savage love (307: *saeuus amor*) she feels for Jason whose life (and, potentially, corporeal integrity) is in her hands (305–8). Medea's internalized *sparagmos* replaces the external cues the scene has built around *physical* bodily rending. Jason will remain 'intact' when Medea chooses love/ Venus, but the savagery of *amor* will prove (extratextually) this decision is ultimately just as shattering (cf. Mopsus' infanticidal prophecy: 1.224–6, cf. 8.247–9; Medea's proleptic nightmare: 5.333–40).

The poem is obsessed with tyranny,[103] and Valerius' tyrants are the characters most explicitly associated with corpse mistreatment. I end my discussion of Valerius' *Argonautica* with his apex tyrant, the Bebrycian king Amycus, who is concocted through a witch's-brew of earlier epic 'villains', especially Homer's Polyphemus, Virgil's Polyphemus, Cacus, Mezentius, and Turnus, and Lucan's Antaeus (etc.).[104] Apollonius' Amycus is brutal and savage (AR 2.1–163) but Debra Hershkowitz is right to stress that Valerius' aim here is 'blurring the line between monstrous men (typified by earlier Amycuses, or Mezentius or Turnus) and anthropomorphic monsters (such as the Cyclops, Cacus, or Antaeus)'.[105] Valerius' Amycus is a *rex*, a *tyrannus* (VF 4.101, 108, 316, 751) but also a *monstrum* (155, 188, 750); he's utterly bereft of 'humanity' (201–2: *mortalia nusquam | signa manent*). And his reign among the Bebrycians is removed from (or a perversion of) 'civil' constructs (laws and treaties: 102–3, 209; sacrificial ritual and observance: 109–11, 146–7, 218–19; *xenia* codes: 109–13, 212 *et passim*).[106] His subjects fear and despise him (200–1, 315–19), in sharp contrast to the Bebrycians in Apollonius who fight to avenge the death of their king (AR 2.98–100).[107]

Amycus welcomes visitors to his land by hurling them off a cliff into the sea as sacrificial offerings to his father, Neptune (VF 4.109–11). If they

---

[103] See McGuire (1997): 154–84 *passim*, Hershkowitz (1998b): 242–74, Ripoll (2003–4), Bernstein (2008): 37–47, Zissos (2009): 360–2, Cowan (2014).

[104] Hershkowitz (1998b): 80–91. See also on Amycus generally: Shelton (1984); Ripoll (1998): 73–9; Zissos (2002): 89–92; Bettenworth (2003); Murgatroyd (2008).

[105] Hershkowitz (1998b): 82; cf. Shelton (1984): 20 n.9, Ripoll (1998): 73–5, Cowan (2014): 231.

[106] E.g. Hutchinson (1993): 117–18; Zissos (2002): 90–1.

[107] Hershkowitz (1998b): 203–4. Cicero characterized *tyranni* precisely like this (*Rep.* 2.48).

appear fit for sport, he challenges them to a boxing match (111–13). He has never lost. All this builds to a crescendo when the Argonauts finally see evidence of Amycus' savagery (177–85):

> litore in extremo spelunca apparuit ingens
> arboribus super et dorso contecta minanti,
> non quae dona deum, non quae trahat aetheris ignem,
> infelix domus et sonitu tremebunda profundi.                    180
> at varii pro rupe metus: hinc trunca rotatis
> bracchia rapta viris strictoque immortua caestu
> ossaque taetra situ <et> capitum maestissimus ordo
> per piceas, quibus aduerso sub uulnere nulla
> iam facies nec nomen erat . . .

> On the edge of the shore there appeared a huge cave,
> roofed over by trees and a projecting ridge
> which doesn't let in the gods' gifts nor the firmament's fire,
> a miserable home quaking from the echoing depths.            180
> But an array of terrors were before the crag: severed arms ripped
> from men whirled away, and withered with boxing-gloves
>     still fastened,
> and bones fouled with decay and a horrific row of heads
> through the pitch-pines, for whom through a direct blow no
> semblance or name now remains.

This is a horror show of corporal abuses. The venue is appropriately a *locus horridus* modelled on Cacus' cave in Virgil (*Aen.* 8.193–7) where too the monster has decorated the entryway with severed heads (196–7): *foribusque adfixa superbis | ora uirum tristi pendebant pallida tabo*, 'and affixed with pride at the entryway were hanging human heads growing pale with grim putrefaction'. Cacus' cave in Ovid's *Fasti* has similar décor and Valerius has blended the descriptions neatly (*Fast.* 1.555–8):[108]

> proque domo longis spelunca recessibus ingens,
>     abdita, uix ipsis inuenienda feris;
> ora super postes adfixaque bracchia pendent,
>     squalidaque humanis ossibus albet humus

> as a home there was a huge cave with deep recesses,
>     so hidden that it could scarcely be found by wild animals.
> Above its door-posts hang tacked-up heads and limbs,
>     and the filthy ground becomes white with human bones.

---

[108] Murgatroyd (2008): 385–6 and (2009): *ad* 4.177–86.

But Valerius' cave is even darker, more precipitous, more infernal, concomitant with the degeneration of his intertextual-monster's activities. It is
a workshop of *post mortem* mutilation. Limbs and bones lie scattered and
rotting (VF 4.181–3), severed hands remain bound in boxing gloves (182).
The reference to the gloves (*caesti*) reminds us that these broken bodies
belong to losers of a *boxing* match, not (e.g.) sword-play. Their mutilation
is not a consequence of the duel, but a grotesque indication of Amycus'
meddling with the dead *à la* Erichtho's necromantic tinkering in *BC* 6.
The details climax with the description of severed heads lined up in trees
(VF 4.183–4). What seemed haphazard and animalistic is undercut by the
notice that Amycus has taken the time to arrange everything deliberately
and methodically (183: *ordo*).[109] The assortment of *membra* are memorial
trinkets; he's 'decorating'.

The displayed heads recall those Cacus flaunts in Virgil and Ovid, along
with Turnus' parading of Nisus' and Euryalus' impaled heads (*Aen.* 9.465–
72). Lucan too is fond of this sort of macabre imagery (e.g. *BC* 2.160; 8.681–
4; 9.136–9), as is Silius (*Pun.* 5.151; 7.704; 15.813; 17.308), and the poetic
material always looks askance at similar trophy heads in Roman civil war
contexts (e.g. Cic. *Phil.* 11.5; Vell. Pat. 2.27.3; Sen. *Suas.* 6.17–19; Tac. *Ann.*
1.61, *Hist.* 1.44; Suet. *Iul.* 85–6, *Aug.* 13.1; App. *B Ciu.* 1.71, etc.). Perhaps
Roman civil war, however, is not the best lens through which to view this
sort of tyrannical head-hunting. Recent history provided Valerius with the
model of Nero's collecting of enemy heads at court in 62 CE; the scenes are
recorded in the final flourish to Tacitus' *Annales* 14. Faustus Cornelius
Sulla Felix (*Ann.* 14.57), Rubellius Plautus (59) – cousins of Nero – and
Nero's wife Octavia (64) are all decapitated, their heads displayed before
the emperor. The first two were potential 'rivals' to Nero's throne via their
lineage, while Octavia is construed as a rival to Nero's mistress Poppaea. In
the pseudo-Senecan (but surely Vespasianic) *Octavia*, Nero's first lines in
the tragedy are a demand to receive the severed heads of Sulla and Plautus
(*Oct.* 437–8: *perage imperata: mitte, qui Plauti mihi | Sullaeque caesi referat
abscisum caput*, 'follow my orders: send someone who can bring back the
severed heads of the slaughtered Plautus and Sulla').[110] If Valerius had Nero
in mind here, the subtle analogy with the king-tyrant-monster Amycus
offers a cutting portrait of the tyranny and monstrosity of the waning years
of Nero's reign and an anticipation of his eventual fall.

---

[109] Noted by Murgatroyd (2008): 384. There is an intricacy and ('serial killer's') attention to detail that
recalls Seneca's Atreus and Lucan's Erichtho in their treatment of corpses in similar dank infernal
hovels (cf. Sen. *Thy.* 749–75; *BC* 6.667–84).

[110] Boyle (2008): *ad Oct.* 437–9.

There is additional literary engagement with ethnographic *materia* from Apollonius' account of Colchian funeral rites. Valerius has Amycus line the heads up 'along the pitch-pines' (VF 4.184: *per piceas*). These *piceae* are 'funereal' trees,[III] and there is ostensibly a grim joke on the complete inversion of traditional death rites overseen by Amycus – these trees are for burning, not hanging the dead. Moreover, branches of pitch-pine (and/ or cypresses) in particular were displayed outside houses in Rome signifying the *collocatio* ('exposition') of the recently deceased.[112] Valerius' use of *piceae* here in the distorted context of corpse exposure, again, seems intentional. Very likely Valerius is thinking also of the Colchian funereal practice of hanging corpses from trees. The scene is worth quoting in full (AR 3.200–9):

> Κίρκαιον τόδε που κικλήσκεται· ἔνθα δὲ πολλαὶ
> ἐξείης πρόμαλοί τε καὶ ἰτέαι ἐκπεφύασιν,
> τῶν καὶ ἐπ' ἀκροτάτων νέκυες σειρῆσι κρέμανται
> δέσμιοι. εἰσέτι νῦν γὰρ ἄγος Κόλχοισιν ὄρωρεν
> ἀνέρας οἰχομένους πυρὶ καιέμεν· οὐδ' ἐνὶ γαίῃ
> ἔστι θέμις στείλαντας ὕπερθ' ἐπὶ σῆμα χέεσθαι,     205
> ἀλλ' ἐν ἀδεψήτοισι κατειλύσαντε βοείαις
> δενδρέων ἐξάπτειν ἑκὰς ἄστεος. ἠέρι δ' ἴσην
> καὶ χθὼν ἔμμορεν αἶσαν, ἐπεὶ χθονὶ ταρχύουσιν
> θηλυτέρας· ἣ γάρ τε δίκη θεσμοῖο τέτυκται.

> This land is, I think, called 'Circe's': wherein many
> willows and tamarisks grow lined up in rows,
> on the highest branches of which hang corpses tied with
> rope. For even now it's a sacrilegious act for Colchians
> to burn dead bodies with fire, nor is it lawful to bury them
> in the ground or to heap a mound up over them,       205
> but instead they wrap them in untanned hide
> and suspend them from trees outside town. The ground receives
> equal portion with the air, since they inter their
> women: for this is the manner of their rites.

From a Greek perspective this custom is barbaric. The description represents our 'introduction' to Colchian ways – this is the very first 'scene' after Apollonius' Argonauts make landfall in the Caucasus – through a complete perversion of one of the most important Greek rituals. This is, prima facie, *othering*. Like Valerius' example of Iazygian filial-euthanasia, the custom establishes the Colchians as 'savage' and strange and posits immediately at

---

[III] Verg. *Aen.* 6.180; Stat. *Theb.* 6.100; Pliny *HN* 16.40, with Murgatroyd (2009): *ad loc.*
[112] Lindsay (2000): 155.

the beginning of the poem's second half a contrast between barbarism and Greek 'civilization'.

The first thing to note here is audience: do the Argonauts actually *see* this spectacle? The present tenses and clear modernizing set off at 3.203 (εἰσέτι νῦν, a variant of the common Apollonian tic ἔτι νῦν περ[113]) put the ethnographic material firmly in the spectrum of narrative 'aside'. Even if functionally we assume the Argonauts passed by such a spectacle on their way to the city from the ships – and they would have, given the clear indication that corpses were to be set in trees 'outside town' (207: ἑκὰς ἄστεος) – the poet does not focalize the scene through their perspective. The ethnographic obtrusion by the narrator collapses the temporal space through an implied aetiological link with the past – implied because we can *imagine* the Argonauts seeing the same thing Apollonius promises he and his audience could see 'even now' at Colchis, though he never tells us explicitly that they encountered this on their walk to the city. This is a neat disruptive narrative trick common in Apollonian aetiology and *praeteritio*.[114]

Whether the Argonauts see the funeral display or not, Apollonius seems to include the material to highlight the otherness (past and present) of the Colchians. But while this is decidedly un-Hellenic in custom, it is nonetheless *themis*; in fact, following the Greek practice (cremation or interment) for Colchian men would defy religious mandates (204–5). This is divinely motivated. The women are buried in the earth in order to balance the cosmic duality of 'female' Earth and 'male' Sky (207–8).[115] There is certainly 'wonderment' in the description,[116] but no obvious judgment on Apollonius' part: this is, simply, 'the manner of their rites' (209). As an audience we are asked to consider not whether this custom is 'right' within a Hellenic moral/ritual framework, but whether the Hellenic construct is the *only* viable system. And if we are to believe the scholiast (*ad* 3.202–9) Apollonius is not innovating here but instead following Nymphodorus' historiographical account concerning Colchian ritual (cf. Aelian *Misc.* 4.1). Perhaps then this *is* 'stranger than fiction'.[117]

We have no doubts about audience in Valerius' scene. The spectacular horror incites the Argonauts' rage and initiates the confrontation between

[113] Goldhill (1991): 292.
[114] See the discussion in Goldhill (1991): 290–333. On Apollonius' use of aetiology in the poem more broadly see Fusillo (1985): 116–58; note also Hutchinson (1988): 94–7. The influence on Lucan's obtrusive narrator seems not unlikely.
[115] Schol. *ad* 202–9; Fusillo (1985): 166, 179 n.15; Hunter (1989): *ad* 3.200–9; Thalmann (2011): 132–3.
[116] Campbell (1994): *ad* 3.205. For Knight (1995): 177 the description of funeral rites is 'sinister'.
[117] Campbell (1994): *ad* 3.200–9. See Fusillo (1985): 178–9 n.14; see Vian (1980): 117–18 for similar modern practices.

Pollux and the savage Amycus. Apollonius provocatively asked us to think outside the (Hellenistic) box about cultural idiosyncrasies. In a scene that wickedly reworks this ethnographic material in Valerius' poem, can anything about Amycus' practice be *themis*?[118]

Despite the obvious grotesquery on display in what is far and away the Flavian *Argonautica*'s most brutal exhibition of corpse mistreatment, this is still an 'aftermath' scene, similar to when Virgil presents Priam's trunk on the shore or Nisus and Euryalus' heads on pikes. As I have indicated repeatedly Valerius, like Virgil, uses silence and pulls back from explicit descriptions of *post mortem* abuses in his poem. We are left to imagine Amycus' necroscopies in the confines of his ghastly abode. Peter Langen long ago recognized the shadow of Virgil's decapitated Priam in Valerius' description of heads whose names and features are blurred in death (*Aen.* 2.557–8: *iacet ingens litore truncus,* | *auulsumque umeris caput et sine nomine corpus*, 'He lies a huge trunk on the shore, a head ripped from his shoulders and a corpse without a name').[119] The coupled *litore* and *ingens* at VF 4.177 to introduce the scene (here describing the setting and size of the cave) anticipate the Virgilian image more fully fleshed out at 183–5. In a post-Lucanian epic landscape, where there is Virgil's Priam there is almost certainly also Lucan's Pompey. Lucan filled Virgil's narrative ellipsis of Priam's decapitation with gruesome details of the sawing of Pompey's head on a skiff's cross-beam (*BC* 8.667–73).[120] A morbid joke caps the description: 'not yet was it a kind of skill to send a head spinning with a sword' (673: *nondum artis erat caput ense rotare*). Amycus has no trouble whirling off limbs (VF 4.181: *rotatis*). This is grisly – *trunca* (181) and *rapta* (182) highlight the interest in mutilation[121] – but there is a wilful distancing from Lucan's sawing and breaking of bones and sinews (*BC* 8.672–3: *tunc neruos uenasque secat nodosaque frangit* | *ossa diu*) signalled by an adherence to the type of corpse treatment (*rotare*) Lucan casts aside.

The spectacle of abuse elicits a threat of retaliatory corpse abuse from Pollux, who will take up the gauntlets against Amycus in a boxing match to the death (VF 4.191–2): '*te tamen hac, quicumque es', ait 'formidine faxo* | *iam tua silua ferat, modo sint tibi sanguis et artus!*', 'whoever you are, I will nevertheless see to it that your trees bear *you* on account of this horrific display, provided you have blood and limbs'. The basic threat of corpse exposure is common in epic, but given the evidence on display there is extra heft behind these words. Another head, it seems, will soon join the

---

[118] Cowan (2014): 243–4 takes a stab at this.  [119] Langen (1896): *ad* 4.185.
[120] See pp. 69–71 above.  [121] Murgatroyd (2009): *ad* 4.181f.

parade in Amycus' perverted forest. This expectation is undercut, however, when Pollux defeats Amycus in the subsequent fight with a right hook that breaks the Bebrycian's neck. Pollux delivers a *euchos* over Amycus that completely undoes his earlier threat of abuse (311–14):

> labentem propulit heros
> ac super insistens 'Pollux ego missus Amyclis
> et Iove natus'. ait 'nomen mirantibus umbris
> hoc referes. sic et memori noscere sepulchro'.

> The hero shoves him as he falls
> and stepping on him from above says: 'I am Pollux from Amyclae,
> son of Jove; to the marvelling shades below
> you will report this name. You'll be remembered like this on your tomb.'

Amycus' mutilations had stripped his victims of their *facies* and *nomina* (185); Pollux's victory will immortalize his *nomen* (314) in spoken word and through an epitaphic marker on Amycus' tomb, displacing Amycus' own *nomen* lost among the shades (313–14).[122] There are a few things of note here. There is wit in the suggestion that Amycus will bring word of Pollux's victory to the shades below since we are told explicitly that the shades of his earlier victims have all been granted license to come up to watch the fight (258–60).[123] The presence of the shades *above* ground cleverly undercuts that standard *topos* of victors instructing victims to deliver messages to the dead (e.g. Verg. *Aen.* 2.547–50, 9.742, 11.688–9, etc.). The sepulchre will function more as a physical memorial of Pollux's victory than a tomb honouring the dead Amycus. It will monumentalize Pollux's *kleos*, actualizing Hector's (unfulfilled) vision of an Achaean tomb at Troy for the warrior he imagines defeating in a duel at *Iliad* 7.84–91. That tomb, like Amycus' here, is meant to immortalize not the name and memory of the victim, but the victor. Pollux's boast is a bit more scornful, but there *will* be a tomb contrary to his earlier threat of corpse exposure (VF 4.191–2). The Argonauts' treatment of Amycus' corpse, then, pointedly juxtaposes 'civilized' and 'barbarian' social customs vis-à-vis death rites.

But the end of book 4 presents a different picture of Amycus' treatment. The Mariandynian king Lycus welcomes the Argonauts to his palace, which is now 'decked with Bebrycian trophies' (4.739: *Bebryciis praefixa tropaeis*). As a fierce rival of the Bebrycians – Amycus had earlier killed his brother in a boxing match – Lycus profusely thanks the Argonauts for ridding them of the monstrous king. His planned war against Amycus was pre-empted by

---

[122] Shelton (1984): 22; Dinter (2009): 542.    [123] Murgatroyd (2009): *ad* 4.313f.

Pollux's victory. Lycus recalls the scene upon his armed arrival in Bebrycia (749–50): *illum in sanie taboque recenti | uidimus aequoreo similem per litora monstro,* 'we spied that one in bloody gore and just beginning to rot, similar to a sea monster stretched out along the shore'. Lycus' praise confirms the sealing of Pollux's *kleos* but there is apparently no physical tomb to monumentalize it. Amycus has been exposed on the shore. Valerius has strangely offered three 'versions' of Amycus' corpse mistreatment: Pollux's pre-fight threat imagined the cruel king's head (or various body parts) lining the pitch-pines like his earlier victims; Pollux's *post mortem* boast necessitated the presence of a sepulchre; Amycus' *actual* treatment is exposure on the shore 'like a sea monster'.

We don't feel particularly sorry for Amycus even if his abuse is surprising to discover after some 450 lines of silence and alternative expectations. He was a monster who treated the dead with vicious disdain and cruelty. That his own corpse is left to rot on the shore feels like poetic justice and is purposefully set in stark contrast to the funerals for Idmon and Tiphys that begin immediately in the next book (5.1–62). Amycus' cave was at the 'limit' of the shore (177: *litore in extremo*); he straddles both domains, geographically and through his descent from the sea-god Poseidon. And the vivid simile comparing his corpse to a beached sea monster (750) combines elements of land and sea, evocative of Apollonius' description of the aftermath of the Argonauts' engagement with the monstrous Gegeneis in book 1.

Apollonius' Argonauts are attacked at Cyzicus by the Gegeneis ('Earth-Born'), monsters with six arms (AR 1.944–6). They hurl boulders at the Argo's crew and try to hem them in the harbour 'like a man aiming to catch a sea-creature' (991). We are told the Gegeneis had been nurtured by Hera as a (non-canonical) labour for Heracles (996–7). Heracles and the Argonauts rout the monsters without much difficulty and leave their bodies stretched out in the harbour half in the water and half on the shore. The odd topographical circumstance gives Apollonius an opportunity to blend the always-separate Homeric images of scavenging animals from the sea and land (1006–11):

ὣς οἱ ἐνὶ ξυνοχῇ λιμένος πολιοῖο τέταντο
ἑξείης, ἄλλοι μὲν ἐς ἁλμυρὸν ἀθρόοι ὕδωρ
δύπτοντες κεφαλὰς καὶ στήθεα, γυῖα δ' ὕπερθεν
χέρσῳ τεινάμενοι· τοὶ δ' ἔμπαλιν, αἰγιαλοῖο
κράατα μὲν ψαμάθοισι, πόδας δ' εἰς βένθος ἔρειδον,    1010
ἄμφω ἅμ' οἰωνοῖσι καὶ ἰχθύσι κύρμα γενέσθαι.

So at the straits of the clear harbour they were stretched out
in a row, some massed together dipping into the salt water
their heads and chests, spreading out above their legs
on dry land; others were the other way around,
heads on the sandy-shore, feet sunk in the deep water,                    1010
both to become fodder for birds and fish at the same time.

The result of the skirmish reverses the hunting metaphor that initiated the encounter, and a parallel simile follows upon their defeat: the monsters are like recently chopped lumber left lying along the sea's edge (half-in, half-out of the water) to absorb moisture and, thus, better receive shipping-pegs (1003–5: ὡς δ' ὅτε δούρατα μακρὰ νέον πελέκεσσι τυπέντα | ὑλοτόμοι στοιχηδὸν ἐπὶ ῥηγμῖνι βάλωσιν, | ὄφρα νοτισθέντα κρατεροὺς ἀνεχοίατο γόμφους). The image of bodies lying in and out of the water like lumber works visually, but the implication of wood needing water to 'swell' and soften to better support pegs for shipbuilding also conjures the grotesquery of corpse-bloating and the ease of access for beaks, teeth, and talons. This is subtle but effective realism that undercuts standard Homeric similes comparing warriors to *falling* not fallen/inert trees.[124] The metaphors mirror, appropriately, the disruptive, liminal status of the Gegeneis and of the scene in general: like a hunter trying to land-lock a sea-creature, the 'Earth-Born' humanoids attempt to cut off the Argo's access to the sea by heaping up stones at the mouth of the harbour; like half-submerged lumber, they lie straddling land and sea, and their corpses become food for scavengers of each element.[125] The phrase κύρμα γενέσθαι is a standard Homeric line-end (*Il.* 17.151, 272; *Od.* 3.271),[126] and the description of death via simile is Homeric, but the mixing of scavenger types is wholly un-Homeric.[127]

The Gegeneis' fate is brutal but, like Valerius' Amycus, these are unquestionably *monsters* (of Hesiodic pedigree: cf. *Theog.* 147–53): they are 'violent' and 'wild' (942: ὑβρισταί . . . ἄγριοι), a 'spectacle' on account of their six arms (943: μέγα θαῦμα περικτιόνεσσιν ἰδέσθαι, 'a great marvel for their neighbours to see'). Their function as creatures 'nurtured' (995: τρέφεν) by Hera as a labour for Heracles, the 'monster-slayer', underscores their bestial status. And their initial attack coupled with the fishing metaphor recalls Homer's simile likening the monstrous Laestrygonians to fishermen spearing Odysseus' crew like fish (*Od.* 10.124).[128] In each case

---

[124] The contrast is noted by Green (1997): 223–4, Effe (2008): 205.
[125] Similarly Thalmann (2011): 96–7.   [126] Ardizzoni (1967): *ad* 1.1011.
[127] See Hunter (1993): 42 for the 'epitaphic' feel of the simile.
[128] Vian (1951): 19–20 n.6; Clauss (1993): 160. See generally Knight (1995): 147–52.

*xenia* codes are horrifically breached, the Argonauts' foul treatment set in sharp contrast to their cordial initial encounter with the neighbouring Doliones. The Argonauts' subsequent exposure of the Gegeneis' corpses is cold but not entirely unfitting for their uncouth and savage nature. Surprisingly Valerius leaves the Argonauts' confrontation with the Gegeneis out of his *Argonautica* entirely. But he seems to have transferred their *post mortem* exposure to Amycus, a *xenia* breaking monster, the details of whose corpse abuse are absent in Apollonius' poem.

Exposure is not as terrible as mutilation, but there is the suggestion of foul play through additional intertextual cues Valerius activates. We are told that Lycus' palace is decked with Bebrycian trophies at VF 4.739. Paul Murgatroyd notes that *praefigere* can mean 'stick to the surface with', and war spoils like chariot wheels and helmets already appeared 'on display' at 1.837.[129] But the verb is also used more commonly of 'impaling', especially of severed heads (*OLD* s.v. *praefigo* 1b): e.g. Nisus and Euryalus' impaled heads (*Aen.* 9.465–7, 471–2); cf., with modified prefix (*adfigere*), the display-heads outside Cacus' cave in Virgil (*Aen.* 8.196–7) and Ovid (*Fast.* 1.557), quoted above. A similarly vague but frightening image appears at the beginning of Euripides' *Iphigenia in Tauris*. As the two men approach the temple of Artemis at Tauris, Orestes asks Pylades: 'Do you see the trophies hanging from the top of the walls?' (*IT* 74: θριγκοῖς δ᾽ ὑπ᾽ αὐτοῖς σκῦλ᾽ ὁρᾷς ἠρτημένα). Pylades acknowledges that these trophies are the 'best' or 'top parts' of foreigners who have been killed (75: τῶν κατθανόντων γ᾽ ἀκροθίνια ξένων). What is explicit in Herodotus' account of these same abuses (4.103; cf. Amm. Marc. 22.8.34) is elided somewhat here: the *akrothinia* are severed human heads.[130] The tragic image may have resonated with Valerius in his description of foreign spoils decking the high walls of the Mariandynian king just across the Black Sea from Tauris.

In any case, the allusions to Nisus and Euryalus and the heads lining Cacus' cave are important intertexts for Amycus' cave of horrors. Now that his own corpse has been left to rot, we are invited to read the 'trophies' Lycus has claimed from his enemy more grimly; this would not be out of step with a poem that has signalled head-hunting and display as symptomatic of monarchical victory, as we've seen (VF 1.52, 7.285–6). Virgil's Priam *ingens* and Lucan's Pompeius *Magnus* lie headless 'on the shore', imagery which casts a shadow over the earlier scenery of Amycus' cave. If we read either of these epic corpses into Amycus *gigans* (4.200) lying stretched-out *per litore* like a 'sea monster' (750: *aequoreo . . . monstro*),

---

[129] Murgatroyd (2009): *ad* 4.738f.    [130] Bremmer (2013): 92–3, 98.

maybe we can feel more comfortable assuming an act of mutilation has occurred – the repeated but altered rehashings of the fate of Amycus' corpse recall Pompey's similar extended demise. And the collocation *sanie tabo* (749) must remind us of Thyestes' execration of Atreus in Ennius' *Thyestes*, that his brother die a shipwreck victim 'spattering rocks with putrefaction, gore, and black blood' (fr. 297 Jocelyn: *saxa spargens **tabo sanie** et sanguine atro*). Virgil reworked the image in part of his description of the *contemptor diuum* Mezentius' foul form of torture which consisted of stitching corpses to living bodies at *Aeneid* 8.487 (***sanie taboque** fluentis*). All of these vignettes of bodily violence converge in the brief description of Amycus' rotting corpse, adding layers of *implicit* abuse through intertextual guides. As often in this provocative poem, however, we are forced to read between the lines.

Both *Argonautica* poems contain evidence of corpse mistreatment. It is a product of circumstance that the most detailed and evocative example of abuse in Apollonius – the *maschalismos* of Absyrtus – doesn't feature in Valerius' incomplete poem. But the Flavian poet does weave sparagmatic violence into his epic in ways that suggest both the influence of Apollonius' frightening scene and hint that the poem's earlier dismemberments function as prolepses for the unfulfilled violence awaiting Absyrtus. But it's telling that there is nothing as gruesome as the *maschalismos* in Valerius' *Argonautica*. However this scene affects our reading of Apollonius' Jason, his butchering of Absyrtus is near the apex of corpse abuse in Greco-Roman epic and is a direct affront to Homeric aesthetics and moral codes. Valerius pulls back significantly from this level of explicit *post mortem* violence. The evidence of abuse in his epic, singed from the recent horrors of Neronian Rome, post-Neronian civil war, and Lucan's poetic *Civil War*, seems self-consciously occluded or blurred through distancing effects (in narrative, syntax, and referential cues) that recall and expand upon Virgilian practice. Valerius flirts with but also shrouds his audience from abuses that occur or might have occurred in the text.

CHAPTER 5

# Funeral 'Rights': Statius' Thebaid

Like Valerius' poem, Statius' *Thebaid* is intensely concerned with the behaviour and activity of tyrants. The *Argonautica*'s tyrants are cruel, manipulative, and monstrous (in the case of the Bebrycian king Amycus this is not simply a characterization). We see on numerous occasions their perceived 'success' made manifest through the subsequent violence they direct at enemy corpses (VF 1.52, 4.177–85, 7.277–8; cf. 4.739). The *Thebaid* follows a similar pattern. Statius' tyrants rage against dead bodies. The dominant leitmotif of the second half of the poem is the issue of the treatment of dead Argive heroes denied rites by the tyrant Creon.[1] There exists throughout the poem a troubling tension between traditional funeral rites and the 'rights' owed to dead bodies by Greco-Roman customs and standards. Funeral denial (and its bludgeoning narrative anticipation) in the poem precipitates a perversion of ritual practice and procedure. The *Thebaid* is bursting with ritually corrupt and distorted funerals whose functional practice reflects the complex *ethical* issues involved in the abnegation of death rites. As we shall see, the context of civil war at Thebes complicates this picture even further, as Statius asks us to consider whose corpse has a *right* to death rites.

After the mutual slaughter of the enemy-brothers Eteocles and Polynices in book 11, Creon, who has now assumed the Theban throne after Eteocles' death, delivers a formal edict banning funeral rites for all slain Argives and their allies, including Polynices (*Theb.* 11.661–4):

> primum adeo saeuis imbutus moribus aulae
> (indicium specimenque sui) iubet igne supremo
> arceri Danaos, nudoque sub axe relinqui
> infelix bellum et tristes sine sedibus umbras.

---

[1] See bibliography on p. 79 n.43.

Right away, soaked in the savage ways of the palace
(evidence and proof of his ways), he orders final funeral fires
be denied to the Danaans, and the unfortunate army left
under the naked sky, sad shades without a home.

Scholars have focused on Creon's inhumane cruelty here as something
specific to his gaining kingship and endemic in rulers at Thebes.[2] Both the
narrator and Oedipus say as much, bookending the notice of Creon's edict
with scathing indictments (11.654–60, 677–82). The point is again hammered home by Antigone who questions Creon's actions as a product of
hatred spawned by the power of kingship (11.724). Creon's funeral ban is
his first act as king, and more telling still is the ban's contrast with his own
very recent concern for the unburied corpses on the battlefield when he
confronts Eteocles at 11.276–80, urging him to end the war by accepting
Polynices' challenge to a duel. Though he rages back at Creon's demand,
Eteocles anticipates that this bombast is a mask for Creon's own ambition
and 'mad hope' for the Theban throne (11.298–302), and this does come to
pass.

Eteocles had earlier refused funeral rites to the augur Maeon, the lone
survivor of Tydeus' massacre of the 50 ambushers in book 2, after he had
denounced the king as a tyrant. Maeon commits suicide as an act of *libertas*
in the face of tyrannical oppression (3.96–8), and his corpse is tossed into
the woods at Eteocles' order.[3] This earlier scene anticipates Creon's ban,[4] as
he too will reject death rites to the dead.[5] But Creon eclipses Eteocles in
sheer scale: instead of denying rites to one man, Creon refuses funerals for
an entire army (the Argive contingent and Polynices), following the footsteps of Euripides' Creon in his *Suppliants*. Maeon will lie beneath the
naked sky (3.112: **nudoque sub axe**) as Creon's ban proposes for all of the
dead Argives (11.663: **nudoque sub axe**, in the same *sedes*).[6] Eteocles' refusal
of Maeon's rites is the first narrative appearance of this theme in the
*Thebaid* which anticipates Creon's edict (here and re-echoed at 12.94–
103; cf. 12.55–9, 692).

Statius, as narrator or through the voices of his characters, repeatedly
refers to Creon's looming ban to the point of obsession. The prologue

---

[2] See Venini (1970): xxiii, *ad* 11.659ss, *ad* 661ss, Ganiban (2007): 198–9, Bessone (2011): 150–1.
[3] I discuss the scene in detail below, pp. 207–10.
[4] Snijder (1968): *ad* 3.71, implicitly. See Vessey (1973): 113–14, 130 n.1, Ripoll (1998): 296, Pollmann
(2004): 35 and *ad* 12.95.
[5] We see this transference of funeral denial in Eur.'s *Phoen.* 775–7, concerning the treatment of
Polynices' corpse, which sets the stage (as it were) for the action of his *Suppliants*.
[6] Snijder (1968): *ad* 3.112.

promises a song of kings' bodies lacking burial (1.36–7: *tumulis . . . carentia regnum | funera*). Laius' ghost presages a guilty decree delaying funeral fires (4.640–1: *ab igne supremo | sontes lege morae*). A prophetic Apollo spares the seer-warrior Amphiaraus the fate of lying naked and forbidden a sepulchre at Creon's command (7.776–7: *certe non perpessure Creontis | imperia aut uetito nudus iaciture sepulcro*, 'surely you won't suffer Creon's orders and lie naked with a tomb forbidden'), and Juno too waxes clairvoyant when she accosts Jupiter at the sight of the drowning Hippomedon (9.517–19): *certe tumulos supremaque uictis | busta dabas: ubi Cecropiae post proelia flammae, | Theseos ignis ubi est?*, 'surely you used to provide tombs and final pyres to the conquered: where are Cecropian flames after battle, where is Theseus' fire?' Her words give the first (and only) indication of the role Theseus will come to play in the poem when he arrives from Athens, defeats Creon in battle, and reverses the funeral ban.[7] Yet even here little is assured and we must wait a further three books for Athenian intervention.

The aged Aletes, lamenting the Theban ambushers slain by Tydeus in book 2, prays for immediate death (i.e. before the outbreak of the formal war in book 7) so that his corpse has an opportunity to be burned and buried, as he anticipates this will not be available to him once the war begins (3.212–13): *ast ego doner | dum licet igne meo terraque insternar auita!*, 'but let me have my fire while it's permitted, let me be covered by ancestral dirt!'[8] The most important prefiguring of Creon's ban is Dis's injunction at 8.72–4, when he orders Tisiphone to infect both sides of the war with madness. Among his list of atrocities is the demand that one deny funeral rites to the dead, looking toward Creon without naming him explicitly (8.72–3): *[sit] quique igne supremo | arceat exanimes et manibus aethera nudis | commaculet*, 'let there be one who deprives the dead the final funeral fire and pollutes the air with naked shades'.[9] While verbal cues tie all of these passages together, we should note here that Dis's anticipation of the language of Creon's initial ban (8.72–3: *quique **igne supremo** | arceat*) is doubled by *iubet **igne supremo** | arceri* at 11.662–3,[10] as Creon finally fulfils the edict Statius has been telegraphing for the first ten and a half books. Dis's words seal the fate of the Argives, but Statius' audience has long seen this coming.

[7] Ripoll (1998): 296; Bessone (2011): 54 and (2013): 88–9.
[8] Snijder (1968): *ad loc.*; Pollmann (2004): 34.
[9] Venini (1970): *ad* 11.661ss; Smolenaars (1994): *ad* 7.776f.; Pollmann (2004): 35–6; van der Keur (2013): 333 n.19.
[10] Venini (1970): *ad* 11.661ss.

If this sort of pre-scripting was not already hammered home, Creon re-emphasizes – he literally repeats himself (12.93: ***iterat***; 100: *quare **iterum repetens iterumque edico***, 'therefore repeating again, I again decree')[11] – his funeral ban at the beginning of book 12 during, of all things, the funeral of his own son Menoeceus, who had committed suicide by hurling himself from Thebes' walls (10.756–82). His rage now fully animalistic,[12] Creon wishes he could do even more than simply leave the Argive bodies to rot on the plain. He would re-animate the corpses (like the galvanistic Erichtho), heap more misery on them, and personally lead animals to tear their flesh. The natural processes of decay and decomposition are a gift compared to what Creon *would* do if he had his way.[13] But denying the dead death rites will have to suffice (12.94–103):

> saeuum agedum inmitemque uocent si funera Lernae
> tecum ardere ueto; longos utinam addere sensus                    95
> corporibus caeloque animas Ereboque nocentes
> pellere fas, ipsumque feras, ipsum unca uolucrum
> ora sequi atque artus regum monstrare nefandos!
> ei mihi, quod positos humus alma diesque resoluet!
> quare iterum repetens iterumque edico: suprema                    100
> ne quis ope et flammis ausit iuuisse Pelasgos;
> aut nece facta luet numeroque explebit adempta
> corpora; per superos magnumque Menoecea iuro.

> Well, let them call me savage and cruel if I forbid Lerna's dead
> to be burned with you; would that I could rightly give lasting feeling  95
> to their corpses and hurl their guilty souls from the sky and
> from Erebus, myself follow the hooked beaks of birds
> and show them the accursed limbs of kings!
> Oh well, the nourishing earth and time will decompose them *in situ*!
> Therefore repeating again, I again decree:                        100
> let no one dare aid Pelasgians with help and flames,
> or he'll pay for this deed with death and he'll replace the snatched-off
>     corpse;
> I swear by the gods and by great Menoeceus.

There is here a cathexic *negative* enjoyment in Creon's rejection of funeral rites for the dead: Creon's preoccupation is not necessarily his own desire, but rather the desire derived from his active rejection of the ultimate 'goal' of a corpse (to be treated properly). Creon's funeral eulogy for his dead son

---

[11] Lovatt (1999): 134–5.
[12] See Rieks (1967): 221–2, Feeney (1991): 360–1, Ripoll (1998): 300–1, Pollmann (2004): *ad* 12.94–103.
[13] Franchet d'Espèrey (1999): 76 is right of course that there is a sort of violence in funeral denial since it represents a second 'symbolic' murder.

culminates in the paradox of a mass funeral ban,[14] distorting the *humanitas* from the act of his son's exequies.[15] This is mistreatment well beyond the threatening and boasting expressed in the *Iliad* (e.g. 21.122–7, 22.256–9, 22.335–6, etc.) and the *Aeneid* (10.557–60), and, as Helen Lovatt has argued, puts Creon on par with – or even worse than – Lucan's Caesar, who denies funerals to all the Pompeian dead at Pharsalus (*BC* 7.787–98).[16] Both Creon and Caesar increase the scale of funereal denial to encompass an entire army. The unfulfilled desire, moreover, to give 'feeling' to corpses (*Theb.* 12.95–6: *addere sensus* | *corporibus*) metapoetically revives another image from Lucan, this one articulated by the 'Erichthonian' apostrophic narrator at the outset of Pharsalus and aimed at itchy-fingered Crastinus whose spear-cast initiates battle (*BC* 7.470–1): *di tibi non mortem, quae cunctis poena paratur,* | *sed* **sensum** *post fata tuae* **dent***, Crastine morti*, 'may the gods grant you not death, Crastinus, a punishment prepared for all, but feeling to your corpse after death'.[17] Creon effectively channels the extremity of the nexus Lucan/ narrator-Caesar-Erichtho in one brutal *post mortem* boast.

There are additional epic allusions. The scene calls to mind Aeneas' granting of rites to both armies on the occasion of Pallas' funeral at the start of *Aeneid* 11, but shatters the collective nature of that reference point since Creon only allows the corpses of slain Thebans to be cremated, the 'traitor' Polynices and his army are left to rot. In the context of a funeral scene, while the scale is significantly greater here, the scene also recalls Achilles' promise to Patroclus at the latter's funeral that he will not allow Hector's corpse to be buried (*Il.* 23.179–83).[18] Further linking the scenes is the hope in both passages that wild animals might have their way with the corpses of the dead men (cf. *Il.* 23.182–3: Ἕκτορα δ' οὔ τι | δώσω Πριαμίδην πυρὶ δαπτέμεν, ἀλλὰ κύνεσσιν, 'I will not give Hector, son of Priam, to the fire but to dogs to devour'). Like Achilles and Aeneas, Creon sacrifices human victims to the shade of a dead man (*Theb.* 12.68–9). Menoeceus' funeral also echoes the funeral of Hector in *Iliad* 24,[19] but instead of the closure of the theme of corpse mutilation that Hector's funeral brings to Homer's poem,[20] Creon demands still more abuses.

What Statius seems to be stressing here is Creon's excessiveness,[21] specifically built upon the theme of funeral denial. Earlier incarnations

---

[14] Burck (1981): 478; Pollmann (2004): *ad* 12.72–92.    [15] Parkes (2013): 168.    [16] Lovatt (1999).

[17] Roche (2015): 404–5 notes the allusion to Lucan's Crastinus.

[18] Juhnke (1972): 158–9; Pollmann (2004): *ad* 12.95. See McNelis (2007): 155–9 for a more thorough examination of Statius' reworking of the end of the *Iliad* here.

[19] Dietrich (1999): 42–3.    [20] Segal (1971): 71; Redfield (1975): 218–23.

[21] On excessiveness in the *Thebaid* generally, see Hershkowitz (1998a): 249–60.

of Creon in Sophocles' *Antigone* and Euripides' *Phoenissae* were satisfied
that Polynices alone remained unburied.[22] By upping the ante here in
terms of the scale of denial, Statius' version of the tyrant fills the role of
Euripides' Creon in *Suppliants*, but by contrast he's very much 'on stage'.[23]
Death should bring an end to hatred and rage, as indicated by Theseus'
comments to the Theban emissary at *Suppliants* 524–41 (cf. Soph. *Aj.* 1347–
9; Eur. fr. 176 Nauck; Stat. *Theb.* 12.573–4). Statius allows *furor* to continue
beyond the terminus of death, signalled to readers by the proemic warning
at *Thebaid* 1.35: *nec furiis post fata modum*, 'no limit to rage after death'.
Creon's edict is judged against the laws of nature and the gods, as Theseus
makes plain; his efforts, he claims (on the side of 'good'), are an attempt to
restore natural and cosmic laws, overturning the excessiveness of Creon's
*furor* (12.642): *terrarum leges et mundi foedera mecum | defensura cohors*,
'troop, prepared to defend the laws of the lands and pacts of heaven with
me'. This cosmic universality underscores the stakes.[24]

Like Caesar in his mistreatment of the Pompeian soldiers after
Pharsalus,[25] scholarship has universally lambasted Creon in the *Thebaid*.
But just how 'excessive' is his edict within the larger system of social and
literary history that Statius is drawing upon here? Despite the open
castigation of Creon by characters within the poem – and indeed the
narrator – it's worth considering whether his edict is backed up by traditional Greco-Roman custom or code concerning the treatment of enemy
dead, particularly in the context of internecine conflict where citizens
become traitors to the crown.

Xenophon makes clear that Athenians denied burial in Attica to both
traitors and temple robbers (*Hell.* 1.7.22: ἐάν τις ἢ τὴν πόλιν προδιδῷ ἢ τὰ
ἱερὰ κλέπτῃ, κριθέντα ἐν δικαστηρίῳ, ἂν καταγνωσθῇ, μὴ ταφῆναι ἐν τῇ
Ἀττικῇ, τὰ δὲ χρήματα αὐτοῦ δημόσια εἶναι, 'if anyone betrays the state or
steals sacred property, he will be tried before a court, and if he's convicted,
he will not be buried in Attica, and his property will be confiscated'), and

---

[22] Coffee (2009): 269.

[23] Statius' Creon follows the model of Creon in Euripides' *Supp.*, who denies funerals for all of the
Argive leaders. But Creon is not an actual character in Euripides' play. For Statius' broad array of
sources, including the tragedians, see Venini (1970): xii–xxvi. For Statius' re-appropriation of images
and themes from *Supp.*, see Bessone (2011): esp. 20–3, 131–5, 151–5, 218–19. See also Braund (1997):
12–16, Heslin (2008), Criado (2015): 294–7.

[24] See Franchet d'Espèrey (1999): 382. The same parameters are articulated in the tragedies on the
subject: funeral rites as customary Panhellenic practice: Soph. *Ant.* 1113–14; Eur. *Supp.* 311, 526–7,
537–41, 671–2; divinely sanctioned practice: Soph. *Ant.* 76–7, 450–60, 519–21, 921–8, 1070–5; Eur.
*Supp.* 19, 123, 301–2, 348, 373, 558–63; Eur. *Phoen.* 1651, 1663; see Mikalson (1991): 126–7, 275 n.304.

[25] See my discussion of *BC* 7 above and the similar issues at play, pp. 148–51.

there is evidence to suggest that this was a more widespread Hellenic practice in treating the corpses of enemies to the polis.[26] Funeral rites could be denied, but they could also be undone as in the case of Phrynichus who was tried and convicted of treason posthumously, whereupon his bones were exhumed and removed from Attica (Lycurg. *Leoc.* 113). A similar situation occurred with the Alcmaeonidae: members of the clan were ousted from Attic land on account of the sacrilege of Megacles, but so too the family dead were exhumed and sent packing with their living relatives (Thuc. 1.126.12).[27] This is not an exclusively Hellenic practice. Similar *post mortem* punishments were imposed on those declared state enemies (*hostes*) in Rome during both rounds of proscriptions and in the imperial period for *lèse-majesté*.[28]

Concomitant with claims for *ataphia* for state enemies was the fifth-century (at the latest) practice of *anairesis*, whereby a military truce granted the losing side the ability to retrieve their dead for purposes of funeral ritual (e.g. Thuc. 5.74.2).[29] Our sources make it clear that the victors were under no legal or moral obligation to offer funeral rites to the enemy dead on their own, but 'ancestral custom' (τὸ πάτριον) dictated that they allow the losing side access to comrade corpses.[30] This is a significant reformulation of the situation in Homeric poetry, which, though it offers proto-examples of practices resembling *anairesis*,[31] in general presents the *prospect* of corpse mistreatment and active funeral denial – almost never granted by the poet, as we've seen[32] – as a common feature of what Vincent Rosivach calls the 'competitive ethic' of heroic warriors. By the fifth century active corpse mistreatment of slain enemies was no longer acceptable.[33]

Even a cursory sketch of the issues reveals the complications a case like Polynices' presents, and this clearly resonated with fifth-century Athenian audiences given the preponderance of tragedies treating this particular subject. In the context of the Athenian tragic conception of the myth (most relevant for our purposes given Statius' indebtedness to the plays)

---

[26] Rosivach (1983): 194 with n.4. For additional scholarship on the *post mortem* treatment of state enemies in Greece see Mikalson (1991): 124–8, Lindenlauf (2001).
[27] Whitehorne (1983): 138.      [28] Nippel (1995): 64–7.      [29] Rosivach (1983): 194–6.
[30] Whitehorne (1983): 136; Mikalson (1991): 125.
[31] Achaeans and Trojans are allowed to collect their side's corpses in *Iliad* 7 during a momentary truce, and again as part of the pact sealed by Achilles and Priam for the funeral rites for Hector in 24. Odysseus moves the suitors' corpses into the courtyard to be collected for funeral in *Odyssey* 22 (the bodies are buried at 24.417).
[32] See Chapter 1.
[33] Plato's Socrates went so far as to suggest that Achilles' treatment of Hector's corpse in the *Iliad* necessitated censorship and even denial, his behaviour deemed x-rated and (literally) not suitable for children of the ideal polis (*Resp.* 3.391b-c); see Kucewicz (2016): 425–6.

Polynices is, at once, a slain enemy whose family is denied Panhellenic *anairesis* rights of collection and funeral by Creon's edict; but he's also a traitor waging civil war against his own people, equally deserving *ataphia* according to law. More broadly, by fighting under Polynices' banner, the Argives implicate themselves in the civil violence, making their own families' claims for funeral rites irreconcilable with claims for *ataphia* for traitors to the state. Although he's resoundingly censured for his actions (the main charge being one of *hubris*: e.g. Eur. *Supp.* 511–12, 630–3, 728–30, 743–4; *Phoen.* 1663), as a traitor and enemy of the state (Soph. *Ant.* 194–206; Eur. *Phoen.* 1628–70), Creon was within legal grounds for denying Polynices (and his army) funeral rites. Our poets betray their (moral/ ethical) leanings – all corpses eventually receive funerals in *Antigone, Suppliants*, and Statius' epic – but the issue is not simply that the Theban throne has 'infected' Creon with a royal madness made manifest in his 'excessive' treatment of corpses. Creon does display a frightening excessiveness in other respects (rage and *furor*, his almost libidinal interest in funeral denial), but his edict is not in itself an act that has crossed a discernible legal or even moral boundary. The situation ultimately boils down to the problems posed by the practice of civil war, which in every way muddies definitions and customs.

We might expect, as in the final book of the *Iliad*, a reversal of the funeral abnegation at the end of the *Thebaid*, and this is exactly the role Theseus plays when he arrives from Athens to undo Creon's edict.[34] The Argive women are told by Ornytus (an Argive survivor) to seek out Theseus' aid in providing funeral rites for their dead relatives (*Theb.* 12.163–5), and Capaneus' widow Evadne's speech to Theseus at the Altar of Clemency is solely an appeal to the laws of humanity, articulated through the very Roman markers *clementia* and *pietas*, which demand proper treatment of the dead (12.546–86).[35] Theseus doesn't hesitate. After rushing to Thebes and piercing Creon with a spear, he delivers a speech immediately abrogating the funeral ban which has echoed throughout the entire poem (12.779–81):

> 'iamne dare extinctis iustos' ait 'hostibus ignes,
> iam uictos operire placet? uade atra dature
> supplicia, extremique tamen secure sepulcri'.

---

[34] I will not focus specifically on the figure of Theseus and his positive and/or negative aspects in the *Theb.*, though there is a glut of scholarship on this point; see Criado (2015) for details.

[35] See Feeney (1991): 361–2, Braund (1997): 12. Argia refers to ensuring the funerals for the dead Argives as a 'pious labour' (12.197).

'Now is it pleasing to give rightful fire to dead enemies?'
He said: 'and to cover the conquered? Go on, you who are awaiting
black punishments, you who are nevertheless secure in a final tomb.'

Martin Helzle has shown how Theseus' words not only undo Creon's edict
literally, by allowing the dead customary rites, but also lexically, as
Theseus' word choice directly avoids Creon's phrasing from his speech in
book 12.[36] Theseus, it appears, is everything Creon is not, even down to
words and syntax. His final word (*sepulcri*) contrasts sharply with Creon's
denial of tombs to the dead,[37] and his ultimate rewriting of the initial ban is
his decision to ensure Creon's corpse receive proper respect.

Statius is doing a number of interesting things here intertextually. He
has disrupted/corrupted the 'Iliadic' ending he had set up by denying
Creon his opportunity of Achillean resipiscence through the introduction
of Theseus, who will rescind the funeral ban. At the same time, as scholars
have noted, Theseus' killing of Creon offers Statius the opportunity to
comment on the end of the *Aeneid*, as the scene is clearly modelled on
Aeneas' 'sacrificial' killing of Turnus (cf. *Theb* 12.771–3; *Aen.* 12.948–9).[38]
But while the *Aeneid* leaves unanswered the fate of Turnus' corpse – will
Aeneas offer him the funeral he requests? – Statius immediately answers
that question with respect to Creon by giving Theseus the final speech
Virgil denied to Aeneas.

In theory the *Thebaid* ends the way the *Iliad* does, with funeral(s) and
lamentation, but Statius warps the atmosphere of the predecessor poems by
distorting these rituals. The backdrop of the entire book is a field of rotting
and smouldering corpses, supplemented by further bloodshed as Theseus
enters the fray and immediately reactivates Statius' war-song. Evadne
immolates herself on the pyre of her dead husband Capaneus (12.800–2)
and Deipyle kisses her husband Tydeus' mouth, which, at last mention,
was stained with Melanippus' bloody brains (12.802–3, with 8.760–2).[39]

While *Iliad* 24 reverberates with speeches of lamentation in remem-
brance of Hector, which serve as the impetus for public and private
healing, the *Thebaid*'s close has no match for this: Statius cannot even
bring himself to recount the songs sung for the dead, not if he had 100

---

[36] Helzle (1996): 149–50.    [37] Braund (1997): 4; cf. Bessone (2011): 156.
[38] E.g. Hardie (1993): 46–7 and (1997): 153; Braund (1997); Ganiban (2007): 226–8; McNelis (2007):
161–3; Erasmo (2008): 148–9.
[39] Ganiban (2007): 230–1 (but not Argia). Franchet d'Espèrey (1999): 313 argues (among other things)
that Deipyle and Evadne erase implicitly (and Statius 'corrects' structurally) the earlier impiety
displayed by the Lemnian women through their loyalty to their dead husbands. The claim is
enticing but says nothing of the disturbing way in which Statius presents this *fidélité*.

voices and Apollo stirring his breast (12.797–9).[40] Instead we get the wild onrush of Argive women from the woods to the city, described as maenads preparing for war (12.786–96). As scholars have noted, this imagery that at once distorts the traditional direction of Bacchic movement also throws a scene of epic ending and funeral rites back into the sphere of madness and warfare. These women are the new warriors, preparing 'Bacchic wars' (791–2: *quales Bacchea ad bella uocate | Thyiades amentes*, 'just like mindless Thyiads called by Bacchus to war').[41] The women compete amongst each other as they search for the corpses of their loved ones with pious uproar (782: *pio . . . tumultu*). What for the *Iliad* was a return to humanity and the ritual healing associated with interment and lamentation is in the *Thebaid* a further nod to the perversions of ritual and war and further wars to come.

The sense of incompletion here is akin to what Elaine Fantham and others have argued is particularly unsatisfying about the end of the *Aeneid*, where there too the poem lacks a formal lament.[42] But this, at least structurally, is a result of Virgil's powerfully chosen endpoint. Statius provides every opportunity for a formal lament, even teasing at it, but eschews it in favour of a convolution of epic-style endings, none of which is particularly prioritized.[43] This choice of ending was not a hasty one, as we know from Statius' own comments regarding the belaboured composition of the *Thebaid*, particularly the conclusion of his epic (*Silu.* 3.2.142–3: *ast ego, deuictis dederim quae busta Pelasgis | quaeue laboratas claudat mihi pagina Thebas*, 'but I [recount] what burial I have given to defeated Pelasgians and what page closes my exhausted *Thebaid*'; cf. similarly *Silu.* 3.5.35–6; 4.4.88–9; 4.7.25–8). Though they get there by different paths, Statius ends his epic as Virgil had by inspiring a similar pull of conflicting emotional responses in his audience and, as Susanna Braund has shown, the ambiguity has similarly inspired 'readings' of the poem that fall at opposite ends of the critical interpretive spectrum.[44]

---

[40]  Feeney (1991): 363; Braund (1997): 5–6. For the *topos* see Hinds (1998): 91–8, Gowers (2005).

[41]  See Ahl (1986): 2897–8, Hardie (1997): 154, Lovatt (1999): 144–5, Ganiban (2007): 230–1, Panoussi (2007): 128–9, Newlands (2012): 116–17. Braund (1997): 5 by contrast sees these Argive women described as Bacchants (in this context, a very Theban association) as 'dissolv[ing] the boundaries that separated the two sides'. On this scene see below pp. 225–6.

[42]  Fantham (1999): 226. Cf. Braund (1997): 8, Hardie (1997): 143–4, Lovatt (1999): 145–6, Erasmo (2008): 149, Fulkerson (2008): 21.

[43]  Newlands (2009): 392–6; Barchiesi (2015): 161–2 n.32. On the *Thebaid*'s ending(s), see Malamud (1995): 22–7, Braund (1997), Dietrich (1999): 42–3. On Statius' *unending* ending, see Hardie (1997): 154–6, Lovatt (1999): 146–7, Pollmann (2004): 27.

[44]  See Braund (1997): 16–18, Bessone (2011): 128–9.

Although Statius certainly adheres to – and manipulates – the frameworks of the *Iliad* and *Aeneid* in their own treatment of the theme of epic funeral, as we've seen, the specific mythological subject offered Statius a means of filtering epic conventions through the lens of the Theban stage plays.[45] My focus for the rest of this chapter will be Statius' appropriation of epic models, but I do want to look briefly at the tragic material again to stress that in terms of the *Thebaid*'s engagement with the complexity of funeral rites and socio-political upheaval, both structurally and atmospherically, Statius often looks to the Greek and Roman stage.[46]

Crucial for our discussion of corpse mistreatment is Euripides' *Suppliants*. The final book of the epic can, as Helzle has argued,[47] be read as a tragedy independent of the previous eleven books, and in many ways the action subsequent to the mutual slaughter of Polynices and Eteocles in book 11 functions as an addendum. Scholars have observed that the duel between the brothers is a climactic reconfiguration of the duel that closes the *Aeneid*.[48] There Virgil left unresolved the issue of Turnus' corpse treatment, but Creon's funeral denial provides a specific reason for a twelfth book, which Statius structures entirely around the resolution of the issue of corpse treatment (this also positions his epic back in line with the *Iliad*).[49] Euripides' *Suppliants*, like the *Thebaid*, concerns the death rites for the fallen Argives and their leaders. But like the *Thebaid* it also struggles with the paradox of creating peace out of war and violence – readers of the *Aeneid* will be familiar with this issue as well. The play, like Statius' epic, ends by compounding the issue with the imposition of martial imagery in scenes of funeral lament, as Athena delivers a prophecy predictive of further warfare and bloodshed, while the Epigoni hold the ashes of their fathers whom they will later avenge (*Supp.* 1183–1226).[50] In both the play and the epic, the ending aims uncomfortably at another beginning and another war, and we exit with a sense of future evils to come (even if, in the play, the war is divinely sanctioned). The seemingly endless repetition

---

[45] On Statius' 'Romanization' of earlier mythic/tragic models, see Braund (1997): 12–16 and (2006), Fantham (1997), Heslin (2008), Bessone (2011).

[46] Feeney (1991): 344 n.107 articulates Statius' 'family-tree' of influences: 'Statius has two mighty progenitors, Vergil and Ovid, together with two godfathers, Seneca and Lucan, and a grandfather, Homer.' I'm not sure how we weave the Attic playwrights into this, but they deserve an invitation to the family reunion.

[47] Helzle (1996): 146–59.

[48] E.g. Venini (1970): xviii–xix, Braund (1997), Ganiban (2007): 190–5.

[49] Hardie (1997): 155 n.58.

[50] Feeney (1991): 363. Cf. Ahl (1986): 2897–8, Hardie (1993): 14, Henderson (1998): 250, Bessone (2011): 33, Newlands (2012): 116–17.

of war is underlined at the opening of Statius' gates of war in book 7. Before war in the *Thebaid* even formally begins, Jupiter looks ahead to a future war beyond the structure of the epic that almost certainly refers to the renewal of hostilities by the Epigoni (*Theb.* 7.219–21): *non hoc statui sub tempore rebus | occasum Aoniis, ueniet suspectior aetas | ultoresque alii*, 'I have not set up a crash of Aonian history at this time; a more critical time will come along with other avengers'.[51]

All of this has implications for Statius and his audience in Flavian Rome. The Theban myths explore powerful issues related to civil war, monarchy and monarchal power, and dynastic succession, all of which resonated with early imperial Rome. The distance provided by a mythic model gave Statius room to negotiate and examine more critically the contemporary problems his Rome faced in ways he could less easily express in the panegyrical *Siluae*. The situation too is similar to the one Virgil faced when he composed his epic after Octavian/Augustus consolidated sole power in Rome out of civil war. Vespasian and the Flavians brought a renewed peace, styled explicitly on the *Pax Augusta*,[52] after the civil wars in 68–69 CE following Nero's suicide, but (no doubt unintentionally) the association with Augustus and the Julio-Claudians provided a painful reminder of the cyclicality of the potential for tyranny, political dissolution, and renewed internecine struggle.[53]

Vespasian, an outsider (i.e. non-Julio-Claudian), entered the Capitol in mid-70 CE from Egypt bringing an end to Roman civil wars in much the same style that the Athenian Theseus enters civil-war-torn Thebes;[54] but this still leaves (in both instances) issues related to political stability, succession, violent repetition, and tyranny. Political reality too often actualized Lucan's 'tragic' vatic conception of the principate as an endless cycle of repeated self-evisceration,[55] and even Flavian Peace risked further negative repetitions: Suetonius calls Saturninus' revolt at Mogontiacum (Mainz) in 89 CE, which sought to overthrow Domitian, a 'civil war' (Suet. *Dom.* 6.2). The heads of Saturninus and others were shipped back to Rome for display at the forum (*Dom.* 6.2; Dio Cass. 11.3). Domitian himself (at

---

[51] The reference, however, is ambiguous; see Smolenaars (1994): *ad* 7.221, Franchet d'Espèrey (1999): 90.

[52] McNelis (2007): 5–8.

[53] Cf. Tac. *Hist.* 1.50 on the civil wars in 69 CE replaying and amplifying the war between Pompey and Caesar.

[54] Vessey (1973): 315 n.1; Ahl (1986): 2819; Henderson (1998): 220; Braund (2006): 271 n.27. Statius is explicit that he means not to link Roman history with events in Thebes (*Theb.* 1.17–31), but his audience cannot have missed the connections.

[55] Henderson (1998): 220.

least according to our sources) seemed a Nero-reborn, and in death, like Nero, he would bring an end to another Roman familial dynasty with no heirs to fill the void.

Flavian authors recognized Virgil's deep interest in tragic elements (e.g. Mart. 5.5.8: *coturnati ... Maronis opus*, 'the buskin-wearing work of Virgil', cf. 7.63.5, 8.18.5–8),[56] and Statius takes this interest to its logical conclusion by crafting an epic entirely around a tragic subject. Yet he goes further than Virgil by mapping a more dismally tragic and Lucanian worldview of cyclical socio-political madness onto a Virgilian epic framework, and the subject matter offered by the very ancient Thebes allowed him to consider the more disturbing elements in Rome's own recent history. We know too that Theban themes resonated with poets writing from the Social Wars through to the Augustan period, a time similarly plagued by civil wars in Rome.[57] Statius seems to be reactivating an interest in Theban civil war themes as his own period was punctuated with a renewal of internecine violence. However we choose to read the end of the *Thebaid* – and (as with Virgil's epic), the whole point is that we do so ambiguously[58] – this is a poem wholly infected with a darkness only ever feared in the *Aeneid*.

## Dead and 'Buried'

The battlefield offers Statius a number of opportunities to play with the funeral theme. I discuss here scenes of funeral perversion on the battlefield, all of which look ahead to Creon's decree in book 11. The battlefield is not a traditional space for epic funeral rites. Patroclus, Hector, Pallas – even Lucan's Pompey – are all granted extra-military space for obsequies. There are clearly demarcated *loci* in epic for waring and its ritual aftermath. Statius utterly destroys these spatial boundaries. As in Lucan's *BC* these funeral rites are distorted and ritually corrupt. But whereas Lucan emphasizes the active disruption of customary rites, Statius' battlefield 'funerals' ape custom through the oddities of circumstance. Among these perversions are what I call 'corpse-tombs' or 'corpse-burials', where a dead body explicitly 'buries' another; Amphiaraus' live-burial or inadvertent *katabasis*

---

[56] Conte (2007): 166. On Virgil's use of Greek tragedy see most recently Panoussi (2009).
[57] Braund (2006): 266.
[58] This is essentially the thrust of Henderson (1998): 212–54. See also Feeney (1991): 362–3, Hardie (1993): 46–8. Braund (1997) takes a more positive view of the ending but is clear that there exists 'the presence of a darker side to the poem' (p.16) as a product of Lucan's influence on Statius' rendering of civil war epic.

in books 7 and 8; and Idas' accidental self-cremation after he stabs himself with his own firebrand after being felled by Tydeus in book 8.

In lieu of the opportunity of offering a proper burial to Hippomedon – who was speared to death by a crowd of Thebans following his battle with the river-god Ismenus – Capaneus covers his comrade Hippomedon's corpse with Hippomedon's own armour, which had been taken by Hypseus as war-spoils (9.540–6). He also heaps on Hippomedon Hypseus' own armour, which Capaneus subsequently despoiled from him (9.560–5):

> tunc ensem galeamque rapit clipeumque reuellit
> Hypseos; exanimumque tenens super Hippomedonta,
> 'accipe' ait 'simul hostiles, dux magne, tuasque
> exuuias, ueniet cineri decus et suus ordo
> manibus; interea **iustos** dum reddimus **ignes**,
> hoc ultor Capaneus operit tua membra **sepulcro**'.

> Then he snatches the sword and helmet, he pulls out Hypseus'
> shield; and holding them above the dead Hippomedon,
> he says: 'Great leader, take yours and your enemy's
> spoils; glory will come to your ashes and its own rank
> to your shade; meantime, until we provide just funeral fire,
> the avenger Capaneus covers your limbs with this tomb.'

That Capaneus refers to this armoured covering explicitly as a tomb (*sepulcro*) is a pointed comment on the difficulty in the *Thebaid* of finding a proper burial. Though he cannot know it, Capaneus' words anticipate Creon's edict and are echoed by Theseus when he finally lifts the funeral ban: the Athenian king will provide the fallen soldiers with the flames that are their due (12.779: *iustos . . . ignes*, with 9.564, same *sedes*) and grant everyone, including Creon, a sepulchre (12.781: *sepulcri*: the same word closes both speeches).

Statius builds on this picture of a corpse literally 'buried' by armour later when he creates a human tomb in the form of the armed soldier Dymas. After failing in his attempt to rescue the corpse of Parthenopaeus, his squire Dymas commits suicide over his body and falls on top of him, groaning these dying words (10.441): *hac tamen interea nece tu potiare sepulchro*, 'nevertheless, meantime, may you receive a tomb with this death'.[59] Karla Pollmann notes that falling dead on a corpse is a relatively common epic trope (e.g. Nisus and Euryalus in *Aeneid* 9), but only Statius 'gives this

---

[59] The text is from Delz's (1974) emendation. The textual corruption has proved a point of scholarly debate; see Delz (1974), followed by Pollmann (2001): 22–3 with n.38.

motif the significance of a surrogate burial'.[60] This same motif does in fact appear in the *Punica*, most explicitly at 5.658–66, and it is repeated elsewhere in Silius' poem (*Pun.* 10.250–9, 504–6), but the point about its rarity is important. The *Thebaid*'s particular obsession with interment denial has such a profound impact that any opportunity for burial is gleefully exploited (*Theb.* 10.444: *leto ... fruuntur*, 'they joy in death'), even if that form of burial would be in any other context unthinkable or perverse. The absurdity of this scene is set against the incredible loyalty Dymas has for the dead Parthenopaeus. He risks his own life in an attempt to rescue the corpse of his leader and when he fails, sacrifices his body as a tomb (again, as at 9.565 and 12.781, a form of *sepulcrum* emphatically closes his brief speech). But even this minor victory over the theme of funeral denial is double edged. By creating a corpse-tomb for his leader, he has also more literally created just another unburied corpse, another 'symbol of Argive defeat'.[61] As in the previous example, this scene should be read in light of Creon's eventual treatment of all the Argive corpses.[62] In the ghastly universe of the *Thebaid*, any semblance of funeral is better than no funeral at all.

Ruth Parkes notes that the six Argive leaders who die in battle all suffer some form of 'warped burial'.[63] In addition to Hippomedon and Parthenopaeus, the god-fighting Capaneus is 'cremated' by Jupiter's lightning bolt (10.927–39), Polynices is killed and then covered by the body of his dead brother Eteocles (11.573) in a way that toys with the example of Dymas and Parthenopaeus, and Tydeus, who seems to have dropped out of Parkes' list, similarly is covered over by the corpse of his squire Hopleus (10.402–4):

> labitur egregii nondum ducis immemor Hopleus,
> exspiratque tenens (felix, si corpus ademptum
> nesciat), et saeuas talis descendit ad umbras.

> Hopleus falls down, not yet forgetful of the extraordinary leader,
> and dies embracing him (happy, if he doesn't know the corpse
> was taken), and he descends to the fierce shades below.

This scene occurs moments before Dymas offers his own body as a tomb for Parthenopaeus, and should be read in concert.[64] Tydeus had earlier

---

[60] Pollmann (2001): 23.   [61] Lovatt (2005): 240.
[62] See Pollmann (2001): 18–27 for more on this passage.
[63] Parkes (2011): 87–8 n.29, and (2013): 168. See also van der Keur (2013): 334–7.
[64] Taisne (1994): 71–2. The efforts of Hopleus and Dymas are for Ganiban (2007): 131: 'the purest act[s] of *pietas* in the poem'.

eschewed interest in his own funeral rites (8.736–8),[65] and so the lack of an explicit perversion of traditional funeral custom squares with his desire to be left unburied in the poem.

Amphiaraus' death is worth considering in more detail. Amphiaraus is sucked down into the underworld at the height of his *aristeia* through a chasm in the earth at the climax of the first major battle of the epic (7.794–823). Statius doesn't offer any real reason for this form of death for Amphiaraus – or rather, he offers six possible explanations[66] – but Apollo justifies it prophetically in terms of Creon's impending funeral denial edict. He tells Amphiaraus that at least this death is free from the horrors of funeral abnegation that await the Argives (7.775–7). His death, Apollo says, is the will of the Parcae (774–5), but when Amphiaraus appears in the underworld everyone (including the Parcae) is shocked – and frightened – to see him there, and they only cut his life thread at 8.11–13.[67] His descent becomes an unintentional *katabasis*, and this breach of boundaries drives Dis to declare open war on the Olympian gods, whom he blames for Amphiaraus' unannounced arrival (8.34–79).

Despite Apollo's efforts, Amphiaraus' death is hollow and perverse. He has left nothing behind for his people to mourn (8.111, 114–15), no ashes to return to his father (8.6, 113), no pyre or tomb (8.5–6, 114). He even strangely laments that he has left nothing for the Thebans to *capture* (112); anything, including corpse abuse, would be better than this current situation, which amounts to being buried alive. He sums up the spectacular nature of his death succinctly in his disconsolate address to Dis, framed around the issue of his (now unattainable) funeral rites (115): *toto pariter tibi funere ueni*, 'I come to you with all there is to bury'. Although Apollo's main objective was to spare Amphiaraus the fate of an unhonoured corpse, his actual fate is not all that dissimilar (8.176): *sic gratus Apollo?*, 'is *this* Apollo's favour?' As he fades into death, his body, warm with sweat and bloody dust from the battlefield, begins to decompose into the form of a shade (8.86–9):

> iam uanescentibus armis,
> iam pedes: exstincto tamen indecerptus in ore
> augurii perdurat honos, obscuraque fronti
> uitta manet, ramumque tenet morientis oliuae

---

[65] See pp. 222–3.   [66] Ahl (1986): 2858–63; Smolenaars (1994): *ad* 7.809–16; Seo (2013): 171–8.
[67] Lovatt (2005): 239 n.77; Ganiban (2007): 118; Seo (2013): 164.

with his weapons already vanishing,
already on foot, still in his lifeless face, unbroken,
the augur's honour endures, and obscuring his brow,
the headband remains, and he holds a branch of dying olive.

J. Mira Seo suggests Amphiaraus' death is a divine reward of physical inviolability along the lines of Maeon's freedom from scavenging beasts.[68] But Amphiaraus' own emphasis on the lack of proper death rites makes the 'gift' decidedly hollow. Statius anticipates this for us when he calls Amphiaraus' glory 'worthless' at 7.692: *decus ... inane*. All divine efforts to provide heroes with a glorious death in the *Thebaid* are unsatisfactory.[69] Apollo's confession after the death of Amphiaraus speaks volumes (9.656–7): *nec tenui currus terraeque abrupta coegi, | saeuus ego inmeritusque coli*, 'I did not hold back his chariot nor did I force together the chasm of the earth; I'm cruel and unworthy of worship!' While his comrades die fighting for glory on the battlefield, Amphiaraus is buried alive.

Statius subtly links Amphiaraus' ending to Pompey's death in Lucan's poem. During Amphiaraus and Melampus' prophecy in book 3 (they are looking for signs concerning the coming war with Thebes), an omen of eagles and swans matches identifiably with the specific characteristic of each of the Argive leaders' deaths. Among these, Amphiaraus recognizes his own demise and addresses Melampus, who weeps as he too understands the sign of Amphiaraus' unavoidable doom (3.546–7): *quid furtim inlacrimas? illum, uenerande Melampu, | qui cadit, agnosco*, 'why do you secretly weep? Honourable Melampus, I recognize that one who is falling.' The final phrase matches the matrona's prophetic anticipation of Pompey's death in Lucan's poem (*BC* 1.685–6): *hunc ego fluminea deformis truncus harena | qui iacet agnosco*, 'I recognize that man, a misshapen trunk who lies on the river sands'.[70] The echo no doubt adds pathos, but it also plays upon imagery of corpse abuse and funeral denial integral to the scene of Pompey's death. Pompey was mutilated and half-burnt on a funeral pyre; Amphiaraus will be denied death rites as his mortal frame withers away in Hell.

This blurring of lines between living and dying expressed in Amphiaraus' bizarre death scene is mirrored by the figure of Oedipus – the first character to appear in the *Thebaid* – who exists in this state of half-life, half-death,[71]

[68] Seo (2013): 164–7. See below pp. 234–40 on Maeon's death.
[69] Ripoll (1998): 226; Lovatt (2005): 238–9.   [70] Fantham (2011): 613; Seo (2013): 148–9.
[71] See Vessey (1973): 72–4, 279–80, Feeney (1991): 345–6, Hardie (1993): 62–3, 77–8. Ganiban (2007): 24: 'Oedipus is a character of impossible contradictions.'

hovering between both worlds, symbolized by his blindness and his hollow-
ing out a place for Hell in the upper world (1.46–52):

> impia iam merita scrutatus lumina dextra
> merserat aeterna damnatum nocte pudorem
> Oedipodes longaque animam sub morte trahebat.
> illum indulgentem tenebris imaeque recessu
> sedis inaspectos caelo radiisque penates                    50
> seruantem tamen adsiduis circumuolat alis
> saeua dies animi, scelerumque in pectore Dirae.

> Having ransacked his wicked eyes already with guilty hands,
> Oedipus had buried his shame, condemned to eternal night,
> and was dragging along his life in an extended death.
> That man, indulging in darkness, and in the lower chamber of
>     his inner
> abode, guarding his hearth unseen by the sky and               50
> sun-rays, still, the fierce day circles around him
> with tireless wings, and the Dirae of crimes are in his heart.

This liminal state of living like a corpse between both worlds recalls and
adjusts Amphiaraus' liminal state of dying as a living man in Hell (also
doubled by his death-scene straddling the *limen* of books 7 and 8).
Moreover, Oedipus' rejection of the upper world and embracing of the
lower and his transitionality between both signals his intimate ties to Lucan's
interstitial Erichtho. Like her, he will direct an appeal to the infernal gods
(not the *superi*) for intervention (1.56–87), precipitating intestine war.
Oedipus is leading a disturbing death-in-life: he's 'dragging along' (*trahebat*)
his life in a drawn-out death (48). Tiresias further articulates Oedipus'
existence as an 'extended funeral' (4.614–17).[72] Lucan's poetic landscape
populated by the 'living-dead' seems to resonate here. Scholars note the
similar liminal status of Seneca's Oedipus (*Oed.* 949–51),[73] and Seneca
expands upon this living-death state of Oedipus in his *Phoenissae*, which
both poetically and structurally works as background material for Statius'
action. From the play's opening speech Oedipus laments that he has long-
since been a cadaver (*Phoen.* 35–6: *olim iam tuum | est hoc cadauer*), that his
death has only been granted part-way, and he 'drags along' (*traho*) life that is
merely the idle delays (*languidas moras*) of death (44–8; cf. 141–3, 169–71, 181).
As in Statius' poem, for Seneca's Oedipus, life is a protracted funeral, as he
complains to Antigone (*Phoen.* 94–6): *funus extendis meum | longasque uiui*

---

[72] Venini (1970): *ad* 11.582; Parkes (2012): *ad locc.*
[73] Venini (1970): *ad* 11.582; Hardie (1993): 63 n.7.

*ducis exequias patris.* | *aliquando terra corpus inuisum tege,* 'you are extending my funeral and prolonging the death rites of your living father. At last, bury this hateful body in the earth.' He's a living corpse that requires burial (97–8: *pietatem uocas* | *patrem insepultum trahere*), though how much life actually exists in his body, he doesn't know (113–14: *in cinerem dabo* | *hoc quidquid in me uiuit,* 'I will turn to ash whatever still lives in me').[74]

The final appearance of the disgraced king in Statius' poem completes this image of his zombie-like status. After the mutual slaughter of Polynices and Eteocles, Oedipus emerges from his cavernous hovel to inspect the corpses of his sons (*Theb.* 11.580–4):

> at genitor sceleris comperto fine profundis
> erupit tenebris saeuoque in limine profert
> mortem imperfectam: ueteri stat sordida tabo
> utraque canities, et durus **sanguine crinis**
> obnubit furiale caput

> But when the outcome was revealed, the father of the crime from the deep
> shadows burst out, and at the fierce threshold revealed
> his unfinished death: foul with aged decay are
> both his hair and beard, stiff with blood his locks
> shroud a Fury-like head.

His death is 'imperfect', unfinished (*mortem imperfectam*). His emergence from the shadows is like a return from Hell, and his appearance recalls the shade of Hector that comes to visit Aeneas at *Aeneid* 2.277: *squalentem barbam et concretos* **sanguine crinis**, 'his beard stiffened and hair caked with blood'.[75] His appearance here is tantamount to a return to the world of the living from his state of perpetual death in life. Directionally, he moves in opposition to Amphiaraus, whose death is akin to a perverse unintended *katabasis*. The zombie-like Oedipus begins the *Thebaid* by praying to the infernal gods for vengeance and cursing his sons (*Theb.* 1.46–87), and later Statius hauls Laius' ghost from Hell to level a curse against his grandchildren Polynices and Eteocles that leads to full-blown civil war (2.102–24). The dead and the death-like do not disappear from the *Thebaid*, they haunt it; they generate it.

My favourite example of Statius' perverse play on the funeral theme comes during Tydeus' second *aristeia*. The warrior Idas breaks through the Argive ranks wielding a smoking torch and comes face to face with Tydeus. Bad idea (8.466–73):

---

[74] Venini (1970): *ad* 11.582; Parkes (2012): *ad* 4.614.   [75] Venini (1970): *ad* 11.583.

ibat fumiferam quatiens Onchestius Idas
lampada per medios turbabatque agmina Graium,
igne uiam rumpens; magno quem comminus ictu
Tydeos hasta feri dispulsa casside fixit.
ille ingens in terga iacet, stat fronte superstes                    470
lancea, conlapsae ueniunt in tempora flammae.
prosequitur Tydeus: 'saeuos ne dixeris Argos,
igne tuo, Thebane, (rogum concedimus) arde!'

Onchestian Idas, wielding a smoky torch, was heading
through the centre and was disturbing the Greek's battleline,
breaking open a pathway with fire; with a heavy blow at close range
the spear of wild Tydeus pierced him, and scattered his helmet.
That huge man is sprawled out on his back, the spear stands straight up  470
from his forehead, the cascading flames engulf his head.
Tydeus assails him: 'Don't you call Argos savage;
burn, Theban, with your own fire: we allow you a tomb!'

As far as *post mortem* boasts go, this one is hard to beat.[76] Tydeus jumps at
the ridiculousness of the circumstance – the torch that gave Idas an opening and caused such turmoil among the Argive troops sets the man himself
on fire as he dies – while also confronting the main issue of funeral denial
that will come to a head in book 11.[77] Like Capaneus, whose body is
'cremated' by the lightning of Jupiter, Idas receives a quasi-funeral fire
inadvertently, through a warping of traditional rites, with his killer Tydeus
acting the part of a sarcastic eulogizer offering the final words over the
corpse. Though he could not possibly know it yet, as with other characters
in the poem, Tydeus' words anticipate Creon's edict, and his own corpse
will have to await Theseus' intervention to receive fire and a tomb.

'Huge Idas' (*ingens*), felled by a wound to his head, lies stretched out on
his back like the headless Priam at *Aeneid* 2.557: **iacet ingens** *litore truncus*,
and like Pompeius **Magnus** in *BC* 8, modelled (as we have seen repeatedly)
on Virgil's scene of Priam's demise.[78] Tydeus recognizes his impending
doom through the pregnant allusion to, again, the matrona's prophecy of
Pompey's death (*BC* 1.685–6; *Theb.* 8.753, cf. 9.2, 9.17). Like Priam and
Pompey, Tydeus will lie unburied, unlike the mocked Idas who receives
something like a cremation here, albeit (typically in the poem) a distorted
one. But while Tydeus understands the importance of funereal rites – Argos

---

[76] Tydeus is an aesthetician of this sort of brutal *euchos*: e.g. the 'emasculating' of the strategically
named Atys (there is surely play with Catull. 63) at 8.588–91. On epic taunting see Dominik (1994a):
180–8. On the scene as emblematic of Tydeus' 'cruelty' see Perutelli (2000): 192–3.

[77] Feeney (1991): 341.    [78] See esp. pp. 68–79.

would be, as Thebes *will* be, *saeuus* not to allow them (*Theb.* 8.472) – this scene anticipates his own dying request at the end of this book. Tydeus is the only character in the poem who actively rejects the importance of funeral rites (8.736–8): *non ossa precor referantur ut Argos | Aetolumue larem; nec enim mihi cura supremi | funeris,* 'I don't beg my bones be carried back to Argos or to Aetolian Lares; for last funeral rites are not important to me'. His cannibalism of Melanippus' severed head will forfeit him immortality when his divine protector Pallas flees in horror at his crime, while with his words he denies his hated body (738–9) even the most basic of rites in death. Tydeus is *saeuus* extraordinaire: his savagery denies his own funeral and anticipates his animalistic cannibalism of Melanippus' brains. As well as Lucan's Scaeva, his Caesar at *BC* 5.668–71 is certainly a model for Tydeus here since Caesar also denies his own funeral rites during Lucan's sea-storm in book 5.[79] With Tydeus, though, *pathos* rips through the madness and theomachic savagery of Lucan's scene because, while Caesar may have anticipated his own apotheosis in the *Bellum ciuile*,[80] Tydeus doesn't care about, nor does he receive his.[81] Only a character with very little respect for funeral rites would freely joke about the circumstances of Idas' 'cremation' here.[82]

## Mothers of Tears

Statius does depict some rituals that outwardly seem to provide relief to the theme of funeral denial and perversion. But even in cases where cremations or burials occur (Hypsipyle's funeral rites for her father Thoas, the lengthy funeral for the slain child Opheltes, and Argia and Antigone's cremation of Polynices) there is an overwhelming emphasis on the same kind of perversion that characterized the mock-funerals in the militaristic sphere. These rites flirt with the semblance of propriety, but are ultimately undercut by the promise of more misery and abuses to come.

As the Argive army regroups in Nemea, they come across the Lemnian refugee Hypsipyle, who recounts her miserable tale of the Argonauts' visit to Lemnos and the madness Venus imposed on the Lemnian women who murdered all of the island's men. Only Hypsipyle managed to avoid

[79] See pp. 143–8. Silius' Hannibal at *Pun.* 17.559–61 should be read in concert (see pp. 259–62). Cf. Diomedes' somber reflection at Ov. *Met.* 14.479–82.

[80] Dinter (2012): 86.

[81] The denial of 'humane' funeral rites is an indicator of Tydeus' fall from humanity, but may also points to his Stoic denial of the importance of death rites; see Ripoll (1998): 298 n.205.

[82] Thanks to Kyle Gervais for helping me think through this scene.

Venus' curse. She describes the events of the night, the slaughter of the island's men, and the escape she alone provided for her father, Thoas, amidst the murder and conflagration that gripped the other Lemnian women. Hypsipyle's mock-funeral for her father (who is not actually dead) constitutes, paradoxically, one of the most successful funerals in the poem (5.313–19):

> ipsa quoque arcanis tecti in penetralibus alto
> molior igne pyram, sceptrum super armaque patris
> inicio et notas regum uelamina uestes,                                    315
> ac prope maesta rogum confusis crinibus asto
> ense cruentato, fraudemque et inania busta
> plango metu, si forte premant, cassumque parenti
> omen et hac dubios leti precor ire timores.
> And I myself, in the secret inner recesses of our house,

> construct a pyre high with fire, I toss the sceptre and arms of
>    my father
> onto it, his robes too, famous clothing of kings.                         315
> But in my grief, I stand beside the pile with dishevelled hair
> and bloody sword, and I lament this fraud, the empty tomb,
> in fear, in case by chance they check on me. For father I pray
>    it's a hollow
> omen and with this that my wavering fears of death go away.

Her deception is necessary because the other Lemnian women had carried out the actual murder of their husbands, fathers, and sons, in one blow robbing the island of her once famous 'arms and men'.[83] Valerius' account of the Lemnian massacre is a horror-show of intestine violence,[84] but he says nothing about a false-pyre for Thoas; the funereal perversion fully suits Statius' poetic agenda.

Although the women cremate the men, these are manifestly 'impious crimes' (5.300–1: *impia ... scelera*). Hypsipyle must feign the funeral rites for her father so as not to appear at variance with the other women. It's a twisted play on the codes of morality in the poem that her crime is protecting her father, her *pietas* the (assumed) act of patricide.[85] For her deception and the appearance of wickedness, she's gifted the throne of Lemnos, which her father had vacated by fleeing, or, in the minds of the other women, which Hypsipyle had violently wrested from him (320–5):

---

[83] 5.305: *armisque uirisque*; Henderson (1998): 246. On the post-Virgilian appropriation of Virgil's *incipit* see Bloch (1970), Cowan (2007b): 26 n.91, Landrey (2014).
[84] See pp. 187–90.    [85] Ahl (1986): 2886–8; Pagán (2000): 437–8; Ganiban (2007): 88.

his mihi pro meritis, ut falsi criminis astu                              320
parta fides, regna et solio considere patris
(supplicium!) datur. anne illis obsessa negarem?
accessi, saepe ante deos testata fidemque
inmeritasque manus; subeo (pro dira potestas!)
exangue imperium et maestam sine culmine Lemnon.        325

For these merit-worthy deeds – as belief in the trick of the false crime   320
grew – my father's kingdom, a seat on the throne, are given to me
(punishment!). Though overwhelmed could I possibly refuse these?
I accepted, often having called the gods to witness my good faith
and guiltless hands before (O awful power!). I shoulder
a bloodless empire and a Lemnos grim without her crown.        325

Victoria Pagán aptly notes how Hypsipyle's 'mock burial of her father is so empty and so contrary to the purpose of the ritual that it becomes a pointed commentary on the final, essential theme of the Theban legend, the refusal of burial by Creon'.[86] Kingship and skewed funeral rites are inseparable in the *Thebaid*.

But the care and mournful touch she puts into a feigned funeral resonate here. Mourning women seeking funerals for men elsewhere in the *Thebaid*, both Thebans and Argives, are hysterical to the point of Bacchic madness.[87] In the aftermath of Tydeus' slaughter of the 50 Theban ambushers, Theban wives and parents fill Cithaeron with howling and compete with one another in their woe (3.116–17). The whole crowd rages at the sight of blood (125: *turba furit*) as they attempt to reattach limbs and severed heads in a perversely inverted Bacchic *sparagmos*. The point is driven home as a 'Pentheus' lies among the fallen (170), and the old man Aletes invokes the story of Agave (188–190) among the deathly reminders of recent Theban (mytho-)history. At the poem's close the Argive women, finally able to cremate their dead husbands, brothers, and fathers, are explicitly compared to Thyiads rushing into Bacchic wars. The recovering and cremation of their husbands is akin to an offensive Maenadic rampage (12.790–6). Bacchants are often associated with corpse dismemberment (e.g. Ov. *Met.* 11.50–1, of Orpheus' *post mortem* abuse[88]), so even here as the women search in earnest for their husbands' bodies to provide funeral rites, we might also imagine they have more sinister plans. The scenes

[86] Pagán (2000): 437.
[87] For more on the Bacchic nature of the *Thebaid*'s women see Panoussi (2007), Augoustakis (2010): 49–51, 86–91, McAuley (2016): 316–18.
[88] Cf. *Met.* 6.587–666 where Procne and Philomela, as 'Bacchants', murder, dismember, and boil Procne's son Itys.

pervert the traditional forms of female lament and funeral rites through the
imposition of maenadic imagery of a particularly militaristic slant.[89]

Maenadic behaviour characterized all the Lemnian women as they
raged, killing their fathers, husbands, and sons before ultimately cremating
them (*Theb.* 5.90–4, 148–51).[90] That is, all the Lemnians act like maenads
except Hypsipyle, even though, ironically, she is the granddaughter of
Bacchus. The burning of her father's *arma* and clothes as a surrogate for his
actual body is reminiscent of Andromache's mournful substitute funeral
for Hector at *Iliad* 22.510–15:

> ἀτάρ τοι εἵματ' ἐνὶ μεγάροισι κέονται
> λεπτά τε καὶ χαρίεντα τετυγμένα χερσὶ γυναικῶν.
> ἀλλ' ἤτοι τάδε πάντα καταφλέξω πυρὶ κηλέῳ
> οὐδὲν σοί γ' ὄφελος, ἐπεὶ οὐκ ἐγκείσεαι αὐτοῖς,
> ἀλλὰ πρὸς Τρώων καὶ Τρωϊάδων κλέος εἶναι'.
> ὣς ἔφατο κλαίουσ', ἐπὶ δὲ στενάχοντο γυναῖκες.

> 'though there is clothing stored in the palace,
> delicate and beautiful, well-made by women's hands.
> But I will burn all of this in a crackling fire,
> since they are useless to you, now that you'll never be wrapped in them;
> but as your glory, from the men and women of Troy'.
> So she spoke weeping, and the women wailed with her.

The sentiment is similar here but the context is, of course, completely
different. Andromache's substitute funeral is aimed at ritual completion
for the corpse of her husband still in Achilles' possession. Hypsipyle's
funeral rites are an attempt to convince her raging coterie that she is as
bloodthirsty as they are, while her father flees the island. Mass Bacchic
madness distorts what would otherwise be the *Iliad*'s scene of mass ritual
mourning and lamentation associated with Andromache's substitute funeral. And we likely have a further nod to Dido's divinely induced 'madness'
as she immolates herself on the substitute pyre of Aeneas' possessions as he
flees Carthage at the end of *Aeneid* 4.[91] There is a hint of Cornelia's
substitute funeral for Pompey at Lucan *BC* 9.174–9 (already modelled in
part on the substitute funeral from *Iliad* 22[92]), which is also bizarrely one of
the more successful funerals in a poem which everywhere fights against

---

[89] Lovatt (1999): 144–5; cf. Franchet d'Espèrey (1999): 310–11.   [90] See e.g. Chinn (2013): 329–31.
[91] See Ganiban (2007): 86–8 for Hypsipyle's connection to Virgil's Dido and her pyre of Aeneas'
possessions. Tasine (1994): 239–44 examines Statius' source material for the larger scene; no mention
of Andromache's substitute funeral.
[92] See pp. 135–6.

proper observance. Similarly in Statius' epic, only a funeral that is not even *real* comes close to adhering to the codes of morality.

But even here this funeral is not situated within the timeline of the main narrative, since Hypsipyle narrates past events over nearly 450 lines (*Theb.* 5.49–498). While the action of Hypsipyle's narrative is certainly contaminated by Venus' curse against the Lemnian women, it's uninfected by the stain of Thebes. Hypsipyle's substitute funeral comes from a place of moral rectitude – better to *not* kill your father and lie to your divinely possessed comrades. But ultimately this is cited as the act that inspires divine retribution when Jupiter's enormous snake kills the infant Opheltes (5.534–9).[93] While Hypsipyle tells her story to the Argives, the child she's supposed to be babysitting is crushed by the accidental flick of the snake's tale (538–9).

When Hypsipyle and the Argives realize Opheltes has been killed, they prepare funeral rites and dedicate games in his honour.[94] Yet even these rites are corrupted by their insistent anticipation of the horrible events of the second war-filled half of Statius' poem. The child's mother, Eurydice, attempts repeatedly to throw herself on the remains of Opheltes (6.35–6), and later demands the Argives place Hypsipyle alive on the pyre to burn with her son as a form of sacrifice (169–73). Even this is not enough. She wants to burn together with Hypsipyle and Opheltes on the pyre, with the lasting satisfaction of revenge for Hypsipyle's negligence sated (169–76):[95]

> 'illam (nil poscunt amplius umbrae),
> illam, oro, cineri simul excisaeque parenti                    170
> reddite, quaeso, duces, per ego haec primordia belli
> cui peperi; sic aequa gemant mihi funera matres
> Ogygiae'. sternit crines iteratque precando:
> 'reddite, nec uero crudelem auidamque uocate
> sanguinis: occumbam pariter, dum uulnere iusto               175
> exsaturata oculos unum impellamur in ignem'.

> 'That woman (the shades demands nothing more),
> give that woman, I beg, to his ashes, along with his slaughtered mother,   170
> commanders, I beseech you, by the origin of the war
> which I spawned. May Ogygian mothers thus mourn deaths
> equal to me!' She rips out her hair and repeats, by begging:
> 'Give her, and don't call me cruel and eager

---

[93] See Ganiban (2007): 93–4 and (2013).
[94] On Opheltes' death and funeral see Burck (1981): 464–73, Erasmo (2008): 127–40, Ganiban (2013).
[95] Burck (1981): 472; Henderson (1998): 245.

for blood: let me die too, as long as after having sated my eyes        175
on the deserving wound we can be tossed on one fire.'

While Statius allows none of this distorted funereal madness to happen, he
is, however, preparing us for the end of the poem when Evadne will, in fact,
immolate herself on her husband Capaneus' pyre (12.800–2).[96] The
expressed vitriol over the cremation of a loved one has resonances with
the 'duel' over the funeral rites of Polynices between Argia and Antigone.[97]
Argia and Antigone also threaten to throw themselves on the (accidental)
joint pyre for Eteocles and Polynices (12.446).[98]

Eurydice even takes direct blame for the coming war between the Thebans
and Argives: it's her 'spawn' (6.171–2, cf. 6.143–8). This image alludes to the
prophecy that Opheltes will be the first death in anticipation of the Theban war
(5.647). The child's ominous alternate name, 'Archemorus' (5.609, 739), speaks
to the ruin awaiting the Thebans as they begin the death-march to Thebes – his
death is 'the beginning of doom'. Eurydice is, then, the first grieving mother in
a series of grieving mothers the coming war will propagate, and the lighting of
Opheltes' pyre initiates an omen of impending disaster, as the seer Amphiaraus
recognizes in the approaching war that will amplify the misery he and the
Argives are witnessing at the funeral for a small child (6.221–6). This first victim
that presages the war is only a microcosm of the many deaths that will follow.[99]

The funeral games for Opheltes/Archemorus that directly follow the
cremation risk everywhere spilling over into *actual* warfare.[100] Statius
threatens activating too early the *horrida bella* that initiated Virgil's change
of subject matter in book 7 of the *Aeneid*. As competitiveness grows to
violence during the chariot race, Statius comments (6.457–8): *bella geri
ferro leuius, bella horrida, credas | is furor in laudes*, 'you would think waging
war, terrible war, with iron, a more trifling affair, this is their frenzy for
glory'. The phrasing echoes the Sibyl's comments in the *Aeneid* – also in
book 6 – about the looming war in Italy in a prophetic speech removed
from a military context (*Aen.* 6.86–7: *bella, horrida bella, | et Thybrim
multo spumantem sanguine cerno*, 'I see wars, terrible wars, and the Tiber
spewing floods of bloodshed'). The phrasing is repeated at the start of
*Aeneid* 7, signalling a change of tone at the onset of war and Virgil's war-
song (7.41–2: *dicam horrida bella, | dicam acies actosque animis in funera
reges*, 'I will speak about terrible warfare, I will speak of battles and kings

---

[96] Augoustakis (2010): 60, 88.     [97] Augoustakis (2010): 59.
[98] See just below, pp. 229–31 on the cremation scene.
[99] Vessey (1973): 195; Ganiban (2013): 259–65.
[100] E.g. 6.618–20, 625–6, 513–17, 531–9, 734–7; see Lovatt (2005): 270.

driven to their graves by their fighting spirit'). By imitating Virgil's language in *Aeneid* 6 and 7 in a pseudo-military context before the actual fighting has begun, Statius uncomfortably straddles the line between the games and the oncoming war,[101] between his 'delay' tactics of the first 6 books,[102] and the Ennian/Virgilian-style beginning of the war in book 7.[103]

The entire funeral and games honouring Opheltes/Archemorus are in the end completely undercut by Jupiter who at the beginning of book 7 passes over these rites due to the dead as – metapoetically – nothing more than a waste of time, a further (narrative) delay. Jupiter even quips that one would think the war had already been fought given how engaged the Argives are in funerary concerns (*Theb.* 7.18–19): *credas bello rediisse, tot instant | plausibus, offensique sedent ad iusta sepulcri*, 'you would think they had returned from war, they contend with such applause as they sit for the funeral rites of the calamitous tomb!' Jupiter is being sarcastic, but his point is clear enough: the sequence of events is all skewed.[104] Funerals like this should be occurring *after* war not as a prelude to it,[105] and this sequencing issue is further compounded by funeral games that all too easily spill over into the semblance of warfare.

The most dramatic funeral scene in the poem is Argia and Antigone's midnight meeting over the corpse of Polynices.[106] Any dishonour associated with a stealthy night-time funeral (e.g. Eur. *Tro.* 446) is outstripped by necessity. The efforts to cremate the *rotting* Polynices (*Theb.* 12.209: *te tabente per agros*, 'you, decomposing in enemy fields'), against Creon's edict, are definitively pious (12.186, 384, 459), and so their motivations come from a positive place in reaction to the ban. Yet their attempts at *pietas* literally reignite the fratricidal madness that set the war in motion, when they accidentally mingle the body of Polynices with his enemy-brother Eteocles on the same pyre. As soon as Polynices comes into contact with Eteocles' smouldering ashes, their duel begins anew, they are 'brothers again' (12.429–36):

> ecce iterum fratres: primos ut contigit artus
> ignis edax, tremuere rogi et nouus aduena busto          430
> pellitur; exundant diuiso uertice flammae
> alternosque apices abrupta luce coruscant.
> pallidus Eumenidum ueluti commiserit ignes

---

[101] See Lovatt (2005): 28–9 with n.16, 269–71.
[102] On delay (*mora*) in the first half of the *Thebaid* see Vessey (1986): 2988–93; McNelis (2004): 269–75.
[103] McNelis (2004): 276.    [104] Pollmann (2004): 33–4.
[105] See Juhnke (1972): 105–8 on Statius' borrowings here from the the *Iliad* and *Aeneid*. See also Erasmo (2008): 127–40.
[106] The bibliography is vast. See helpfully Augoustakis (2010): 80–5 with 83 n.123.

Orcus, uterque minax globus et conatur uterque
longius; ipsae etiam commoto pondere paulum                    435
secessere trabes.

Look, they're brothers again: as the ravenous fire first
seized his limbs, the pile quaked and the new arrival is driven    430
from the pyre; flames poured out when the summit broke in half,
and flared-up each tip with the light severed.
As if pale Orcus joined Eumenides' fires,
and each orb menaced and each tried to outmatch
the other; its weight displaced, the wooden mass itself       435
slid apart a bit.

As in Hypsipyle's mock funeral for her father, the scene plays with the confusion in this poem of *pietas* and *nefas*. Through a concerted act of love and piety, the sisters-in-law come together to cremate Polynices, but the act morphs into a renewal of fratricidal crimes (12.441): *uiuunt odia improba, uiuunt*, 'their wicked hatred lives, it *lives!*'[107]

The scene reworks an earlier death-scene and cremation linking brothers in a bloody embrace.[108] As the Theban mother Ide scans the field of battle after Tydeus' annihilation of the 50 Theban ambushers, she finds her twin sons locked in death, pierced together by a spear through each heart (3.147–9).[109] Ide mourns her loss and promises her sons an eternal fraternal bond on the pyre and in a funeral urn (3.165–8):

quin ego non dextras miseris complexibus ausim
diuidere et tanti consortia rumpere leti:
ite diu fratres indiscretique supremis
ignibus et caros urna confundite manes!

But I would not dare separate your hands from this pitiful
grasp and rend the brotherhood of such death:
go as brothers indefinitely, indistinguishable even in the final
funeral fires, and mingle your dear remains in one urn!

Ide promises – the funeral is only *anticipated* in the narrative – that she will purposefully unite her sons on the pyre, and their fraternal *pietas* 'indistinguishable', or maybe better 'unsevered' (*indiscreti*), will last forever. This prefigures and contrasts the fraternal *nefas* of Polynices and Eteocles and their accidental reunion. The pyre fractures in two as their smouldering corpses compete with one another past the limits of life and death,

[107] See Ganiban (2007): 208–12 on the issues of *pietas* and *nefas* in this scene.
[108] Vessey (1973): 126–7; Newlands (2012): 115; van der Keur (2013): 341. Cf. Henderson (1998): 240–1.
[109] See McAuley (2016): 316–19.

mimicking the intestine violence that still plagues their ghostly Earth-Born ancestors, as Manto observes at 4.556–60.

Charles McNelis has shown how the renewal of brotherly strife between Polynices and Eteocles on the pyre perverts the sentiments of Achilles and Patroclus (via the request of the latter's ghost) in the *Iliad* that their bones be mingled together in death (*Il.* 23.82–92) and that the Achaeans construct a burial mound to hold both of them (23.243–8).[110] We are prepared for some allusion to the *Iliad* scene moments before this when Argia is driven to find Polynices' corpse by the image of her husband's ghost demanding a funeral (*Theb.* 12.191–3): *sed nulla animo uersatur imago | crebrior Aonii quam quae de sanguine campi | nuda uenit poscitque rogos*, 'but no image disturbs her mind more frequently than the naked ghost which comes from Aonia's bloody field, and demands a tomb'. The scene replays Patroclus' ghost appearing to Achilles to demand burial at *Iliad* 23.59–107.[111] Patroclus wants his bones mingled with Achilles' (whose impending death is assured at Troy) in a fraternal bond. Argia (and Antigone) will inadvertently mingle her husband's remains with his brother in fraternal strife.

Statius' play with the sentiments in the *Iliad* finds further engagement with and perversion of how those sentiments play out in the complementary passage in *Odyssey* 24, when the ghost of Agamemnon describes Achilles' funeral rites at Troy. Achilles is cremated, his white bones and those of Patroclus are 'mingled' (*migda*) in a golden urn (Hom. *Od.* 24.76–7): ἐν τῷ τοι κεῖται λεύκ' ὀστέα, φαίδιμ' Ἀχιλλεῦ, | μίγδα δὲ Πατρόκλοιο Μενοιτιάδαο θανόντος.[112] By alluding to a moment representing profound friendship in the *Iliad*, and the execution of Patroclus and Achilles' demand to have their remains united in the *Odyssey*, Statius destroys the sentiments of the model scenes and highlights the boundless madness of his own depiction of 'fraternity'. While Achilles and Patroclus sought to cement their bond beyond the limits of mortality, Polynices and Eteocles' enmity proves equally limitless.

Scholars have noted how the brothers' hatred 'infects' Argia and Antigone who, when Creon's guards apprehend them, begin fighting with one another to take the blame for the crime of cremating Polynices (*Theb.* 12.456–63):[113]

---

[110] McNelis (2007): 157–8. Cf. Burck (1981): 480.

[111] Pollmann (2004): *ad* 12.191–3; van der Keur (2013): 341.

[112] On these lines and their dialogue with *Il.* 23 see Heubeck (1992): *ad* 24.76–9, Burgess (2009): 16–17, 104–6.

[113] Burck (1981): 480; Hardie (1993): 45–6; Hershkowitz (1998a): 292–6; Franchet d'Espèrey (1999): 318; Ganiban (2007): 208–12. Heslin (2008): 118 argues the women fight to play the famous role of Sophocles' Antigone, here divided between them; cf. Bessone (2011): 210–11.

ambitur saeua de morte animosaque leti
spes furit: haec fratris rapuisse, haec coniugis artus
contendunt uicibusque probant: 'ego corpus', 'ego ignes',
'me pietas', 'me duxit amor'. deposcere saeua
supplicia et dextras iuuat insertare catenis.                    460
nusquam illa alternis modo quae reuerentia uerbis,
iram odiumque putes; tantus discordat utrimque
clamor, et ad regem qui deprendere trahuntur.

They seek savage death and spirited hope of destruction enrages
them: this one insists she'd stolen her brother's limbs, the other
   her husband's,
proving the case in succession: 'I have the corpse', 'I the fire',
'devotion drove me', 'for me it was love'. They demanded brutal
punishments and delighted to put their hands in chains.          460
No longer was there that earlier respect in alternating words,
you'd think it all anger and hatred, such shouting opposed
on each side, and those who seized them were dragged to the king.

Whatever love and piety led the women to the corpse of Polynices and
allowed them to work together to cremate him is suddenly blown apart.
Their mutual respect descends into agonistic anger and hatred and in their
madness they hurry to claim the reward of death for defying Creon's edict.
Like Menoeceus' funeral at the start of book 12 that ended with a re-
emphasis of Creon's ban, Polynices' funeral only brings a continuation of
the fraternal strife that ignited the war in the first place.[114] Time and again
Statius highlights the perverted blurring of misery and violence as scenes of
grieving everywhere spill over into violent acts, confrontations, and open
warfare. Nowhere is this more apparent than in scenes of funeral rites that
repeatedly accomplish little more than a continuation of militant savagery
and chaos. Funerals in the *Thebaid* bring anything but a peaceful
resolution.

## Some Exceptions?

And yet there is a sense that Statius will not allow things to get too far out of
hand. We might recall that despite the insistence that the gods have averted
their gaze from events on earth at the beginning of book 12 – a product of
the impiety of the fratricidal duel between Polynices and Eteocles – Statius
almost immediately contradicts himself. The poet describes a series of
goddesses sharing in the misery of the Argive women and assisting in

---

[114] Lovatt (1999): 144.

their journey to Athens to seek aid from Theseus at the Altar of Clemency (12.129–40). Capping this list is Iris, who is tasked with 'refreshing' the decaying corpses of the Argive leaders as they await funeral rites (12.137–40):

> nec non functa ducum refouendi corpora curam
> Iris habet, putresque arcanis roribus artus
> ambrosiaeque rigat sucis, ut longius obstent
> expectentque rogum et flammas non ante fatiscant.

> Iris has the care of refreshing the dead bodies of the leaders,
> and she moistens the rotting limbs with secret dew
> and ambrosial liquor so that they might keep longer
> and hold out for the pyre, and not fall apart before they get the flames.

The scene is subtly introduced but shocking to the thematic picture of corpse abuse and funeral denial (as well as divine action) that Statius' poem has incessantly expounded. The heroes are rotting (*putres . . . artus*); Iris 'refreshes' them through some form of moistening agent (*rigat*), keeping them in their present rot, not allowing them to rot *too much* (140). There is an odd mixture here of divine, human, and witchy elements in Iris' behaviour: her actions evoke the preservation of heroes in the *Iliad* like Sarpedon (*Il.* 16.680), Patroclus (19.38–9), and Hector (23.184–7, 24.411–23), whose corpses are preserved, importantly, from even reaching a point of decay by ambrosia, divine oils, and nectar, and made pristine again for funeral rites. Iris also recalls, at the opposite end of the spectrum, the servile Roman funerary *pollinctor* ('embalmer') tasked with perfuming the corpse with various preservative ingredients to delay putrefaction.[115] There is additionally a touch of the sort of arcane nefarious 'magic' that preserves Pompey's severed head in its state of mutilation (*BC* 8.688–91) and reanimates Erichtho's corpse-soldier in Lucan's epic (6.667–84). The use of *refoueo* here hints at a macabre Lucanesque 'revivification' of rotting flesh.

The poem ends with an extended discourse on *humanitas*, as gods give way to human actors in book 12, and humans play out the final action of the poem and provide their own form of resolution. Here Statius creates an epic universe that suddenly nods to Lucan's portrait of a godless realm.[116] No god interferes with Theseus' actions, no god forces his hand. But before

---

[115] See Lindsay (2000): 157–8 for the profession.
[116] See Feeney (1991): 355–91 for a brilliant unravelling of Statius' handling of divinity; Statius 'ends up in Lucan's camp' by essentially removing the gods from the end of the poem (p.358).

they become abstractions, the gods' last truly 'divine' action concerns the
treatment of those dead and rotting bodies strewn on the Theban plain.

The first act that sets the stage for the leitmotif of funeral denial in the
poem is Eteocles' refusal of funeral rites for Maeon, the lone survivor of
Tydeus' annihilation of the Theban ambushers (*Theb.* 3.97–8: [Eteocles]
*uetat igne rapi, pacemque sepulcri | impius ignaris nequiquam manibus arcet*,
'Eteocles prohibits fire be taken, and impiously (and in vain) prevents the
unknowing shade the peace of a tomb'). Eteocles' act is reprehensible, but
Maeon's bravery in facing the tyrant and his suicide in the face of tyranny
allow Statius room to bestow considerable praise upon the dead man as a
form of narratorial *laudatio funebris* (3.99–113):[117]

> tu tamen egregius fati mentisque nec umquam
> (sic dignum est) passure situm, qui comminus ausus          100
> uadere contemptum reges, quaque ampla ueniret
> libertas, sancire uiam: quo carmine dignam,
> quo satis ore tuis famam uirtutibus addam,
> augur amate deis? non te caelestia frustra
> edocuit lauruque sua dignatus Apollo est,                    105
> * * *                                                        105A
> et nemorum Dodona parens Cirrhaeaque uirgo                   106
> audebit tacito populos suspendere Phoebo.
> nunc quoque Tartareo multum diuisus Auerno
> Elysias, i, carpe plagas, ubi manibus axis
> inuius Ogygiis nec sontis iniqua tyranni                     110
> iussa ualent; durant habitus et membra cruentis
> inuiolata feris, nudoque sub axe iacentem
> et nemus et tristis uolucrum reuerentia seruat.

> You, exceptional in destiny and spirit, never
> to suffer neglect (this is fitting), you who dared          100
> to despise kings face to face; wherever copious freedom might
> appear, you established a way. By what song, by what
> word can I sufficiently add worth and fame to your virtues,
> augur, dear to the gods? Not in vain did Apollo teach you divine
> wisdom, worthy of the laurels he offered . . .              105
> * * *                                                        105A
> And Dodona, parent of groves, and the Cirrhaean virgin      106
> will dare to keep the people in suspense, since Phoebus is silent.
> Now also, well separated from Tartarean Avernus,
> go, take Elysian tracts, where the heavens are inaccessible to shades

---

[117] The text is corrupted somewhat; see Hill (1983): *ad loc.*

of Ogygia, and the oppressive commands of the criminal tyrant       110
do not carry weight. Garments and limbs are preserved, by bloody
beasts unharmed, and lying under the naked sky
both the grove and the sad reverence of birds guards you.

Again like the corpses Iris preserves or solidifies in their decay, Maeon is
kept in a state of perpetual preservation. He's not buried or cremated and
so Eteocles' command is upheld, but the aim of this command is denied
since Maeon's corpse will remain intact, unmutilated by beasts, and even
protected by birds that elsewhere in epic serve as the (threatened) agents of
corpse abuse (Maeon was an augur after all: 3.104[118]). Tydeus' corpse can
later be said to avoid the abuse by beasts and birds (even funereal fire), but
only because his animal savagery makes him impervious and opposed to
natural law (9.101–2). Maeon will remain a corpse but he will not be subject
to the normal, natural fate of corpses on account of his tyrant-defying
heroism. He's preserved physically and this preservation is doubled by
Statius' *makarismos* that immortalizes him in this state of inviolability.
Maeon is 'splendid of fate and soul, never to suffer oblivion' (99–100: *tu
tamen egregius fati mentisque nec umquam* | . . . *passure situm*).

The extension of the 'life' of Maeon's corpse nods to Lucan's interest in
the processes of death and dying, preservation and decay, and the *makarismos* overall has a Lucanian Stoic political tinge.[119] Statius' praise of Maeon
derives from his ability to carve out a space for 'copious freedom' (101–2:
*ampla . . . libertas*) through his challenge to tyranny and his Stoical suicide.
This interest in *libertas* set in opposition to broadly defined 'kings' (3.101:
*reges*) is very much a Lucanian flourish and largely atypical of Statius' poetic
programme.[120] It might strike us as a touch bold for Statius to glorify
exuberantly (he's nearly speechless, 102–4) a character set in opposition to a
monarch, no matter how despotic. Lucan had explored the vatic power of
characters doubling as voices for the poet himself or for poetry-makers in

---

[118] Hutchinson (1993): 306.
[119] For the Stoic thrust of Maeon's suicide see Vessey (1973): 114–16, Dominik (1994a): 159 and (1994b):
154. *Contra* Ahl (1986): 2831 n.33. Seo (2013): 156–60 notes the association with the famous Stoic
suicide of Cato, linking this back to allusions to Cato-style suicides in Lucan's poem.
[120] Note, however, the case of Aletes. After Maeon's speech and suicide, Statius inserts the vitriolic
speech of an elderly Theban named Aletes, who condemns the invidious actions of Eteocles (3.179–
213). Statius as narrator questions from where this man conjured such *libertas*, here something like
'freedom of speech' (3.216: *unde ea libertas?*). Statius quickly answers his own question: the man is
acting so boldly because he's old and close to death. He might have been killed or forced to suicide
like Maeon, but his own natural death is approaching; he has no fear (216–17: *iuxta illi finis et aetas* |
*tota retro, seraeque decus uelit addere morti*, 'His end was near, his whole life in the rear, and he would
like to add glory to his death at this late hour').

his epic (*uates* as both 'seer' and 'poet', *OLD* s.v. 1–2),[121] and Statius goes out of his way to identify Maeon as a *magnanimus uates* (82) the moment before he plunges his sword into his own side. Is there a deeper political comment at work in here? Is Maeon acting out a role relatable to a Roman and/or Flavian context?

Donka Markus has argued that Maeon acts as a metaphorical/metaliterary stand-in for Statius, and that his suicide recalls the silent protests that characterized political discourse in the Flavian period.[122] There is much to recommend this reading, but I'm also tempted to read Maeon as a Statian prototype for his poetic predecessor Lucan, particularly when set against Statius' own praise of Lucan in his *post mortem genethliakon* (birthday poem) for the dead poet at *Siluae* 2.7.[123] This poem – presenting a newborn Lucan in the arms of the muse Calliope who sings of his poetic genius and grim fate – glorifies Lucan as a Neronian *uates* (2.7.41–2) acting out a role in life that mirrored the efforts of the champions of Republican *libertas* that he depicts in his poem. In *Siluae* 2.7, Lucan's Pompey-like 'great shade' (116: *magna . . . umbra*, cf. Luc. *BC* 1.135) will reminisce in Elysium with Pompeys and Catos, a hero as they were, one of Rome's *summi uiri* (111–15).[124] Together they watch the tortured shade of Nero pale at the torches brandished by his mother in Tartarus (117–19). Lucan's song was silenced by Nero's 'tyrannical wickedness' (100), and Statius symbolizes this by cutting short and punctuating Calliope's song predicative of Lucan's brilliant but abbreviated life (appropriately) with 'Lucanian' apostrophic *furor*,[125] condemning the poet to silence (100–4):

> sic et tu (rabidi nefas tyranni!)
> iussus praecipitem subire Lethen,
> dum pugnas canis arduaque uoce
> das solacia grandibus sepulcris,
> (o dirum scelus! o scelus!) tacebis.

> Thus you too (wickedness of a crazed tyrant!)
> ordered to plunge headfirst to Lethe,
> while you sing battles and with mighty voice
> give comfort to grand tombs
> (o horrible crime! o crime!) you will be silent/silenced.

---

[121] See O'Higgins (1988), Masters (1992): 205–15, Finiello (2005): 178–82.

[122] Markus (2003): 466–7. Lovatt (2007) lays out some further implications of this type of reading particularly in Statius' use of the vatic figure of Orpheus in the *Siluae*. On (suicidal) silence as political protest in the *Thebaid* see McGuire (1997): 17–25, 197–205.

[123] See Quint (1993): 131–3, Malamud (1995), Newlands (2011a) on Statius' birthday poem for Lucan.

[124] Lovatt (2007): 152; Newlands (2011a): 441.     [125] Seo (2013): 156.

The phrase *rabidi nefas tyranni* is a virtual tagline for both Lucan's and Statius' epics, and the poems are further linked by their interests in (perversions of) tombs, as well as crimes. The description here points also directly to Statius' presentation of Maeon's suicide before the 'face of a savage tyrant' (*Theb.* 3.82: *trucis ora tyranni*).

The *uates* Lucan plunged headfirst into the Pisonian conspiracy, aiming to overthrow the emperor Nero, but was, along with his poem, silenced in the face of a tyrant. In the bizarre staging of Maeon's suicide, Statius has Maeon cut short his own speech with a suicidal sword-blow that brings him down (a striking aposiopesis: 3.87). He kills himself mid-prophecy, silencing a song ready to predict the duel that destroys Eteocles and his brother Polynices (*Theb.* 3.85–8):

> 'uado equidem exsultans ereptaque fata
> insequor et comites feror exspectatus ad umbras.
> te superis fratrique – ' et iam media orsa loquentis
> absciderat plenum capulo latus

> 'I leave truly revelling and destiny snatched away,
> I pursue it and I'm borne away, expected, to comrade shades.
> You, to gods and brother –' And now mid-speech
> he's cut short, his side pierced to the hilt.

A suicide that cuts short a vatic verse predicting civil war has resonant parallels with Lucan's (physical and poetic) demise following the botched Pisonian conspiracy. Claims to *libertas* and a Stoic release from tyranny through suicide also point to Lucan and to the claims of the victorious conspirators Vindex and Galba who championed the return of *libertas* following the overthrow of Nero in 68 CE.[126]

Lucan was silenced by his forced suicide, but also the recitation of his poem before Nero famously caused the emperor to walk out, prompting a subsequent universal ban on the performance of his poetry (Suet. *Vita Luc.* 332.11–13 Hosius; Tac. *Ann.* 15.49). Whatever political claims Statius is making here, he reserves singularly 'excessive and overly enthusiastic praise' for Maeon which balloons into an interest in his corpse's special preservation.[127] Like Lucan in Statius' praise poem, Maeon's *umbra*, joined with other like-minded shades, escapes the assaults of tyrants in Tartarus through its access to Elysium. Maeon is not buried in the *Thebaid*, but

[126] See Gallia (2012): 12–46, McClellan (2018): 64, 74 n.22.
[127] Markus (2003): 366; cf. Seo (2013): 156: the poet's 'disproportionately effusive *makarismos*' of Maeon.

like Lucan in *Siluae* 2.7, he achieves something more: poetic immortality in song, matching his corporeal preservation in death.

There is surely in Statius' *nec umquam . . . passure situm* (*Theb.* 3.99–100) an allusion to another expression of poetic immortality: Horace's poetic *monumentum* outlasting/outstripping the (*situs* of the) royal pyramids (*Carm.* 3.30.2: <u>regalique **situ** pyramidum altius</u>). As in Horace's poem, there is a play on two possible (but different) meanings of the word *situs*.[128] Maeon will not suffer 'neglect', in not being remembered, but also – reading back from *Thebaid* 3.111–13 – he will not suffer 'physical decay' beneath the naked sky. Maeon's contempt for kings in the following image (101: *contemptum <u>reges</u>*) seals the allusion: like Horace, Maeon too, in his own way, can despise *reges*.

Horace is likely also on Statius' mind at the close of *Siluae* 2.3.76–7, in the immortal praise of one Blaesus – a friend of the poem's dedicatee, Atedius Melior – who was killed during the civil war in 69 CE:[129] *quae te sub teste **situm** fugitura tacentem | ardua **magnanimi** reuirescet gloria Blaesi*, 'the lofty glory of great-souled Blaesus which, under your surveillance, will flee silent neglect/decay and be renewed again'. Statius' poem will forestall Blaesus' literary oblivion,[130] Blaesus who, like Maeon (*Theb.* 3.82), is *magnanimus* and guarded (*te sub teste*) from 'decay' – again, the double meaning of *situs* is clear. The Horatian allusions here in commemorative and funereal contexts in Statius' *Siluae* reinforce Maeon's status in the *Thebaid* as a silvan figure for another deceased poet: Lucan.[131]

Helen Lovatt has claimed that Statius presents himself in the *Siluae* (with implications for the *Thebaid*) as a failed post-Augustan *uates*, unable to achieve the goals of a 'political poet' effectively in Flavian society. This failure is indicated in his poetry, which implicitly bemoans the political silences he's forced to deploy as a product of a poetics by necessity structured around the rhetoric of monarchal praise.[132] My reading is not quite so pessimistic and grants Statius rather more poetic and political freedom and effectiveness. Still this argument is a powerful one and is a useful guide for unpacking Statius' interests in heroic political-suicides like Maeon and Lucan.

*Siluae* 2.7, a programmatic poem among Statius' occasional poetry (it closes book 2), stages a dialogue concerning the poetics of political engagement, presenting Lucan's bombastic 'Republican' political recalcitrance to

---

[128] See Nisbet and Rudd (2004): *ad loc.* for the range of meaning of *situs* in Hor. *Carm.* 3.30.2.
[129] Hardie (1983): 66–7.    [130] Newlands (2011b): *ad loc.*
[131] Thanks to Philip Hardie for insight here.
[132] Lovatt (2007): 160–3, following Markus (2003).

Neronian tyranny as something worthy of praise but ultimately personally, artistically, and politically disastrous, quite literally suicidal for the man and his art. As Carole Newlands argues, Statius' birthday poem for Lucan presents this form of politico-poetic engagement as unsuccessful and extremely dangerous. There were better ways to confront or critique Roman politics that did not result in the silencing of one's poetic voice: 'In the *Siluae*, as well as in the *Thebaid*, yet in an entirely different way, Statius attempts to avoid silence, the fate of Lucan. He establishes and maintains his poetic authority through a "poetics of Empire" that constitutes the art of obliquity practiced in extravagant and stylish ways.'[133] There is at least some understanding in Statius' 'poetics of Empire' of Seneca's warnings about avoiding the wrath of kings through one's own expressions of wrathful dissent (e.g. *De ira* 2.14.4, 2.30.1, 2.33.1), warnings Lucan seems not to have heeded.

Maeon and Lucan unsheathe tyrannicidal weapons (*Theb.* 3.81: *sed iam nudauerat ensem; Silu.* 2.7.53: *carmen . . . exseres togatum*), but these are both (Lucan's war-making poem, Maeon's sword) self-destructive implements that cut short their wielder's (political) voices. Statius immortalizes both vatic figures through the praise of his songs, which insinuates the inviolability and preservation of each. Lucan will return from death for one day to his widow Polla (2.7.120–3),[134] he will be worshipped not in the image of a false god but as 'himself' (126: *ipsum . . . ipsum*), and protected by his widow just as the reverence of birds preserves Maeon's corpse (124–31); he will be a semi-divine figure. And the reverence of birds in particular *matters* here. Like Maeon, Lucan was an augur (Vacca *Vita Lucani* 335.16 Hosius: *sacerdotium etiam accepit auguratus*). Moreover, 'Deaths' are banished from a poem about a dead man (131–2: *securae procul hinc abite, Mortes:* | *haec uitae genialis est origo*, 'get far from here, carefree Deaths: here is the source of birthday life'). These men are in a sense deathless through their efforts to (re-)attain *libertas* and through Statius' commemoration of them in song. But they are also dead and silent, their voices severed before their songs reach an endpoint.

Open political dissension is courageous in the face of tyranny because it necessitates death, and this courage must be honoured and respected.[135] But it's not Statius' path. Statius will find a voice of dissent, but often,

---

[133] Newlands (2002): 44 and (2011a): 445–7.
[134] Initially, Maeon's 'wife and faithful parents' (*coniunx fidique parentes*) bring his body home before Eteocles ultimately denies him funeral fires (*Theb.* 3.93–8). Again, if we read Lucan into Statius' Maeon, we might read Polla between the lines here too.
[135] See Ahl (1986): 2832.

cleverly, this dissension is refracted through anti-tyrannical voices like Lucan's (more literally Calliope's prophecy of Lucan), Maeon's, like the vitriol of the elderly Aletes in book 3, or the endless mourning and grieving voices of women in his poems,[136] all of which serve to destabilize any univocal politicized reading of his poetry. Statius chooses a safer but still sharply critical path, a path that will not by necessity leave the treatment of one's corpse and poetic *corpus* to the whims of a mercurial tyrant.

---

[136] On the destabilizing role of female lament in the *Theb.* see Malamud (1995): 20–1, Newlands (2002): 44–5.

# CHAPTER 6

# Grave Encounters: Silius Italicus' Punica

At perhaps the height of Lucan's apostrophic fury in the *Bellum ciuile*, after Caesar's bloodsoaked victory at Pharsalus and his refusal to provide customary death rites for the fallen Pompeian soldiers, Lucan contrasts Caesar's savagery with Hannibal's humane and almost reverential treatment of L. Aemilius Paulus, the Roman general at Cannae (*BC* 7.799–801): *non illum Poenus humator | consulis et Libyca succensae lampade Cannae | conpellunt hominum ritus ut seruet in hoste*, 'the Carthaginian burier of the consul, and Cannae lit by Libyan light do not convince him to honour the customs of humanity towards the enemy'.[1] Even Hannibal, Rome's greatest enemy, understood the 'customs of humanity' (*hominum ritus*) concerning the treatment of enemy corpses. Caesar comes off badly here. But what about Hannibal? At its core this is, of course, criticism with faint praise. Lucan had earlier grouped the two men, comparing Caesar's approach on Rome with Hannibal's crossing of the Alps (*BC* 1.303–5): *non secus ingenti bellorum Roma tumultu | concutitur, quam si Poenus transcenderit Alpes | Hannibal*, 'Rome is shaken by the huge disturbance of war, just as if the Carthaginian Hannibal were surmounting the Alps'. Rome's most lethal threat to internal stability conjures images of her greatest external enemy.[2] But at least Hannibal showed *respect* to the enemy dead, Lucan complains.[3] This chapter explores Silius' unpacking of this material, both the historical evidence of and rationale for Hannibal's treatment of Roman corpses, and the Carthaginian's juxtaposition to Lucan's Caesar and, more broadly, Rome's 'Caesars' in the subsequent context of more recent civil strife. Though Hannibal remains an unsuccessful foreign invader repelled from Rome's walls, Silius provocatively casts him (and his nemesis Scipio Africanus) as a disturbing prototype for

---

[1] I discuss the passage in detail below, pp. 248–50.   [2] See Ahl (1976): 107–8.
[3] E.g. Gioseffi (1995): 506–7.

the Roman scourge ultimately actualized in the home-grown Caesars who rip Rome to pieces.

## 'Carthaginian' Roman Funerals

Our ancient historiographers provide evidence that Hannibal on occasion went out of his way to oversee funeral rites for dead Roman generals. The claim is made for three generals killed in battle against the Carthaginians during the Second Punic War: L. Aemilius Paulus,[4] T. Sempronius Gracchus,[5] and M. Claudius Marcellus.[6] Livy's accounts are full of contradiction and he provides little explanation for Hannibal's motivation in seeking out the bodies for death rites. We should not underestimate the oddity of Hannibal's actions here. He was under no customary obligation to provide funeral rites for the enemy dead: this was the purview of the defeated military commander, who was expected to recover the bodies of men of rank and simple soldiers, and offer obsequies either individually or *en masse*.[7]

More helpful than Livy for assessing Silius' handling of these funerals – though strangely under-analyzed[8] – is Valerius Maximus, who provides a detailed analysis of Hannibal's death rites for the three Roman generals. After cataloguing the funerals for Paulus, Gracchus, and Marcellus, Valerius elaborates (5.1.ext. 6):

> ergo humanitatis dulcedo etiam in <ef>ferata barbarorum ingenia penetrat toruosque et truces hostium mollit oculos ac uictoriae insolentissimos spiritus flectit. nec illi arduum ac difficile est inter arma contraria, inter destrictos conminus mucrones placidum iter reperire. uincit iram, prosternit odium hostilemque sanguinem hostilibus lacrimis miscet. quae etiam Hannibalis admirabilem uocem pro funeribus Romanorum ducum arbitria

---

[4] Livy 22.52.6: *consulem quoque Romanum conquisitum sepultumque quidam auctores sunt*, 'some writers say that the Roman consul was also sought out and given burial'.

[5] Livy 25.17.4–7. Livy offers a variety of different accounts of the funeral for Gracchus, none of which he prioritizes (though he says most sources believe Hannibal conducted the funeral rites). Cf. Dio. Sic. 26.16.

[6] Cic. *Cato Maior* 75; Livy 27.28.1–2; App. *Hann.* 50; Plut. *Marc.* 30.1–2. The accounts all contain inconsistencies. On the historiographic models Silius manipulates in all three funeral scenes see Augoustakis (2017): 305–15.

[7] See Onas. *Strat.* 36.1; Hope (2015): 162–70, with additional bibliography. See p. 150 above.

[8] Burck (1984): 66 n.274; Tschiedel (2011): 240 n.25; van der Keur (2013): 340 n.45. Stocks (2014): 29, 31 notes the passage as an example of Valerius' blending of positive and negative features of Hannibal, equating the positives with 'Roman' qualities and the negatives with 'Punic', in what she rightly argues is a complex construction of Hannibal as an *exemplum* of the enemy 'who is also a reflection of Rome at its ideological best' (p.32). She doesn't consider this particular passage in terms of Silius' own accounts of the funerals for Roman generals. See the useful sketch in Hope (2015): 165–6.

statuentis expressit. quin aliquanto ei plus gloriae Paulus et Gracchus et Marcellus sepulti quam oppressi attulerunt, si quidem illos Punico astu decepit, Romana mansuetudine honorauit. uos quoque, fortes ac piae umbrae, non paenitendas sortitae estis exequias: nam ut optabilius in patria, ita speciosius pro patria conlapsae supremi officii decus infelicitate amissum uirtute recuperastis.

Therefore the sweetness of humanity even penetrates the savage nature of barbarians, softens the wild and fierce eyes of enemies, and deflects the excessive pride of victory. It's not hard or difficult among enemy arms, among swords bared in conflict, to find a calm path. It conquers wrath, it lays-low hatred and mixes enemy blood with enemy tears. It even brought an admirable speech of Hannibal when he was deciding what funeral honours to give to Roman leaders. In fact, Paulus, Gracchus, and Marcellus brought him even more glory through their funerals than did his victories over them, since he had deceived them with Carthaginian cunning but honoured them with Roman gentleness. But you brave and loyal spirits, you did not receive obsequies you would be upset about: you might have hoped to have died in your country, but it was even more splendid to die *for* your country, you lost the glory of a proper funeral through bad luck, you regained it through your courage.[9]

Much of this squares with Silius' descriptions of these funeral rites in the *Punica*. Hannibal seems to fight through his enmity for the leaders, displaying kindness and *humanitas* through recognition of the importance of obsequies (*Pun.* 10.518–20; 12.473–4; 15.385–7, 394–6). Silius puts into words the *laudatio funebris* Valerius mentions Hannibal provided as part of the funeral services, in the case of Paulus and Marcellus, and Hannibal's words in each echo Valerius' own claim that the men should not be ashamed of these atypical rites, that they died proudly for their country and gained honour in death (10.572–4; 15.383–5).

The point of departure here, and what Silius seems to latch onto, is the issue of the *glory* Hannibal attained through these funerals. Valerius says nothing about Hannibal's motivation, only the result of his actions: glory achieved through the very 'Roman' way in which he honoured the dead (via *humanitas* and *mansuetudo*), set in contrast to his specifically 'Carthaginian' cunning and guile in acquiring military victory. Silius warps the sentiments of Valerius' account by making Hannibal's lust for praise and glory the only real goal of these funerals.

---

[9] Valerius also claims that Hannibal recovered the corpse of Flaminius and oversaw the funeral rites (1.6.6). Silius follows Livy 22.7.5 and Plut. *Fab.* 3.3 in claiming that Hannibal was unable to find Flaminius' body.

The source of Hannibal's inspiration to offer funeral rites for the Roman generals is L. Cornelius Scipio's treatment of the Carthaginian Hanno's corpse (from the First Punic war) depicted in *ekphrasis* in *Punica* 6.[10] Silius prepares us for all of these later funeral rites (and Hannibal's particular motivation) during the famous scene at Liternum, as Hannibal views images of Roman glory from the earlier war immortalized on the temple walls of an unidentified deity. Among the scenes is the elder Scipio's funeral for Hanno (6.670–2):[11]

> cernit et extremos defuncti ciuis honores:
> Scipio ductoris celebrabat funera Poeni,
> Sardoa uictor terra.

> [Hannibal] also saw the last honours of a dead countryman:
> Scipio was leading the funeral of a Carthaginian general,
> as victory in the Sardinian land.

Gesine Manuwald has argued that the scenes on the temple walls are described from an omniscient Roman perspective, though we view them initially with Hannibal as he looks on (6.653–7). Only with the description of Scipio's funeral for Hanno does the perspective shift back to Hannibal, as he becomes the focalizer for the images we are viewing: 'this focalization underscores how Hannibal is confronted with Roman conduct and Roman power'.[12] The shift of focalization marks the importance of this particular image as Hannibal learns that piety or *humanitas* – in this case through offering an enemy proper funeral rites – can earn glory and praise as lasting as military triumph. Silius does not explicitly tell us that Scipio's actions are a sign of *humanitas*, but again Valerius provides a model that identifies Scipio's intent (5.1.2):[13]

> atque ut ab uniuersis patribus conscriptis ad singulos ueniam, L. Cornelius consul primo Punico bello, cum Olbiam oppidum cepisset, pro quo fortissime dimicans Hanno dux Karthaginiensium occiderat, corpus eius e tabernaculo suo amplo funere extulit nec dubitauit hostis exequias ipse celebrare, eam demum uictoriam et apud deos et apud homines minimum inuidiae habituram credens, <quae> quam plurimum humanitatis habuisset.

[10] Note Stocks (2014): 222: '[Hannibal's] intention is to reinvent these images – an aim that will be partially realised when he buries Rome's generals, replaying the image of Scipio Maior's burial of a Carthaginian commander in Sardinia (6.671–2).'

[11] See Fowler (2000): 93–107, Barchiesi (2001): 138–9, Fröhlich (2000): *ad locc.*, Marks (2003), Manuwald (2009) on the scene at Liternum.

[12] Manuwald (2009): 42–3. Cf. Fröhlich (2000): *ad* 6.670–2, 671, Marks (2003): 137 n.20.

[13] Fowler (2000): 100–1.

And, that I might move from the senate as a whole to individual members of it, L. Cornelius [Scipio], consul in the First Punic War, when he captured the city of Olbia, the Carthaginian general Hanno had died fighting very bravely in its defence, Scipio gave his body a full military funeral from his own tent. He himself did not hesitate to perform the obsequies of an enemy, believing that victory would elicit the least envy from both gods and men which involved the greatest humanity.

Scipio's actions are grounded in a deep respect for the gods and a fear of overreaching, which might result in divine and human envy (*inuidia*). Respect for the gods and fear of overreaching are not things we can easily associate with Hannibal in Silius' poem; his speech, in fact, after viewing these Roman images on the Liternum temple ends with a promise to construct his own Carthaginian victory monument whose *coup de grâce* will depict Jupiter hurled down from the Tarpeian rock (*Pun.* 6.713: *deiectum Tarpeia rupe Tonantem*). And from the outset of Silius' poem Hannibal is construed as a *contemptor diuum*, like Mezentius, Caesar, and Capaneus (*Pun.* 1.58): *armato nullus diuum pudor*, 'armed, he had no respect for Heaven'. Hannibal has recognized the immortal power of *humanitas*, but has warped its sentiments and purpose. The scenes of the temple monumentalize, and thus immortalize, Roman victory, piety, humanity, and glory, and consequently Hannibal orders them to be destroyed (714–16). But these images become a model for Hannibal's own imagined monument once his (unrealized) defeat of Rome is complete (700–13).

Keeping this scene from Liternum in mind, we can look in more detail at Hannibal's funeral rites for Paulus, Gracchus, and Marcellus, and particularly at the ways in which Hannibal attempts to appropriate the sort of *humanitas* that yielded fame and glory for L. Cornelius Scipio,[14] as a calculated means of bringing lasting fame to his own name. In this way we will be able to see that Silius distorts the claims of 'Roman kindness' Valerius ascribes to Hannibal, setting the Carthaginian leader up as an emblem of false exemplarity.

It's worth stressing, first, that leading up to Hannibal's visit to Liternum the issue of funeral rites for Roman soldiers has been building steadily in the poem. The first action attributed to a Carthaginian in real-time in the poem is Hasdrubal's (the son-in-law of Hamilcar) abuse and display of the Spanish king Tagus' corpse and funeral denial (1.152–4): *Tagum superumque*

---

[14] Kißel (1979): 106 n.14 is right that Scipio Maior's treatment of Hanno is the only obvious funeral in the poem without clear negative connotations (though it doesn't occur in the narrative present).

*hominumque | immemor erecto suffossum robore maestis | ostentabat ouans populis sine funere regem*, 'heedless of gods and men, exulting, [Hasdrubal] displayed Tagus pierced to a wooden cross to his miserable people, their king lacking a funeral'. This scene follows a lengthy prophecy by Juno predicting the Roman losses at Ticinus, Trebia, Trasimene, and Cannae, whose rivers and lakes will be inundated with Roman corpses and severed limbs (1.43–54). Cannae will be the 'tomb of Italy' (50: *tumulum Hesperiae*), even though Hannibal will leave the Roman bodies unburied: Italy herself will be forced to subsume the suppurating corpses of the dead (cf. 15.530–1).

A second prophecy similarly predicts fields and rivers covered with corpses (1.125–6). We have seen Hannibal deny Theron's funeral rites along with the mass suicidal pyre of the Saguntine citizens that ends book 2 (a funeral of sorts, but wholly distorted and infected by Tisiphone's intervention).[15] Flaminius is haunted by a ghost-army of the unburied Roman soldiers from Trebia (5.127–9), and is himself only granted a 'tomb' through the corpses of his own suicidal troops (5.658–66). The horror of post-battle carnage at Trasimene eclipses even Juno's own predictions for the same battle (6.1–61), and the only real funerary ritual recorded is Bruttius' bizarre burial of the Roman legionary eagle in the blood-soaked earth (34–40). The first six books of the poem offer little comfort to the dead, and until he views the scene of Hanno's funeral led by Scipio at Liternum, Hannibal shows no interest at all in the corpses of his enemies.

In the case of Gracchus' funeral in book 12, Silius is particularly scathing. After destroying a Roman blockade in his defence of Capua, Hannibal and his troops ride over the bodies of fallen Romans (12.471–2), and only halt their horses when they come upon Gracchus' corpse (12.473–4, 477–8):

> exequiae tantum famam nomenque uolentem
> mitificae mentis tenuerunt funere laeto.
> . . .
>
> Gracchus caeco circumdatus astu
> occiderat, laudemque Libys rapiebat humandi.

> They detained him wanting the fame of so great a funeral
> and the reputation of a gentle mind, though happy with the death.
> . . .
>
> besieged by hidden cunning, Gracchus had been
> murdered, and Hannibal seized the glory of burying him.

---

[15] See the discussion of activities at Saguntum above pp. 97–112.

Trampling over the corpses of the dead in order to offer funeral rites to only one of them is disturbing, but that the sole funeral comes as a means of self-aggrandizement and personal gain betrays Hannibal's lack of interest in the rites themselves and in Gracchus in particular.[16]

Silius is less damning of Hannibal in the description of Marcellus' funeral in book 15, though here too the rites function explicitly as a vehicle to bolster Hannibal's own reputation and glory; the dead Roman is of secondary concern. Hannibal equates himself with Marcellus as his peer in battle (15.385–6), the pyre prepared for Marcellus might have brought some to imagine that Hannibal himself had fallen (389–90), and Marcellus' death is a bringer of *laus* ('glory' or 'praise') to Hannibal and his men (392). Before Hannibal's eulogy, Silius himself praises Marcellus, but again bemoans the glory that his death brought to Hannibal (339): *heu quantum Hannibalem clara factura ruina*, 'alas, about to make Hannibal so great by a famous fall'. Scholars have noted that the scene is full of contradictions. It's hard to square Hannibal's apparent magnanimity here with his calculation of the importance of glory expressed in his earlier funeral for Gracchus (and Paulus, as we shall see).[17] Hannibal performs the rites over Marcellus, but his own interests are of chief concern.[18]

Paulus' funeral is the most detailed and the most fraught. Carthaginian troops discover Paulus' corpse after the battle of Cannae and a joyous Hannibal immediately announces that the Roman leader (as well as Hannibal's troops and allies) must be granted proper funeral rites (*Pun.* 10.503–23). Hannibal orders the construction of funeral pyres, which precipitates a typical epic tree-felling scene, and the bodies of the Carthaginian corpses are cremated (524–43). Hannibal burns an offering of collected armour to Mars, the 'first fruits of battle', as payment for the god's harkening to his prayers (545–57), and subsequently oversees the rites for Paulus, offering a *laudatio funebris* over the corpse before the flames take Paulus' body and his spirit rises triumphant into the sky (558–77).

Erich Burck has detailed Silius' borrowings in this scene from the early action of *Aeneid* 11.[19] Both Aeneas and Hannibal offer funeral rites to the dead, dedicate war spoils to Mars, and personally oversee the extensive rites

---

Burck (1981): 464, Spaltenstein (1990): *ad* 12.473, Manuwald (2009): 43 n.26, van der Keur (2013): 340. *Contra* Augoustakis (2017): 311–12, who takes a kinder view of Hannibal, generally. Dio. Sic. 26.16 contrastingly applies no *arrière-pensée* to Hannibal's treatment of Gracchus, and even that he repelled the desires of his troops to cut up the corpse and scatter its parts.

Burck (1984): 67–8; Tipping (2010): 75–6. Cf. the prophecy of Marcellus' death at *Pun.* 1.132–3.

Whether Marcellus was buried at all has been seriously questioned; see Flower (1996): 146–7.

Burck (1981): 460–2 and (1984): 67–8; Spaltenstein (1990): *ad* 10.527, 543.

for a fallen individual (Aeneas for Pallas; Hannibal for Paulus). Silius'
acknowledgment of Virgil's scene is clear, but the atmosphere is distorted.
Aeneas had allowed both sides of the conflict (his own and the Rutulian
contingent) to gather and provide funerals for the dead during an agreed-
upon ceasefire. The model is a similar scene from *Iliad* 7, wherein a truce
allows Trojans and Achaeans to collect and cremate their dead *en masse*.
Hannibal says and does nothing about the Roman corpses here, but makes
explicit his plan to construct pyres for his own dead soldiers.

    Silius had made much of Paulus' 'one-for-all' relationship with Rome in
the lead-up to and during the battle of Cannae (he's a 'synecdochic' hero:
*Pun.* 10.48–51, 270–5, etc.),[20] and Hannibal rearticulates that association
here (10.521–2): *qui tot mihi milibus unus | maior laetitiae causa es*, 'you
alone are the source of more joy to me than so many thousands'. This scene
prepares us for the funeral Hannibal performs over Paulus' corpse at the
expense of, or in place of, the thousands of Roman dead Hannibal and his
men trample underfoot and leave to rot. As in Gracchus' case, while we
may be excused for reading Paulus' funeral as similarly a synecdochic
funeral for all of his soldiers, the issue of rotting Roman corpses looms
large (e.g. 10.449–54).

    While *Aeneid* 11 provides a meaningful backdrop that Silius is aiming to
distort, the stain of Lucan's Caesar in *BC* 7 represents another powerful
intertext for Silius in his efforts to add elements of perversity to the funeral
rites. As I mentioned at the start of this chapter, Lucan had chosen this
precise moment of Hannibal's campaign (his funeral for Paulus after
Cannae) to highlight Caesar's mania at Pharsalus, comparing the Roman
general unfavourably to Rome's greatest historical enemy (*BC* 7.799–801):

> non illum Poenus humator
> consulis et Libyca succensae lampade Cannae
> conpellunt hominum ritus ut seruet in hoste

> The Carthaginian burier
> of the consul, and Cannae lit by Libyan light do not
> convince him to honour the customs of humanity towards the enemy.

Caesar is made to look worse than a 'humane' Hannibal – a Hannibal
similarly praised by Valerius Maximus – though evidence for Caesar's
denial of funeral rites for the dead Pompeians at Pharsalus is not corrobo-
rated anywhere in our sources.[21] Lucan's scene is both a deliberate

---

[20] Marks (2005a): 79–80; Cowan (2007b).
[21] See Gioseffi (1995): 503, Narducci (2002): 228, Radicke (2004): 429.

corruption of an epic *topos* (humanitarian ceasefire and funeral rites for the dead) and a historical fabrication aimed at amplifying Caesar's monstrousness. Silius utilizes the allusion instigated by his epic predecessor and turns the comparison back implicitly, retrojecting Caesar's feasting his eyes on the slaughter post Pharsalus (*BC* 7.728–824, esp. 786–95) onto Hannibal's bloodthirsty scanning of the battlefield after his victory at Cannae (*Pun.* 10.450–4):[22]

> **lustrabat campos** et saeuae tristia dextrae
> facta recensebat pertractans uulnera uisu
> Hannibal et magna circumstipante caterua
> dulcia praebebat trucibus **spectacula** Poenis.
> quas inter strages . . .

> Hannibal was traversing the battlefield and counting-up dreadful
> deeds of his savage hand, investigating wounds with his gaze;
> and with a large band surrounding him,
> he offered a delightful spectacle to the ferocious Carthaginians.
> Amid which slaughter . . .

Both of these scenes play up the horrid spectacle and the leaders' lust for viewing it. Both Caesar and Hannibal ride over the fields of battle (*Pun.* 10.450: **lustrabat campos**; *BC* 7.795: **lustrare** . . . **campos**);[23] Hannibal's surveying eyes (*Pun.* 10.451: *pertractans uulnera uisu*) match Caesar's eyes, which cling to the deathly fields of Pharsalus (*BC* 7.788–9: *feralibus aruis | haerentis oculos*); both 'calculate' death statistics (*Pun.* 10.451: *recensebat*; *BC* 7.792: *numerat*); and the slaughter is pleasing to them (*Pun.* 10.453: *dulcia . . . spectacula*, with *BC* 7.797: *laeta . . . spectacula*).[24]

Silius had already created a link between his battle at Cannae and Lucan's climactic battle at Pharsalus. Among many allusions, Silius inserts soldiers into his Italian catalogue whose names evoke the major participants of Rome's civil wars (*Pun.* 8.352–621); he includes a prophetic soldier (8.656–76) reminiscent of Lucan's matrona who predicts the future civil bloodshed (*BC* 1.673–95), as well as pre-battle omens (*Pun.* 8.622–5) which

---

[22] Fucecchi (1990): 164; Tipping (2010): 64 n.32; Littlewood (2017): 200 and *ad locc.* For more on Silius' Hannibal and Lucan's Caesar see Kißel (1979): 108–11, Ahl, Davis, and Pomeroy (1986): 2511–16, Tipping (2010): 89–92, Bessone (2013): 93–6, Chaudhuri (2014): 240–3. Stocks (2014): 67–8 compares Caesar's viewing of the post-Pharsalus slaughter with Hannibal's viewing of dead Romans after Trasimene (*Pun.* 5.666–76), though this less directly relies on Lucan's scene than the fields of Cannae.

[23] Littlewood (2017): *ad* 10.450–2.

[24] Pagán (2000) notes certain 'tyrannical' associations with the joy of viewing battlefield aftermath scenes.

match those at *BC* 1.522–83 and 7.151–213 (both anticipating Pharsalus as the nadir of the civil war).[25] The battle itself is replete with allusions to civil war and to Lucan's depiction of it more specifically.[26] Caesar left Pharsalus heaped with unburied Roman corpses, as Hannibal likewise leaves Cannae, but both single out the opposing leader for special death rites. Caesar's burial of Pompey comes at the end of *BC* 9 when he's presented with Pompey's severed head in Egypt and demands that it receive special treatment and proper disposal (9.1089–93). Lucan assures us that Caesar veiled his joy at the sight of Pompey's head (1035–41, 1062–3), and that the rites over it, including a quasi-funeral speech (1064–1104), and his indignant tears function as a contrivance of his infamous *clementia*. Caesar's main concern is his own reputation (1080: *famae cura uetat*), and the appearance of *humanitas*. No one believes him (1104–8).[27]

This scene at the end of *BC* 9, coupled with Lucan's description of the battle of Pharsalus in book 7, is crucial to Silius' handling of Paulus' death and Hannibal's treatment of his corpse. Silius casts Paulus as a double for Lucan's Pompey through their synecdochic association with the collective state body: they are the 'heads' of Rome's military corps(e). But Silius creates a more detailed connection than scholars have observed, which bears on the issue of funeral rites and corpse treatment and deserves deeper engagement.

Paolo Marpicati and others have argued that Silius' epitaph for Paulus (*Pun.* 10.305–11) evokes the decapitation of Lucan's Pompey as well as Virgil's epitaph for the headless Priam (*Aen.* 2.554–8). Paulus is not decapitated, of course, but his death is articulated through analogy with the severing of his army's head (*Pun.* 10.309–11): *postquam spes Italum mentesque in consule lapsae, | ceu truncus capitis saeuis exercitus armis | sternitur*, 'after the hope and minds of the Italians collapsed with the consul, as if its head was severed, the army is overthrown by ferocious arms'.[28] Further details link Paulus to Lucan's Pompey,[29] including Paulus' *nomen* climbing up to the stars (10.308), doubly reworking Pompey's catasterism at *BC* 9.1–14 and Lucan's (and Pompey's own) insistence on the importance of Pompey's famous *nomen* in the poem (cf. Mago's

---

[25] McGuire (1997): 92–3, 133–9; Marks (2005a): 275 n.104 and (2009): 135–9; Tipping (2010): 36–7.

[26] See Tipping (2010): 36–9, 42–3 for details.     [27] See pp. 138–40 above.

[28] See Marpicati (1999), Marks (2008): 70–5 and (2009): 138–9, Cowan (2007b): 31–2, Littlewood (2017): *ad* 10.305–6, 310–11.

[29] For some of these and other allusions Silius creates between his Paulus and Lucan's Pompey see Spaltenstein (1990): *ad locc.*, Marpicati (1999): 195–6, 199, Marks (2008): 70–5, Cowan (2007b): 16, 27–32, Littlewood (2017): xxix.

description of Paulus at *Pun.* 11.511–12: *magnum Latia inter nomina Paulus | nomen*). Paulus' ghost does, like Pompey, literally rise from his tomb and fly into the sky (*Pun.* 10.577). A Lentulus advises Pompey after his defeat at Pharsalus to seek Egypt's aid (*BC* 8.328–455), as does another Lentulus who encourages Paulus to flee Cannae (*Pun.* 10.267–75). Like Pompey (*BC* 8.622–35), Paulus uses his death as an opportunity for exemplarity, to show future ages how a hero ought to die (*Pun.* 10.283–5): *amplius acta | quid superest uita, nisi caecae ostendere plebi | Paulum scire mori?*, 'what more can be done with what life remains in me, except to demonstrate to the ignorant plebs that Paulus knows how to die?' Silius' Egyptian boat simile (10.321–5) recalls Pompey's death in a boat off Egypt. The death of each man is drawn out to almost operatic lengths. And Paulus' corpse, uncovered by Hannibal's troops beneath a pile of corpses, recalls Pompey's corpse-like appearance at Lesbos following his loss at Pharsalus (*BC* 8.56–7: *deformem pallore ducem uultusque prementem | **canitiem** atque **atro squalentis puluere** uestes*, 'the leader, misshapen by pallor, white hair concealing his face, and his clothes stiff with black dust'; *Pun.* 10.510–11: ***puluere canities atro** arentique cruore | **squalebat** barba*, 'his white hair was stiff with black dust, and his beard with dried gore').

These allusions prompted Raymond Marks to comment: 'Silius wants us to read the defeat at Cannae and, especially, the death of Paulus there in relation to the death of Pompey and, in doing so, invites us to see Paulus as a kind of Pompey figure or, perhaps, Rome as the Pompey figure and Paulus as the equivalent of Pompey's head.'[30] This assertion can be strengthened, particularly the association between Paulus and Pompey's head, when we examine Paulus' funeral rites. I mentioned that Hannibal's troops recover Paulus' corpse in the aftermath of the battle at Cannae in book 10, but the manner in which he's found casts an element of perversion over the subsequent funeral rites that Hannibal oversees (10.504–6):

> permixta ruina
> inter et arma uirum et lacerata cadauera Pauli
> eruerant corpus media de strage iacentum.

> mixed with destruction
> amid both arms of men and mutilated corpses, they had extracted
> the body of Paulus from the middle of the heap of the slain.

Silius here and elsewhere in his epic (cf. 5.658–66, 10.250–9), like Statius, constructs bizarre 'corpse-tombs', heaps of dead men and weapons which

---

[30] Marks (2009): 139.

functionally form *tumulus*-like structures over fallen generals or warriors when the opportunity for proper interment seems remote.[31] When Hannibal's soldiers find Paulus, they effectively *exhume* him from a tomb constructed of the 'arms and men' (505: *arma uirum*) he stands for;[32] he's the army's *caput* entombed in its own *corpus*.

Paulus' distorted double-burial resonates with the multiple quasi-funerals for Pompey in the *BC*, funerals that do not work individually but collectively come some way toward a unified whole. Lucan articulates the inadequacy of Pompey's individual funerals most poignantly through his use of negative enumeration, whereby Lucan as narrator or his characters describe in detail the funeral display or paraphernalia or custom that is traditionally conducted over a Roman corpse, as a means of highlighting the paucity of Pompey's actual rites. Different scenes focus on different missing elements, including the roles of the widow and family, an enormous mourning crowd, the funeral pomp and procession, and so on (e.g. *BC* 7.37–44, 8.729–35, 739–42, 806–15, 9.55–62).[33] We find the same system at work during Paulus' funeral,[34] where the negative enumeration of traditional rites contrasts sharply his actual funeral conducted by Hannibal (*Pun.* 10.565–8):

> non coniunx natiue aderant, non iuncta propinquo
> sanguine turba uirum, aut celsis de more feretris
> praecedens prisca exequias decorabat imago,
> omnibus exuuiis nudo

> No actual wife was present, no crowd of men linked
> by familial blood, nor on customary lofty litters
> did the ancestral mask leading the way beautify the procession:
> it was stripped of all adornments.

The list Silius offers condenses the series of negative enumerations Lucan provides for Pompey over the course of 3 books (*BC* 7–9), and highlights the jarringly odd circumstance of Paulus' funeral at the hands of his Carthaginian enemy.

Paulus' corpse may lack all the traditional elements of a Roman funeral, but Silius tells us that 'Hannibal as eulogizer was by itself glory enough'

---

[31] On the motif in Statius, see pp. 215–17.
[32] On the Virgilian collocation here see Cowan (2007b): 26 with n.91, Landrey (2014): 627–9.
[33] See pp. 127–43.
[34] Littlewood (2017): *ad* 10.565–6 notes that 'Paulus' funeral is strongly reminiscent of Lucan's sequences of reiterated negatives', though the example she provides is of the re-wedding of Cato and Marcia in Book 2. Cf. Augoustakis (2017): 307: 'What Silius emphasizes in his narrative of Paulus' burial is absence: the lack of pomp and ceremony expected on such an occasion'.

(*Pun.* 10.568–9: *iamque Hannibal unus | sat decoris laudator erat*). Nods to Aeneas' funeral for Pallas in *Aeneid* 11 abound here,[35] but again Lucan's Caesar provides the most immediate model, structurally and atmospherically. Pompey's *truncus* is left half-burnt on the Egyptian shore, but his head finds its way to Caesar who assumes the singular role of witness, *laudator*, and mourner over Pompey's final funeral rites (*BC* 9.1089–1104), a duty he performs over the remains of his enemy. The oddity of these rites, their nontraditional nature, is surpassed only by the oddity of Caesar's eulogy, which shifts the focus from the deceased to the eulogizer. This is typical of Caesar's megalomania in Lucan's poem, as he everywhere steals the focus of attention. But it stands out here in a funereal context where the focus should fall upon the dead man.

By Silius' own analogy, Paulus is the head severed from its military *truncus* (left to rot on the battlefield) which is recovered and brought to the victorious Hannibal by his minions. Like Caesar's rites over Pompey's head, those Hannibal provides for Paulus aim to impress upon the reader the absurdity and abnormality of the situation. Hannibal alone (*Pun.* 10.568: *Hannibal unus*), the victorious enemy, usurps the role of witness, *laudator* (explicitly at 569), and mourner. But again, as was the case during his funerals for Gracchus and Marcellus, the focus (as with Caesar) is largely self-involved with a view to the future (573–5): *tibi gloria leto | iam parta insigni. nostros Fortuna labores | uersat adhuc casusque iubet nescire futuros*, 'fame is already acquired by you through a notable death. Fortune still vexes my efforts, and orders me to not know future disasters.' There is a neat inversion of Aeneas' words to Helenus concerning *his* future at *Aeneid* 3.493–7 in the 'ghostly' Buthrotum: Aeneas must leave behind the shadow of Troy to found Rome; Hannibal will try to parlay his victory at Cannae into a Caesar-style *destruction* of Rome.

Lucan pulls no punches in his description of Caesar's agenda when he demands burial for Pompey's severed head. Caesar sheds mawkish tears (*BC* 9.1037–41, 1104–6), his scorn and derision a ploy to conceal his brimming joy at the circumstances of this bizarre *tête-à-tête*. The funeral rites granted to Pompey and his *laudatio* are a cheap attempt to gain credence and recognition for his *clementia* and *humanitas*. Contrastingly in the *Punica*, in the scene itself, Silius offers little overt criticism of Hannibal's actions, and only subtly hints at a deeper agenda. We might be tempted to read sarcasm into the claim that Hannibal's praise alone was enough to compensate for the lack of traditional Roman elements in his

---

[35] See Burck (1981): 462, Spaltenstein (1990): *ad locc.*, Littlewood (2017): *ad locc.*

funeral. Silius is not explicit. He tells us Hannibal was 'proud' (*Pun.* 10.559: *iactabat*) to honour his dead enemy Paulus, and we should read this pejoratively. But is Hannibal boasting of killing Paulus, of honouring him, or of showing off by honouring him?[36] The most we can say for certain is that Hannibal seems courteous, if self-aggrandizing too.

Yet this all changes as we continue reading. We are confronted with Hannibal's treatment of Gracchus' corpse (12.472–8), which Silius denounces explicitly as aimed solely at enhancing Hannibal's reputation for *humanitas*, in language strongly reminiscent of Caesar's motivations in Egypt in *BC* 9. And then we meet Paulus one more time in the underworld during Scipio Africanus' *katabasis*, where Silius fills in the gaps left unsaid in the initial funeral scene. Paulus' shade approaches Scipio, drinks the blood offering, and asks what he's doing in Hell, to which Scipio replies mournfully (*Pun.* 13.711–17):

> 'armipotens ductor, quam sunt tua fata per urbem
> lamentata diu! quam paene ruentia tecum
> traxisti ad Stygias Oenotria tecta tenebras!
> tum tibi defuncto tumulum Sidonius hostis
> constituit laudemque tuo quaesiuit honore'.      715
> dumque audit lacrimans hostilia funera Paulus,
> ante oculos iam Flaminius, iam Gracchus

> 'Powerful leader, throughout the city your death
> was mourned for so long! With your collapse you nearly
> dragged the Oenotrian city down to the Stygian shadows!
> Then the Sidonian enemy built a tomb for your dead body
> and aimed at glory by honouring you.'      715
> And while Paulus in tears hears about the hostile burial,
> before his eyes now is Flaminius, now Gracchus . . .

Despite his seemingly pious actions, Hannibal's aim, like Caesar's, is glory through a reputation for *humanitas*. This is Hannibal's attempt at mimicking L. Cornelius Scipio who – less calculatingly or sinisterly – gained immortality at Liternum in *Punica* 6 for his funeral rites over the Carthaginian enemy Hanno. Hannibal's calculation, by contrast, casts a shadow over his actions. Moreover, Paulus' tears make it clear that Hannibal's presence was little comfort despite Silius' earlier claim (10.568–9).[37]

Paulus' weeping (13.716) may betray a deeper loss: Hannibal's appropriation of praise from Paulus (715: *laudem*), whose *laus* should have come

---

[36] See Spaltenstein (1990): *ad* 10.558.    [37] *Contra* Augoustakis (2017): 310.

via a traditional Roman funeral. Just before Scipio meets Paulus, he speaks
with the shades of his father and uncle. In stark contrast to the funeral for
Paulus, Scipio describes the state-sponsored funerals Rome granted his kin
(13.658–60):

> quantos funeribus uestris gens Italia passim
> dat gemitus! tumulus uobis censente senatu
> Mauortis geminus surgit per gramina campo.

> So greatly at your death the entire Italian nation
> groans! By senatorial decree a tomb for you
> rises, a double one, on the grassy field of Mars.

The pattern follows Scipio's exchange with Paulus, noting how Rome wept
at the deaths of Scipio's father and uncle (as Rome had for Paulus, 13.711–
12), followed by his detailing of their last *post mortem* rites (cf. 13.714–15).
The elder Scipio's response is telling (13.663–5):

> ipsa quidem uirtus sibimet pulcherrima merces;
> dulce tamen uenit ad manes, cum gratia uitae
> durat apud superos, nec edunt obliuia laudem.

> Indeed virtue itself is its own most glorious reward;
> but nevertheless sweetly it comes to the shades when the influence
>     of their lives
> endures among the living, and oblivion doesn't devour their praise.

Hannibal, it seems, has 'devoured' the *laus* from Paulus by positing himself
as the focal point of the funerary rites. Scipio confirms this implicitly by
going out of his way to highlight Hannibal's role in Paulus' funeral,
capping his comments to Paulus with what is almost gossipy anecdotal
information.[38]

That the ownership of *laus* is at stake here, more than Paulus' concern
for exactly how his body has been disposed of, can be gleaned from some of
Silius' earlier contextually relevant references to funeral ritual. During the
rites Hannibal conducts over his dead soldiers and allies at Cannae, and
moments before he cremates Paulus, Silius comments that the building
and lighting of funeral pyres are 'a miserable duty and a meaningless
kindness to the dead' (10.536: *officium infelix et munus inane peremptis*).
Later during Scipio's exchange in the underworld with Appius Claudius,
he meets an unburied shade who asks Scipio to offer his corpse obsequies.
The shade lists his preferred form of disposal: cremation over inhumation.

---

[38] Cf. Juhnke (1972): 288 n.238, with the response from Kißel (1979): 175.

Scipio responds with a learned ethnographic survey of various funeral rituals employed by different cultures around the world (13.468–87). His speech functions as a disquisition indicating that exactly how a corpse is dealt with is irrelevant to the corpse and the dead man.[39] Both of these comments share Stoic sensibilities about death and disposal with Cicero's *Tusculan Disputations* (esp. 1.42–5) and Lucan's *ekpyrotic* philosophizing post-Pharsalus on the uselessness of funeral rites in the greater scheme of the impending cosmic conflagration (esp. *BC* 7.809–19), both clear models for Silius here.[40] Scipio promises to cremate Appius, but the manner in which he carries out the rites is unimportant; it matters only that Appius has been provided some semblance of funeral at all. Though Silius does not explain the exact cause of Paulus' tears at hearing of his own funeral conducted by Hannibal, he's less distraught over the manner of his last rites than that Hannibal managed to steal his *laus*, the ultimate aim of epic heroes, in the process.

### Hannibal's Bloody Homecoming

Hannibal cares little for the mass dead and only seems to offer death rites for the corpses of Roman generals as a means of validating his own illusory *humanitas* and appropriating the praise and glory associated with the funerals. As we've seen, this is a crude imitation of L. Cornelius Scipio's funeral for the Carthaginian Hanno depicted on the Roman temple at Liternum in book 6. Hannibal's interest in his own funeral rites in *Punica* 17, as the issue of Carthage's loss in the war (and Scipio's and Rome's victory) and Hannibal's own 'ending' take centre stage in Silius' narrative, imbricating allusions that create something of a cacophony of dizzying intertextuality. This compounds the image Silius has presented throughout the epic of Hannibal as simultaneously an epic hero and villain.

With Carthage under threat of destruction from Scipio and his forces, Carthaginian envoys beg Hannibal to return from Italy to defend his own country and city (17.170–83). He hesitates but ultimately agrees to save Carthage, recognizing that he represents their only hope for survival (197–8): *nunc patriae decus et patriae nunc Hannibal unus | subsidium, nunc in nostra spes ultima dextra*, 'now Hannibal is the glory of the country, now its only source of protection, now the last hope is in my right arm'. Hannibal leaves Italy by ship (211–17), his eyes longingly clinging to the sight of his unfulfilled epic conquest

---

[39] See Bassett (1963): 77.
[40] Bassett (1963) details Silius' borrowings from these and other texts; Littlewood (2017): *ad* 10.536.

and the land he has come to regard as his own. In this respect, as we have seen, he resembles Aeneas leaving Troy in defeat at *Aeneid* 3.10–12, and Pompey fleeing Italy at *BC* 3.1–7.[41]

Suddenly Hannibal changes his mind and decides to return to Italy, to aim at epic glory one last time. He turns his fleet's sails back toward the Italian shore (*Pun.* 17.230–9). Silius slyly constructs out of this decision to attack Italy again an allusion to the Achaeans' feigned flight from Troy in *Aeneid* 2 and Seneca's *Agamemnon*. The Italians come out to the shore to inspect the now empty Carthaginian camp, a gift from the gods (*Pun.* 17.204–7), recalling the Trojans' gleeful examination of the empty Achaean camp on the abandoned shoreline (*Aen.* 2.21–30). Verbal links tie Silius' formulation with Seneca's articulation of the same scene, but from a different angle (*Ag.* 435–6): *iuuat **uidere nuda** Troiae **litora**, | iuuat relicti sola Sigei loca*, 'it was a delight to see the empty shores of Troy, a delight to see the lonely land of deserted Sigeum'; *Pun.* 17.206–7: *et **litora** ab hoste | **nuda uidere** sat est*, 'it was enough to see the shore empty of the enemy'. Eurybates describes the happy sight of the empty Achaean camps from the view of the fleeing ships; Silius describes the same happy sight but from the perspective of those remaining on the shore. Silius evokes this earlier mythic ruse, sealing the association when, just before Hannibal decides to turn around, he recalls the destruction of Troy and Rome's ancestors (17.228–9): *gentique superbae | Iliacum exitium et proauorum fata dedissem*, 'I should have given to that haughty nation the destruction of Troy and the fate of their ancestors'. This repetition of destruction is itself a repetition of Hannibal's initial childhood oath to visit upon Rome the fate of Troy, and the ring-composition ties the poem's beginning with its (near) end through Hannibal's obsession with Troy's/Rome's destruction (1.114–15): *Romanos terra atque undis, ubi competet aetas, | ferro ignique sequar Rhoeteaque fata reuoluam*, 'when I reach the appropriate age, on land and sea I will hound the Romans with sword and flame, and replay the fate of Troy'. Venus voices the same fear of destructive repetition in her complaint to Jupiter at 3.567–9: *parumne est, | exilia errantes totum quaesisse per orbem? | anne **iterum** capta **repetentur** Pergama Roma?*, 'Is it insufficient, wandering through the whole earth in search of exile? Or with Rome taken will Troy be attacked *again*?'

The young Hannibal continues (1.116–17), 'the gods will not oppose me', but by now it's obvious that Italy is not so easily conquered. Neptune,

---

[41] See pp. 111. Cf. Jason sailing off in tears from home at AR 1.534–5, with the reading in Hutchinson (2013): 333.

like Poseidon and Aeolus (*Od.* 5.299–312; *Aen.* 1.94–101), stirs up a typhoon
and blasts Hannibal and his ships back towards Carthage (Aeneas too is
driven from Italy to Carthage), crashing waves over the fleet (*Pun.* 17.236–
58).[42] There is an inversion here, since these earlier scenes in Homer and
Virgil represent the first appearance of Odysseus and Aeneas in their epics,
while this will be among Hannibal's last in the *Punica*: this is the end of his
epic journey. Sailing imagery in epic is typically associated with beginnings
or at least 're-beginnings', and Silius offers here a disruption of an epic
voyage by breaking it off before it has really even begun.

Despite the inversions, Hannibal's fear is still the same as his epic
predecessors: that he will die at sea and not on some field of battle
(17.260–7):

> felix, o frater, diuisque aequate cadendo,
> Hasdrubal! egregium fortis cui dextera in armis
> pugnanti peperit letum, et cui fata dedere
> Ausoniam extremo tellurem adprendere morsu.
> at mihi Cannarum campis, ubi Paulus, ubi illae
> egregiae occubuere animae, dimittere uitam                                    265
> non licitum uel, cum ferrem in Capitolia flammas,
> Tarpeio Iouis ad manes descendere telo.

> How fortunate, brother, by your death made equal to the gods,
> Hasdrubal! You for whom the right hand of a brave enemy granted
> an excellent death in battle; and whom Fate allowed
> to take the Ausonian land with a final bite.
> But to me, in the fields of Cannae, where Paulus, where those
> excellent souls fell, it was not permitted to abandon                         265
> my life or, when I bore flames against the Capitol,
> to descend to the shades by the Tarpeian bolt of Jupiter.

Aeneas (*Aeneid* 1.96–8) wishes he had died by Diomedes' hand, recalling
their duel in *Iliad* 5. Further, he wishes he were dead like his comrades
Hector and Sarpedon (*Aen.* 1.99–100; cf. *Iliad* 16 and 22). This is how epic
heroes, or at least Homeric heroes, should die, on the battlefield. Hannibal
begins similarly on the mortal plane, but ends with the stunning reference
to his 'duel' with Jupiter in *Punica* 12 – when he had attempted to storm
Rome's walls despite divine warnings and Jupiter's lightning bolts – placing himself on par with the gods and thus eclipsing mortal standards of
epic combat. Hannibal, then, inverts Aeneas' allusion to Diomedes, who

---

[42] Silius' reworking of these earlier epic sea storms has been well documented: see Marks (2005a): 59
n.117 for bibliography; also Tipping (2010): 87–8, Lovatt (2013): 260, Stocks (2014): 61–4.

himself fought with gods at Troy, but more directly recalls Capaneus (or Salmoneus or Locrian Ajax) who felt the wrath of Jupiter's thunderbolt during the height of his theomachic madness.[43] Moments before, the Carthaginian envoys had kissed Hannibal's hands 'as if he were a god' (*Pun.* 17.183: *effundunt lacrimas dextramque ut numen adorant*). Venus demands that Neptune calm the storm lest Hannibal's and the Carthaginians' deaths by divine intervention make them seem invincible against humans and thus 'godlike' (284–9). And earlier, during his attack on Rome, the Romans believe only Jupiter has the power to defeat Hannibal (12.643–5). Silius imposes this godlikeness into Hannibal's own characterization of himself.[44]

While Hannibal recalls the frightened and (for a time) defeated Odysseus and Aeneas at sea, his decision to turn back to attack Rome coupled with his theomachic pretensions strongly point to the tempestuous Caesar at sea in *BC* 5, who similarly battled the (divine) elements and challenged the gods to strike him down in his attempt to cross from Epirus into Italy.[45] The teasing allusion here is more fully articulated near the end of the poem when Hannibal regrets not dying at sea and seems to align himself more definitely with Caesar in rejecting his own funeral rites (17.559–60): *aequore mersum | texissent scopuli, pelagusque hausisset et undae!*, 'the crags should have buried me, plunged in the deep, and the sea, the waves should have swallowed me whole'.

Caesar had eschewed the permanence of a pyre or tomb so long as he was always 'feared and anticipated by every land' (*BC* 5.671: *dum metuar semper terraque expecter ab omni*). Hannibal delivers a parallel threat and further challenges to Jupiter later as he watches from afar his army's destruction against Scipio and the Roman army at the battle of Zama. These are his last lines before exiting the epic stage (*Pun.* 17.606–15; cf. 12.729–30):

> caelum licet omne soluta
> in caput hoc compage ruat terraeque dehiscant,
> non ullo Cannas abolebis, Iuppiter, aeuo,
> decedesque prius regnis, quam nomina gentes
> aut facta Hannibalis sileant. nec deinde relinquo          610

---

[43] See Ripoll (1998): 340–8 on Hannibal and Capaneus; Marks (2014): 134–5, generally; Chaudhuri (2014): 252, and 232–55 on the theomachic qualities of Hannibal in the *Punica*.

[44] Hannibal's aims were sublimely celestial: surpassing the Alps, burning Rome's Capitol, usurping the rule/role of Jupiter the Thunderer; his wish here – not without wit – implies that he ought to have trodden a more traditional (downward) path, like Scipio (17.267): *ad manes descendere*.

[45] See Ahl, Davis, and Pomeroy (1986): 2514–15, Fucecchi (1990): 165 and (2011a): 331, Mills (2009): 56–60, Bessone (2013): 93–4. On the scene in *BC* 5, see pp. 143–8 above.

securam te, Roma, mei, patriaeque superstes
ad spes armorum uiuam tibi. †nam modo pugna
praecellis, resident hostes† mihi satque superque,
ut me Dardaniae matres atque Itala tellus,
dum uiuam, expectent nec pacem pectore norint.

Although the whole sky collapses
onto this head with its structure loosened, and the earth split open,
you will never, Jupiter, erase Cannae from any age,
you will abdicate the throne sooner than nations
silence the name and deeds of Hannibal. Nor do I leave                    610
you safe from me, Rome. Though you stand victorious over my country,
I'll live on in the hope of warring against you. For only in this battle
are you superior: enemies remain. For me it's enough and more
that Roman mothers and the land of Italy,
while I still live, should await me and not know peace in their heart.

This eternal fame through the imposition of fear and a challenge to divinity permeates each boast and supersedes the limits of mortality.[46] Like Caesar's speech, Hannibal's functions as a self-eulogy,[47] modelled on his own speeches at the funerals for Paulus and Marcellus. Hannibal eyed his own future and fate during these funeral speeches, selfishly usurping the praise and glory from the dead Romans. Here his eulogy also looks forward, blending (or blurring) a sense of atemporal dread with the *telos* of his own lifespan (612: *uiuam*; 615: *dum uiuam*). Hannibal will be a menace to Rome 'while he's alive', but like Caesar his infamy will live 'forever', longer than Jupiter's reign (608–10) and beyond even cosmic *ekpyrosis* (606–7).[48]

Yet unlike Lucan's Caesar in his war with Rome, Hannibal is ultimately a 'defeated' epic character. Everywhere Silius builds up his pretensions to Caesarism, he also undercuts the association with allusions to other defeated epic characters. While his desire to have died at sea challenges his earlier association with Aeneas and looks instead to Lucan's Caesar, his sense of helplessness, his guilt, and thoughts of suicide link Hannibal

---

[46] Both threats rely on Accius' tyrant *ethos: oderint, dum metuant*, 'let them hate me, as long as they fear me' (Acc. *Atr.* fr. 203–4 Ribbeck).

[47] Stocks (2014): 216–17, 229–30 also refers to Hannibal's speech as a self-eulogy.

[48] This claim to eternal epic *fama* reworks similar claims to poetic immortality that we see in *sphragides* like Hor. *Carm.* 3.30, *Aen.* 9, *Met.* 15, *BC* 9, etc., but crucially Hannibal himself voices his own prophecy of poetic eternity, usurping the role of epic narrator and writing his own epic 'ending'; his, however, will not be the last words of the *Pun.* For this inversion of the *sphragis topos* see Tipping (2010): 69–70, 104, Bessone (2013): 95–6, Chaudhuri (2014): 254–5, Stocks (2014): 229–30 n.23.

intimately to Turnus lost at sea at *Aeneid* 10.668–86.[49] The context is similar too: both Turnus and Hannibal attack phantoms contrived by Juno as a means of leading them from battle and delaying their deaths (*Aen.* 10.633–88, attacking a phantom-Aeneas; *Pun.* 17.522–66, a phantom-Scipio); and each watches helplessly away from the battlefield, hearing the groans of their comrades, and unable to return to fight.[50] Turnus wishes god-driven winds would smash his boat against the rocks and crags and cast him into the Syrtian shallows of North Africa (*Aen.* 10.676–8). Hannibal, reflecting back on his earlier plight at sea, in retrospect wishes he had suffered the fate Turnus desired off the North African coast.

Although Hannibal's defeat prompts a further Caesar-style incentive to rage and vengeance through his threat to Jupiter, his actual position more closely resembles Pompey during the battle at Pharsalus, who similarly watches the destruction of his army and his own claims to victory from a safe distance on land (*BC* 7.647–53; *Pun.* 17.597–603).[51] Juno in disguise refers to him as 'Hannibal the Great' (17.572: *magnus ... Hannibal*), lying that the Carthaginian leader is routing the Roman army while leading Hannibal himself away from his own and Carthage's defeat. A reference to Lucan's 'Mr Big' as a leader whose reputation for victory ultimately outshines his actual battlefield success seems clear here.[52]

More striking still are the allusions linking Hannibal's wish to have been a shipwreck victim to the actual fate of Pompey as a quasi-shipwreck victim also off the coast of North Africa in Lucan's poem. Here is Silius' passage again (*Pun.* 17.559–60): *aequore mersum | texissent **scopuli, pelagus**que **hausisset** et undae!*, 'the crags should have buried me, plunged in the deep, and the sea, the waves should have swallowed me whole'. The reworking of Lucan's description of Pompey's corpse floating in the waves is explicit (*BC* 8.708–10): *pulsatur harenis, | carpitur in **scopulis** hausto per uolnera fluctu, | ludibrium **pelagi**, nullaque manente figura | una nota est Magno capitis iactura reuolsi*, 'he's battered on the sands, ripped apart on the rocks, taking in waves through his wounds, the plaything of the sea, and with no form remaining the one identifiable feature of Magnus is the loss of a severed head'. Pompey's decapitation also resonates because

[49] Burck (1984): 165; Spaltenstein (1990): *ad* 17.555; Stocks (2014): 64–5.
[50] See Marks (2005a): 196 with n.85; Klaassen (2009): 102, Fucecchi (2011a): 326–7, Lovatt (2013): 260.
[51] See Fucecchi (1990): 163–4 and (2011a): 330, Mills (2009): 60, Stocks (2014): 228. For more on the similarities between Silius' Hannibal and Lucan's Pompey generally, see Ahl, Davis, and Pomeroy (1986): 2513–17, Fucecchi (1990): 157–66, Marks (2008): 81–5, Stocks (2014): 68–70.
[52] Stocks (2014): 216.

Hannibal refers to the destruction of his own *caput* (along with a Pompey-like distinctive interest in his *nomen*) moments later during his theomachic boast to Jupiter (*Pun.* 17.606–10, cited above). This recalls unmistakably the fate of Pompey.[53] The point is clear: Hannibal is willing to die *exactly* like Pompey (headless, unburied, beaten by waves) so long as his name and fame live on. Silius catches Lucan's own blending of the fates of Caesar and Pompey as they seek immortality in the face of 'death at sea' (Caesar: *BC* 5.653–71; Pompey: 8.610–36). Hannibal will survive and threaten the gods like Caesar, but he will lose the war and conjure images of death, mutilation, and defeat like Pompey.

Hannibal flees the epic undercover (*Pun.* 17.616–17): *sic rapitur paucis fugientum mixtus et altos | inde petit retro montes tutasque latebras*, 'so he hurries off, mixed in with a few refugees, and from there seeks the high mountains behind him and safe hiding-places'. Again he resembles Pompey after his defeat at Pharsalus, though more inconspicuous (*BC* 8.12–13: *deserta sequentem | non patitur tutis fatum celare latebris | clara uiri facies*, 'though he follows deserted paths, the man's famous face doesn't let him conceal his fate in safe hiding-places'). The allusion is signalled earlier by the Sibyl's prophecy to Scipio about Hannibal's fate, though here his flight from battle into the shadows will degenerate further into a hiding place offered by the Bithynian king Prusias (13.889–90): *altera seruitia imbelli patietur in aeuo | et latebram munus regni*, 'in powerless old age he will suffer another slavery and a hiding-place in service of the king'. Hannibal's exit also recalls Aeneas fleeing Troy for the mountains at *Aeneid* 2.804: *cessi et sublato montis genitore petiui*,[54] and Turnus grudgingly fleeing life into the shadows at the close of Virgil's poem (*Aen.* 12.952: *fugit ... sub umbras*).[55] These are all exits marked powerfully by defeat (singular and communal), and in the case of Pompey and Turnus, also by death, which Silius intricately weaves together into one multi-layered snapshot.

That the exit is meant to signify death – and decapitation – for Hannibal and Carthage is strengthened by the allusion in the line immediately following Hannibal's flight (*Pun.* 17.618): *hic finis bello*, 'this was the end of the war'. This phrase recalls Silius' epitaph for the dead Paulus at Cannae (10.305: *hic finis Paulo*, 'this was the end of Paulus'),[56] and the moment of Hannibal's greatest victory and Rome's teetering on the brink of destruction, articulated through the analogy of Rome's 'decapitation' (309–11):

---

[53] See Narducci (2002): 363 n.170, Marks (2008): 82–3.
[54] Spaltenstein (1990): *ad* 17.616; Hardie (1997): 162.    [55] See Hardie (1993): 39 and (1997): 162.
[56] Marks (2008): 83–4.

*postquam spes Italum mentesque in consule lapsae,* | *ceu truncus capitis saeuis exercitus armis* | *sternitur,* 'after the hope and minds of the Italians collapsed with the consul, as if its head was severed, the army is overthrown by ferocious arms'. The epitaphic signifier ultimately derives from Virgil's comment on the headless Priam emblematizing the 'decapitation' of Troy at *Aeneid* 2.554: *haec finis Priami,* 'this was the end of Priam'.[57] What follows is Silius' description of Carthage's surrender to Rome (tantamount to decapitation), the symbolic funeral procession of her wealth, power, weaponry, war elephants (*Pun.* 17.618–24) transferred and translated to Scipio (literally, as he encompasses the land via his cognomen 'Africanus', 17.625–6) as a procession of Scipio's now triumphant return to Italy (17.628: *sublimi . . . triumpho,* and generally: 625–54).

The traitorous Numidian king Syphax, along with Hanno, are drawn in chains through Rome as prisoners, as are Carthaginian youths, Macedonian leaders, Moors and Numidians, the Garamantes, and so on. Moreover, effigies of cities, mountains, rivers, conquered and subjugated, follow in order: Carthage, Spain, Gades, Calpe, Baetis, Pyrene, Ebro, all once emblems of Hannibal's and Carthage's expansive power and control, now under the aegis of Scipio and Rome. These – as I demonstrate below – are all simultaneously elements of victory parade (for Scipio/Rome) and funeral pomp (for Hannibal/Carthage).

Hannibal watches his army's destruction at Zama from the vantage point of a hill like Pompey at Pharsalus. But the language also combines and reworks two additionally famous scenes of epic gaze from the *Aeneid,* both inherently funereal. For Hannibal the scenery is grim (*Pun.* 17.597–9): *at fessum* **tumulo** *tandem regina propinquo* | *sistit Iuno ducem,* **facies unde omnis** *et atrae* | **apparent** *admota oculis uestigia pugnae,* 'but finally queen Juno sat the tired leader down on a nearby mound, from where the whole sight came to view, traces of the gloomy battle moved before his eyes'. The scene recalls the parade of 'future-heroes' in Virgil's underworld, where Anchises shows Aeneas the future of his race atop a hill (*Aen.* 6.754–5): *et* **tumulum** *capit* **unde omnis** *longo ordine posset* | *aduersos legere et uenientum discere uultus,* 'he takes position on a mound from where he might distinguish those turned toward him in a long procession and study the faces of them as they come by'. Juno's presence here also points to *Aeneid* 2 where another goddess (Venus) shows Aeneas the destruction of his city (2.622–3): **apparent** *dirae* **facies** *inimicaque Troiae* | *numina magna deum,* 'there appeared the grim faces and mighty divine forces of gods hostile to

Troy'. Silius has blended and perverted the Virgilian scenes. Whereas Anchises shows Aeneas the future of his race from the perspective of the underworld, Juno – like Venus at Troy – shows Hannibal not the future of his race (and city), but its death and destruction.

The funereal feel stains the scene with death. Hannibal's soldiers fear their leader is *already* dead since they cannot locate him on the battlefield, or else that he has fled in despair at the ill-will of the gods (*Pun.* 17.581–4). Both opinions are more or less true, as Silius has constructed it in the later *pompa* of Hannibal's ekphrastic journey through the streets of Rome. Hannibal watches Carthage's destruction from the vantage point of a *tumulus*, a 'mound' or 'hill', of course, but we may be tempted to read some grim symbolism between the lines. Following Hannibal's self-eulogy, Silius' postscript of the triumph of Scipio doubles as a funeral procession for Hannibal and Carthage, as indicated by the epitaphic marker *hic finis* and the virtual 'death' of Hannibal and his Carthage through their defeat at Zama.

The final 'image' in Scipio's triumphal parade (17.644: *imago*) which commands everyone's attention is an effigy of Hannibal in flight over the fields (643–4): *sed non ulla magis mentesque oculosque tenebat, | quam uisa Hannibalis campis fugientis imago*, 'but no other sight held minds and eyes more than the image of Hannibal fleeing over the plains'. Hannibal is not there *per se*, but that his *imago* is paraded along with other 'images' comprising his once mighty Mediterranean influence point to a funeral procession and the public display of ancestral *imagines*. Silius is blending long-held Greco-Roman associations linking funeral and triumphal processions (e.g. Sen. *Consol. ad Marc.* 3.1: *funus triumpho simillimum*),[58] complete with painted battle-scenes, masks, other artistic representations, all meant to be viewed as public spectacle. Lucan had done similar things by construing Pompey's parade of troops as a quasi-funeral procession for their leader in *BC* 3, and the parading of his severed head on a pike in books 8 and 9 apes cruelly the parades of ancestral *imagines* in *pompa*.[59] Funeral and triumphal processions are both powerfully suggestive of closure in Greco-Roman literature. Statius combines both in *Thebaid* 12, though triumph is 'interrupted' by a return to war, and the funerals are not really described (*Theb.* 12.519–39, 797–809). By warping elements of each, Silius is teasing at both at the same time.

---

[58] See Flower (1996): 107–9, 123–4, 244, Beard (2007): 284–6 for the funeral absorbing elements of triumphal procession.

[59] See pp. 128–9, 138–9.

Claire Stocks also views this scene from the poem's close as evocative of a funeral procession, but argues that Hannibal is subsumed into Scipio's triumph as a pseudo-ancestor with seniority over Scipio, and that he threatens to 'steal the show' by attracting the attention of Rome's audience.[60] Implicit in her claim is the idea that Hannibal is appropriating Scipio's glory and praise by infiltrating his triumph and dominating the crowd's attention. I agree that the conflict between conqueror and conquered, triumph and funeral, praise/glory, and immortality is certainly at the heart of Silius' construction of his epilogue, but the layering of allusive imagery requires us to read the ending in multiple ways.

The poem also ends with Scipio infiltrating and dominating a pseudo-funeral for Hannibal and Carthage, recalling and inverting the way in which Hannibal had earlier insinuated himself into the odd anti-Roman funerals for Paulus, Gracchus, and Marcellus, by leading the rites and appropriating the praise and glory owed to the dead. Hannibal's *imago* draws the attention of the crowd, detracting from Scipio's triumph. But it is Scipio in full triumphal regalia who dominates our attention over the final 10 lines of the poem, which equally detracts from our attention to Hannibal's funereal effigy (*Pun.* 17.645–54). Scipio's triumph is tantamount to *apotheosis*.[61] The poem ends with a nod to 'mythologizing' and Scipio enters a space familiar to readers of Cicero's *Somnium*. By the poem's close, Scipio has mastered the realms of Hell, earth, and (through allusion to *apotheosis*) sky. Silius' encomium of Scipio approximates an encomium of a Roman emperor, son-of-a-god, and foreshadows the divinity of future Roman *principes* (cf. 3.625–9 of Jupiter's prophecy of Domitian's future *apotheosis*).[62] Scipio is Bacchus, Hercules, not inferior in glory (652: *laudibus*) to Quirinus, or in services (652: *meritis*) to Camillus, draped in purple and gold, a spectacle of military excellence (645–6). The glory he has gained is ageless (625: *mansuri compos decoris per saecula rector*).

Scholars have noted that the last two lines of the *Punica* echo the final lines of *BC* 8 and Lucan's eulogy for Pompey (*Pun.* 17.653–4): *nec uero, cum te memorat de stirpe deorum, | prolem Tarpei,* **mentitur** *Roma,* **Tonantis**, 'nor in truth does Rome lie when she speaks about your divine lineage as offspring of the Tarpeian Thunderer'; *BC* 8.871–2: *atque erit Aegyptus populis fortasse nepotum | tam* **mendax** *Magni tumulo quam Creta* **Tonantis**, 'and Egypt perhaps will be to our descendants as deceptive

---

about the grave of Magnus as Crete is of the Thunderer's'.[63] Hannibal had left Zama and the *Punica* like Pompey fleeing Pharsalus in the opening lines of *BC* 8, and at the poem's close Silius alludes to the ending of *BC* 8, with Pompey now a mutilated corpse receiving a warped funeral. But whereas Lucan had construed these lines as a symbol of Pompey's atemporal, immortal *fama* as part of his narrator's *laudatio funebris*, Silius reassigns the lines to Scipio in triumph, arrogating the claims to immortality that the intertext ought to be ascribing to (the 'dead') Hannibal. This functions as a stunning reversal that directly recalls Hannibal's appropriation of Roman generals' funeral rites earlier in the poem.

At Liternum in *Punica* 6, Hannibal had seen images of past Roman victory from the First Punic War against Carthage on the temple there, and envisioned future images he himself would commission commemorating his victory against Rome. The final scene of Silius' poem is a recapitulation of the *ekphrasis* from book 6, which functions as another 'monument' of the Punic War – a triumph in *ekphrasis* (book 6) replaced by an *ekphrasis* in triumph (book 17) – but one that replays so closely the scenes Hannibal had tried to destroy and supplant with his own Carthaginian victory monument.[64] Like that of his father, Hamilcar, Hannibal's *imago* attracts the attention of all (6.689–91; 17.643–4),[65] and a 'Scipio' is immortalized for leading the funeral rites over a 'Carthaginian general' (6.670–2). Hannibal's fortunes mirror those of his defeated ancestors as displayed at Liternum, which powerfully contrast his own idealized, but unrealized, imaginary future monument (cf. 6.700–13).

Consider Hannibal's final imagined scene of future-vision for his Carthaginian monument (6.712–13): *flagrantem effinges facibus, Carthago, Libyssis | Romam et deiectum Tarpeia rupe Tonantem*, 'Carthage, you will portray Rome burning with Libyan torches and the Thunderer thrown from the Tarpeian Rock'. Hannibal's aim here becomes something of a theomachic refrain throughout the poem: cf. 10.335–6: *moenia flamma | occupat et iungit Tarpeia incendia Cannis*, 'he attacks blazing walls and unites the burning Tarpeian Rock with Cannae'; 12.516–17: *quam tanti fuerit cadere, ut Palatia cernas | et demigrantem Tarpeia sede Tonantem*,

[63] Hardie (1997): 159–60; Marks (2008): 84–5; Tipping (2010): 190.
[64] The relationship between the temple *ekphrasis* and the scenes described in Scipio's parade has received some scholarly attention: see Fowler (2000): 101–2, Marks (2003), Manuwald (2009): 49–50, Stokes (2014): 228–9. Marks (2003) has shown convincingly that the final parade that closes the *Punica* functions as a virtual *ekphrasis* recalling the images on Dido's temple at Carthage as well as the earlier scenes at Liternum.
[65] Marks (2003): 133; Stocks (2014): 221.

'such a fall [of Capua] was worth it if you see the Palatine and the Thunderer driven from his seat on the Tarpeian Rock'; 17.225–7: *tunc sat compos, qui non ardentia tela | a Cannis in templa tuli Tarpeia Iouemque | detraxi solio?*, 'was I sane then when I did not bring blazing weapons from Cannae to the Tarpeian Rock or drag Jupiter down from his throne?' (cf. also 15.800–5).[66] This is Hannibal's ultimate goal, to burn Rome and throw Jupiter down from the Capitol, then immortalize his victory in stone. Here again are the last lines of the poem, the last lines of Silius' commemoration of Scipio *triumphator* (17.653–4): *nec uero, cum te memorat de stirpe deorum, | prolem **Tarpei**, mentitur **Roma, Tonantis***, 'nor in truth does Rome lie when she speaks about your divine lineage as offspring of the Tarpeian Thunderer'.[67] We've seen how Silius usurps the funereal context of these lines (from Pompey in *BC* 8), superimposing them onto Scipio's triumph and undermining Hannibal's pseudo-funeral. But the lines also form a devious intratextual seizure of Hannibal's claims to theomachic immortality. The closest he will come to torching Rome and defeating Jupiter is his destruction of the Liternum temple depicting Roman victory in the line that closes the book (6.716): *in cineres monumenta date atque inuoluite flammis*, 'turn these images to ashes and wrap them in flames'. The poem ends not with Hannibal's overthrow of Jupiter the Thunderer and the conflagration of the Capitol, but of Rome's firm solidification and immortalizing assurance established by the association between Scipio and his divine father Jupiter.

We have to weigh two conflicting commemorative 'images' of Hannibal at the poem's close, both contextually funereal: that of his self-eulogy depicting eternal fame through fear, outlasting Jupiter's reign and cosmic *ekpyrosis*, and of his funeral *imago* crystalized in shameful flight and defeat over the fields of Zama, in a quasi-funeral pomp through the city he had failed to destroy. This conflict is in large part a product of the clashing of intertextual models aimed at destabilizing our reading of Hannibal and our interpretation of the end of the poem more broadly. Especially powerful are the competing allusions between Lucan's Caesar and Pompey in Silius' characterization of Hannibal throughout *Punica* 17.[68] Hannibal everywhere battles allegiances to Lucan's protagonists, in what Marco Fucecchi has described as a 'pattern of the synchronic coexistence of opposites'.[69] Broadly speaking, Silius has constructed Hannibal as an

---

[66] Chaudhuri (2014): 248 n.45 notes some of these.
[67] Harrison (2009): 288 spots the verbal connection between *Pun.* 6.713 and 17.654.
[68] Fucecchi (1990) and (2011a).
[69] Fucecchi (2011a): 313: 'schema della coesistenza sincronica di opposti'.

epic anti-hero aiming to conquer Rome like Caesar, but fated to failure like Pompey.

Our analysis of Hannibal's characterization necessitates mediation through Silius' handling of his nemesis Scipio, and scholars have debated just how positively we should view Scipio as a purveyor of *Romanitas*, of *uirtus*, and as something like a proto-*princeps* in the poem as a whole, and in his description in the epilogue in particular.[70] Like reading(s) of Hannibal, not surprisingly arguments have hinged on allusions pitting 'positive' models from earlier epic (and history) against 'negative' ones. Hannibal is clearly an enemy of Rome and always by definition a villain, but if we feel a strong urge to read Lucan's Pompey into his demise, then there must be at least a hint of Lucan's victorious, villainous Caesar in the Scipio who defeats him.

Scipio's victory over Hannibal and Carthage is symbolized in the *Punica*'s final image by his familial connection to Jupiter and Rome's control of the Tarpeian rock and the Capitol, the precise features and focal point of Hannibal's imagined destruction of Rome at Liternum (6.712–13). Hannibal is never able to burn the Capitol; as Jupiter promises Venus, her 'bloodline holds the Tarpeian citadel and will hold it for a long time' (3.572–3: *tenet longumque tenebit | Tarpeias arces sanguis tuus*), looking ahead to Domitianic Rome and Silius' present.

Yet Jupiter's prophecy betrays a more disturbing reality of future-history more in line with Hannibal's unfulfilled wish. Despite the oracular response from Jupiter Ammon claiming that no man will 'penetrate the guts' of Italy more deeply than Hannibal (3.708–9: *nullique relinques | altius Ausoniae penetrare in uiscera gentis*; cf. 1.64, 12.569–70), Jupiter reveals the horrors of the civil war of 68–69 CE following the death of Nero. During this brutal conflict Romans themselves (Vitellians and Flavians) destroyed the Capitol – most importantly the temple of Jupiter Optimus Maximus – and nearly killed the young future emperor Domitian hiding inside (3.609–10): *nec te terruerint Tarpei culminis ignes; | sacrilegas inter flammas seruabere terris*, 'the fires on the Tarpeian temple cannot frighten you; amid impious flames you will be preserved for the world'. Tacitus and Statius (in his *Siluae*) offer additional details: *et urbs incendiis uastata, consumptis antiquissimis delubris, ipso Capitolio ciuium manibus incenso*, 'and the city was wasted by fire, with the most ancient shrines consumed, the Capitol itself torched by citizen hands' (Tac. *Hist.* 1.2; cf. *Hist.* 3.71–4); *sacrilegis lucent Capitolia taedis*, 'the Capitol glows with

---

[70] See the very useful overview in Dominik (2010): 444–5.

impious torches' (Stat. *Silu.* 5.3.197). The destruction was devastating and clearly had a significant impact on Silius who was in Rome on December 17 when the Capitol burned (Tac. *Hist.* 3.65).

The image of Hannibal penetrating Italy's guts is a clear allusion to Lucan's conception of Roman civil war as corporeal self-evisceration (e.g. *BC* 1.3; 7.221–2, 293–4, 491, 578–80, etc.), and Lucan himself had contrasted the prying sword-hand of Hannibal (and Pyrrhus) with Rome's more deadly self-inflicted wounds (*BC* 1.30–2):

> non tu, Pyrrhe ferox, nec tantis cladibus auctor
> Poenus erit: nulli penitus descendere ferro
> contigit; alta sedent ciuilis uolnera dextrae
>
> Neither you, ferocious Pyrrhus, nor the Carthaginian will be
> the author of such slaughter: no sword has reached the innermost
> parts. It's wounds of a civil hand that sink so deep.

By only scratching the surface of Rome's civic bodily integrity, Hannibal provides a limit to destruction that later Romans aspiring to autocracy will shatter: Hannibal is a model for how a tyrant can conquer Rome, his only problem being paradoxically (and disturbingly) that he's not Roman enough to pull it off.[71] Rome awaits Caesar(s) for Hannibal's threats to reach fulfilment; what Hannibal could not do in Silius' poem and in history, Caesars can and did do, in Lucan's poem, in history.[72] Scipio's emergence as a proto-*princeps* in the *Punica* sets the ball rolling towards monarchy.[73]

Scipio's success in defeating Hannibal in large part derives from his becoming something like another Hannibal – they are interchangeable even (*Pun.* 17.401–5)[74] – rejecting the limitations imposed by State authority and the burdens of the divided, fractious consular command of disparate armies that nearly brought about Rome's defeat, shown in the civil-war-heavy imagery of the first half of the *Punica*.[75] By consolidating power in the final five books of the poem (*Pun.* 13–17; a *Scipiad*, as Hardie has it[76]) Scipio becomes the *unus uir* to challenge Hannibal (e.g. 3.590–1; 17.399) and a paradigm of monarchal leadership. Scipio is a powerful model for future

---

[71] See Chaudhuri (2014): 234, 241–3, 248 for similar sentiments.
[72] Henderson (1998): 197: '[Lucan's] Caesar plays a Hannibal that *takes* Rome.'
[73] The temple of Jupiter Optimus Maximus Capitolinus also burned in 83 BCE, again during a time of civil war (Tac. *Hist.* 3.72; Plut. *Sull.* 27; App. *B Ciu.* 1.86). Jupiter in Silius' poem refers to the events of 69 CE, but the idea holds firm that only Romans themselves can destroy the Capitol.
[74] Hardie (1993): 24–5.    [75] On the civil war imagery see Marks (2005b), Landrey (2014).
[76] Hardie (1993): 97.

Roman autocracy. This likeness between a monarchal Scipio and Rome's present Flavian monarchs is symbolized by Jupiter's prophecy which jumps staggeringly from Scipio's defeat of Hannibal to the exploits of the Flavians (3.590–629),[77] erasing the history in between and collapsing the sizeable temporal distance. But Scipio's association with monarchy also makes him unavoidably a forerunner of Caesarism and all of its negative implications, its 'dangerous individualism'.[78]

Although Scipio will hold the Capitol at the end of the poem (looking ultimately to Domitian's rebuilding of the temple of Jupiter Optimus Maximus after another fire destroyed it in 81 CE), *Punica* 16 closed with his willingness to abandon Rome's walls and temples to Hannibal in order to bring the war to Carthage (16.690–7: cf. the senators' fears of leaving Rome unprotected at 16.597–9). There is some obvious grandstanding here as he attempts to incite the senate to action, but Scipio, taking over Hannibal's imperative as the 'invading enemy leader' when he attacks Carthage, does in the end go further even than Hannibal, who had finally, reluctantly left Italy in order to protect his Carthage from destruction (17.170–98). Rome is eventually victorious, but this more and more seems incidental to Scipio's interest in his own glory and praise,[79] reminiscent of Hannibal's interest in 'Carthage's' victory over Rome. The poem ends with Scipio's triumph, not Rome's; Scipio's fame is raised to the sky through the forward-looking imagery of imperial *apotheosis*, not Rome's, reformulating the promise of Silius' proem (1.1–2: *ordior arma, quibus caelo se gloria tollit* | *Aeneadum*, 'I begin the war through which the fame of the Aeneadae lifted itself to the sky').

The conflicting glory of Hannibal and Scipio brings the poem to a close, and casts an eye forward to a future where Rome is ruled by powerful individuals who are in many ways more fully formed versions of the prototypes for monarchy offered by leaders on both sides of the *Punica*. Though Scipio occupies a secure Capitol in the poem's final image, Hannibal's eternal/infernal goal of its destruction and conflagration reaches fruition in the civil wars that brought about the establishment of the Flavian dynasty, as presaged by Jupiter in book 3. Silius' poem ends

---

[77] Marks (2005a): 213–17 sees this jarring historical compression rightly as a means of tying Scipio teleologically with the future Roman *principes* of the Flavian period (Domitian in particular).

[78] See Tipping (2010): 188–92.

[79] See Ahl, Davis, and Pomeroy (1986): 2555–7, McGuire (1997): 141–2, Tipping (2010): esp. 176–85. Various 'divine' figures even encourage Scipio to pursue individual glory without mention of State authority: 13.772–5 (Alexander the Great); 15.113–20 (Virtus); 15.199 (Scipio Maior); cf. 3.590–2 (Jupiter's prophecy); see Fucecchi (1993): 38–44, Ripoll (1998): 248–53, Bernstein (2008): 156.

where Lucan's begins, anticipating and pre-writing Lucan's view towards Rome's self-eviscerating internecine madness, more destructive than the worst exogenous enemies could bring to the Capitol. Scipio anticipates Rome's *principes*, but so too does Hannibal, and both combine to form a frightening image of the downside to future Caesarism. While relative peace may have allowed Silius' Flavian panegyric to sit more comfortably with his Roman audience, the cost of that peace could never be far from the surface.

# *A* post mortem

In an important recent piece, Kyle Gervais valuably compares the spectacle of violence in Statius' *Thebaid* and the films of Quentin Tarantino, particularly concerning the dynamics of spectatorship and our cognitive involvement as an audience in visually attuned filmic or literary scenery.[1] Gervais' argument is twofold. Statius, through violent imagery, aims to inspire ekplectic 'body-first' affective reactions in his audience (*phantasia*: physical and emotional responses to violence), with the goal of occluding the audience's role as 'audience' and thereby involving them more intimately and viscerally in the action. But simultaneously Statius' intense (and dense) allusive agenda 'compromises' the effects of *phantasia* through constant referential games that invite readers/listeners to play along in spotting the panoply of allusions to poetic predecessors. The effect of intertextuality then mitigates the affective impact engendered by violent depictions by reminding the audience that they are, indeed, an audience and not part of the fictive drama; Statius' allusiveness provides a distancing effect. Our extratextual reaction to the drama is a blend of repulsion and attraction, the safety of distance weighed against the allure of affective parasocial simulations. This tension or conflict between *phantasia* and allusion constitutes a sort of Statian 'poetics of violence' that shares striking similarities with Tarantino's violent aesthetic, as Gervais deftly details through examination of a number of scenes from the filmmaker's oeuvre and from comments Tarantino has made in interviews articulating his approach to graphic violence. The argument is made, seductively, for Statius, but it could equally apply to the other Latin epicists, all of whom, as we've seen, similarly labour over the visual spectacle of violence – particularly in the context of violence against corpses – refracted through a cascading series of earlier epic setpieces. The thesis, I suspect, has wider applications. But let me push on it just a bit in closing.

[1] Gervais (2013).

Gervais' argument is one of aesthetics buttressed by a combination of cognitive theory and Iserian reader(/audience)-response theory. The suggestion here for Statius' poetry is that audiences will have – and are expected to have – only *literary* cues or intertexts in mind when confronting a scene of violence in the *Thebaid*. Gervais does make reference to the Roman arena as a marker for 'cultural meaning',[2] which he argues adds additional distancing effects, but this is less of a focus. What about other allusions? Can we stretch the referential network to include additional real-life contemporary Roman violence, to expand this notion of cultural meaning that might direct an audience to more visceral comparanda beyond the relative safe-space provided by a playful literary or 'staged' aesthetic? Must 'cultural meaning' always juxtapose affect? I have argued that these epics present a (sometimes uneasy) mixture of literary and historical precedents in their presentation of corpse mistreatment, that scenes of violence are very often 'fictionalized' refashionings of historical abuses visited upon Roman citizens during periods of political upheaval. I suggest we are invited to recognize these historical referents and that the nods to real-world violence in an epicized literary landscape corrupt the distinction between reality and fiction, problematizing our role as 'detached' audience. If we read these historical allusions as a further critical interpretative lens, perhaps the cultural 'intertexts' would not exactly remind the audience that the violence is fictional but rather that it masks *reality*, which might elicit quite a different reaction than Gervais suggests.

In other words, I think there's a purpose here beyond aesthetics and the pleasures of viewing/reading violence. If art, by a sort of Nietzschean 'veil', masks the violence and horror of reality, perhaps as an audience we have a moral imperative to examine the realities it conceals. By allowing the violence and abuse of post-Neronian civil war, of the later Saturninian revolt in 89 CE and its aftermath, of state-sponsored activity, and of an array of horrors back through Roman history into the irresistibly 'unreal' world of the *Thebaid*, Statius inveigles us into (re-)establishing an emotional connection with actual violence via literary fiction, like a Hamlet holding a 'mirror up to nature' (*Ham.* 3.2.23–4), crafting memetic reality as a mechanism for revealing dark truths. Maybe epic violence too can snap us back to reality.

---

[2] Gervais (2013): 154–5.

# Bibliography

Adamietz, J. (1970), 'Jason und Hercules in den Epen des Apollonios Rhodios und Valerius Flaccus', *A&A* 16: 29–38.

Ahl, F. (1976), *Lucan: An Introduction*. Ithaca.

(1986), 'Statius' Thebaid: a reconsideration', *ANRW* 2.32.5: 2803–912.

(2007), *Virgil: Aeneid*. Oxford.

Ahl, F., M.A. Davis, and A. Pomeroy (1986), 'Silius Italicus', *ANRW* 2.32.4: 2492–561.

Albrecht, M. von (1964), *Silius Italicus*. Amsterdam.

Ambühl, A. (2015), *Krieg und Bürgerkrieg bei Lucan und in der griechischen Literatur: Studien zur Rezeption der attischen Tragödie und der hellenistischen Dichtung im Bellum ciuile*. Berlin.

Anderson, M.J. (1997), *The Fall of Troy in Early Greek Poetry and Art*. Oxford.

Anderson, W.S. (1990), 'Vergil's second *Iliad*', in Harrison (ed.), *Oxford Readings in Vergil's Aeneid*. Oxford: 239–52.

(1999), '*Aeneid* 11: the saddest book', in Perkell (ed.), *Reading Vergil's Aeneid: An Interpretive Guide*. Norman: 195–209.

Ardizzoni, A. (1967), *Apollonio Rodio: le Argonautiche libro I*. Athens.

Arweiler, A. (2006), 'Erictho und die Figuren der Entzweiung – Vorüberlegungen zu einer Poetik der Emergenz in Lucans *Bellum ciuile*', *Dictynna* 3. Available: http://journals.openedition.org/dictynna/202.

Ash, R. (1997), 'Severed heads: individual portraits and irrational forces in Plutarch's *Galba* and *Otho*', in Mossman (ed.), *Plutarch and His Intellectual World: Essays on Plutarch*. London: 189–214.

(2015), '"War came in disarray . . . " (*Thebaid* 7.616): Statius and the depiction of battle', in Dominik, Newlands, and Gervais (eds.), *Brill's Companion to Statius*. Leiden: 207–20.

Augoustakis, A. (2003), '"*Rapit infidum victor caput*": ekphrasis and gender-role reversal in Silius Italicus' *Punica*', in Thibodeau and Haskell (eds.), *Being There Together: Essays in Honor of Michael C.J. Putnam in the Occasion of His Seventieth Birthday*. Afton: 110–27.

(2010), *Motherhood and the Other: Fashioning Female Power in Flavian Epic*. Oxford.

(2011), '*Sine funeris ullo ardet honore rogus*: burning pyres in Lucan and Silius Italicus' Punica', in Asso (ed.), *Brill's Companion to Lucan*. Leiden: 185–98.

(2016), *Statius, Thebaid 8.* Oxford.

(2017), 'Burial scenes: Silius Italicus' *Punica* and Greco-Roman historiography', in Bessone and Fucecchi (eds.), *The Literary Genres in the Flavian Age.* Berlin: 299–315.

Auhagen, U. (2001), 'Lukans Alexander-Darstellung im bellum ciuile (10, 20–52) – ein antineronischer Exkurs', in Faller (ed.), *Studien zu antiken Identitäten.* Würzburg: 133–44.

Austin, R.G. (1964), *P. Vergili Maronis Aeneidos Liber Secundus, with a Commentary.* Oxford.

Bagnani, G. (1955), '*Sullani manes* and Lucan's rhetoric', *Phoenix* 9: 27–31.

Bahrani, Z. (2008), *Rituals of War: The Body and Violence in Mesopotamia.* Cambridge, MA.

Baier, T. (2001), *Valerius Flaccus Argonautica Buch VI: Einleitung und Kommentar.* Munich.

Balibar, É. (2002), *Politics and the Other Scene,* trans. Jones, Swenson, and Turner. London.

(2015), *Violence and Civility: On the Limits of Political Philosophy.* New York.

Barchiesi, A. (1984), *La traccia del modello: effetti omerici nella narrazione virgiliana.* Pisa.

(1997), 'Otto punti di una mappa dei naufragi', *MD* 39: 209–26.

(2001), *Speaking Volumes: Narrative and Intertext in Ovid and Other Latin Poets,* ed. and trans. Fox and Marchesi. London.

(2015), *Homeric Effects in Vergil's Narrative,* trans. Marchesi and Fox. Princeton.

Barnes, W.R. (1995), 'Virgil: the literary impact', in Horsfall (ed.), *A Companion to the Study of Virgil.* Leiden: 257–92.

Barry, W.D. (2008), 'Exposure, mutilation, and riot: violence at the "Scalae Gemoniae" in early imperial Rome', *G&R* 55: 222–46.

Barton, C. (1993), *The Sorrows of the Ancient Romans: The Gladiator and the Monster.* Princeton.

Bartsch, S. (1994), *Actors in the Audience: Theatricality and Doublespeak from Nero to Hadrian.* Cambridge, MA

(1997), *Ideology in Cold Blood: A Reading of Lucan's Civil War.* Cambridge, MA.

(2010), 'Lucan and historical bias', in Devillers and Franchet-d'Espèrey (eds.), *Lucain en débat: rhétorique, poétique et histoire.* Bordeaux: 21–31.

(2015), *Persius: A Study in Food, Philosophy, and the Figural.* Chicago.

Bassett, E.L. (1959), 'Silius *Punica* 6.1-53', *CPh* 54: 10–34.

(1963), 'Scipio and the ghost of Appius', *CPh* 58: 73–92.

(1966), 'Hercules and the hero of the *Punica*', in Wallach (ed.), *The Classical Tradition: Literary and Historical Studies in Honor of H. Caplan.* Ithaca: 258–73.

Basson, W.P. (1984), 'Vergil's Mezentius: a pivotal personality', *AClass* 27: 57–70.

Beard, M. (2007), *The Roman Triumph.* Cambridge, MA.

Beazley, J.D. (1947), 'The Rosi krater', *JHS* 67:1–9.

Berno, F.R. (2004), 'Un "truncus", molti re: Priamo, Agamennone, Pompeo, Virgilio, Seneca, Lucano', *Maia* 56: 79–84.

Bernstein, N. (2004), '*Auferte oculos*: modes of spectatorship in Statius *Thebaid* 11', *Phoenix* 58: 62–85.

(2008), *In the Image of the Ancestors: Narratives of Kinship in Flavian Rome.* Toronto.

(2011), 'The dead and their ghosts in the *Bellum Ciuile*: Lucan's vision of history', in Asso (ed.), *Brill's Companion to Lucan*. Leiden: 257–79.

(2014), '*Romanas ueluti saeuissima cum legions Tisiphone regesque mouet*: Valerius Flaccus' *Argonautica* and the Flavian era', in Heerink and Manuwald (eds.), *Brill's Companion to Valerius Flaccus*. Leiden: 154–69.

(2017), *Silius Italicus, Punica 2*. Oxford.

Berti, E. (2000), *M. Annaeus Lucanus: Bellum ciuile, liber X*. Florence.

Bessone, F. (2011), *La Tebaide di Stazio: epica e potere*. Pisa.

(2013), 'Critical interactions: constructing heroic models and imperial ideology in Flavian epic', in Manuwald and Voigt (eds.), *Flavian Epic Interactions*. Berlin: 87–105.

Bettenworth, A. (2003), 'Giganten in Bebrykien: Die Rezeption der Amykosgeschichte bei Valerius Flaccus', *Hermes* 131: 312–22.

Bexley, E. (2010), 'The myth of the Republic: Medusa and Cato in Lucan, *Pharsalia* 9', in Hömke and Reitz (eds.), *Lucan's 'Bellum ciuile': Between Epic Tradition and Aesthetic Innovation*. Berlin: 135–54.

Bleibtreu, E. (1991), 'Grisly Assyrian record of torture and death', *BAR* 17: 52–61.

Bloch, A. (1970), 'Arma virumque als heroisches Leitmotiv', *MH* 27: 206–11.

Bond, P. (2017), 'ISIS using Hollywood movies in recruiting propaganda', *The Hollywood Reporter*, 31 May. Available: www.hollywoodreporter.com/news/isis-using-more-hollywood-movies-recruiting-propaganda-1008796.

Bouckaert, P. (2013), 'Is this the most disgusting atrocity filmed in the Syrian civil war?: what we know about the Syrian rebel commander captured on video ripping out and eating the heart of a pro-Assad fighter', *Foreign Policy*, 14 May. Available: http://foreignpolicy.com/2013/05/14/is-this-the-most-disgusting-atrocity-filmed-in-the-syrian-civil-war/.

Bowie, A.M. (1990), 'The death of Priam: allegory and history in the *Aeneid*', *CQ* 40: 470–81.

Boyle, A.J. (1986), *The Chaonian Dove: Studies in the Eclogues, Georgics and Aeneid of Virgil*. Leiden.

(2006), *An Introduction to Roman Tragedy*. London.

(2008), *Octavia: Attributed to Seneca*. Oxford.

Bramble, J.C. (1983), 'Lucan', in Kenney and Clausen (eds.), *The Cambridge History of Classical Literature, Vol. II: Latin Literature, Part 4: The Early Principate*. Cambridge: 37–61.

Braund, S. (1992), *Lucan: Civil War*. Oxford.

(1997), 'Ending epic: Statius, Theseus and a merciful release', *PCPhS* 42: 1–23.

(2006), 'A tale of two cities: Statius, Thebes, and Rome', *Phoenix* 60: 259–73.

Braund, S., and G. Gilbert (2003), 'An ABC of epic *ira*: anger, beasts, and cannibalism', in Braund and Most (eds.), *Ancient Anger: Perspectives from Homer to Galen*. Cambridge: 250–85.

Bremmer, J.N. (1997), 'Why did Medea kill her brother Apsyrtus?', in Clauss and Johnston (eds.), *Medea: Essays on Medea in Myth, Literature, Philosophy, and Art*. Princeton: 83–100.

(2013), 'Human sacrifice in Euripides' *Iphigenia in Tauris*: Greek and barbarian', in Bonnechere and Gagné (eds.), *Sacrifices humains: perspectives croiseés et representations*. Liège: 87–100.

Bruère, R.T. (1951), 'Lucan's Cornelia', *CPh* 46: 221–36.

Buckley, E. (2010), 'War-epic for a new era: Valerius Flaccus' *Argonautica*', in Kramer and Reitz (eds.), *Tradition und Erneuerung: Mediale Strategien in der Zeit der Flavier*. Berlin: 431–55.

(2013), 'Visualizing Venus: epiphany and *anagnorisis* in Valerius Flaccus' *Argonautica*', in Lovatt and Vout (eds.), *Epic Visions: Visuality in Greek and Latin Epic and its Reception*. Cambridge: 78–98.

Burck, E. (1981), 'Epische Bestattungsszenen: Ein litterarhistorischer Vergleich', in Lefèvre (ed.), *Vom Menschenbild in der römischen Literatur II*. Heidelberg: 429–87.

(1984), *Historische und epische Tradition bei Silius Italicus*. Munich.

Burgess, J.S. (2001), *The Tradition of the Trojan War in Homer and the Epic Cycle*. Baltimore.

(2009), *The Death and Afterlife of Achilles*. Baltimore.

Butler, S. (2011), *The Matter of the Page: Essays in Search of Ancient and Medieval Authors*. Madison.

Byre, C.S. (1996), 'The killing of Apsyrtus in Apollonius Rhodius' *Argonautica*', *Phoenix* 50: 3–16.

Calonne, N. (2010), '*Cadauer* dans le *Bellum Ciuile*', in Devillers and Franchet-d'Espèrey (eds.), *Lucain en débat: rhétorique, poétique et histoire*. Bordeaux: 215–23.

Campbell, M. (1994), *A Commentary on Apollonius Rhodius Argonautica III 1–471*. Leiden.

Camps, W.A. (1969), *An Introduction to Virgil's Aeneid*. Oxford.

Carr, D. (2014), 'With videos of killings, ISIS sends medieval message by modern method', *The New York Times*, 7 Sept. Available: www.nytimes.com/2014/09/08/business/media/with-videos-of-killings-isis-hones-social-media-as-a-weapon.html?_r=1.

Carrié, J.-M. (1993), 'The soldier', in Giardina (ed.), *The Romans*, trans. Cochrane. Chicago: 100–37.

Carroll, N. (1990), *The Philosophy of Horror: Or, Paradoxes of the Heart*. New York.

Casali, S. (2011), 'The *Bellum ciuile* as an anti-*Aeneid*', in Asso (ed.), *Brill's Companion to Lucan*. Leiden: 81–110.

Castelletti, C. (2014), 'A hero with a sandal and a buskin: the figure of Jason in Valerius Flaccus' *Argonautica*', in Heerink and Manuwald (eds.), *Brill's Companion to Valerius Flaccus*. Leiden: 173–91.

Cavarero, A. (2002), *Stately Bodies: Literature, Philosophy, and the Question of Gender*, trans. de Lucca and Shemek. Ann Arbor.

(2009), *Horrorism: Naming Contemporary Violence*, trans. McCuaig. New York.

Ceulemans, R. (2007), 'Ritual mutilation in Apollonius Rhodius' *Argonautica*: a contextual analysis of IV, 477–479 in search of the motive of the μασχαλισμός', *Kernos* 20: 97–112.

Chaudhuri, P. (2014), *The War with God: Theomachy in Roman Imperial Poetry*. Oxford.

Chiesa, G. (2005), 'La rappresentazione del corpo nel *Bellum ciuile* di Lucano', *Acme* 58: 3–43.

Chinn, C.M. (2013), 'Orphic ritual and myth in the *Thebaid*', in Augoustakis (ed.), *Ritual and Religion in Flavian Epic*. Oxford: 319–34.

Chulov, M. (2016), 'Media jihad: why Isis's leaders bow to its propagandists', *The Guardian*, 4 Jan. Available: www.theguardian.com/world/2016/jan/04/med ia-jihad-why-isiss-leaders-bow-to-its-propagandists.

Clare, R.J. (2002), *The Path of the Argo*. Cambridge.

Clark, J. (2014), *Triumph in Defeat: Military Loss and the Roman Republic*. Oxford.

Clausen, W. (2002), *Virgil's Aeneid: Decorum, Allusion, and Ideology*. Munich.

Clausewitz, C. von (1976), *On War*, ed. and trans. Howard and Paret. Princeton.

Clauss, J.J. (1993), *The Best of the Argonauts: The Redefinition of the Epic Hero in Book One of Apollonius' Argonautica*. Berkeley.

Coffee, N. (2009), *The Commerce of War: Exchange and Social Order in Latin Epic*. Chicago.

Coleman, K.M. (1990), 'Fatal charades: Roman executions staged as mythological enactments', *JRS* 80: 44–73.

Cole, S.G. (2004), *Landscapes, Gender, and Ritual Space: The Ancient Greek Experience*. Berkeley.

Conte, G.B. (1968), 'La guerra civile nella rievocazione del popolo: Lucano II.67–233', *Maia* 20: 224–53.

(1999), *Latin Literature: A History*, trans. Solodow, revised by Fowler and Most. Baltimore.

(2007), *The Poetry of Pathos: Studies in Virgilian Epic*, ed. Harrison. Oxford.

Cottee, S. (2014), 'The pornography of jihadism: what ISIS videos and x-rated movies have in common', *The Atlantic*, 12 Sept. Available: www.theatlantic.com/interna tional/archive/2014/09/isis-jihadist-propaganda-videos-porn/380117/.

(2015), 'ISIS and the logic of shock: why each Islamic State video is more horrifying than the last', *The Atlantic*, 6 Feb. Available: www.theatlantic.co m/international/archive/2015/02/isis-and-the-logic-of-shock-jordan-video/3 85252/.

Cowan, R. (2007a), 'The headless city: the decline and fall of Capua in Silius Italicus' Punica', *ORA* 1542. Available: https://ora.ox.ac.uk/objects/uuid:dce b6b5a-980c-46ca-ac9e-088615e7fbea.

(2007b), 'Reading Trojan Rome: illegitimate epithets, avatars and the limits of analogy in Silius Italicus' Punica', *ORA* 1559. Available: https://ora.ox.ac.uk/ objects/uuid:11faca95-f158-4cef-a109-48b676c15baf.

(2014), 'My family and other enemies: Argonautic antagonists and Valerian villains', in Heerink and Manuwald (eds.), *Brill's Companion to Valerius Flaccus*. Leiden: 229–48.

Criado, C. (2015) 'The constitutional status of Euripidean and Statian Theseus: some aspects of the criticism of absolute power in the *Thebaid*', in Dominik, Newlands, and Gervais (eds.), *Brill's Companion to Statius*. Leiden: 291–306.

D'Alessandro Behr, F. (2007), *Feeling History: Lucan, Stoicism, and the Poetics of Passion*. Columbus.

Davies, M. (1989), *The Epic Cycle*. Bristol.

(1994), '*Odyssey* 22.474–7: murder or mutilation?', *CQ* 44: 534–6.

Day, H.J.M. (2013), *Lucan and the Sublime: Power, Representation and Aesthetic Experience*. Cambridge.

Dearden, L. (2017), 'Isis kills dozens of civilians caught attempting to flee Mosul and hangs bodies up on electricity poles: militants cracking down on attempted escapes while using human shields', *Independent*, 8 Apr. Available: www.indepen dent.co.uk/news/world/middle-east/mosul-offensive-latest-isis-advance-killing-c ivilians-fleeing-display-bodies-human-shields-iraq-a7674411.html.

Dekel, E. (2012), *Virgil's Homeric Lens*. New York.

De Grummond, N.T. (2006), *Etruscan Myth, Sacred History and Legend*. Philadelphia.

De Luna, G. (2006), *Il corpo del nemico ucciso: violenza e morte nella guerra contemporanea*. Turin.

Delvigo, M.L. (2013), '*Per transitum tangit historiam*: intersecting developments of Roman identity in Virgil', in Farrell and Nelis (eds.), *Augustan Poetry and the Roman Republic*. Oxford: 19–39.

Delz, J. (1974), 'Vorläufige Bestattung: zu Statius, Thebais 10,441; mit einem Anhang zu 4,750', *MH* 31: 42–5.

(1987), *Sili Italici Punica*. Stuttgart.

Derrida, J. (1985), 'Two words for Joyce', trans. Bennington, in Attridge and Ferrer (eds.), *Post-Structuralist Joyce: Essays from the French*. Cambridge: 145–60.

Dewar, M. (1991), *Statius: Thebaid IX*. Oxford.

Dietrich, J.E., (1999), '*Thebaid*'s feminine ending', *Ramus* 28: 40–53.

Dinter, M. (2009), 'Epic from epigram: the poetics of Valerius Flaccus' *Argonautica*', *AJPh* 130: 533–66.

(2012), *Anatomizing Civil War: Studies in Lucan's Epic Technique*. Ann Arbor.

Dominik, W.J. (1994a), *Speech and Rhetoric in Statius' Thebaid*. Hildesheim.

(1994b), *The Mythic Voice of Statius: Power and Politics in the Thebaid*. Leiden.

(2003), 'Hannibal at the gates: programmatising Rome and *romanitas* in Silius Italicus' *Punica* 1 and 2', in Boyle and Dominik (eds.), *Flavian Rome*. Leiden: 469–97.

(2006), 'Rome then and now: linking the Saguntum and Cannae episodes in Silius Italicus' *Punica*', in Nauta, Van Dam, and Smolenaars (eds.), *Flavian Poetry*. Leiden: 113–27.

(2010), 'The reception of Silius Italicus in modern scholarship', in Augoustakis (ed.), *Brill's Companion to Silius Italicus*. Leiden: 425–47.

Dowden, K. (2004), 'The epic tradition in Greece', in Fowler (ed.), *The Cambridge Companion to Homer*. Cambridge: 188–205.

Duff, J.D. (1928), *Lucan: The Civil War*. Cambridge, MA.

Dunn, F. (2018), 'The mutilation of Agamemnon (A. *Ch.* 439 and S. *El.* 445)', *Mnemosyne* 71: 195–208.

Dyson, J.T. (2001), *King of the Wood: The Sacrificial Victor in Virgil's Aeneid*. Norman.

Eagleton, T. (2008), *Literary Theory: An Introduction*. Minneapolis.

Edgeworth, R. (1986), 'The ivory gate and the threshold of Apollo', *C&M* 37: 145–60.

   (2005), 'The silence of Vergil and the end of the *Aeneid*', ed. by Stem, *Vergilius* 51: 3–11.

Edmunds, L. (2001), *Intertextuality and the Reading of Roman Poetry*. Baltimore.

Edwards, C. (2007), *Death in Ancient Rome*. New Haven.

Effe, B. (2008), 'The similes of Apollonius Rhodius: intertextuality and epic innovation', in Papanghelis and Rengakos (eds.), *Brill's Companion to Apollonius Rhodius*, 2nd ed. Leiden: 199–220.

Elmer, D.F. (2008), '*Epikoinos*: the ball game *episkuros* and *Iliad* 12.421-23', *CPh* 103: 414–23.

   (2013), *The Poetics of Consent: Collective Decision Making and the Iliad*. Baltimore.

Erasmo, M. (2008), *Reading Death in Ancient Rome*. Columbus.

Erskine, A. (2002), 'Life after death: Alexandria and the body of Alexander', *G&R* 49: 163–79.

Esposito, P. (1996), 'La morte di Pompeo in Lucano', in Brugnoli and Stok (eds.), *Pompei exitus: variazioni sul tema dall'Antichità alla Controriforma*. Pisa: 75–124.

Estèves, A. (2010), 'Les têtes coupées dans le *Bellum Ciuile* de Lucain: des guerres civiles placées sous l'emblème de Méduse', in Devillers and Franchet-d'Espèrey (eds.), *Lucain en débat: rhétorique, poétique et histoire*. Bordeaux: 203–13.

Evans, B., and H.A. Giroux (2015), *Disposable Futures: The Seduction of Violence in the Age of Spectacle*. San Francisco.

Fagan, G.G. (2011), *The Lure of the Arena: Social Psychology and the Crowd at the Roman Games*. Cambridge.

Fantham, E. (1992a), *M. Annaei Lucani de Bello Ciuili Liber Secundus*. Cambridge.

   (1992b), 'Lucan's Medusa-excursus: its design and purpose', *MD* 28: 95–119.

   (1997), '"Envy and fear the begetter of hate": Statius' *Thebaid* and the genesis of hatred', in Braund and Gill (eds.), *The Passions in Roman Thought and Literature*. Cambridge: 185–212.

   (1999), 'The role of lament in the growth and eclipse of Roman epic', in Beissinger, Tylus, and Wofford (eds.), *Epic Traditions in the Contemporary World: The Poetics of Community*. Berkeley: 221–35.

   (2011), *Roman Readings: Roman Responses to Greek Literature from Plautus to Statius and Quintilian*. Berlin.

Farrell, J. (1999), 'The Ovidian corpus: poetic body and poetic text', in Hardie, Barchiesi, and Hinds (eds.), *Ovidian Transformations: Essays on Ovid's 'Metamorphoses' and its Reception*. Cambridge: 126–41.

(2005), 'Intention and intertext', *Phoenix* 59: 98–111.

(2007), 'Horace's body, Horace's books', in Heyworth (ed.), *Classical Constructions: Papers in Memory of Don Fowler, Classicist and Epicurean.* Oxford: 174–93.

Farron, S.G. (1985), 'Aeneas' human sacrifice', *AClass* 28: 21–33.

(1986), 'Aeneas' revenge for Pallas as a criticism of Aeneas', *AClass* 29: 69–83.

Faust, M. (1970), 'Die künstlerische Verwendung von κύων "Hund" in den homerischen Epen', *Glotta* 48: 8–31.

Feeney, D. (1986), 'History and revelation in Vergil's underworld', *PCPhS* NS 32: 1–24.

(1991), *The Gods in Epic: Poets and Critics the Classical Tradition.* Oxford.

(1999), 'Epic violence, epic order: killings, catalogues, and the role of the reader in *Aeneid* 10', in Perkell (ed.), *Reading Vergil's Aeneid: An Interpretive Guide.* Norman: 178–94.

(2010), '"*Stat magni nominis umbra*": Lucan on the greatness of Pompeius Magnus', in Tesoriero (ed.), *Lucan: Oxford Readings in Classical Studies.* Oxford: 346–54.

Fenik, B. (1968), *Typical Battle Scenes in the Iliad.* Wiesbaden.

Ferenczi, A. (1995), '*Sine honore labores*: Zum Virtusbegriff bei Valerius Flaccus', *Philologus* 139: 147–56.

Finiello, C. (2005), 'Der Bürgerkrieg: Reine Männersache? Keine Männersache! Erictho und die Frauengestalten im *Bellum Ciuile* Lucans', in Walde (ed.), *Lucan im 21. Jahrhundert/Lucan in the 21st Century.* Munich: 155–85.

Fitch, J.G. (1976), 'Aspects of Valerius Flaccus' use of similes', *TAPhA* 106: 113–24.

Flower, H. (1996), *Ancestor Masks and Aristocratic Power in Roman Culture.* Oxford.

Fowler, D. (1987), 'Vergil on killing virgins', in Whitby, Hardie, and Whitby (eds.), *Homo Viator: Classical Essays for John Bramble.* Bristol: 185–98.

(1990), 'Deviant focalisation in Virgil's *Aeneid*', *PCPhS* 36: 42–63.

(1997a), 'On the shoulders of giants: intertextuality and classical studies', *MD* 39: 13–34.

(1997b), 'Virgilian narrative: story-telling', in Martindale (ed.), *The Cambridge Companion to Virgil.* Cambridge: 259–70.

(2000), *Roman Constructions: Readings in Postmodern Latin.* Oxford.

Franchet d'Espèrey, S. (1999), *Conflit, violence et non-violence dans la Thébaïde de Stace.* Paris.

Fraenkel, E. (1964), *Kleine Beiträge zur klassischen Philologie.* Vol. 2, Zur römischen Literatur. Rome.

Frame, D. (2009), *Hippota Nestor.* Washington, DC.

Francken, C.M. (1896–1897), *M. Annaei Lucani Pharsalia. Cum commentario critico.* Utrecht.

Fränkel, H. (1968), *Noten zu den Argonaitika des Apollonios.* Munich.

Fratantuono, L. (2007), *Madness Unchained: A Reading of Virgil's Aeneid.* Lexington.

(2012), *Madness Triumphant: A Reading of Lucan's Pharsalia.* Lexington.

Freudenburg, K. (1993), *The Walking Muse: Horace on the Theory of Satire.* Princeton.

Friedrich, W.-H. (2003), *Wounding and Death in the Iliad: Homeric Techniques of Description*, trans. Jones and Wright. Bristol.

Fröhlich, U. (2000), *Regulus, Archetyp römischer Fides: Das sechste Buch als Schlüssel zu den Punica des Silius Italicus. Interpretation, Kommentar und Übersetzung.* Tübingen.

Fucecchi, M. (1990), 'Il decline di Annibale nei *Punica*', *Maia*, 42: 151–66.

    (1993), 'Lo spettacolo delle virtù nel giovane eroe predestinato: analisi della figura di Scipione in Silio Italico', *Maia* 45: 17–48.

    (1996), 'Il restauro dei modelli antichi: tradizione epica e tecnica manieristica in Valerio Flacco', *MD* 36: 101–65.

    (1997), *La teichoskopia e l'innamoramento di Medea: saggio di commento a Valerio Flacco Argonautiche 6, 427–760.* Pisa.

    (2006), *Una guerra in Colchide: Valerio Flacco, Argonautiche 6, 1–426.* Pisa.

    (2011a), '*ad finem uentum*: considerazioni sull'ultimo libro dei *Punica*', in Castagna, Biffino, and Riboldi (eds.), *Studi su Silio Italico*. Milan: 299–333.

    (2011b), 'Partisans in civil war', in Asso (ed.), *Brill's Companion to Lucan.* Leiden: 237–56.

    (2012), 'Epica, filosofia della storia e legittimazione del potere imperiale: la profezia di Giove nel libro III dei *Punica* (e un'indicazione di percorso per l'epos storico)', in Baier (ed.), *Götter und menschliche Willensfreiheit: Von Lucan bis Silius Italicus.* Munich: 235–54.

Fulkerson, L. (2008), 'Patterns of death in the *Aeneid*', *SCI* 27: 17–33.

Fusillo, M. (1985), *Il tempo delle Argonautiche: un'analisi del racconto in Apollonio Rodio.* Rome.

Gale, M. (2000), *Virgil on the Nature of Things: The Georgics, Lucretius and the Didactic Tradition.* Cambridge.

Gale, M., and J. Scourfield (2018), 'Introduction: reading Roman violence', in Gale and Scourfield (eds.), *Texts and Violence in the Roman World.* Cambridge: 1–43.

Gallia, A.B. (2012), *Remember the Roman Republic: Culture, Politics, and History Under the Principate.* Cambridge.

Galtier, F. (2010), 'Un tombeau pour un grand nom: le traitement de la dépouille de Pompée chez Lucain', in Devillers and Franchet-d'Espèrey (eds.), *Lucain en débat: rhétorique, poétique et histoire.* Bordeaux: 193–202.

Ganiban, R.T. (2007), *Statius and Virgil: The Thebaid and the Reinterpretation of the Aeneid.* Cambridge.

    (2013), 'The death and funeral rites of Opheltes in the *Thebaid*', in Augoustakis (ed.), *Ritual and Religion in Flavian Epic.* Oxford: 249–66.

Gantz, T. (1993), *Early Greek Myth: A Guide to Literary and Artistic Sources.* 2 vols. Baltimore.

Garland, R. (1985), *The Greek Way of Death.* Ithaca.

Georgy, M. (2017), 'Iraqi forces wage psychological war with jihadist corpses', *Reuters*, 6 Feb. Available: www.reuters.com/article/us-mideast-crisis-mosul-corpses-idUSKBN15L1OT.

Gervais, K. (2013), 'Viewing violence in Statius' *Thebaid* and the films of Quentin Tarantino', in Lovatt and Vout (eds.), *Epic Visions: Visuality in Greek and Latin Epic and its Reception.* Cambridge: 139–67.

(2015), 'Tydeus the hero? Intertextual confusion in Statius, *Thebaid* 2', *Phoenix* 69: 56–78.

(2017), *Statius, Thebaid 2.* Oxford.

Gibson, B., (2008), 'Battle narrative in Statius, *Thebaid*', in Smolenaars, van Dam, and Nauta (eds.), *The Poetry of Statius.* Leiden: 85–110.

Gioseffi, M. (1995), 'La "deprecatio" lucanea sui cadaveri insepolti a Farsalo (b. civ. VII 825–846)', *BStudLat* 25: 501–20.

Giusti, E. (2016), 'Did somebody say Augustan totalitarianism? Duncan Kennedy's "Reflections", Hannah Arendt's *Origins*, and the continental divide over Virgil's *Aeneid*', *Dictynna* 13. Available: http://journals.openedi tion.org/dictynna/1282.

Glei, R.F. (2008), 'Outlines of Apollonian scholarship 1955–1999', in Papanghelis and Rengakos (eds.), *Brill's Companion to Apollonius Rhodius*, 2nd ed. Leiden: 1–28.

Goldhill, S. (1991), *The Poet's Voice: Essays on Poetics and Greek Literature.* Cambridge.

Gordon, R. (1987), 'Lucan's Erictho', in Whitby, Hardie, and Whitby (eds.), *Homo Viator. Classical Essays for John Bramble.* Bristol: 231–41.

Gowers, E. (2005), 'Virgil's Sibyl and the "many mouths" cliché (*Aen.* 6.625–7)', *CQ* 55: 170–82.

Gowing, A. (2005), *Empire and Memory: The Representation of the Roman Republic in Imperial Culture.* Cambridge.

(2010), '"Caesar grabs my pen": writing civil war under Tiberius', in Breed, Damon, and Rossi (eds.), *Citizens of Discord: Rome and its Civil Wars.* Oxford: 249–60.

Grayling, A.C. (2017), *War: An Inquiry.* New Haven.

Green, C.M.C. (2010), '*Stimulos dedit aemula uirtus*: Lucan and Homer reconsidered', in Tesoriero (ed.), *Lucan: Oxford Readings in Classical Studies.* Oxford: 149–83.

Green, P. (1997), *The Argonautika.* Berkeley.

Grenade, P. (1950), 'Le mythe de Pompée et les Pompéiens sous les Césars', *REA* 52: 28–63.

Griffin, J. (1977), 'The epic cycle and the uniqueness of Homer', *JHS* 97: 39–53.

(1980), *Homer on Life and Death.* Oxford.

Griffiths, F.T. (1990), 'Murder, purification, and cultural formation in Aeschylus and Apollonius Rhodius', *Helios* 17: 25–39.

Guyer, P., ed. (2000), *Immanuel Kant: Critique of the Power of Judgment*, trans. Guyer and Matthews. Cambridge.

Håkanson, L. (1973), *Statius' Thebaid: Critical and Exegetical Remarks.* Lund.

(1979), 'Textual problems in Lucan's *De bello ciuili*', *PCPhS* 205: 26–51.

Hammond, P., and Hopkins, D. (2000), *The Poems of John Dryden, Volume 4: 1693–1696.* New York.

Hardie, A. (1983), *Statius and the Siluae: Poets, Patrons and Epideixis in the Graeco-Roman World.* Liverpool.

Hardie, P. (1986), *Virgil's Aeneid: Cosmos and Imperium*. Oxford.

(1989), 'Flavian epicists on Virgil's epic technique', *Ramus* 18: 3–20.

(1993), *The Epic Successors of Virgil*. Cambridge.

(1994), *Virgil, Aeneid: Book IX*. Cambridge.

(1997), 'Closure in Latin epic', in Roberts, Dunn, and Fowler (eds.), *Classical Closure: Reading the End in Greek and Latin Literature*. Princeton: 139–62.

(2002), *Ovid's Poetics of Illusion*. Cambridge.

(2008), 'Lucan's song of the earth', in Congano and Milano (eds.), *Papers on Ancient Literatures: Greece, Rome and the Near East*. Padova: 305–30.

Harper Smith, A. (1987), 'A commentary on Valerius Flaccus' Argonautica II'. Diss., University of Oxford.

Harrison, S.J. (1988), 'Vergil as a poet of war', *PVS* 19: 46–68.

(1991), *Vergil Aeneid 10*. Oxford.

(2009), 'Picturing the future again: proleptic ekphrasis in Silius' Punica', in Augoustakis (ed.), *Brill's Companion to Silius Italicus*. Leiden: 279–92.

Heerink, M. (2016), 'Virgil, Lucan, and the meaning of civil war in Valerius Flaccus' *Argonautica*', *Mnemosyne* 69: 511–25.

Heinze, R. (1993), *Virgil's Epic Technique*, trans. Harvey, Harvey, and Robertson. Berkeley.

Helzle, M. (1996), *Der Stil ist der Mensch: Redner und Reden im römischen Epos*. Stuttgart.

Henderson, J.G.W. (1998), *Fighting for Rome: Poets and Caesars, History and Civil War*. Cambridge.

Hershkowitz, D. (1995), 'Patterns of madness in Statius' *Thebaid*', *JRS* 85: 52–64.

(1998a), *The Madness of Epic: Reading Insanity from Homer to Statius*. Oxford.

(1998b), *Valerius Flaccus' Argonautica: Abbreviated Voyages in Silver Latin Epic*. Oxford.

Heslin, P.J. (2008), 'Statius and the Greek tragedians on Athens, Thebes, and Rome', in Smolenaars, van Dam, and Nauta (eds.), *The Poetry of Statius*. Leiden: 111–28.

Heubeck, A. (1992), 'Books XXIII–XXIV', in Heubeck, West, and Hainsworth (eds.), *A Commentary on Homer's Odyssey* vol. 3. Oxford: 311–418.

Heuzé, P. (1985), *L'image du corps dans l'œuvre de Virgile*. Paris.

Hill, D.E (1983), *P. Papini Stati Thebaidos Libri XII*. Leiden.

Hinard, F. (1984), 'La male mort: exécutions et statut du corps au moment de la première proscription', in *Du châtiment dans la cité*. Rome: 295–311.

(1985), *Les proscriptions de la Rome républicaine*. Rome.

Hinds, S. (1998), *Allusion and Intertext*. Cambridge.

Holmes, B. (2010), *The Symptom and the Subject: The Emergence of the Physical Body in Ancient Greece*. Princeton.

Hömke, N., (2010), 'Bit by bit towards death: Lucan's Scaeva and the aesthetisization of dying', in Hömke and Reitz (eds.), *Lucan's 'Bellum ciuile': Between Epic Tradition and Aesthetic Innovation*. Berlin: 91–104.

Hope, V.M. (2000), 'Contempt and respect: the treatment of the corpse in ancient Rome', in Hope and Marshall (eds.), *Death and Disease in the Ancient City*. London: 104–27.

(2015), 'Bodies on the battlefield: the spectacle of Rome's fallen soldiers', in Bakogianni and Hope (eds.), *War as Spectacle: Ancient and Modern Perspectives on the Display of Armed Conflict*. London: 157–77.

Hopkins, K. (1983), *Death and Renewal*. Cambridge.

Horsfall, N.M., ed. (1995), *A Companion to the Study of Virgil*. Leiden.

(2003), *Vergil, Aeneid 11*. Leiden.

(2008), *Virgil, Aeneid 2: A Commentary*. Leiden.

(2010), 'Pictures from an execution', in Dijkstra, Kroesen, and Kuiper (eds.), *Myths, Martyrs, and Modernity: Studies in the History of Religions in Honour of Jan N. Bremmer*. Leiden: 237–47.

(2016), *The Epic Distilled: Studies in the Composition of the Aeneid*. Oxford.

Housman, A.E. (1927), *M. Annaei Lucani Belli ciuilis libri decem*. 2nd ed. Oxford.

Hübner, U. (1987), 'Vergilisches in der Amyclasepisode der Pharsalia', *RhM* 130: 48–58.

Hunink, (1992), *M. Annaeus Lucanus: Bellum ciuile Book III: A Commentary*. Amsterdam.

Hunter R. (1989), *Apollonius of Rhodes: Argonautica III*. Cambridge.

(1993), *The Argonautica of Apollonius: Literary Studies*. Cambridge.

(2015), *Apollonius of Rhodes: Argonautica Book IV*. Cambridge.

Hutchinson, G.O. (1988), *Hellenistic Poetry*. Oxford.

(1993), *Latin Literature from Seneca to Juvenal*. Oxford.

(2013), *Greek to Latin: Frameworks and Contexts for Intertextuality*. Oxford.

Jacobs, J. (2010), 'From Sallust to Silius Italicus: Metus Hostilis and the fall of Rome in the *Punica*', in Miller and Woodman (eds.), *Latin Historiography and Poetry in the Early Empire*. Leiden: 123–40.

James, S.L. (1995), 'Establishing Rome with the sword: *condere* in the *Aeneid*', *AJPh* 116: 623–37.

Janko, R. (1992), *The Iliad: A Commentary: Vol. 4, Books 13–16*. Cambridge.

Jenkins, B.M. (1974), 'International terrorism: a new kind of warfare', *The Rand Paper Series*. Available: www.rand.org/pubs/papers/P5261.html.

Jenkyns, R. (1985) 'Pathos, tragedy and hope in the *Aeneid*', *JRS* 75: 60–77.

Jervis, A.E. (2001), 'Talking heads: the iconography of mutilation in the Roman Republic'. Diss., Stanford.

Johnson, W.R. (1987), *Momentary Monsters: Lucan and His Heroes*. Ithaca.

Johnston, S.I. (1999), *Restless Dead: Encounters between the Living and the Dead in Ancient Greece*. Berkeley.

Jones, P. (2005), *Reading Rivers in Roman Literature and Culture*. Lexington.

de Jong, I.J.F. (1987), *Narrators and Focalizers: The Presentation of the Story in the Iliad*. Amsterdam.

(2012), *Homer: Iliad Book 22*. Cambridge.

Joyce, J.W. (2008), *Thebaid: A Song of Thebes*. Ithaca.

Juhnke, H. (1972), *Homerisches in römischer Epik flavischer Zeit: Untersuchungen zu Szenennachbildungen und Strukturentsprechungen in Statius' Thebais und Achilleis und in Silius' Punica*. Munich.

Kang, J.C. (2014), 'ISIS's call of duty', *The New Yorker*, 18 Sept. Available: www .newyorker.com/tech/elements/isis-video-game.

Keith, A.M. (1999), 'Slender verse: Roman elegy and ancient rhetorical theory', *Mnemosyne* 52: 41–62.

(2002), 'Ovidian personae in Statius' *Thebaid*', *Arethusa* 35: 381–402.

(2008), 'Lament in Lucan's *Bellum ciuile*', in Suter (ed.), *Lament: Studies in the Ancient Mediterranean and Beyond*. Oxford: 233–57.

Kelly, G.P. (2014), 'Battlefield supplication in the *Iliad*', *CW* 107: 147–67.

Kennedy, D.F. (2018), 'Dismemberment and the critics: Seneca's *Phaedra*', in Gale and Scourfield (eds.), *Texts and Violence in the Roman World*. Cambridge: 215–45.

van der Keur, M. (2013), 'Of corpses, carnivores and cecropian pyres: funeral rites in Silius and Statius', in Manuwald and Voigt (eds.), *Flavian Epic Interactions*. Berlin: 327–42.

Kierdorf, W. (1979), 'Die Leichenrede auf Pompejus in Lucans Pharsalia (9, 190ff.)', *WJA* 5: 157–62.

(1980), *Laudatio Funebris: Interpretationen und Untersuchungen zur Entwicklung der römischen Leichenrede*. Meisenheim.

King, K.C. (1982), 'Foil and fusion: Homer's Achilles in Vergil's *Aeneid*', *MD* 9: 31–57.

Kirk, G.S. (1990), *The Iliad: A Commentary: Vol 2, Books 5–8*. Cambridge.

Kißel, W. (1979), *Das Geschichtsbild des Silius Italicus*. Frankfurt.

Klaassen, E.K. (2009), 'Imitation and the hero', in Augoustakis (ed.), *Brill's Companion to Silius Italicus*. Leiden: 99–126.

Klay, P. (2014), *Redeployment*. New York.

Kleywegt, A.J. (2005), *Valerius Flaccus, Argonautica Book 1: A Commentary*. Leiden.

Knauer, G.N. (1964), *Die Aeneis und Homer: Studien zur poetischen Technik Vergils mit Listen der Homerzitate in der Aeneis*. Göttingen.

Knight, V. (1995), *The Renewal of Epic: Responses to Homer in the Argonautica of Apollonius*. Leiden.

Korenjak, M. (1996), *Die Ericthoszene in Lukans Pharsalia: Einleitung, Text, Übersetzung, Kommentar*. Frankfurt.

Korsmeyer, C. (2011), *Savoring Disgust: The Foul and the Fair in Aesthetics*. Oxford.

Krischer, T. (1971), *Formale Konventionen der homerischen Epik*. Munich.

Kristeva, J. (1982), *Powers of Horror: An Essay on Abjection*, trans. Roudiez. New York.

(2012), *The Severed Head: Capital Visions*, trans. Gladding. New York.

Kubiak, D. (1990), 'Cornelia and Dido (Lucan 9, 174–9)', *CQ* 40: 577–8.

Kucewicz, C. (2016), 'Mutilation of the dead and the Homeric gods', *CQ* 66: 425–36.

Kullmann, W. (2015), 'Motif and source research: neoanalysis, Homer, and the Cyclic epic', in Fantuzzi and Tsagalis (eds.), *The Greek Epic Cycle and its Ancient Reception: A Companion.* Cambridge: 108–25.

Küppers, J. (1986), *Tantarum causas irarum: Untersuchungen zur einleitenden Bücherdyade der Punica des Silius Italicus.* Berlin.

Kyle, D.G. (1998), *Spectacles of Death in Ancient Rome.* London.

Landrey, L. (2014), 'Skeletons in armor: Silius Italicus' *Punica* and the *Aeneid*'s proem', *AJPh* 135: 599–635.

Langen, P. (1896), *C. Valeri Flacci Setini Balbi Argonauticon Libri Octo.* Berlin.

Larson, F. (2014), *Severed: A History of Heads Lost and Heads Found.* New York.

(2015), 'ISIS beheadings: why we're too horrified to watch, too fascinated to turn away', *CNN*, 13 Jan. Available: www.cnn.com/2015/01/13/opinion/beh eadings-history/index.html.

Lausberg, M. (1985), 'Lucan und Homer', ANRW 2.32.3: 1565–1622.

Leigh, M. (1997), *Lucan: Spectacle and Engagement.* Oxford.

Lindenlauf, A. (2001), 'Thrown away like rubbish: disposal of the dead in ancient Greece', *Papers from the Institute of Archaeology* 12: 86–99.

Lindsay, H. (2000), 'Death-pollution and funerals in the city of Rome', in Hope and Marshall (eds.), *Death and Disease in the Ancient City.* London: 152–73.

Littlewood, R.J. (2017), *A Commentary on Silius Italicus' Punica 10.* Oxford.

Livrea, E. (1973), *Apollonii Rhodii Argonauticon Liber Quartus.* Florence.

Lohmar, J.M. (2013), 'The anatomy of Roman epic: a study of poetic violence'. Diss., University of Florida.

Loupiac, A. (1998), *La poétique des éléments dans La Pharsale de Lucain.* Brussels.

Lovatt, H. (1999), 'Competing endings: re-reading the end of Statius' *Thebaid* through Lucan', *Ramus* 28: 126–51.

(2005), *Statius and Epic Games: Sport, Politics and Poetics in the Thebaid.* Cambridge.

(2007), 'Statius, Orpheus and the post-Augustan *uates*', *Arethusa* 40: 145–63.

(2010), 'Cannibalising history: Livian moments in Statius' *Thebaid*', in Miller and Woodman (eds.), *Latin Historiography and Poetry in the Early Empire.* Leiden: 71–86.

(2013), *The Epic Gaze: Vision, Gender, and Narrative in Ancient Epic.* Cambridge.

Lyne, R.O.A.M. (1989), *Words and the Poet: Characteristic Techniques of Style in Vergil's Aeneid.* Oxford.

(1990), 'Vergil and the politics of war', in Harrison (ed.), *Oxford Readings in Vergil's Aeneid.* Oxford: 316–38.

Ma, A. (2018), 'ISIS ripped off a scene from "The Lord of the Rings" in its latest propaganda video', *Business Insider*, 24 May. Available: www.businessinsider .com/isis-rips-off-lord-of-the-rings-scene-for-propaganda-video-2018-5.

MacKay, L.A. (1963), 'Hero and theme in the *Aeneid*', *TAPhA* 94: 157–66.

Macleod, C.W. (1982), *Homer: Iliad Book 24.* Cambridge.

MacSwan, A. (2016), 'Both sides accused of abuses in battle for Mosul', *Reuters*, 15 Nov. Available: www.reuters.com/article/us-mideast-crisis-iraq-abuses-idUSKBN13A1I4.

Malamud, M. (1995), 'Happy birthday, dead Lucan: (P)raising the Dead in *Siluae* 2.7', *Ramus* 24: 1–30.

   (2003), 'Pompey's head and Cato's snakes', *CPh* 98: 31–44.

Manuwald, G. (2009), 'History in pictures: commemorative ecphrases in Silius Italicus' *Punica*', *Phoenix* 63: 38–59.

   (2015), *Valerius Flaccus: Argonautica Book III*. Cambridge.

Marincola, J. (2010), 'Eros and empire: Virgil and the historians on civil war', in Kraus, Marincola, and Pelling (eds.), *Ancient Historiography and its Contexts*. Oxford: 183–204.

Marks, R.D. (2003), 'Hannibal in Liternum', in Thibodeau and Haskell (eds.), *Being There Together: Essays in Honor of Michael C.J. Putnam on the Occasion of his Seventieth Birthday*. Afton: 128–44.

   (2005a), *From Republic to Empire: Scipio Africanus in the Punica of Silius Italicus*. Frankfurt.

   (2005b), '*Per uulnera regnum*: self-destruction, self-sacrifice, and *deuotio* in *Punica* 4-10', *Ramus* 34: 127–51.

   (2008), 'Getting ahead: decapitation as political metaphor in Silius Italicus' *Punica*', *Mnemosyne* 61: 66–88.

   (2009), 'Silius and Lucan', in Augoustakis (ed.), *Brill's Companion to Silius Italicus*. Leiden: 127–54.

   (2014), 'Statio-Silian relations in the *Thebaid* and *Punica* 1-2', *CPh* 109: 130–9.

Markus, D. (2003), 'The politics of epic performance in Statius', in Boyle and Dominik (eds.), *Flavian Rome*. Leiden: 431–68.

Marpicati, P. (1999), 'Silio "delatore" di Pompeo (Pun. 5, 328 ss.; 10, 305 ss.)', *MD* 43: 191–202.

Martindale, C.A. (1976), 'Paradox, hyperbole, and literary novelty in Lucan's *De bello ciuili*', *BICS* 23: 45–54.

   (1993), *Redeeming the Text: Latin Poetry and the Hermeneutics of Reception*. Cambridge.

Masters, J. (1992), *Poetry and Civil War in Lucan's Bellum Ciuile*. Cambridge.

Matthews, M. (2008), *Caesar and the Storm: A Commentary on Lucan, De Bello Ciuili, Book 5, lines 476–721*. Oxford.

Mayer, R. (1981), *Lucan Civil War VIII*. Warminster.

Mayor, J.E.B. (1979), *Thirteen Satires of Juvenal, with a Commentary*. New York.

Mazzocchini, P. (2000), *Forme e significati della narrazione bellica nell'epos virgiliano: i cataloghi degli uccisi e le morti minori nell'Eneide*. Fasano.

McAuley, M. (2016), *Reproducing Rome: Motherhood in Virgil, Ovid, Seneca, and Statius*. Oxford.

McClellan, A.M. (2017), 'The death and mutilation of Imbrius in *Iliad* 13', in Ready and Tsagalis (eds.), *Yearbook of Ancient Greek Epic, vol. 1*. Leiden: 159–74.

(2018), 'The politics of revivification in Lucan's *Bellum ciuile* and Mary Shelley's *Frankenstein*', in Weiner, Stevens, and Rogers (eds.), *Frankenstein and Its Classics: The Modern Prometheus from Antiquity to Science Fiction.* London: 59–75.

(Forthcoming), 'Lucan's Neronian *res publica restituta*,'' in Thorne and Zientek (eds.), *Lucan's Imperial World.* London.

McGuire, D.T. (1997), *Acts of Silence: Civil War, Tyranny, and Suicide in the Flavian Epics.* Hildesheim.

McKeown, J.C. (1987), *Ovid's Amores I: Text and Prolegomena.* Liverpool.

McNelis, C. (2004), 'Middle-march: Statius' *Thebaid* and the beginning of battle narrative', in Kyriakidis and De Martino (eds.), *Middles in Latin Poetry.* Bari: 261–310.

(2007), *Statius' Thebaid and the Poetics of Civil War.* Cambridge.

Mebane, D. (2009), 'The Nisus and Euryalus episode and Roman friendship', *Phoenix* 63: 239–59.

Mebane, J. (2016), 'Pompey's head and the body politic in Lucan's *De bello ciuili*', *TAPA* 146: 191–215.

Mikalson, J.D. (1991), *Honor Thy Gods: Popular Religion in Greek Tragedy.* Chapel Hill.

Miller, S. (2014), *War After Death: On Violence and Its Limits.* New York.

Miller, W.I. (1993), *Humiliation: And Other Essays on Honor, Social Discomfort, and Violence.* Ithaca.

(1997), *The Anatomy of Disgust.* Cambridge, MA.

Mills, F. (2009), 'The agony of departure: Silius Italicus' *Punica* 17.149-290', *Antichthon* 43: 50–63.

Monro, D.B., and Allen, T.W. (1920), *Homeri Opera.* Oxford.

Moretti, G. (1985), 'Truncus ed altro: appunti sull'immaginario filosofico e scientifico-didascalico nella *Pharsalia*', *Maia* 37: 135–44.

Morford, M.P.O. (1967), *The Poet Lucan: Studies in Rhetorical Epic.* Oxford.

Mori, A. (2008), *The Politics of Apollonius Rhodius' Argonautica.* Cambridge.

Morrison, J.V. (1992), *Homeric Misdirection: False Predictions in the Iliad.* Ann Arbor.

Most, G.W. (1992), '*Disiecti membra poetae*: the rhetoric of dismemberment in Neronian poetry', in Hexter and Selden (eds.), *Innovations of Antiquity.* New York: 391–419.

Mozley, J.H. (1934), *Valerius Flaccus.* Cambridge, MA.

Mueller, M. (1984), *The Iliad.* London.

Murgatroyd, P. (2008), 'Amycus' cave in Valerius Flaccus', *CQ* 58: 382–6.

(2009), *A Commentary on Book 4 of Valerius Flaccus' Argonautica.* Leiden.

Murnaghan, S. (1997), 'Equal honor and future glory: the plan of Zeus in the *Iliad*', in Roberts, Dunn, and Fowler (eds.), *Classical Closure: Reading the End in Greek and Latin Literature.* Princeton: 23–42.

Murray, G. (1961), *The Rise of the Greek Epic.* 4th ed. Oxford.

Myers, M.Y. (2011), 'Lucan's poetic geographies: center and periphery in civil war epic', in Asso (ed.), *Brill's Companion to Lucan.* Leiden: 399–415.

Mynors, R.A.B (1969), *P. Vergili Maronis Opera*. Oxford.

Narducci, E. (1973), 'Il tronco di Pompeo (Troia e Roma nella *Pharsalia*)', *Maia* 25: 317–25.

(2002), *Lucano: un'epica contro l'impero*. Rome.

Neal, T. (2006a), *The Wounded Hero: Non-Fatal Injury in Homer's Iliad*. Frankfurt.

(2006b), 'Blood and hunger in the *Iliad*', *CPh* 101: 15–33.

Nelis, D.P. (1991), 'Iphias: Apollonius Rhodius, *Argonautica* 1.311-16', *CQ* 41: 96–105.

Newlands, C.E. (2002), *Statius' Siluae and the Poetics of Empire*. Cambridge.

(2009), 'Statius' self-conscious poetics: hexameter on hexameter', in Dominik, Garthwaite, and Roche (eds.), *Writing Politics in Imperial Rome*. Leiden: 387–404.

(2011a), 'The first "biography" of Lucan: Statius *Siluae* 2.7', in Asso (ed.), *Brill's Companion to Lucan*. Leiden: 435–51.

(2011b), *Statius: Siluae Book 2*. Cambridge.

(2012), *Statius, Poet Between Rome and Naples*. London.

Nicolson, A. (2014), 'Homer and ISIS: what the author of the *Iliad* tells us about blood on the sand', *Slate*, 29 Dec. Available: www.slate.com/articles/arts/cu lturebox/2014/12/homer_and_isis_what_the_iliad_tells_us_about_the_mo dern_middle_east.html.

Nippel, W. (1995), *Public Order in Ancient Rome*. Cambridge.

Nisbet, R.G.M. (1978–80), '*Aeneas imperator*: Roman generalship in an epic context', *PVS* 17: 50–9.

Nisbet, R.G.M., and N. Rudd (2004), *A Commentary on Horace: Odes Book III*. Oxford.

Nix, S.A. (2008), 'Caesar as Jupiter in Lucan's "Bellum ciuile"', *CJ* 103: 281–94.

Noy, D. (2000), '"Half-burnt on an emergency pyre": Roman cremations which went wrong', *G&R* 47: 186–96.

Nünlist, R. (2009), *The Ancient Critic at Work: Terms and Concepts of Literary Criticism in Greek Scholia*. Cambridge.

O'Hara, J.J. (1990), *Death and the Optimistic Prophecy in Vergil's Aeneid*. Princeton.

(2007), *Inconsistency in Roman Epic*. Cambridge.

O'Higgins, D. (1988), 'Lucan as *uates*', *ClAnt* 7: 208–26.

Oliensis, E. (1998), *Horace and the Rhetoric of Authority*. Cambridge.

Ormand, K. (1994), 'Lucan's *auctor uix fidelis*', *ClAnt* 13: 38–55.

Osgood, J. (2006), *Caesar's Legacy: Civil War and the Emergence of the Roman Empire*. Cambridge.

O'Sullivan, T. (2009), 'Death *ante ora parentum* in Virgil's *Aeneid*', *TAPhA* 139: 447–86.

Pagán, V.E. (2000), 'The mourning after: Statius *Thebaid* 12', *AJPh* 121: 423–52.

Panoussi, V. (2007), 'Threat and hope: women's rituals and civil war in Roman epic', in Parca and Tzanetou (eds.), *Finding Persephone: Women's Rituals in the Ancient Mediterranean*. Bloomington: 114–34.

(2009), *Greek Tragedy in Vergil's Aeneid: Ritual, Empire, and Intertext.* Cambridge.

Papaioannou, S. (2005), 'Epic transformation in the second degree: the decapitation of Medusa in Lucan, BC 9.619-889', in Walde (ed.), *Lucan im 21. Jahrhundert/Lucan in the 21st Century.* Munich: 216–36.

Parker, R. (1983), *Miasma: Pollution and Purification in Early Greek Religion.* Oxford.

Parkes, R. (2011), 'Tantalus' crime, Argive guilt and desecration of the flesh in Statius' *Thebaid*', *Scholia* 20: 80–92.

(2012), *Statius, Thebaid 4.* Oxford.

(2013), 'Chthonic ingredients and thematic concerns: the shaping of the necromancy in the *Thebaid*', in Augoustakis (ed.), *Ritual and Religion in Flavian Epic.* Oxford: 165–80.

Parkin, S. (2016), 'How Isis hijacked pop culture, from Hollywood to video games', *The Guardian*, 29 Jan. Available: www.theguardian.com/world/201 6/jan/29/how-isis-hijacked-pop-culture-from-hollywood-to-video-games.

Parret, H. (2009), 'The ugly as the beyond of the sublime', in Madelein, Pieters, and Vandenabeele (eds.), *Histories of the Sublime.* Cambridge. Available: www.her manparret.be/media/articles-in-print/21_The-Ugly-as-the-Beyond.pdf.

Pellucchi, T. (2012), *Commento al libro VIII delle Argonautiche di Valerio Flacco.* Hildesheim.

Penwill, J. (2009), 'The double visions of Pompey and Caesar', *Antichthon* 43: 79–96.

Perutelli, A. (2000), *La poesia epica latina: dalle origini all'età dei Flavi.* Rome.

(2004), 'Dopo la battaglia: la poetica delle rovine in Lucano (con un'appendice su Tacito)', in Esposito and Ariemma (eds.), *Lucano e la tradizione dell'epica latina.* Naples: 85–108.

Petrone, G. (1996), *Metafora e tragedia: immagini culturali e modelli tragici nel mondo romano.* Palermo.

Pollmann, K.F.L. (2001), 'Statius' *Thebaid* and the legacy of Vergil's *Aeneid*', *Mnemosyne* 54: 10–30.

(2004), *Statius, Thebaid 12: Introduction, Text, and Commentary.* Paderborn.

Pomeroy, A.J. (2000), 'Silius' Rome: the rewriting of Vergil's vision', *Ramus* 29: 149–68.

Poortvliet, H. (1991), *C. Valerius Flaccus, Argonautica Book II: A Commentary.* Amsterdam.

Porter, J.R. (1990), 'Tiptoeing through the corpses: Euripides' *Electra*, Apollonius, and the *bouphonia*', *GRBS* 31: 255–80.

Putnam, M.C.J. (1965), *The Poetry of the Aeneid.* Ithaca.

(1995), *Virgil's Aeneid: Interpretation and Influence.* Chapel Hill.

(2011), *The Humanness of Heroes: Studies in the Conclusion of Virgil's Aeneid.* Amsterdam.

Quinn, K. (1968), *Virgil's Aeneid: A Critical Description.* London.

Quint, D. (1993), *Epic and Empire: Politics and Generic Form from Virgil to Milton.* Princeton.

Radicke, J. (2004), *Lucans poetische Technik: Studien zum historischen Epos*. Leiden.

Redfield, J. (1975), *Nature and Culture in the Iliad: The Tragedy of Hector*. Chicago.

Richardson, N. (1993), *The Iliad: A Commentary: Vol. 6, Books 21–24*. Cambridge.

Richardson, S. (2007), 'Death and dismemberment in Mesopotamia: discorporation between the body and the body politic', in Laneri (ed.), *Performing Death: Social Analyses of Funerary Traditions in the Ancient Near East and Mediterranean*. Chicago: 189–208.

Richlin, A. (1999), 'Cicero's head', in Porter (ed.), *Constructions of the Classical Body*. Ann Arbor 190–211.

Rieks, R. (1967), *Homo, Humanus, Humanitas: Zur Humanität in der lateinischen Literatur des ersten nachchristlichen Jahrhunderts*. Munich.

Rimell, V. (2002), *Petronius and the Anatomy of Fiction*. Cambridge.

(2015), *The Closure of Space in Roman Poetics: Empire's Inward Turn*. Cambridge.

Ripoll, F. (1998), *La morale héroïque dans les épopées latines d'époque flavienne: tradition et innovation*. Paris.

(2003–4), '*Perfidus tyrannus*: le personnage d'Eétès dans les *Argonautiques* de Valérius Flaccus', *L'Information Littéraire* 55: 3–10.

(2008), 'Jason au chant VIII des *Argonautiques* de Valérius Flaccus: héros ou anti-héros ?', *Pallas* 77: 173–84.

Roach, M. (2003), *Stiff: The Curious Lives of Human Cadavers*. New York.

Roche, P. (2009), *Lucan: De Bello ciuili Book 1*. Oxford.

(2015), 'Lucan's *De bello ciuili* in the *Thebaid*', in Dominik, Newlands, and Gervais (eds.), *Brill's Companion to Statius*. Leiden: 393–407.

Rohmann, D. (2006), *Gewalt und politischer Wandel im 1. Jahrhundert n. Chr.* Munich.

Rosivach, V.R. (1983), 'On Creon, *Antigone*, and not burying the dead', *RhM* 126: 193–211.

Rossi, A. (2001), 'Remapping the past: Caesar's tale of Troy (Lucan BC 9.964–999)', *Phoenix* 55: 313–26.

(2004), *Contexts of War: Manipulation of Genre in Virgilian Battle Narrative*. Ann Arbor.

(2005), '*sine fine*: Caesar's journey to Egypt and the end of Lucan's *Bellum ciuile*', in Walde (ed.), *Lucan im 21. Jahrhundert/Lucan in the 21st Century*. Munich: 237–60.

Rudich, V. (1997), *Dissidence and Literature Under Nero: The Price of Rhetoricization*. London.

Sansone, D. (2000), 'Iphigeneia in Colchis', in Harder, Regtuit, and Wakker (eds.), *Apollonius Rhodius*. Leuven: 155–72.

Saramago, J. (2008), *Death with Interruptions*, trans. M.J. Costa. New York.

Scafoglio, G. (2012), 'The murder of Priam in a tragedy by Pacuvius', *CQ* 62: 664–70.

Schein, S.L. (1984), *The Mortal Hero: An Introduction to Homer's Iliad*. Berkeley.

Schenk, P. (1999), *Studien zur poetischen Kunst des Valerius Flaccus: Beobachtungen zur Ausgestaltung des Kriegsthemas in den Argonautica*. Munich.

Schettino, M.T. (2011), 'Sagunto e lo scoppio della guerra in Silio Italico', in Castagna, Biffino, and Riboldi (eds.), *Studi su Silio Italico*. Milan: 41–51.

Schlunk, R.R. (1974), *The Homeric Scholia and the Aeneid: A Study of the Influence of Ancient Literary Criticism on Vergil*. Ann Arbor.

Schmit-Neuerburg, T. (1999), *Vergils Aeneis und die antike Homerexegese: Untersuchungen zum Einfluss ethischer und kritischer Homerrezeption auf imitatio und aemulatio Vergils*. Berlin.

Schnepf, H. (1970), 'Untersuchungen zur Darstellungskunst Lucans im 8. Buch der *Pharsalia*', in Rutz (ed.), *Lucan*. Darmstadt: 380–406.

Segal, C. (1971), *The Theme of the Mutilation of the Corpse in the Iliad*. Leiden.

Seo, J.M. (2013), *Exemplary Traits: Reading Characterization in Roman Poetry*. Oxford.

Shackleton Bailey, D.R. (1988), *M. Annaei Lucani De Bello ciuili libri X*. Stuttgart.

Sharrock, A. (2011), 'Womanly wailing? The mother of Euryalus and gendered reading', *EuGeStA* 1: 55–77.

Shelton, J.E. (1984), 'The Argonauts at Bebrycia: preservation of identity in the Latin *Argonautica*', *CJ* 80: 18–23.

Skutsch, O. (1985), *The Annals of Quintus Ennius*. Oxford.

Smith, S.C. (1999), 'Remembering the enemy: narrative, focalization, and Vergil's portrait of Achilles', *TAPhA* 129: 225–62.

Smolenaars, J.J.L., ed. (1994), *Statius Thebaid VII: A Commentary*. Leiden.

Snijder, H. (1968), *Thebaid: A Commentary on Book III*. Amsterdam.

Spaltenstein, F. (1986), *Commentaire des Punica de Silius Italicus. Livres 1 à 8*. Geneva.

(1990), *Commentaire des Punica de Silius Italicus. Livres 9 à 17*. Geneva.

(2002), *Commentaire des Argonautica de Valérius Flaccus. Livres 1 et 2*. Brussels.

(2005), *Commentaire des Argonautica de Valérius Flaccus. Livres 6, 7 et 8*. Brussels.

Spencer, D. (2005), 'Lucan's follies: memory and ruin in a civil war landscape', *G&R* 52: 46–69.

Spencer, R. (2013), 'Cannibalism in Syria: why is this a bigger story than the routine slaughter of children?', *Telegraph Online, Business Insights: Essentials*, 15 May. Available: http://bi.galegroup.com/essentials/article/GALE%7C A329860309?u=tall85761

Spentzou, E. (2018), 'Violence and alienation in Lucan's *Pharsalia*: the case of Caesar', in Gale and Scourfield (eds.), *Texts and Violence in the Roman World*. Cambridge: 246–68.

Stanley, K. (1993), *The Shield of Homer: Narrative Structure in the Iliad*. Princeton.

Stocks, C. (2014), *The Roman Hannibal: Remembering the Enemy in Silius Italicus' Punica*. Liverpool.

Stover, T. (2011), 'Unexampled exemplarity: Medea in the "Argonautica" of Valerius Flaccus', *TAPhA* 141: 171–200.

(2012), *Epic and Empire in Vespasianic Rome: A New Reading of Valerius Flaccus' Argonautica*. Oxford.

(2014), 'Lucan and Valerius Flaccus: rerouting the vessel of epic song', in Heerink and Manuwald (eds.), *Brill's Companion to Valerius Flaccus*. Leiden: 290–306.

Strand, J. (1972), *Notes on Valerius Flaccus' Argonautica*. Göteborg.

Sydenham, E.A. (1952), *Coinage of the Roman Republic*. London.

Syme, R. (1939), *The Roman Revolution*. Oxford.

Taisne, A.-M. (1994), *L'esthétique de Stace: la peinture des correspondances*. Paris.

Tarrant, R. (2012), *Virgil: Aeneid Book XII*. Cambridge.

Tesoriero, C. (2004), 'The middle in Lucan', in Kyriakidis and De Martino (eds.), *Middles in Latin Poetry*. Bari: 183–215.

  (2005), 'Trampling over Troy: Caesar, Virgil and Lucan', in Walde (ed.), *Lucan im 21. Jahrhundert/Lucan in the 21st Century*. Munich: 202–15.

Thalmann, W.G. (2011), *Apollonius of Rhodes and the Spaces of Hellenism*. Oxford.

Thierfelder, A. (1970), 'Der Dichter Lucan', in Rutz (ed.), *Lucan*. Darmstadt: 50–69.

Thomas, R.F. (1986), 'Virgil's *Georgics* and the art of reference', *HSPh* 90: 171–98.

  (2000), 'A trope by any other name: "polysemy", ambiguity and *significatio* in Virgil', *HSPh* 100: 381–407.

  (2001), *Virgil and the Augustan Reception*. Cambridge.

Thompson, L., and R.T. Bruère (1968), 'Lucan's use of Vergilian reminiscence', *CPh* 63: 1–21.

Thorne, M. (2011), '*Memoria redux*: memory in Lucan', in Asso (ed.), *Brill's Companion to Lucan*. Leiden: 363–81.

Tipping, B. (2010), *Exemplary Epic: Silius Italicus' Punica*. Oxford.

Tomassi Moreschini, C.O. (2005), 'Lucan's attitude towards religion: stoicism vs. provincial cults', in Walde (ed.), *Lucan im 21. Jahrhundert/Lucan in the 21st Century*. Munich: 130–154.

Toynbee, J.M.C. (1971), *Death and Burial in the Roman World*. Baltimore.

Tracy, J. (2014), *Lucan's Egyptian Civil War*. Cambridge.

Tschiedel, H.J. (2011), 'Annibale come padre e marito', in Castagna, Biffino, and Riboldi (eds.), *Studi su Silio Italico*. Milan: 231–44.

Uccellini, R. (2006), 'Soggetti eccentrici: Asbyte in Silio Italico (e altre donne pericolose del mito)', *GIF* 57: 229–53.

Van Nortwick, T. (1980), 'Aeneas, Turnus, and Achilles', *TAPhA* 110: 303–14.

Venini, P. (1970), *Thebaidos liber undecimus*. Florence.

Vermeule, E. (1979), *Aspects of Death in Early Greek Art and Poetry*. Berkeley.

Vernant, J.-P. (1991), 'A "beautiful death" and the disfigured corpse in Homeric epic', in Zeitlin (ed.), *Mortals and Immortals: Collected Essays*. Princeton: 50–74.

Vessey, D.W.T.C. (1973), *Statius and the Thebaid*. Cambridge.

  (1982), 'The dupe of destiny: Hannibal in Silius, *Punica* III', *CJ* 77: 320–35.

  (1985), 'Lemnos revisited: some aspects of Valerius Flaccus, *Argonautica* II', *CJ* 80: 326–39.

  (1986), 'Pierius menti calor incidit: Statius' epic style', *ANRW* 2.32.5: 2965–3019.

Vian, F. (1951), 'Les ΓΗΓΕΝΕΙΣ de Cyzique et la grande mère des dieux', *RA* 37: 14–25.

  (1974), *Apollonios de Rhodes: Argonautiques. Tome I: Chant I–II*. Paris.

  (1980), *Apollonios de Rhodes: Argonautiques. Tome II: Chant III*. Paris.

(1981), *Apollonios de Rhodes: Argonautiques. Tome III: Chant IV.* Paris.

Vinchesi, M.A. (2005), 'Tipologie femminili nei *Punica* di Silio Italico: la *fida coniunx* e la *virgo belligera*', in Gasti and Mazzoli (eds.), *Modelli letterari e ideologia nell'età flavia.* Pavia: 97–126.

Voisin, J.-L. (1984), 'Les Romains, chasseurs de têtes', in *Du châtiment dans la cité.* Rome: 241–93.

Wachsmuth, D. (1967), ΠΟΜΠΙΜΟΣ Ο ΔΑΙΜΩΝ: Untersuchungen zu den antiken Sakralhandlungen bei Seereisen. Berlin.

Walters, B.C. (2011), 'Metaphor, violence, and the death of the Roman Republic'. Diss., UCLA.

Walsh, T.R. (2005), *Feuding Words and Fighting Words: Anger and the Homeric Poems.* Lanham, MD.

van Wees, H. (1992), *Status Warriors: War, Violence and Society in Homer and History.* Amsterdam.

Weil, S. (2003), *The Iliad, or the Poem of Force: A Critical Edition*, ed. and trans. Holoka.New York.

Weiss, M. and Hassan, H. (2016), *ISIS: Inside the Army of Terror*, 2nd ed. New York.

Whitehorne, J.E.G. (1983), 'The background to Polyneices' disinterment and reburial', *G&R* 30: 129–42.

Wick, C. (2004), *M. Annaeus Lucanus, Bellum Ciuile, liber IX. I: Einleitung, Text und Übersetzung: Kommentar*, 2 vols. Munich.

Wijsman H.J.W. (2000), *Valerius Flaccus Argonautica Book VI: A Commentary.* Leiden.

Williams, G.W. (1978), *Change and Decline: Roman Literature in the Early Empire.* Berkeley.

Zanker, P. (1988), *The Power of Images in the Age of Augustus.* Ann Arbor.

Zissos, A. (1993), 'Lucan 6.719–830: a commentary'. Diss., University of Calgary.

(2002), 'Reading models and the Homeric program in Valerius Flaccus' *Argonautica*', *Helios* 29: 69–96.

(2004), '*L'ironia allusiva*: Lucan's *Bellum ciuile* and the *Argonautica* of Valerius Flaccus', in Esposito and Ariemma (eds.), *Lucano e la tradizione dell'epica Latina.* Naples: 21–38.

(2008), *Valerius Flaccus' Argonautica: Book 1.* Oxford.

(2009), 'Navigating power: Valerius Flaccus' *Argonautica*', in Dominik, Garthwaite, and Roche (eds.), *Writing Politics in Imperial Rome.* Leiden: 351–66.

Žižek, S. (2008), *Violence.* New York.

(2016), *Disparities.* London and New York.

Zwierlein, O. (1988), 'Statius, Lucan, Curtius Rufus und das hellenistische Epos', *RhM* 131: 67–84.

(2010), 'Lucan's Caesar at Troy', in Tesoriero (ed.), *Lucan: Oxford Readings in Classical Studies.* Oxford: 411–32.

# Index Locorum

# General Index

horror, 4–5, 8–11, 46, 69–70, 79–84, 151–2,
191, 223
'Horror Paradox', 8, 152
Hypseus, 216
Hypsipyle, 25, 223–8, 230

Iazygian 'euthanasia', 172–3, 195
Idas (Apollonius), 183
Idas (Statius), 216, 221–3
Ide, 230–1
Idmon, 179, 183, 199
*imagines*, 128, 139, 264, 267
Imbrius, 23, 27, 34–41, 175
Iolchis, 184
Iphigenia, 184
Iris, 25, 31, 47, 76, 101, 233, 235
Iser, Wolfgang, 57, 273
Islamic State (ISIS), 1–6, 8
Ismenus, 216

Janko, Richard, 40
Jason, 25, 170
and Agamemnon, 174–5
and human sacrifice, 182–6
and Locrian Ajax, 175
and Mezentius, 177
as corpse abuser, 173–9, 180–1
Jenkins, Bryan, 5
John of Salisbury, 12
Juno, 59, 92, 104, 106, 108, 176, 177, 178, 205, 246,
261, 263–4
Jupiter, 58, 81, 82, 111, 133, 148, 175, 205, 214, 217, 222,
229, 245, 257, 258–9, 260, 261–2, 265, 266–71
Jupiter Optimus Maximus, temple, 26, 268–70

Kant, Immanuel, 5, 10, 82
Keith, Alison, 89, 126
*kleos*, 38, 178, 198–9
Korenjak, Martin, 166
Korsmeyer, Carolyn, 10
Kristeva, Julia, 10, 82

Laestrygonians, 3, 200
Laius, 205, 221
Langen, Peter, 197
Larson, Frances, 4–5, 6
*laudatio funebris*, 128, 132–3, 137, 146–8, 234–5,
243, 247, 253, 266
Lausus, 50, 51, 59–60, 161
*Leichenkampf*, 28–9, 91, 95, 120–1, 173
Leigh, Matthew, 151
Lemnian women, 176, 187–90, 223–7
Lentulus, 73, 251
*libertas*, 137, 167–9, 204, 235–40
Liternum, temple, 244–5, 246, 254, 256, 266–8

Livy, 11, 12, 45, 52, 110, 242
Lovatt, Helen, 207, 238
Lucan (*see* Index Locorum)
and Maeon, 236–40
apostrophic narrator, 69, 73, 125, 132, 151,
207, 241
Lucilius, 13
Lucretius, 14
Lycaon, 32, 51
Lycus, 198–9, 201

Macrobius, 14
Maeon, 25, 89, 204, 219, 234–40
Mago (*Aeneid*), 173
Mago (*Punica*), 250
Malamud, Martha, 138
Manilius, 121
Manto, 231
Manuwald, Gesine, 244
Marcellus, Marcus Claudius, 25, 242–3, 245, 247,
253, 260, 265
Marius Gratidianus, 44, 62, 117–18, 119
Marius, Gaius, 23, 24, 42–4, 72, 115, 116,
119–20, 137
Marks, Raymond, 109, 251
Markus, Donka, 236
Marpicati, Paolo, 250
*maschalismos*, 180–1, 183, 185–6, 202
Masters, Jamie, 8
McNelis, Charles, 231
Medea, 25, 171, 173, 178–9, 180, 182–5, 186–7,
191–2
Medesicaste, 36
Medusa, 82–4, 138
Melampus, 219
Melanthius, 186
Meleager, 89–90
Menelaus, 100
Menenius Agrippa, 11
Menoeceus, 206, 207, 232
Mercury, 148
Mezentius, 42, 51–2, 59–60, 62, 65, 93–5, 114, 116,
144, 177, 192, 202, 245
and Caesar, 62, 144
and Hector, 49, 51–2, 59–60, 114
and Jason, 177
and torture, 52, 93, 116, 202
and Tydeus, 93–5, 114
*miasma*, 180
Miller, William Ian, 10, 81
Minerva (*see* Pallas, goddess)
Misenus, 50, 57
Mopsus, 179, 192
Morrison, James, 40
Mozley, J.H., 174